ABORTION IN THE EUROPEAN UNION

The Foundation for European Progressive Studies (FEPS) is the think tank of the progressive political family at EU level. Our mission is to develop innovative research, policy advice, training and debates to inspire and inform progressive politics and policies across Europe. We operate as hub for thinking to facilitate the emergence of progressive answers to the challenges that Europe faces today.

FEPS works in close partnership with its members and partners, forging connections and boosting coherence among stakeholders from the world of politics, academia and civil society at local, regional, national, European and global levels.

Today FEPS benefits from a solid network of 68 member organizations. Among these, 43 are full members, 20 have observer status and 5 are ex-officio members. In addition to this network of organisations that are active in the promotion of progressive values, FEPS also has an extensive network of partners, including renowned universities, scholars, policymakers and activists.

Our ambition is to undertake intellectual reflection for the benefit of the progressive movement, and to promote the founding principles of the EU – freedom, equality, solidarity, democracy, respect of human rights, fundamental freedoms and human dignity, and respect of the rule of law.

The Karl Renner Institute is the political academy of the Austrian Social Democratic movement. In this capacity, it foremostly aims at

- involving experts from various fields in the development and realisation of new political positions by establishing a discourse between experts from various fields and the Austrian Social Democratic Party;
- generating a forum for political discussion and thus helping to introduce social democratic positions into public discussion;
- training representatives of the Austrian Social Democratic Party so that they are optimally prepared for their present and future tasks;
- fostering the organisational development of the Austrian Social Democratic Party in order to open up and modernize party structures.

In order to fulfill these tasks as well as possible, the Karl Renner Institute and its nine regional offices (one in each of Austria's federal provinces) try to orient and modify their individual programmes according to their customers' demands, needs and wishes. A broad variety of publications, debate evenings, seminars and lectures appeal at a politically interested public while special conventions and seminars aim to invite experts, teachers and educators. Besides this, the Karl Renner Institute is involved in educational work on an international level.

ABORTION IN THE EUROPEAN UNION

ACTORS, ISSUES AND DISCOURSE

Bérengère Marques-Pereira

Book published in March 2023 by the Foundation for European Progressive Studies and the Karl Renner Institute in association with London Publishing Partnership

FOUNDATION FOR EUROPEAN PROGRESSIVE STUDIES (FEPS)

Avenue des Arts 46 – 1000 Brussels, Belgium
www.feps-europe.eu
@FEPS_Europe

KARL RENNER INSTITUTE

Karl-Popper-Straße 8 – 1100 Vienna, Austria
www.renner-institut.at
@RennerInstitut

Project coordinators: Laeticia Thissen (Policy Analyst on Gender Equality, FEPS) and Barbara Hofmann (Head of Equal Rights and Talent Development, Karl Renner Institute)
Supervision: Dr Hedwig Giusto (Senior Research Fellow and Editor in Chief of the *Progressive Post*)
Translation: BeTranslated
Layout and editing: T&T Productions Ltd, London
Cover photo: Tryptique

This book was published with the financial support of the European Parliament. It does not represent the view of the European Parliament.

ISBN: 978-1-913019-82-2

www.carbonbalancedprint.com
CBP2250

Table of contents

Foreword

Despite numerous earlier warnings by grassroots movements and the international community, the growing risks for women's rights have suddenly become very real and painfully tangible. In the midst of turbulent times marked by Covid-19 and other subsequent crises bearing a heavy toll for women, the ongoing regressions have been particularly visible for one of the most iconic and most essential of those rights: the right to safe abortion. The US Supreme Court's decision in June 2022 to overturn the landmark ruling of Roe vs. Wade most emblematically illustrates the sort of backpedalling of women's rights currently at work. However, this attack on women's right to choose is rooted in well-funded actors with tentacles stretching far beyond America to the other side of the ocean. Europe is not immune to similar developments, with a steady rise of anti-gender movements trampling on women's most fundamental rights. This trend presents us with a sobering reminder of the widely cited words of Simone de Beauvoir, who famously warned: "Never forget that it only takes a political, economic or religious crisis for women's rights to be called into question. These rights can never be taken for granted. You must remain vigilant throughout your life." Concerned about the impact this trend may have in the European Union, the European Parliament has called on member states to decriminalise abortion and to remove the remaining legal, financial, social and practical restrictions hindering access, while also calling for the right to abortion to be included in the EU Charter of Fundamental Rights.

Against this backdrop, the Foundation for European Progressive Studies and the Karl Renner Institute seek to address the right to abortion as an indispensable condition for social justice and gender equality. Particularly in an era tormented by disinformation and its gendered consequences, this politically divisive and socially complex issue calls, in the first place, for the development of a well-informed understanding of the moral and social concerns it raises. The essential work conducted by Professor Bérengère Marques-Pereira on abortion in the EU is therefore not only very timely but also highly relevant.

Originally published in French by the Brussels-based socio-political research centre CRISP (Centre de recherche et d'information socio-politiques), our foundations sensed that the ideas discussed in this substantial and original research called for a much broader dissemination among EU-wide audiences. That is why we are first and foremost immensely grateful to the author, Bérengère Marques-Pereira, for her enthusiasm in embarking with us on this journey, which has meant much more than a mere translation exercise. On the contrary, the republication has opened a range of new questions in the face of a constantly developing political landscape, while also proving useful in complementing the book with some of the most recent events and applicable legal frameworks. Most notably, Chapter 2 refers to the European Parliament's report on reproductive and sexual rights by social democratic Member of the European Parliament Fred Matić, which was hailed as a major victory for the right to abortion.

As a culmination of true teamwork resulting from many hours of discussion with the author herself on the new meaning acquired by each word in their translated form, this publication project would never have been thinkable without the precious contributions of all those directly and indirectly involved in the process. In particular, we are grateful to Marc Rayet for the endless hours of revision, to Jean Faniel, the director of CRISP, for his enthusiasm and feedback about this republication, and to Sam Clark, at London Publishing Partnership, and Alex Chambers for their editing work and for making this publication possible.

This book constitutes a unique tool for a well-informed contribution to debates on abortion at both national and EU levels. For instance, by distinguishing between five types of abortion regime in the EU in Chapter 1, Bérengère Marques-Pereira helps us to navigate through the bewildering complexities of the various legislative and policy frameworks in place by offering a comprehensive panorama of the different journeys a woman needs to undertake in order to have access to basic health care in the form of an abortion. Depending on her country of residence and her own socio-economic background, she may find more or fewer hurdles in her way compared with her fellow European citizens.

By forcing us to take a step back from the emotionally charged and ethically contentious debates spurred by abortion, the author aptly untangles the underlying strategies and approaches adopted at the opposite ends of the spectrum. This understanding is all the more relevant as it avoids harmfully instrumentalising such a multifaceted topic at the cost of women's bodies. Contrary to what one might imagine from the highly antagonistic positions that the issue of abortion still generates in current public debates, it is a very ancient practice that knows no geographical borders. Historians have demonstrated that, from antiquity to the present day, women have always resorted to abortion through various methods passed on from generation to generation, regardless of whether abortion was legal or not. In addition, unintended pregnancy and abortion rates among European women are not necessarily always correlated with the income level of their country of residence. In fact, most countries with higher abortion rates in Europe are considered high-income, which attests to the fact that barriers to accessing reproductive rights and services do not disappear with greater resources. Abortion is one of the safest medical procedures, even more so than childbirth itself. However, when governments restrict access, they deprive people of basic health care, compelling them to resort to clandestine, unsafe methods. This is particularly true for those who cannot afford to travel or to seek private care. And yet abortion remains an issue that divides like no other. Emerging from a background of traditional views on gender roles, it is fraught with many profound points of contention that are implicated in wider political agendas. In that sense, the work of Bérengère Marques-Pereira in this book has the potential to serve as a go-to reference for anyone wishing to gain a more nuanced and refined grasp of the specific narratives at play.

Bérengère Marques-Pereira comprehensively depicts the various actors, each playing their role in the general picture. Chapter 3, for instance delineates the role of religious actors such as the Catholic Church and the Holy See, while Chapter 4 lays out how both supporters and opponents of abortion rights mobilise human rights narratives. Additionally, she familiarises the reader with the relevant intergovernmental bodies that endorse the need to guarantee access to abortion as a matter of equality and non-discrimination. The appendices the author has provided in the second half of the book are particularly convenient for directly accessing the existing landmark legal bases, ranging from the United Nations Committee on the Elimination of Discrimination Against Women (CEDAW) to the Council of Europe and the European Union. In that sense, her contribution lies in the detailed description of each actor and how their respective positions are framed in a carefully chosen way.

Our hope is that readers − whether in their personal, professional, academic or political capacities − may use this book as a springboard for ideas to preserve women's fundamental rights and to meaningfully advance gender equality. We therefore very warmly recommend this book to anyone who, like the women behind the "Manifesto of the 343" in 1971 (see Chapter 5), recognises that the moment for action is long past due.

Laeticia Thissen
Policy Analyst on Gender Equality,
Foundation for European Progressive Studies

Barbara Hofmann
Head of Equal Rights and Talent Development,
Karl Renner Institute

Introduction

A medical procedure with multiple social, psychological and emotional implications, abortion has been a socio-political issue in its own right for several decades. In particular, the right to access abortion is a source of tension, opposition and conflict between different stakeholders and schools of thought, which sometimes take extremely antagonistic positions.

Why return to the issue of abortion rights in the European Union today? Is access to abortion not a given compared with Africa, the Americas and Asia? Religious fundamentalists and right-wing populists in the United States and Latin America relentlessly attack these rights. On the other hand, countries such as Belgium, France, Luxembourg and Spain have recently amended their legislation. In the case of Belgium, this translated to removing abortion from the criminal code (even if the spirit of the previous law largely remains). In the cases of France and Luxembourg, it resulted in the integration of abortion into their national health codes, whereas in Spain the most recent legislative developments enshrine the right to have an abortion in a public hospital and lift the parental consent obligation for teenagers. Even Cyprus and Ireland ended their near-total bans on abortion in 2018. Europe is the continent where access to safe and legal abortion appears to be improving in line with the medical and public health recommendations of bodies such as the World Health Organization and the International Planned Parenthood Federation, as well as international recommendations from the United Nations, the Council of Europe and the European Parliament.

However, the governments of several EU countries – namely, Hungary, Italy and Poland – are questioning this access. Meanwhile, in the United States, access to abortion has been severely restricted by recent laws passed in Alabama, Arizona, Florida, Georgia, Idaho, Kentucky, Louisiana, Mississippi, Missouri, Ohio, Oklahoma, Tennessee and Texas. It is worth noting the particularity of the restrictions imposed by Texas. As of 1 September 2021, Texan law around abortion is the most draconian in the United States. Not only does it prohibit abortion as soon as the heartbeat of the embryo can be detected (usually after six weeks of pregnancy) – even in cases of foetal malformation incompatible with sustainable life after birth, or in cases of incest or rape – but it also allows any citizen to file a civil suit against organisations or individuals who help women have an abortion. In the event of a conviction, the plaintiffs receive a bonus of at least $10,000 in "compensation". It is therefore no longer up to public authorities to enforce the law, since in practice the legal proceeding can be initiated through denunciations made by citizens. The US Supreme Court handed down a major victory to opponents of abortion rights by refusing to suspend this law and refusing to rule on its constitutionality. The European Parliament adopted a resolution on 7 October 2021 strongly condemning such laws.[1] Then, on 24 June 2022, the Supreme Court overturned the Roe v. Wade decision, which since 1973 had guaranteed the constitutional right to abortion during the first two trimesters of pregnancy. Since the 2022 ruling, almost half of the states have outlawed or severely restricted abortion. More broadly, attempts to restrict abortion, whether successful or not, highlight the possible reversibility of the right to access it. Consequently, this right remains a highly sensitive public issue and the subject of much heated political debate at the national,[2] international and supranational levels.[3]

In general, the conflict between self-proclaimed *pro-choicers* (abortion rights advocates) and self-proclaimed *pro-lifers* (abortion rights opponents) is antagonistic and skewed. Pro-choicers incorporate access to abortion into reproductive and sexual rights. Pro-lifers, who are opposed

---

1   European Parliament, 2021, "European Parliament Resolution on the state law relating to abortion in Texas, USA, 2021/2910 (RSP)", 7 October.

2   For analysis of decision-making processes at the national level and comparisons between national cases, see, for example, Engeli, Isabelle, 2009, "The challenges of abortion and assisted reproductive technologies policies in Europe", *Comparative European Policies* 7(1), 56–74; Engeli, Isabelle, and Fréderic Varone, 2012, "Governing morality issues through procedural policies", *Swiss Political Science Review* 17(3), 239–258; Engeli, Isabelle, 2012, "Political struggles on reproduction: doctors, women and Christians", *Political Research Quarterly* 2(65), 330–345.

3   With regard to European parliamentary debates, see Mondo, Émilie, and Caroline Close, 2018, "Morality politics in the European Parliament: a qualitative insight into MEPs' voting behaviour on abortion and human embryonic stem cell research", *Journal of European Integration* 40(7), 1001–1018. With regard to the role of religion in the European Parliament, see Foret, François, 2014, "Introduction: religion at the European Parliament; purposes, scope and limits of a survey on the religious beliefs of MEPs", *Religion, State and Society* 42(2–3), 108–129; Foret, François (ed.), 2015, *The Secular Canopy*, Cambridge: Cambridge University Press.

to these new reproductive and sexual rights, instead consider the question to be whether access to abortion is a human right, and they take a restrictive view of human rights that excludes any access to abortion whatsoever. Although these two advocacy groups clash along an "us versus them" divide, it is the shared language of human rights at the international and supranational levels that characterises their discourses of legitimisation (for one side) or delegitimisation (for the other) with regard to the right to abortion. However, this divide renders the conflict asymmetrical, as pro-choicers see pro-lifers as adversaries (with whom one can argue and negotiate) while pro-lifers see pro-choicers as enemies (who are beyond argument and must be destroyed). For pro-lifers an ethical–political stance can only be considered in the light of natural law, which is immutable because it is transcendental and binding on believers and non-believers alike.

This is the starting point. What questions does it raise in terms of political sociology? Should we use the terms "pro-choice" and "pro-life" employed by the protagonists themselves at the risk of ignoring the axiological neutrality advocated in political science? How can we use the terms "sexual and reproductive rights", "abortion rights" or "human rights" without sounding prescriptive? What approach should be used to account for the legislation of the different EU countries and its application, and to understand the antagonistic use of the language of human rights?

If we are aware that neutrality is impossible because academic knowledge is always situated in a social, cultural and political context marked by normative presuppositions, we can nevertheless expect a scientific approach to implement a form of reflexivity that leads to a distinction between constative and normative aims. However, these are only two ends of a continuum. For between the factual observation and the normative position there are several milestones: the analytical milestone, where explanations, understanding and interpretations come into play, and the political milestone, which introduces evaluations and prescriptions of public policies. The reflexive view also requires us to bear in mind the ever-present shifts between the different registers available to us (indeed, it is not uncommon to shift unconsciously from one register to another): the empirical register (the statement of facts), the explanatory and interpretative registers (the establishment of causalities and correlations between facts, and the interpretation of these through the prism of the conceptualisations linked to the approaches and paradigms used), the evaluative register (the evaluation of public policy), the prescriptive register (the prescription of reforms) and the normative register (the enumeration of norms for what is desirable and undesirable – advocacy and indictment). Nevertheless, the scientific approach remains linked to a context. The history of the construction of scientific issues is inseparable from the history of social realities and social representations, and of how these have been supported by the practices of actors and institutions driven by particular commitments.

This book does not intend to endorse those categories of everyday or political language that validate the status quo of the gendered and sexual order, nor those that, in contrast, try to modify it in either a radical or a gradual way. Instead we will focus on identifying the discursive logic of both sides in the international and European context of the 1990s to today – a context in which we have witnessed an ongoing backlash against women's rights, which goes hand in hand with an anti-feminism inherent in the religious fundamentalisms favoured by right-wing identity-based populist movements. In this sense, objectivity and neutrality are not equivalent. Where sociological and political analysis takes the right to abortion as its object – an object that primarily concerns women's bodies – it must also decipher the mechanisms at work in maintaining or changing social relations, and gender relations in particular.

The terms "pro-choice" and "pro-life" describe the discourses of voluntary associations that respectively support or oppose abortion rights. These terms also encompass other issues, all of which are related to the dissociation between sexuality and procreation, such as sexual orientation and gender identity, or, in the field of reproduction, medically assisted reproduction and surrogacy. This book focuses solely on the issue of abortion rights.

In this context, "pro-choice" refers to the notion of free self-determination in the sense of self-ownership, privacy and habeas corpus. It is thus an extension of liberal individualism to women's bodies, and also of the neutrality of the state in relation to philosophical–religious conceptions. The term also refers to women's autonomy to decide for themselves on the use of their bodies in the dual register of freedom and equality. It is thus based not only on the feminist demands for women's freedom from men and for gender equality, but also on social, political, medical and public health concerns, namely, eradicating clandestine abortions and ensuring equality for all women considering abortion. In this sense the term "pro-choice" is at the intersection of two currents: secular liberal individualism and a feminism that has undergone both libertarian and egalitarian shifts since the early 1970s. However, the emphasis on the notion of choice in current progressive discourses, and on gender equality as something said to be already achieved in Western societies, indicates an invisibilisation of the socio-economic, political and cultural constraints that are linked to the gendered division of labour.

The term "pro-life" encompasses the idea of an absolute right to life from the moment of conception – that is, the right to life of the embryo or foetus regardless of the health of the pregnant woman or the circumstances of her unwanted pregnancy (e.g. rape, incest or malformation of the foetus) and, a fortiori, regardless of the socio-economic conditions in which the pregnancy takes place. In this respect, the Holy See, both in its religious discourse and in its position as a non-member permanent observer to the UN, is setting itself up as the voice of ethical–political discourse, which could lead to alliances being formed with evangelical and Islamic fundamentalist groups within the UN. Its state, voluntary association and political relays ignore the concept of gender equality, choosing to focus on the themes of moral decadence and the West's decline. The term "pro-life" thus refers to a religious doctrinal corpus and a conservative, even reactionary, rhetoric based on natural law.

In this book we will avoid, as far as possible, these two normative expressions and employ the terms "supporters of the right to abortion" and "opponents of the right to abortion", which are more factual.

With regard to the terms "sexual rights" and "reproductive rights" and their inclusion in the field of human rights, we will endeavour to reproduce their social construction from a socio-historical perspective, highlighting the ideas, actors and institutions that contributed to their emergence (Chapter 2). To grasp the full extent of this social construct, it will be contrasted with the discursive opposition of the Holy See in international forums and its doctrinal positions (Chapter 3).

To defend legislative change in this area – whether that change is restrictive or permissive – the arguments of the various parties refer to the legislation of the different countries of the EU and to its application; hence, an overview of these laws is an essential prerequisite. Chapter 1 therefore proposes a typology ranging from the regimes that are most liberal on abortion to the more or less permissive ones through to restrictive regimes and those that prohibit abortion outright. This typology shows that, to date, no country in the EU has recognised women's right to abortion as a free choice, but only as a right to access abortion (in differing degrees) in the name of public health. It also highlights some hesitant advances and recognised setbacks with regard to this access. In this sense, the empirical evidence is objective but not neutral. It is objective because there is no way of getting around the facts, namely, the legal criteria that allow or prohibit abortion and the socio-medical factors that make access to abortion more or less effective. But it is not neutral because the reasoning that links the facts is problematic, chiefly because of the social construction of the notion of reproductive health and its hybridisation with sexual and reproductive rights. Therefore, there are no hard-and-fast facts.[4]

The body of analysis in Chapter 2 examines international and European political, legal and judicial bases: on the one hand, the international conferences organised by the UN on the themes of human rights, population and development, and women's rights, as well as the resolutions of the Council of Europe and the European Parliament; and, on the other hand, the covenants, conventions and charters relating to human rights and the work of their monitoring committees. It also includes the judicial bases related to the European Court of Human Rights, the Court of Justice of the European Union and, in Appendix B, the revised Social Charter. Chapter 2 shows that in the EU there is consensus in two areas: the predominance of women's right to life over the foetus's and the recognition of the right to access safe, legal abortion. In the absence of consensus about the beginning of life, European judges grant a wide margin of appreciation to individual states, while reminding some of them of the need to apply their own legislation, which is already very restrictive in some cases. However, it should be noted that no right has ever been recognised in the European Union for women to have full control over their own bodies.

In Chapter 3 the corpus of analysis is based on the Catholic Church's doctrine as expressed in the encyclicals, apostolic letters and general audiences of Popes Paul VI, John Paul II, Benedict XVI and Francis. It is also based on the secular discourse of the Holy See at the UN, specifically in its reservations expressed at the international conferences in Cairo in 1994 and Beijing in 1995, at the General Assembly, in the UN Commission on the Status of Women and in the monitoring committees of the various conventions. Chapter 3 shows that the positions of the Holy See, whether doctrinal or ethical–political, are based on the naturalisation, alterisation and hierarchisation of men as the norm of reference and reverence for women. These positions arise from structural anti-feminism, and they propose a "new feminism" that is a reactivation of traditionalist maternalism.

Chapters 2 and 3 explain the context of meaning in which the discourses of European voluntary associations in favour of or opposed to the

---

4   Revault d'Allones, Myriam, 2018, *La faiblesse du vrai*, Paris: Seuil, p. 77.

right to abortion take place; these voluntary associations are presented in Chapter 4. More than 500 voluntary associations calling themselves pro-life exist in the EU. However, it would be impossible to discuss them all here. Thus, the focus is on two "transnational advocacy networks"[5] that were set up following the submission of two major issues to the EU: the "One of us" petition to ban embryo research and funding for family planning from inclusion in development and cooperation programmes, and the Estrela Report on sexual and reproductive rights. The first network is called the One of Us Federation and the second the High Ground Alliance for Choice and Dignity in Europe. In Appendices C and D the associations that are part of these networks and/or have taken a position on the two aforementioned issues are presented. Each voluntary association is described in a summary table to help situate it.

The corpus of analysis in Chapter 4 brings together the main academic contributions of authors who develop the positions of the Commission of the Bishops' Conferences of the European Union (COMECE) and the Holy See, as well as the writings of radical activists campaigning for the inclusion of natural law in positive law. The corpus also includes academic contributions related to the High Ground Alliance network and the positions of its connected voluntary associations and their presidents. Chapter 4 shows that the normative framework of anti-abortion associations resonates cognitively with the doctrine of the Catholic Church and employs the language of human rights to safeguard a natural order. On the other hand, associations defending the right to abortion rely on a dynamic conception of human rights – that is, on the dissociation between sexuality and procreation in line with the legacy of Enlightenment philosophy. In other words, it is a conception that envisages that human rights are not fixed per se but can be extended by taking into account that sexuality is no longer reduced to procreation, since contraception, abortion and homosexuality are now recognised rights.

Chapters 2, 3 and 4 take as their object of analysis the normative framework in which the issue of abortion is embedded in the EU. The analysis of the substantive reasons given for the inclusion or exclusion of abortion in the field of human rights highlights the values and norms that are attached to the political actions of legitimising or delegitimising the right to abortion. For one side these values and norms are the rights to health, physical and psychological integrity, privacy, autonomy and

---

5   The concept of transnational advocacy networks refers to Keck, Margaret, and Kathrijn Sikking, 1998, *Activists Beyond Borders: Advocacy Networks in International Politics*, Ithaca (NY): Cornell University Press, pp. 1–38.

equality, in accordance with the principle of the neutrality of the state in ethical matters and with the social role of the state in public health matters; for the other they are the rights to life from the moment of conception, to human dignity and to freedom of conscience reduced to the freedom of religion through the prism of natural law.

While Chapter 1 deals with the issue at the national level of each EU country, and the following three chapters focus on the supranational level, the last chapter (Chapter 5) focuses on Belgium. The particular complexity of this case within the EU, both historically and currently, is linked to the deep porosity between civil and political society in Belgium. An analysis of the politicisation of the abortion issue enables us to define the significance of the law that Belgium adopted in 2018 and to understand why Belgium maintains a de facto status quo that prevents the recognition of a true right to abortion. The analysis also examines the various attempts to reform the 2018 law and their status in autumn 2020.

Naturally, it is impossible to trace here the politicisation and decision-making processes in this area for all the countries in the EU. Without ignoring the national activism that led to changes in legislation regulating access to abortion, we will focus on the supranational level, where, in an era of globalisation, normative ideas on this issue are expressed. However, the aim is not to analyse the impact of institutional configurations on the way actors construct their discourse per se.[6]

Abortion is about women's bodies as the reproductive site of the human species. For opponents of the right to abortion, the focus of debates over rights should be the foetus and its qualification as a person with the associated human rights.[7] In the latter context, the conscience clause[8] is used to obstruct access to abortion. For the doctor Johannes Bitzer, the ethical conflict can be resolved only by taking into account women's bodies:

---

6   On this subject, see Schmidt, Vivien, 2008, "Discursive institutionalism: the explanatory power of ideas and discourse", *Annual Review of Political Science* 12, 303–326. With regard to abortion, see Mondo, Emilie, 2018–2019, "European culture wars? Abortion and human embryonic stem cells research (1998–2015)", PhD Thesis, Université libre de Bruxelles.

7   According to the monitoring committee of the European Convention on Human Rights, the right to life does not apply before birth (see European Court of Human Rights, 2004, "Vo v. France", Application no. 53924/00, judgement of 8 July, paragraphs 75 and 82; see Appendix B).

8   A conscience clause is a provision that allows a medical practitioner to not perform a procedure (abortion, euthanasia, etc.) that he or she considers to go against his or her religious, moral, philosophical or ethical beliefs. See below.

The conscientious objector within me would tell me that I am destroying life and therefore acting against a fundamental moral and ethical value. This is true: there is indeed a conflict between my professional and ethical duties towards the woman and my general professional and ethical duties towards emerging life (embryo, foetus). In this conflict however, my duties towards the woman override all others, because without her body there would be no new life and without her support there would be no good life.[9]

In the eyes of the sociologist Luc Boltanski, abortion currently refers to the existence of a "parental project", while the question of whether the foetus is a person plays on the ambiguity between the moral and legal meanings of personhood.[10] In both cases, such an approach ignores social and power relations, and sex relations in particular – or to put it differently, gender relations.[11] Taking these relations into account, the sociologists Nathalie Bajos and Michèle Ferrand point out that it is not the parental project that undergoes abortion, gives birth, breastfeeds or, more often than not, raises children. They also point out that not distinguishing between the different stages of gestation (embryonic – i.e. up to ten weeks of amenorrhoea – and foetal) and only considering the "foetal condition" in terms of the parental project leads to the idea of a

---

9   Bitzer, Johannes, 2016, "Conscientious objection: to be or not to be", *European Journal of Contraception and Reproductive Health Care* 21(3), 195.

10   Boltanski, Luc, 2004, *La condition fœtale: une sociologie de l'engendrement et de l'avortement*, Paris: Gallimard, pp. 215–259.

11   On this theme, see Scott, Joan W., 2012, *De l'utilité du genre*, Paris: Fayard, pp. 17–54. Reasoning in terms of gender relations means emphasising the dynamic, conflictual, relational and transversal nature of the various actors. *Dynamic:* establishing a simple factual observation with regard to the inequalities between actors does not go far enough; it is also important to understand the historical and socio-political processes that shape the actors and how they act and constitute themselves into social classes or gendered classes of men and women. *Conflictual:* it is not enough to simply identify gender roles; it is also important to understand power asymmetries (the phenomena of oppression, exploitation and domination arising from the gendered division of labour). *Relational:* power asymmetries situate men and women as gendered categories. *Transversal:* social relations cross all spheres of society; thus, gender relations cannot be reduced to the family space alone – these relationships are also present in different public spaces. Thinking in terms of gender relations also means emphasising four dimensions: partition, hierarchisation, variability and division. The division between masculine and feminine overlaps with the partition between private and public, and between production and reproduction. The hierarchisation of the masculine over the feminine is a strategic power relationship placing men over women as gendered classes. The variability in time and space of gender relations is based on the gendered division of labour.

potential child or an "unborn child" and reduces the woman's role to that of a mother.[12]

Focusing on the issue of gender relations, several sociologists and political scientists see the struggles for abortion rights as a process of individuation and subjectivation at the very heart of women's citizenship.[13] This issue can therefore be analysed in terms of the concept of the citizenship regime.[14] However, it is not the language of citizenship but the language of human rights (and sometimes social rights) that is used by both proponents and opponents of abortion rights. Therefore, the substantive content of the language of human rights will be examined here in order to identify the normative frameworks at play following the major international conferences that directly or indirectly concerned women's rights and the issue of abortion in particular. The analysis of the framing[15] of positions on abortion seems all the more important as women's bodies remain a field of conflict within the EU.[16]

---

12   Bajos, Nathalie, and Michèle Ferrand, 2006, "La condition fœtale n'est pas la condition humaine", *Travail, genre et société* 1(15), 176–182.

13   See, for example, Lister, Ruth, 2002, "Sexual citizenship", *Handbook of Citizenship Studies*, edited by Engin Isin and Bryan Turner, London: Sage, pp. 191–208; Outshoorn, Joyce (ed.), 2015, *European Women's Movements and Body Politics: The Struggle for Autonomy*, Basingstoke: Palgrave Macmillan.

14   Marques-Pereira, Bérengère, 2018, "Abortion rights: rights and practices in a multilevel setting", in *Citizenship as a Regime: Canadian and International Perspectives*, edited by Mireille Paquet, Nora Nagels and Aude-Claire Fourot, Montreal: McGill–Queen's University Press, pp. 238–254. The chapter in the previous reference is based on the concept of the citizenship regime introduced by Jenson, Jane, 2007, "Des frontières aux lisières de la citoyen-neté", in *L'état des citoyennetés en Europe et dans les Amériques*, edited by Jane Jenson, Bérengère Marques-Pereira and Éric Remacle, Montreal: Presses de l'Université de Montréal, pp. 23–30; see below.

15   The sociology of social movements considers the process of framing as the work of signification and construction of meaning that a movement carries out to understand an issue and popularise a cause. For the concept of framing, see Snow, David A., 2004, "Framing processes, ideology, and discursive fields", in *The Blackwell Companion to Social Movements*, edited by David A. Snow, Sarah A. Soule and Hanspeter Kriesi, Oxford: Blackwell Publishing, pp. 380–412; Benford, Robert D., and David A. Snow, 2012, "Processus de cadrage et mouvements sociaux : présentation et bilan", *Politix* (99), 219–255.

16   It is sufficient to bear in mind that the Convention on Preventing and Combating Violence against Women and Domestic Violence (better known as the Istanbul Convention), adopted by the Committee of Ministers of the Council of Europe in 2011 and signed in 2017 by the EU, remains only partially implemented to date. In fact, it has entered into force in only thirty-four of the forty-five signatory countries. Its ratification is currently at a standstill. This convention is the first binding European legal instrument in this field.

Indeed, since the 1990s, women's citizenship rights have been the target of conservative and even reactionary anti-feminism, a torch that is now being carried by religious fundamentalisms. Two phobias characterise these movements, namely, equality between women and men, and women's freedom and autonomy; sexism and misogyny are their breeding ground. The right-wing identity-based populism[17] that currently marks many European, North American and Latin American countries is exacerbating the pervasiveness of the issue through verbal attacks and the setbacks it is imposing on women's rights. The fear of a lack of differentiation between the sexes, the rejection of equality and power sharing, and the fear that women may be in control of their own sexuality are factors that often drive measures aimed at hindering or even eliminating access to safe and legal abortion, and they are expressed with a verbal virulence that makes feminism the number one target of conservatism.[18]

Each chapter in this book raises the question of social citizenship with regard to abortion (around topics such as public health policy and free medical treatment for nationals, residents, migrants and undocumented women). Women have gained their emancipation through the acquisition of civil, political, economic and social citizenship rights. However, extending these citizenship rights to reproductive freedom remains a challenge when it comes to women's control over their own sexuality.

Beyond this observation, the study of the articulations and tensions between human rights and citizenship rights within the issue of abortion would allow for a greater understanding of how these two types of rights can be used by supporters and opponents of abortion. But it would also make it possible to remove any confusion – whether intentional or not – between seeing the right to access safe and legal abortion as fundamental to women's autonomy and seeing it as essential in terms of public health.

The demand for the right to abortion is about obtaining reproductive freedom for women, a freedom that would treat abortion as an act of privacy and personal conscience. When abortion is recognised as a medical procedure with an associated right to health, it goes hand in hand with an obligation to provide pre- and post-abortion care – if the state guarantees

---

17   Dieckhoff, Alain, 2019, "Les populistes au pouvoir: perspective comparée", in *Populismes au pouvoir*, edited by Alain Dieckhoff, Christophe Jaffrelo and Élise Massicard, Paris: Presses de Sciences Po, pp. 13–21.

18   Lamoureux, Diane, 2019, "L'antiféminisme comme conservatisme", in *Antiféminismes et masculinismes d'hier et d'aujourd'hui*, edited by Christine Bard, Mélissa Blais and Francis Dupuis-Déri, Paris: Presses universitaires de France, pp. 51–77.

the provision of such services – including in the event that the conscience clause is invoked by the doctor or health care professional. Only at the point when that care is ensured can we talk about an achieved right of access to safe and legal abortion.

Beyond the overview this book provides of the abortion context in Europe, and more specifically in Belgium, it focuses on the normative frameworks underpinning the positions of actors in favour of or opposed to the right to abortion and its access. These normative frameworks are accompanied by doctrinal references, legal categorisations, and pragmatic and controversial arguments. This book, therefore, aims to highlight the complexity of this ever-present issue by revealing the symbolic representations of women's autonomy and control over their bodies at work in the European Union.

1 | Access to abortion in the European Union

Europe has one of the lowest abortion rates in the world: out of every 1,000 women aged 15 to 44, 29 have had an abortion. This places Europe in third place behind North America (17) and Oceania (19), and ahead of Africa (34), Asia (36) and Latin America (44).[1]

Decriminalising abortion is once again becoming an issue for supporters of the right to abortion in the face of legislative and de facto setbacks driven by opponents of abortion since the 2000s.[2] Before examining how this issue is framed by the various parties (in Chapters 2, 3 and 4), it is essential to provide an overview of access to abortion in the European Union. From the outset, it can be seen that access to abortion varies greatly across the EU (see Appendix A). This is unsurprising, since the issue of abortion falls under the principle of subsidiarity, which limits the legislative competence of the EU (Article 5.3 of the Treaty on European Union).[3] This means that abortion is a matter of national sovereignty and that the EU does not in principle guarantee women the right to abortion. However, insofar as freedom of movement and free purchase of services

---

1   Singh, Susheela, Lisa Remez, Gilda Sedgh, Lorraine Kwok and Tsuyoshi Onda, 2018, "Abortion worldwide 2017: uneven progress and unequal access", Guttmacher Institute, p. 9 (www.guttmacher.org).

2   Decriminalisation is a "legal technique that either makes the conditions of the offence more restrictive (the offence will no longer exist in certain cases) or reduces the penalties. Decriminalisation occurs when the law and social realities no longer correspond. Decriminalisation also occurs when, in order to circumvent a legal prohibition, serious undesirable effects arise, such as having a clandestine abortion or travelling abroad because the procedure is permitted there (medical tourism)" (Locoge, Thérèse, 2018, "Le passage de la réflexion éthique vers le biodroit", paper presented at World Bioethics Day, UNESCO Chair, Ghent, 19 October).

3   According to the principle of subsidiarity, public health falls within the remit of individual EU member states. However, Article 8 of the Treaty on the Functioning of the European Union provides for the possibility of the EU taking actions to encourage cooperation and coordination between states in order to improve public health as well as information and education around health and disease prevention.

are guaranteed to all European citizens, such freedoms allow the most materially well-off women, and those women helped and supported by family planning centres, to access abortion – at least in theory.

Yet access to abortion in the EU is subject to various cumulative legal conditions and de facto barriers. A distinction should therefore be made between reproductive freedom – which would be recognised by a total decriminalisation of abortion – and access to abortion, which remains largely unequally distributed and is positioned on a continuum ranging from fairly easy access to an outright criminal ban, passing through more or less permissive legal derogation regimes.

Full decriminalisation requires the removal of all criminal sanctions from the law regulating abortion, and the amendment of the law (and related policies and regulations) so that, first, no doctor is sanctioned for performing a safe and consensual abortion and no woman for under-going one; second, legal proceedings are not brought about by, and the courts are not involved in, the decision on whether to obtain a consen-sual abortion; and third, any risks involved in partially decriminalising a consensual abortion are eliminated, so that the service is provided in accordance with current good practice.[4] Attempts to obstruct, restrict or prohibit access to abortion, on the other hand, have been recognised as making it unsafe: "Outlawing contraception and abortion results in fewer healthy, fertile women capable of bearing children, reduced fertility from widespread pelvic infection, the birth of more babies with congenital anomalies, and, ultimately, less healthy citizens for the future."[5]

In order to consider the legal regimes in each country and establish a typology, it is useful to consider the setbacks and legislative advances that took place in the decades of the 2000s and 2010s, as well as some significant cases that have been heard by the European Court of Human Rights (ECHR), the Committee on the Elimination of Discrimination against Women (CEDAW)[6] and the European Committee of Social Rights (ECSR).

---

4   Berer, Marge, 2017, "Abortion law and policy around the world: examples from Latin America", *Health and Human Rights Journal* 19(1), 14–53. For good practice in this area, see World Health Organization, 2013, *Safe Abortion: Technical and Policy Guidance for Health Systems*, 2nd edition, Geneva: WHO.

5   Amy, Jean-Jacques, 2009, "The shortest lecture on fertility control", *European Journal of Contraception and Reproductive Health Care* 14(5), 322.

6   This acronym refers both to the committee and to the Convention on the Elimination of All Forms of Discrimination against Women; here, only the committee will be referred to as CEDAW.

Appendix A tabulates a set of criteria for profiling the legal regimes in each of the twenty-eight countries of the EU prior to Brexit, plus Northern Ireland, which, though part of the United Kingdom, had its own legislation until 21 October 2019 that was radically different from that of the rest of the United Kingdom.[7] The presentation of the countries mainly follows the presentation established by the documentation centre of the Mouvement français pour le planning familial (the French Movement for Family Planning) in April 2017,[8] supplemented and updated by other references mentioned in the appendix. A few comments chosen for their particular interest support the raw data. The manner in which the countries are distributed into the five tables is explained later in this chapter. It should be noted that these tables include only the data available in the sources consulted, i.e. they may be incomplete and contradict other sources. An attempt has been made here to provide the most reliable versions, but naturally we were unable to examine all the legal texts and, a fortiori, all in their original languages.

1.1 Multi-speed access to abortion

Some countries and regions prohibit abortion altogether (see below). In others the conditions for accessing abortion vary based on several criteria.

Legal criteria

The time limit for requesting an abortion is probably the main criterion for access. In the EU an "on-request" abortion can be obtained up to between ten and twenty-four weeks of pregnancy: twelve weeks in most countries; ten weeks in Croatia, Portugal and Slovenia; fourteen weeks in Austria, France, Romania and Spain; eighteen weeks in Sweden; between twenty and twenty-two weeks (effectively) in the Netherlands; and twenty-four weeks in the United Kingdom (excluding Northern Ireland before 2019). The choice of the time limit is political rather than medical, as the World Health Organization (WHO) defines the threshold between miscarriage

---

7 On 21 October 2019, British members of parliament voted to allow abortion in Northern Ireland. From January 2017, Northern Ireland – as a constituent country of the United Kingdom – did not have an executive, and its day-to-day business was managed from Westminster.

8 Mouvement français pour le planning familial, 2017, "Tableau comparatif des législations sur l'avortement dans l'Union européenne".

(i.e. the embryo stage) and delivery as twenty-two weeks from conception or 500 grams for the weight of the foetus.[9]

Financial affordability is another important factor. The cost of an abortion for the woman varies greatly. While France is the only country where abortion is completely free for all, some countries limit free abortions to residents only (such as the Netherlands, Denmark and, since 2019, the Republic of Ireland). In other countries where access is in principle easy, abortion is reimbursed under the social security system but is very expensive outside it (e.g. Belgium, Luxembourg and the United Kingdom, excluding Northern Ireland before 2019). Most Central and Eastern European countries limit free abortions to "medically prescribed" ones, which no doubt reflects a desire to discourage on-request abortions, which are very expensive for women in these lower-income countries. In addition, some states deny free-of-charge (or even reimbursed) abortion services to migrant women, undocumented women, foreign and non-resident women, and underage girls (this is the case for most EU countries, with the exception of Austria, Belgium, Finland, France, the Netherlands and Sweden). Hungary excludes migrant and undocumented women from all but emergency health care.

The accumulation of legal requirements that must be met before a pregnant woman can obtain a consensual abortion is a proven barrier to its timely access. Indeed, stipulations related to the state of distress, the obligatory interview with doctors or a multidisciplinary team, the waiting time between the first consultation and the procedure, the use of the conscience clause by the doctor and/or health personnel (without the legal obligation to inform the pregnant woman of this from the outset or to refer her to another doctor who performs abortion) and the need for parental authorisation in the case of underage girls are all obstacles that need to be overcome, especially if failure to comply with these conditions leads to criminal sanctions for the doctor and/or the woman. Only Bulgaria and the United Kingdom (excluding Northern Ireland before 2019) do not have any criminal sanctions for the doctor or the woman. Slovakia does not mention any such sanctions in its laws. Women are not subject to criminal sanctions for an abortion outside the legal framework in Denmark, France, Lithuania, the Netherlands, Poland, Portugal, Romania, Slovenia and, since 2019, the Republic of Ireland.

---

9   World Health Organization, 1977, *International Classification of Diseases: Manual of the International Statistical Classification of Diseases, Injuries and Causes of Death; Revision 1975*, volume 1, Geneva: WHO, pp. 773–774.

The totally or extremely restrictive laws in place in Cyprus until 2018, in the Republic of Ireland and Northern Ireland until 2019, and in Malta and Poland to date maintained or still maintain de facto illegal, unsafe and clandestine abortions. This encourages abortion tourism, as these laws allow abortion for only a very small proportion of involuntary pregnancies, especially as the application of the law by doctors and private or public hospitals is often faulty. Women's right to life is at stake: for example, the UN Human Rights Committee has pointed out in relation to Ireland (at the time), Malta and Poland that the obligation of these states to respect this right to life compels them to liberalise their highly restrictive abortion rights.[10] CEDAW's observations with regard to Germany, Hungary and Slovakia have been consistent in highlighting the laws and policies that partially or fully deny women their right to sexual and reproductive health, through the prohibition of – or for certain groups of women, the prevention of access to – certain sexual and reproductive health services.[11]

Attempts to undermine the legal regime of abortion – whether partially or totally successful, direct or indirect – are also likely to hamper access to abortion. This is the case in some Central and Eastern European countries, such as Hungary, Latvia, Lithuania, Poland, Romania and Slovakia. On the other hand, some legislative advances have been made in the EU in Cyprus, France, the Republic of Ireland, Luxembourg and, very recently, Spain.[12] We will come back to this when we discuss the categorisation of the different countries in the EU with regard to legal regimes and the practice of abortion.

Outside the legal criteria

Misuse of the conscience clause is prevalent in Italy, where more than 70% of the country does not offer access to abortion. In Spain and Portugal

10   UN Human Rights Committee, Concluding Observations: Ireland, CCPR/C/IRL/CO/4, 19 August 2014, paragraph 9; Malta, CCPR/C/MLT/CO/2, 20 November 2014, paragraph 13; Poland, CCPR/POL/CO/6, 15 November 2010, paragraph 12. See Chapter 2 and Appendix B.

11   Committee on the Elimination of Discrimination against Women, Concluding Observations: Germany, CEDAW/C/DEU/CO/7-8, 9 March 2017, paragraphs 37b and 38b; Hungary, CEDAW/C/HUN/CO/7-8, 26 March 2013, paragraphs 30–31; Slovakia, CEDAW/C/SVK/CO/5-6, 25 November 2015, paragraph 31. See Chapter 2 and Appendix B.

12   In response to attempts by the right-wing party to knock down legislation from 2010 allowing abortion within the first fourteen weeks of pregnancy, the Spanish Constitutional Court rejected the challenge in February 2023 and the parliament approved a new law expanding abortion rights shortly after (Appendix A, Table A.3).

misuse of the conscience clause is increasing in public hospitals. The same is true in Austria, where four regions do not provide any access to abortion, and where it is difficult to obtain one outside the main urban centres. In France abortion is not performed in many hospitals and fewer and fewer of the new generation of doctors are willing to perform one. In the United Kingdom the use of the conscience clause is increasing among young obstetricians. The countries of Central and Eastern Europe are also seeing an increasingly frequent and excessive use of the conscience clause.

The conscience clause

Invoking the conscience clause, or conscientious objection clause, is an individual act; that is, it is the refusal of an individual to participate in an activity that he or she considers incompatible with his or her religious, moral, philosophical or ethical beliefs. Where it is employed by entire institutions or in departments whose head requires it of his or her staff, its use can be described as abusive.[13] In an international comparative study based on English, Italian, Norwegian and Portuguese cases, it was found that "the ingredients that appear necessary for a functional health system that guarantees access to abortion while still permitting conscientious objection include clarity about who can object and to which components of care; ready access by mandating referral or establishing direct entry; and assurance of a functioning abortion service through direct provision or by contracting services".[14] Sweden, Finland and Iceland do not provide for a conscience clause in their abortion legislation. Some doctors of the European Society of Contraception and Reproductive Health consider that these three cases ensure that women have a genuine right to abortion.[15] From this perspective, the con-

13   Rowlands, Sam, 2014, "A global view of conscientious objection in abortion care provision", paper presented at the European Society of Contraception and Reproductive Health, May, Lisbon.

14   Chavkin, Wendy, Laurel Swerdlow and Jocelyn Fifield, 2017, "Regulation of conscientious objection to abortion: an international comparative multiple-case study", Health and Human Rights Journal 19(1), 64.

15   Fiala, Christian, Kristina Gemzell Danielsson, Oskari Heikinheimo, Jens A. Guðmundsson and Joyce Arthur, 2016, "Yes we can! Successful examples of disallowing 'conscientious objection' in reproductive health care", European Journal of Contraception and Reproductive Health Care 21(3), 201–206.

science clause is understood as "dishonourable disobedience".[16] In this context, it represents an abandonment of professional duties towards patients.[17]

A legal regime alone does not guarantee access to abortion; financial barriers, bureaucratic requirements and legal procedures may hinder the availability of the health services that ensure safe and legal abortion, as well as compromising a woman's autonomy with regard to decision making. The weight of stereotypes and the stigma attached to having an abortion and even using contraception also act as a deterrent. Highly restrictive laws also lead to the denial of abortion care and post-abortion care.

Among the barriers to accessing sexual and reproductive health care, the gender stereotype that a woman's primary role is or should be motherhood has a significant impact on access to abortion and contraceptive services. Thus, these services are often excluded from health insurance, subsidies and reimbursements. This implies that a woman's sexual behaviour based on a dissociation between sexuality and procreation is outside the norm. While the WHO's standards define contraception as an essential medicine,[18] the majority of EU countries do not reimburse contraception, even though the cost can be prohibitive for the poorest women and underage girls, particularly in Central and Eastern European countries, where the cost is relatively high compared with the median monthly income. Only Belgium, Croatia, France, Portugal, Slovenia, Sweden and the United Kingdom reimburse contraception as a medicine,[19] and in Belgium it has been free for women under 25 since 2019. The proportion of women of reproductive age using modern contraception is highest in Germany, Belgium, France, the Netherlands and the United Kingdom, ranging from 75.7% to 90.1%, while it is below 50% in Central and Eastern European countries (except Croatia and Romania), as well as in Cyprus and Greece.[20] Moreover, in some countries and regions informa-

---

16   Arthur, Joyce, Christian Fiala, Kristina Gemzell Danielsson, Oskari Heikinheimo and Jens A. Guðmundsson, 2017, "The dishonourable disobedience of not providing abortion", *European Journal of Contraception and Reproductive Health Care* 22(1), 81.

17   Fiala, Christian, and Joyce H. Arthur, 2017, "There is no defence for 'conscientious objection' in reproductive health", *European Journal of Obstetrics and Gynecology and Reproductive Biology* 216, 254–258.

18   World Health Organization, 2021, "Model list of essential medicines: 22nd list".

19   European Parliamentary Forum on Population and Development, 2022, "European contraception policy atlas".

20   Ibid.

tion about contraception mazy be lacking, be biased or require parental consent. CEDAW has made numerous observations in this respect in relation to Croatia, Hungary, Poland and Slovakia.[21]

Finally, the stigmatising effect of particularly restrictive legislation can lead to the fear of criminal sanctions for the doctor and/or the woman, the suppression of any medical practice of abortion even in the rare cases permitted by law, a lack of training for doctors and health personnel, misleading information on the effects of abortion, and even the refusal of care following abortion.[22] CEDAW's comments on the need to ensure access to safe and legal abortion services in Germany, Croatia, Hungary and Slovakia have not been lacking,[23] nor have the observations made by the UN Committee on the Rights of the Child and the UN Committee on Economic, Social and Cultural Rights on the need to safeguard access to care – statements that thus repudiate the practice of denying abortion.[24]

1.2 Categorisation of EU countries: the legal regime and the practice of abortion

Access to abortion in EU countries can be categorised by cross-referencing two sets of criteria: on the one hand, the legal regime regulating abortion, and on the other, effective access to abortion (as discussed

---

21 Committee on the Elimination of Discrimination against Women, Concluding Observations: Croatia, CEDAW/C/HRV/CO/4-5, 28 July 2015, paragraphs 30–31; Hungary, CEDAW/C/HUN/CO/7-8, 26 March 2013, paragraph 31b; Poland, CEDAW/C/POL/CO/7-8, 14 November 2014, paragraphs 36–37; Slovakia, CEDAW/C/SVK/CO/5-6, 25 November 2015, paragraph 31. See Chapter 2 and Appendix B.

22 Singh et al., *Abortion Worldwide 2017*, pp. 20–33.

23 Committee on the Elimination of Discrimination against Women, Concluding Observations: Germany, CEDAW/C/DEU/CO/7-8, 9 March 2017, paragraphs 37b and 38b; Croatia, CEDAW/C/HRV/CO/4-5, 28 July 2015, paragraph 31; Hungary, CEDAW/C/HUN/CO/7-8, 26 March 2013, paragraph 30. See Chapter 2 and Appendix B.

24 Committee on the Elimination of Discrimination against Women, Concluding Observations: Croatia, CEDAW/C/HRV/CO/4-5, 28 July 2015, paragraph 31; Hungary, CEDAW/C/HUN/CO/7-8, 26 March 2013, paragraphs 30–31. UN Committee on the Rights of the Child, Concluding Observations: Slovakia, CRC/C/SVK/CO/3-5, 25 November 2015, paragraph 41f. UN Committee on Economic, Social and Cultural Rights, Concluding Observations: Poland, E/C.12/POL/CO/5, 2 December 2009, paragraph 28. See Chapter 2 and Appendix B.

---

above).[25] Comparing different countries in terms of these criteria (as they appear in the different columns of the tables in Appendix A) is not straightforward, since only by cross-referencing all such criteria for a particular country is it possible to assess how difficult or easy it is for a pregnant woman to legally and effectively obtain an abortion.

The Guttmacher Institute categorises legal regimes into six categories based solely on the grounds (social, psychological, medical, etc.) given for authorising an abortion.[26] These regimes range from those imposing a total ban with no exceptions (category 1) to those providing unrestricted on-request access (category 6), through four intermediate categories for regimes that allow abortion on grounds that are considered increasingly less restrictive, i.e. to save the pregnant woman's life (category 2), to protect her physical health (category 3), to protect her mental health (category 4) and on socio-economic grounds (category 5).[27] With the exception of those in category 1, countries also allow abortion in cases of pregnancy resulting from rape or incest, or in the case of severe foetal abnormality, but these three conditions do not affect their positioning in the various categories.[28] Similar categorisations are available online for the whole world in the WHO's Global Abortion Policies Database.[29] However, using the WHO tool we can see that, if we look for European countries that allow abortion

---

25   The empirical information is mainly derived from the following sources: Heino, Anna, Mika Gissler, Dan Pater and Christian Fiala, 2013, "Conscientious objection and induced abortion in Europe", *European Journal of Contraception and Reproductive Health Care* 18(4), 231–233; Avortement Info, 2013, "Abortion clinics in Europe" (http://avortement.info); Library of Congress, 2013, "Abortion law of jurisdictions around the world" (www.loc.gov); Law Library of Congress, Global Legal Center, 2015, "Abortion legislation in Europe" (www.law.gov); Heinen, Jacqueline, 2015, "Assauts tous azimuts contre le droit à l'avortement. La Pologne fait-elle école?", in *Genre et religion : des rapports épineux. Illustration à partir des débats sur l'avortement*, Paris: L'Harmattan, pp. 55–90; Mouvement français pour le planning familial, "Tableau comparatif des législations sur l'avortement dans l'Union européenne"; United Nations, 2017, Global Abortion Policies Database (https://abortion-policies.srhr.org); Center for Reproductive Rights, 2017, "The world's abortion laws", (http://worldabortionlaws.com); Council of Europe, Commissioner for Human Rights, 2017, "Women's sexual and reproductive health and rights in Europe", Strasbourg; Centre d'action laïque, 2019, "État des lieux de l'avortement en Europe" (www.laicite.be); Séhier, Véronique, 2019, *Droits sexuels et reproductifs en Europe : entre menaces et progrès*, Paris: Conseil économique, social et environnemental.

26   The Guttmacher Institute is the research arm of the International Planned Parenthood Federation.

27   Singh et al., *Abortion Worldwide 2017*, p. 14.

28   Ibid., p. 50.

29   See https://abortion-policies.srhr.org.

on request, we find that Hungary meets this criterion, even though it is one of the most repressive countries in the EU when it comes to abortion. In contrast, the Netherlands, where access to abortion is by far the easiest, only allows abortion "on social grounds". Hence, oversimplified categorisations may result in misleading conclusions.

A typological classification of EU countries will be given here that attempts to better reflect the reality of the conditions under which abortion can effectively be performed in EU countries, not only by comparing the various criteria (medical, social, economic, etc.) that allow or restrict abortion within the legal regime of each country concerned but also by taking into account the historical and political developments in these countries that condition effective access to abortion. We quickly realise that countries that apply the same criterion for authorising abortion (e.g. the health of the mother) can find themselves in very different categories when it comes to evaluating the ease or difficulty of accessing an abortion.

Thus, five types of regime can be distinguished.

(1) An authorisation regime that provides easy access to abortion on request with few restrictive conditions (e.g. time limits). This category includes Denmark, Finland, the Netherlands and Sweden (see Appendix A, Table A.1).

(2) An authorisation regime that partially or totally decriminalises abortion subject to certain criteria (e.g., time limits and social or medical indications), but where standards of access to abortion remain high. This includes Belgium, France, Luxembourg and the United Kingdom, with the exception of Northern Ireland until October 2019 (see Appendix A, Table A.2).

(3) An authorisation regime in a Southern or Central European country where access to abortion is restricted and/or de facto obstructed: Germany, Austria, Cyprus since 2018, Spain, Greece, Italy, Portugal and the Republic of Ireland since 2019 (see Appendix A, Table A.3).

(4) An authorisation regime that permits abortion, but where access is hampered (sometimes severely) by restrictive procedures. This is the case to varying degrees in former Soviet countries in Central and Eastern Europe (with the exception of Poland, which is in category 5) and parts of the former Yugoslavia, i.e. Bulgaria, Croatia, the Czech Republic, Estonia, Hungary, Latvia, Lithuania, Romania, Slovakia and Slovenia (see Appendix A, Table A.4).

(5) A prohibition regime that prohibits abortion by imposing very restrictive conditions on its access and making it extremely difficult

in practice. Following legislative developments in Cyprus and the Republic of Ireland in 2018, only Malta and Poland remain in this category. Northern Ireland has also been left in, as the legislative situation in that region, which changed in October 2019, is still rather uncertain (Appendix A, Table A.5).

The map in Figure 1.1 summarises the distribution of the twenty-eight countries considered in this typology (plus Northern Ireland).

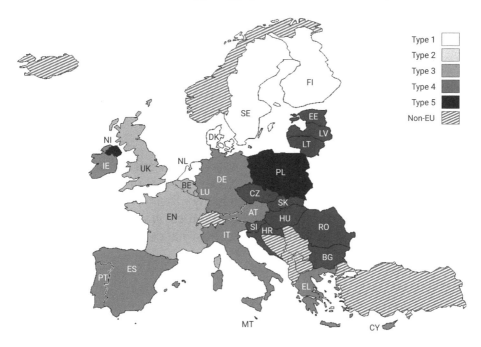

Figure 1.1. Legal regimes and the practice of abortion in the European Union.

The cases of the Southern European countries (excluding Italy) and Central and Eastern European countries could have been combined into a single case, but it was decided to treat them separately. Though the countries of Central and Eastern Europe transitioned to political democracies following the fall of the Berlin Wall in 1989, this transition strengthened the influence of the Catholic and Orthodox churches, resulting in significant restrictions and impediments to accessing abortion, which were unknown during the Soviet era. In contrast, Southern Europe (excluding Italy) transitioned to political democracy in the 1970s, following the fall of dictatorships. In Spain and Portugal, this transition led to a deconfessionalisation of the law, even though the influence of the Catholic Church in ethical matters remains strong, as in Italy, where the Lateran agreements have been in force since 1929. Greece remains under the control of the Orthodox Church, including in civil law. For Cyprus and the Republic of Ireland, and especially for Northern Ireland, the legislative changes are too recent to assess whether the practice of abortion is free from the obstacles that prevent easy access.

1.3 Safe and legal access to abortion (types 1 and 2)

The first two categories of countries offer relatively easy access to abortion (see Appendix A, Tables A.1 and A.2).

**A Northern European authorisation regime that
provides easy access to abortion on request
and less restrictive conditions (type 1)**

Denmark, Finland, the Netherlands and Sweden ensure access to safe and legal abortion, reliable and affordable contraception, sex education, and information on sexual and reproductive health, as well as respecting free choice and consent. In these countries, women won the right to abortion in the 1970s and '80s and can easily access information and all forms of contraception.

Denmark allows abortion on request up to twelve weeks of pregnancy and Sweden up to eighteen weeks. The Netherlands does not set a time limit and performs abortions up to twenty-two weeks on social grounds. In addition, clinics in the Netherlands cater for European and non-European women who have exceeded the legal time limit in their own country of residence. Finland allows abortion up to twelve weeks on social grounds and in cases of rape. For minors, this period is extended to twenty weeks. These different time limits may be extended on medical grounds. These countries reimburse the cost of the abortion, but only for residents in the cases of Denmark and the Netherlands. Denmark and the Netherlands provide for a conscience clause; however, in the Netherlands the doctor is obliged to inform the woman of his or her conscientious objection. However, this clause is not mentioned in Finnish and Swedish laws.[30]

---

30   The existence of the conscience clause does not allow full recognition of a right to abortion or even safe and legal access to it, since there is no ethical misconduct in not performing an abortion. Thus, it is the state's obligation to guarantee abortion care services in order to respect a right to health.

Sweden was the respondent in a court case in which the complainant sought to extend the possibilities for a doctor to refuse to perform an abortion on the basis of the conscience clause and freedom of religion, but these applications were rejected.[31]

In addition, these countries do not require the woman to undergo a waiting period between requesting an abortion and the actual procedure, except in the Netherlands, where this period is five days unless there is a serious risk to the woman's health.

In general, these countries enshrine a genuine right to access abortion on request, which comes close to a right to abortion that recognises women's reproductive freedom, since the conditions of access are not very restrictive, including in application.

A North-Western European authorisation regime that allows abortion on the basis of partial or total decriminalisation, subject to criteria, but where standards of access to abortion remain high (type 2)

Belgium, France, Luxembourg and the United Kingdom provide relatively effective access to abortion. However, in France it is not equally effective throughout the country.

In the United Kingdom abortion is available to non-resident women, which mainly concerns Irish women. However, the United Kingdom's Abortion Act of 1967 did not apply to Northern Ireland, where access to abortion was criminally prohibited unless there was a risk to the life of the pregnant woman. As mentioned above, the legislative situation recently changed (in October 2019), but it is probably still too early to say whether this will change the practice of abortion significantly.

France (in 2016) and Luxembourg (in 2014) removed abortion from their criminal codes to add it to their health codes, as well as removing the concept of a "state of distress". This concept was also removed from Belgium's abortion legislation in 2018, after abortion was taken out of its criminal code and made the subject of a special law (while paradoxically remaining subject to criminal sanctions). France and Luxembourg have allowed abortion since the late 1970s, unlike Belgium (1990) and the United Kingdom (1960).

---

31 European Committee of Social Rights, 2015, "Federation of Catholic Family Associations in Europe (FAFCE) v. Sweden", Complaint no. 99/2013, decision on the merits of 17 March. See Chapter 2 and Appendix B.

Access to on-request abortion is possible in Belgium and Luxembourg up to twelve weeks, in France up to fourteen weeks and in the United Kingdom up to twenty-four weeks. A waiting period is required only in Belgium and Luxembourg.

In the United Kingdom the procedure is free under the National Health Service but very expensive in the private sector. It is free in France and reimbursed in Belgium and Luxembourg for women with social security coverage.

All of these countries provide for a conscience clause, but the United Kingdom prohibits its use if the woman's life is in danger. In Belgium, if a doctor does not wish to perform an abortion, he or she is obliged to inform the woman of this during the first consultation and, since October 2018, to refer the woman to another doctor willing to perform an abortion; this is also the case in France. It is interesting to note that in France an offence of obstruction to abortion was introduced in 2016 to combat information about abortion (particularly online) that intentionally misleads or exerts psychological pressure on women and their circle in relation to abortion, as well as to prevent the intimidation of women going to hospitals for abortions and of the doctors who perform them. In October 2018 Belgium also introduced this offence into its legislation.

The Belgian case will be the subject of Chapter 5, which will examine the legislative initiatives that led to the law of October 2018 in the context of the initiatives of civil society actors. It will also discuss attempts to reform this law up to 2020.

In summary, these eight countries provide unevenly effective access to abortion, and do not recognise a real right to abortion for women.

1.4 Restricted or impeded access to abortion (types 3 and 4)

Access to abortion is clearly more restricted in the next two categories of countries (see Appendix A, Tables A.3 and A.4).

A Southern or Central European authorisation regime where access to abortion is restricted and/or effectively impeded (type 3)

Even in some Southern and Western European countries where abortion is legal, access is often hampered by lengthy procedures, high costs and geographical disparities in the availability of health services. Moreover, the number of doctors and health professionals refusing to perform abortions is increasing in Southern Europe, especially in Spain and Italy.

In Spain, at the end of 2013, a bill tabled by the Rajoy I government (Partido Popular; 22 December 2011–4 November 2016) virtually prevented access to abortion, which had been legalised in 2010 after decades of struggle. The bill allowed abortion only in cases of serious danger to the life or physical and mental health of the woman, and in cases of reported rape but not in cases of foetal malformation. The Spanish right wing clearly announced its determination to change the 2010 law, which allowed abortion up to fourteen weeks at the request of the woman and up to twenty-two weeks in the case of a health risk to the woman or serious foetal abnormality. The Church hierarchy and bodies such as Opus Dei criticised the Spanish prime minister for not moving fast enough to honour his 2011 general election promise to reverse the law. With the support of thousands of participants in the "Marches for Life", the Rajoy government's bill (inspired by the Hazte Oir association; see Chapter 4 and Appendix C) seemed to be a milestone in the total ban on abortion in a context where the European Parliament had rejected the report presented by Edite Estrela on sexual and reproductive rights.[32] Faced with very strong national and international opposition, and with divisions within the Partido Popular, Prime Minister Rajoy withdrew the bill in September 2014, but a law was passed in the autumn of 2015 restricting access to abortion for underage girls (aged 16 or 17) and obliging them to notify their parents, and for girls aged 15 or younger, who needed parental consent. This restriction was defied in February 2023 when the new Spanish parliament approved legislation that expanded abortion rights and allowed 16- and 17-year-olds to undergo an abortion without parental consent.

In Italy more than 80% of medical and health personnel refuse to perform an abortion, invoking the conscience clause. This situation is coupled with a lack of training for interns in hospitals. Thus, direct obstacles to abortion are multiplying, and difficulties in finding a doctor willing to perform an abortion, longer delays and denial of pre- and post-abortion care are commonplace. As a result, women who do not have the financial means to circumvent these obstacles are increasingly resorting

---

32   This rejection was seen as a success by fundamentalist factions and linked to the submission of a petition to the European Parliament by the One of Us organisation. We will examine the European context further in Chapter 4, which focuses on how the claims of abortion rights supporters and opponents at the EU level are framed.

to clandestine abortions. In addition to the dangers to their health, such practices expose them to financial penalties: in February 2016 the Italian Council of Ministers approved a legislative decree increasing the fines for women finding themselves in this situation from €50 to €10,000. In 2016 a complaint was lodged with the ECSR alleging a violation of several articles of the Revised European Social Charter; the committee found a violation of the right to health (Article 11, paragraph 1).[33] The minister for the family in the Conte I government (Lega Nord/Movimento 5 Stelle; 1 June 2018–5 September 2019), Lorenzo Fontana (Lega Nord), claimed to be promoting a natalist policy that would combat abortion, which in his view was the world's leading cause of femicide.

In Portugal the July 2015 law added more conditions to accessing abortion, namely, charging women relatively small costs and, most significantly, introducing a compulsory psychological consultation during which the various state benefits to which women are entitled, if they decide to continue their pregnancy, are detailed orally and in writing.

As can be seen, effective access to abortion in these three Southern European countries has tended to decline over the past decade. For other reasons, the same is true in Greece. CEDAW expressed concern in 2013 about "the very low use of effective methods of contraception, which means that women resort to abortion as a method of family planning".[34] The austerity measures applied in the country have not improved the situation.

In other countries, although access to the right to abortion has tended to increase, it is still subject to significant difficulties. In Germany there is evidence of illegal obstruction to abortion. Since 2012 the BKK IHV health insurance fund in Wiesbaden has been granting a birth bonus of €300 to women who join the Pro Life association. In December 2013 two Catholic clinics in Cologne turned away a 25-year-old female drug user and rape victim who had walked into the emergency room because they might have had to advise her on pregnancy risks and prescribe emergency contraception as part of the post-rape consultation procedure.

---

33 European Committee of Social Rights, 2015, "Confederazione Generale Italiana del Lavoro (CGIL) v. Italy", Complaint no. 91/2013, decision on admissibility and merits of 12 October; European Committee of Social Rights, 2013, "International Planned Parenthood Federation European Network (IPPF EN) v. Italy", Complaint no. 87/2012, decision on merits of 10 September. See Chapter 2 and Appendix B.

34 Committee on the Elimination of Discrimination against Women, Concluding Observations: Greece, CEDAW/C/GRC/CO/7, 26 March 2013, paragraphs 30 and 31a and d. See Chapter 2 and Appendix B.

In addition, until recently Article 219a of the German criminal code prohibited doctors from disseminating information about abortion. In November 2017 a gynaecologist was fined €6,000 for providing this information on her website. (It is interesting to note that in France and Belgium this information is available on the Ministry of Health's website.) At the time, two articles in the German criminal code regulated abortion: Articles 218 and 219, which were found in the section titled "Crimes against life". Article 218 establishes a legal derogation to the criminal prohibition by authorising abortion within twelve weeks of pregnancy if the woman has a medical consultation certificate and respects a three-day waiting period intended to encourage protection of unborn life. However, Article 219, which prohibited the advertising of abortion services, was repealed in March 2022. This vaguely worded article, adopted in 1933 under Nazism, made it very difficult to distinguish between advertising and information. In the courts, most charges relating to this article were brought by voluntary associations opposed to the right to abortion or by Christian fundamentalists. But it was the aforementioned gynaecologist's refusal to remove the information from her website and her willingness to appeal her conviction that allowed the issue of information about abortion to enter into the current public and political debate.

The issue divided the political parties: the SPD, Bündnis 90/Die Grünen and Die Linke were in favour of repealing the law requiring doctors to remain silent about abortion; the liberal FDP was divided on the issue; and CDU/CSU and the far-right Alternative für Deutschland party did not want any changes to the law. From February 2019 a legislative reform relaxed the ban and allowed doctors and centres that perform abortions to make their service known. The current issue for supporters of abortion rights in Germany is to remove them from the criminal code altogether. Similarly, in Austria, where abortion can be requested by the woman during the first three months of pregnancy, abortion remains embedded in the criminal code. In practice, abortion is difficult to obtain in Austria outside large urban centres, as the conscience clause is frequently employed.

Finally, Cyprus and the Republic of Ireland, which prohibited abortion until 2018, have now partially decriminalised it. However, it is still too early to judge the implementation of this decriminalisation in practice as their laws only came into force in 2018 and 2019, respectively.

In 1983 the Republic of Ireland enshrined in its constitution an Eighth Amendment that placed the right to life of the pregnant woman and the "unborn child" on an equal footing. This amendment has been interpreted as a ban on abortion in all circumstances, including rape, incest and foetal abnormality. As a result, between 1980 and 2015, 166,951 Irish women practiced abortion tourism (with 165,438 of these women travelling to England and Wales), according to Planned Parenthood Ireland. In 1992 the Irish Supreme Court reinterpreted the constitutional ban by allowing abortion when the life of the pregnant woman is in danger, after a 14-year-old girl was prevented by a court from obtaining an abortion in England, despite the fact that she had been raped and was threatening to commit suicide. This recommendation, however, has been largely ignored by successive Irish governments. Two decades later, in 2012, a public hospital admitted a young pregnant woman whose foetus could not have survived, and who subsequently died of sepsis because the doctors refused to perform an abortion. From 2013 a new law allowed abortion if there was a danger of death for the woman, but the still highly restrictive nature of the law forced women either to continue a pregnancy – even if it was known that the foetus would die *in utero* or not survive after birth – or to have an abortion abroad.

Between 2013 and 2017, similar cases relating to Ireland were submitted to the UN Committee for Human Rights, which considered that the criminalisation of abortion combined with the shame and stigmatisation surrounding it exacerbated women's suffering.[35] In 2010 the ECHR condemned Ireland, even though the court leaves a margin of appreciation to member states in order to respect the principle of their sovereignty in health matters.[36] As a result of the growing abortion rights movement, the Irish prime minister, Leo Varadkar, announced in January 2018 that a referendum would be held on the removal of the Eighth Amendment to the Constitution. In May 2018 over 66% of the Irish population voted in favour of its removal and in favour of changing the law. It should be noted that the credibility of the Irish Catholic Church in ethical matters had greatly diminished following the revelations of paedophilia scandals and the abduction of children from unmarried mothers. A law passed in December 2018 and in force from 1 January 2019 now allows unconditional access to abortion up to the twelfth week of pregnancy, and beyond that

---

35   UN Human Rights Committee, 2016, "Communication submitted by Amanda Jane Mellet (represented by the Center for Reproductive Rights) v. Ireland", CCPR/116/D/2324/2013, 17 November, paragraph 9; UN Human Rights Committee, 2017, "Communication submitted by Siobhán Whelan (represented by the Center for Reproductive Rights) v. Ireland", CCPR/C/119/D/2425/2014, 11 July, paragraph 9. See Chapter 2 and Appendix B.

36   European Court of Human Rights, 2010, "A, B and C v. Ireland", Application no. 25579/05, judgement of 16 December. See Chapter 2 and Appendix B.

time on medical grounds. While the law contains a conscience clause, it also provides for the obligation to refer the woman to a doctor willing to perform an abortion.

In March 2018, despite the constant opposition of the Orthodox Church,[37] Cyprus adopted a new law allowing abortion up to twelve weeks of pregnancy after a compulsory medical–psychological consultation but without having to justify a risk to the woman's health. The period can be extended to nineteen weeks, especially in cases of rape or incest. Minors must obtain and prove parental consent.

An Eastern European authorisation regime where access to abortion is hampered (sometimes severely) by restrictive procedures (type 4)

With the exception of Poland, the laws of Central and Eastern European countries (that are members of the EU) allow abortion. However, access to abortion in most of these countries since joining the EU has undergone multiple setbacks due to the imposition of complicated or restrictive authorisation procedures. In addition, in these countries the medical procedure is very expensive and is not usually covered by health insurance. Similarly, access to contraception is also limited because of its price. Difficulty in accessing abortion results in expensive and dangerous clandestine abortions that discriminate against women who are already the most disadvantaged and who cannot afford to travel abroad to have an abortion.

Bulgaria is so concerned about its population decline that it is campaigning against teenage pregnancies that end in abortion. Poor sex education, the influence of the Orthodox Church and a prevailing conservatism are all factors that hinder women's autonomy with regard to decision making in this respect.

In Croatia, although its Constitutional Council has reaffirmed the right of access to abortion, practical obstacles are multiplying as a result of anti-abortion campaigns, excessive use of the conscience clause and the failure of sex education.[38]

---

37 Diamantopoulou, Elisa, 2005, "Les enjeux politico-religieux de la corporéité féminine en Grèce, à travers les questions de la contraception et de l'avortement", *Revista de Estudos da Religião* (3), 63–77.

38 Committee on the Elimination of Discrimination against Women, Concluding Observations: Croatia, CEDAW/C/HRV/CO/4-5, 28 July 2015, paragraphs 30–31. See Chapter 2 and Appendix B.

Hungary is also demonstrating a clear regression. In 2012 the Orbán II government (Fidesz-MPSz/KDNP) introduced "the protection of life from conception" into its constitution and took new measures to restrict access to abortion by extending the waiting period and requiring women seeking an abortion to attend two counselling sessions aimed at discouraging them from having an abortion. This policy has been condemned by CEDAW.[39] In spite of these warnings, Hungary further tightened access to abortion in September 2022 by introducing a new decree forcing women to "listen to the foetal heartbeat" before they can access the procedure. Since 2017 Hungary has been pursuing a natalist policy focused on promoting traditional family values and childbearing (including for underage pregnant girls) through anti-gender-equality and anti-abortion campaigns, and campaigns against NGOs that support women's rights.

Since 2014, Slovakia, like Hungary, has imposed new conditions for accessing abortion by introducing longer compulsory waiting times and increased requirements for counselling sessions, which are mostly non-neutral. CEDAW's 2015 observations have so far gone unheeded.[40] Conversely, the ECHR has noted that Roma women have been sterilised without informed consent and are exposed to particular forms of torture and ill-treatment related to their reproductive capacities and decisions, which may constitute a serious and lasting impairment of their personal and bodily integrity, physical and mental health, and psychological well-being.[41]

Finally, Latvia, Lithuania and Romania have seen calls for similar procedures aimed at extending compulsory waiting periods and increasing requirements with regard to advice, which is often non-neutral, but to date these have not been successful. There have also been several attempts to roll back legislation in order to achieve an almost total ban on abortion in Lithuania and Slovakia. These attempts sparked massive demonstrations, which have so far been successful. Moreover, in Estonia, the Czech Republic and Slovenia various restrictive measures were incrementally

---

39 Committee on the Elimination of Discrimination against Women, Concluding Observations: Hungary, CEDAW/C/HUN/CO/7-8, 26 March 2013, paragraph 2. See Chapter 2 and Appendix B.

40 Committee on the Elimination of Discrimination against Women, Concluding Observations: Slovakia, CEDAW/C/SVK/CO/5-6, 25 November 2015, paragraphs 30–31. See also UN Committee on the Rights of the Child, Concluding Observations: Slovakia, CRC/C/SVK/CO/3-5, 25 November 2015, paragraph 41. See Chapter 2 and Appendix B.

41 European Court of Human Rights, 2012, "I. G. and others v. Slovakia", Application no. 15966/04, judgement of 13 November, paragraphs 143–144; European Court of Human Rights, 2011, "V. C. v. Slovakia", Application no. 18968/07, judgement of 8 November, paragraphs 143 and 154. See Chapter 2 and Appendix B.

adopted during the 1990s and into the 2010s. For example, since its independence in 1991, Estonia has reduced the time limit for the possibility of having an abortion on medical grounds from twenty-eight to twenty weeks of pregnancy, in the Czech Republic abortion on non-medical grounds has not been reimbursed since 1993, and Slovenia has added the conscience clause into its legislation.

1.5 A prohibition regime that bans abortion (type 5)

In contrast to the other types of regimes, Malta and Poland still prohibit all abortions, or provide only for rare exceptions (in cases of danger to the life of the pregnant woman, rape, incest and/or malformation of the foetus). Until 2019, this also applied to Northern Ireland. Malta and Poland have had protocols and unilateral declarations restricting access to abortion annexed to their EU accession treaties. They provide for criminal sanctions for anyone who assists a woman in having an abortion outside the exceptions and, in Malta, for the woman as well. The penalties can be severe. Northern Ireland, which was among the most draconian countries in the EU, provided for life imprisonment for women and doctors, even in cases of rape, incest and lethal foetal malformation.

In Poland the cultural and religious influence of the Catholic Church, the hostility of the medical profession to abortion, and the silence of the left and liberals explain the adoption in 1993 (well before its accession to the EU) of the law on "family planning, the protection of the human foetus and the conditions under which the termination of pregnancy is authorised".[42] Commonly referred to as the "anti-abortion law", it totally prohibits abortion, with very few exceptions, i.e. in cases of rape, malformation of the foetus, or a danger to the life or health of the pregnant woman. But even in these cases, abortion has become virtually impossible because of the frequent use of the conscience clause by doctors and health professionals, and because of the various administrative obstacles that prevent abortions from being carried out within the required time limits.

All efforts by women's groups to liberalise the law in Poland (with the most prominent being those of the Women's Rights and Planning Federation) have so far failed. Neither the observations made against

---

42 For more details on Poland, see Heinen, "Assauts tous azimuts contre le droit à l'avortement"; Tartakowsky, Eva, and Paul Zawadski, 2017, "Politique et religion en Pologne", in *Religion et politique*, edited by Alain Dieckhoff and Philippe Portier, Paris: Presses de Sciences Po, pp. 297–305.

Poland by CEDAW[43] and the UN Committee on Economic, Social and Cultural Rights[44] nor the successive condemnations by the ECHR from 2007 onwards[45] have had any effect. On the contrary, recurrent campaigns by the Polish Church and its interventions in the public sphere to toughen the law resulted in the tabling of a bill by religious movements to ban abortion altogether. Following the rejection of this bill, legislative initiatives to ban all abortion rights were repeated in 2011, 2015 and 2016. In September 2016 the Polish Sejm again considered a bill to fully criminalise abortion except in cases of imminent danger to the pregnant woman's life. This bill was the result of a petition with more than 450,000 signatures initiated by the Polish ecclesiastical hierarchy and drafted by the Ordo Iuris association (see Chapter 4 and Appendix C). Following massive demonstrations by the Polish Women's Strike, and the Black Protests in Poland and elsewhere in Europe, the Sejm rejected the bill. However, at the end of June 2017 the Polish president endorsed a law limiting access to the morning-after pill, which is now available only on prescription.

In March 2018, with the support of the Polish episcopate, a new bill garnering more than 100,000 signatures in three months was tabled in parliament that aimed to ban abortion in cases of serious pathologies or disability in the foetus (which represents 96% of abortion cases in Poland). Again the bill was rejected after it provoked massive demonstrations organised by two networks – the Polish Women's Strike and the Gals for Gals platform – and supported by a mass movement, the Committee for the Defence of Democracy. Finally, however, on 22 October 2020, the Polish Constitutional Court ruled that abortion in cases of serious and irreversible foetal malformation or incurable and life-threatening illness was unconstitutional. This ruling, from a court whose members were mostly appointed by the government of the day, made virtually all abortions illegal. The president of the Polish Bishops' Conference, Stanisław

---

43   Committee on the Elimination of Discrimination against Women, Concluding Observations: Poland, CEDAW/C/POL/CO/7-8, 14 November 2014, paragraphs 36–37. See Chapter 2 and Appendix B.

44   UN Committee on Economic, Social and Cultural Rights, Concluding Observations: Poland, E/C.12/POL/CO/5, 2 December 2009, paragraph 28. See Chapter 2 and Appendix B.

45   European Court of Human Rights, 2007, "Case of Tysiąc v. Poland", Application no. 5410/03, judgement of 20 March; European Court of Human Rights, 2011, "R. R. v. Poland", Application no. 27617/04, judgement of 26 May; European Court of Human Rights, 2012, "P. and S. v. Poland", Application no. 57375/08, judgement of 30 October. See Chapter 2 and Appendix B.

Gądecki, thanked the court for the ruling. In the face of this setback, massive demonstrations were staged all over Poland, and in particular in Warsaw. In view of the scale of the protests, the ruling did not come into force until 27 January 2021.

One of the first medical consequences of this ruling was the death of a 30-year-old woman from septic shock in her twenty-second week of pregnancy. The doctors preferred to wait until the foetus's heart had stopped beating rather than perform an abortion, even though the foetus was dying and the woman's life was in danger. This event provoked several demonstrations under the slogan "Not one more," echoing the slogan "*Ni una menos*" first used by Latin American feminists fighting against femicide.

However, the offensive taken up by Catholic fundamentalists resumed in the form of a citizens' bill to ban all abortions and to punish women and doctors with 5–25 years' imprisonment. This project was supported by the Ordo Iuris association (see Appendix C, Table C.13). In the wake of this, Poland decided to withdraw from the Council of Europe Convention on Preventing and Combating Violence against Women and Domestic Violence (better known as the Istanbul Convention) (CETS no. 210), which it had ratified on 27 April 2015. These developments occurred against the backdrop of tensions between the Polish government and the European Commission, following the Constitutional Court's decision on 7 October 2021 to reject the binding nature of EU law.

1.6 Impact of the Covid-19 pandemic

The Covid-19 pandemic has not changed how abortion regimes are categorised in this book.[46] In general, it should be noted that health care systems were overwhelmed during the initial lockdown, resulting in reduced access to abortion services. These reduced services were

---

46   The information in this section is mainly derived from the following sources: Hickson, Caroline, and Neil Datta, 2020, "Sexual and reproductive rights during the COVID-19 pandemic", 22 April, European Parliamentary Forum for Sexual and Reproductive Rights and International Planned Parenthood Federation, European Network, pp. 5–9; Moreau, Caroline, et al., 2021, "Abortion regulation in Europe in the era of COVID-19: a spectrum of policy responses", *BMJ Sexual and Reproductive Health* 47(14), 1–8; Wenham, Clare, 2020, "The gendered impact of the COVID-19 crisis and post-crisis period", European Parliament, September, pp. 47–48; Profeta, Paola, Ximena Calo and Roberto Occhiuzzi, 2021, "Covid-19 and its economic impact on women and women's poverty: insights from 5 European countries", European Parliament, May, pp. 40–43.

also due to the closure of borders. In countries where sexual and reproductive health services were considered essential, there was still a significant drop in attendance, owing to the risk of infection. The use of telemedicine services was undoubtedly useful, but this was not possible for people who did not have access to or were unable to use computer tools. In the countries that considered sexual and reproductive health services non-essential, it is clear that unplanned pregnancies are likely to have long-term effects on the lives of the women and families in question.

Sweden, which falls into the category of providing easy access to abortion on request with few restrictive conditions, has not seen significant changes in this respect, as it mitigated the effects of the pandemic by allowing medical abortions at home beyond the ninth week of pregnancy. In addition, telemedicine services were already in use before the pandemic.

France, an authorisation regime that allows abortion on the basis of partial or total decriminalisation (subject to criteria), but where standards of access to abortion remain high, permitted the use of contraceptive prescriptions that have passed their use-by date, as well as the use of telemedicine for medical appointments. It should also be noted that, during the pandemic, France extended the time limit for abortion from twelve to fourteen weeks, and the time limit for medical abortions was extended from seven to nine weeks. Belgium, which is in the same category, allowed medical abortions at home up to nine weeks and six days, as well as the use of telemedicine appointments for prescriptions and pre-abortion interviews. In addition, it introduced the free morning-after pill for all women who needed it. The United Kingdom and Ireland also allowed the use of telemedicine.

Germany and Italy fall into the category of Central and Southern European countries where access to abortion is restricted or effectively hindered. While in Germany the time limit for performing an abortion was extended from twelve to fourteen weeks during the pandemic, and the use of telemedicine was allowed for the mandatory pre-abortion interviews, it should be noted that several clinics refused to perform abortions. In Italy gynaecology departments were closed as they were considered non-essential. Austria and Cyprus also considered sexual and reproductive health services non-essential.

Poland falls into the category of countries with a ban on abortion. It was during the pandemic that Poland banned abortion almost completely.

Hungary, which falls into the category of countries where abortion is authorised but access is severely restricted, suspended abortions in both the public and private sectors. Slovakia, like other Central and Eastern European countries, considered sexual and reproductive health services non-essential. In Bulgaria and Romania programmes supporting the sexual and reproductive health of Roma girls and women were terminated.

During the pandemic, access to safe and legal abortion was more variable than ever in the EU.

*

In conclusion, an analysis of access to abortion in the EU shows that no country, even the most permissive, recognises women's control over their bodies in the way that feminist movements have been demanding since the 1970s. However, in practice, Sweden has a right to access to abortion that comes close to a right to abortion as a reproductive freedom for women. Elsewhere, when safe and legal access to abortion is recognised, it is in the name of public health. It is true that, in the EU (unlike in the United States, Latin America and Asia) abortion is generally possible at the request of the woman, with a few exceptions. However, a detailed approach to the legal regimes and their implementation highlights that the cumulative nature of the legal conditions – which are far from being solely health-related – constitutes an obstacle, sometimes severe, to women's decision-making autonomy, as do the practices of circumventing or even transgressing the law in certain states. An analysis of the normative frameworks that underpin the demand for and opposition to abortion rights in the European Union provides the key to understanding the scope of these obstacles.

2 | Sexual and reproductive health and sexual and reproductive rights in the field of human rights

Access to abortion, the issue at the heart of this book, invites debate about sexual and reproductive health and sexual and reproductive rights. This chapter focuses on the social construction of these issues. The concepts of sexual and reproductive health and of sexual and reproductive rights are part of an ongoing evolution of ideas around sexuality and reproduction. This evolution is taking place in organisations led by actors who are committed to international law and human rights.

As the focus of this volume is abortion, these two concepts will be considered only from the reproductive perspective (an issue developed at the international level in the 1980s and 1990s) and not from a gender identity or sexual orientation perspective (debated internationally since the 2000s).

The right to sexual and reproductive health, and its hybridisation with sexual and reproductive rights, have their political, legal and judicial foundations in international and European human rights norms (see Appendix B). Thus, current views around procreation and sexuality are legitimised through the use of legal and rights-based language. However, a legal analysis of sexual and reproductive rights with regard to human rights and the law will not be developed here. Taking a socio-historical approach, this chapter traces the trajectory of the notions of reproductive health and reproductive rights. In addition, it considers the political and legal inclusion of access to abortion in the field of human rights.

2.1 From sexual and reproductive health to sexual and reproductive rights

Between 1980 and 1995, international feminist groups focusing on women's health contributed to the emergence of the concepts of sexual and reproductive health. At the same time, organisations such as the

WHO and the International Planned Parenthood Federation (IPPF) were institutionalising these concepts.[1] The dialogue between international health institutions and feminist activists began in the run-up to the United Nations' 1994 International Conference on Population and Development, in Cairo.[2]

Reproductive health includes access to health care, medication and education in order to prevent unwanted pregnancies, ensure safe deliveries, and provide abortion and post-abortion care as well as family planning services and contraception counselling.

Sexual health refers, based on the WHO's definition of health, to a state of physical, mental and social well-being in terms of sexuality. This state of well-being chiefly includes the prevention and treatment of sexual diseases, freedom from sexual violence (including female genital mutilation and gender-based violence) and freedom from human trafficking.

However, as early as 1987 the WHO Regional Office for Europe did not consider sexual health as a state but instead linked it to the rights of individuals:

> Concepts of sexual health or sexual well-being recognise the variety and uniqueness of individual sexual experience and needs, affirming the rights of individuals to be free from all sexual exploitation, oppression and abuse. The goal of sexuality policies, programmes and services is not to achieve a measurable level of "sexual health" in a population, but to empower individuals to meet their needs and give them the personal resources to deal with their problems and difficulties.[3]

The notion of reproductive rights was first developed through the activism of transnational feminist actors. Of particular note is the

---

1   The World Health Organization (WHO) is the United Nations' specialised agency for health. Its constitution came into force in 1948, and it is headquartered in Geneva. The International Planned Parenthood Federation (IPPF) was founded in 1952 at the Third International Conference on Planned Parenthood, in Bombay. Its headquarters are in London. It brings together national family planning associations and currently has 134 associations in 145 countries.

2   Corrêa, Sonia, 1997, "From reproductive health to sexual rights: achievements and future challenges", *Reproductive Health Matters* 5(10), 107–116.

3   World Health Organization, Regional Office for Europe, 1987, *Concepts of Sexual Health: Report on a Working Group*, Copenhagen: WHO, p. 4.

creation of the Women's Global Network for Reproductive Rights[4] at the first transnational conference on this theme, in Amsterdam in 1984,[5] and the creation (in the same year) of Development Alternatives with Women for a New Era (DAWN).[6] These two organisations have greatly enriched feminist approaches to reproductive rights across the Global North and the Global South. The first network focuses more on abortion and contraceptive rights, while the second focuses on a notion of reproductive health that is less individualistic and more attuned to the needs of poor, marginalised women in the South. Nevertheless, in the preparatory work for the Cairo Conference, feminist activists from the North and South agreed on the link between reproductive health and reproductive rights.

The International Women's Health Coalition has also carried out intensive lobbying, advocacy and expert assessments.[7] Furthermore, the transnationalisation of the issue of reproductive rights is supported by international efforts for the recognition of women's human rights. This includes the work of the Center for Women's Global Leadership at Rutgers University (New Jersey, USA). The Center has campaigned intensively and internationally for the ratification of the Convention on the Elimination of All Forms of Discrimination against Women, which was signed in New York in 1979 during a session of the UN General Assembly. Through the

---

4   The Women's Global Network for Reproductive Rights (WGNRR) is a non-governmental organisation (NGO) established in 1984 at the Fourth International Women's Health Meeting under the theme "No to population control... women decide". WGNRR played a decisive role in making women's voices heard at the 1994 Cairo Conference.

5   Corrêa, Sonia, 1994, *Population and Reproductive Rights: Feminist Perspectives from the South*, London: Zed Books.

6   Founded in 1984 in Bangalore, India, DAWN is a feminist network of researchers, academics and activists from the Global South, developing expertise, advocacy and training on global issues, and sustainable and democratic development. This network was launched between 1984–94 in preparation for the Cairo and Beijing Conferences. DAWN's secretariat is alternately based in different countries in Africa, Asia, Latin America, the Caribbean and the Pacific.

7   The International Women's Health Coalition was established in 1984 and is based in New York. This NGO focuses on the sexual and reproductive health of women and girls in Africa, Asia, Latin America and the Middle East. It aims to build bridges between women in the South and decision makers, and it carries out advocacy work based on achievements ranging from the 1994 Cairo Conference to the document "Transforming our world: the 2030 agenda for sustainable development", which was unanimously adopted in September 2015 by all 193 UN member states.

work of these institutions, human rights gradually came to incorporate the notion of reproductive rights between 1984 and 1994.[8]

Three major UN conferences in the 1990s recognised the inclusion of reproductive rights in human rights (see Appendix B). The 1993 World Conference on Human Rights in Vienna, in its Declaration and Programme of Action (paragraph 18), considered that the rights of women and girls constitute an inalienable, integral and indivisible part of universal human rights. This principle was reaffirmed in the Programme of Action (principle 4) of the 1994 Cairo conference and in the Declaration (paragraph 9) of the Fourth World Conference on Women, held in Beijing in 1995. With the adoption of this perspective, forced pregnancies came to be considered a violation of women's human rights.

The Convention on the Elimination of All Forms of Discrimination against Women clarified the concept of reproductive rights: the preamble prohibits discrimination on the basis of women's reproductive roles and the following articles provide for maternity protection and childcare (Article 4), access to family planning education (Article 10, paragraph h) and access to reproductive health services (Article 12; Article 14, paragraph b), as well as the same rights for women as for men to "decide freely and responsibly" on the number and spacing of their children (Article 16). However, this conception of reproductive rights as affirmed by the Convention is not a recognition of a right to abortion.

Furthermore, the notion of reproductive rights, which was absent from the 1994 Cairo Conference, was mentioned in the 1995 Beijing Conference's Platform for Action (paragraph 96). These two conferences mark an important political turning point in the field of reproduction. The Programme of Action of the Cairo Conference explicitly addresses abortion in the framework of reproductive health, while recognising that only national laws can regulate the practice of abortion. It also enshrines reproductive control as a human right, for both individuals and couples (principle 8). This departed from the perspective of other international conferences on population and development or women's rights. While the 1968 Proclamation of Tehran legitimised the right of couples (not individuals) to choose the number and spacing of their children, it was not until the 1990s that the major international conferences on population (Cairo, 1994) and women's rights (Beijing, 1995) focused on the rights of

---

8   See Cook, Rebecca J., 1994, *Women's Health and Human Rights*, Geneva: WHO; Freedman, Lynn P., and Stephen L. Isaacs, 1993, "Human rights and reproductive choice", *Studies in Family Planning* 24(1), 18–30.

individuals with regard to family planning and reproduction.[9] There was, therefore, a paradigm shift from the previous focus on the demographic objective, which instrumentalises women's bodies.

In the history of international conferences on women's rights, the Platform of Action of the Beijing Conference in 1995 was a turning point in recognising the sociological fact of the dissociation between sexuality and procreation. This had not been the case at the conferences in Mexico (1975) and Nairobi (1985).[10] The Mexico Conference did not mention abortion but only access to contraception, and it stated that only couples could decide on the number of children they wanted. The Nairobi Conference, which was equally silent on the subject of the right to abortion, nevertheless welcomed the notions of bodily integrity and fertility control, stating that women should have the right to choose whether to have children.

It must therefore be emphasised that, although the Programme of Action and the Platform of Action resulting, respectively, from the Cairo and Beijing conferences constituted a breakthrough in their recognition of reproductive freedom and even of the right to choose whether to become a parent, neither conference proclaimed a right to abortion as an expression of the realisation of a right not to become a parent.[11] However, these texts do recognise the protection of reproductive health as a matter of social justice that should be guaranteed by human rights enshrined in national laws and international treaties. In this context, the Cairo Programme of Action highlighted the issue of unsafe abortion as a public health problem, and it called for states to actively expand and improve family planning services. Consensus emerged that where abortion is legal it should be safe and accessible (see Appendix B, the section on the Cairo Conference, paragraph 8.25). The Programme of Action also recommended that states ensure women's access to high-quality abortion and post-abortion care services, including counselling, education and family planning services.

Through these conferences, supporters of the right to abortion found an international political basis for legitimising both their status as advocates and their demands. We will come back to this in Chapter 4 by

---

9   Gautier, Arlette, 2012, *Genre et biopolitiques. L'enjeu de la liberté*, Paris: L'Harmattan, Chapter 7.

10   These were respectively named the World Conference of the International Women's Year and the World Conference to Review and Appraise the Achievements of the United Nations Decade for Women.

11   Gautier, *Genre et biopolitiques*.

examining the discourse of European voluntary associations involved in these issues. At this point it is important to emphasise that the consensus arrived at during these conferences was focused on women's physical health in order to legitimise access to safe and legal abortion, and it was not related to women's self-determination or equality with men.

With regard to women's sexual rights, a reference to sexuality entered the field of human rights through the discussion of family planning and the denunciation of social discrimination and violence against women at the 1968 UN Conference on Human Rights in Tehran. The 1993 Vienna Conference resumed this theme by developing the issue of violence against women, and by denouncing the cultural and religious prejudices that serve to legitimise such violence and attacks on women's rights. However, it was not until the Cairo Conference in 1994 that the notion of "a satisfying and safe sex life" and the reference to well-being first appeared (see Appendix B, the section on the Cairo Conference, paragraph 7.2). This wording would be used in other international texts to signify a dissociation between sexuality and procreation. For example, the right to an autonomous sexual life free from procreative obligations was affirmed at the 1995 Beijing Conference (see Appendix B, the section on international political bases, point 2, paragraph 96).[12]

A year later, in 1996, the IPPF published its declaration on sexual rights, which was revised in 2008.[13] This declaration is primarily about recognising the freedom to manage reproductive health within the framework of gender relations. In that context, the IPPF highlights the following rights.

(1) The right to life (to protect women whose lives are endangered by pregnancy).
(2) The right to liberty and security of the person.
(3) The right to equality and freedom from all forms of discrimination.
(4) The right to privacy.
(5) The right to freedom of thought.
(6) The right to education and information.

---

12   In this respect, the resolution adopted by the UN General Assembly on 25 September 2015 on the 2030 Agenda for Sustainable Development was a step backwards. See Appendix B, the section on international policy bases, point 3.

13   International Planned Parenthood Federation, 2008, "Revised charter on sexual and reproductive rights"; International Planned Parenthood Federation, 2009 "Sexual rights: an IPPF declaration".

(7) The right to choose whether or not to marry and to found and plan a family.
(8) The right to decide whether or not – and how and when – to have children.
(9) The right to access health care and social protection.
(10) The right to the benefits of scientific progress.
(11) The right to association and political participation.
(12) The right to be free of torture and cruel, inhuman and degrading treatment.

While the IPPF is less focused on the recognition of non-reproductive sexual life, the WHO issued a declaration of sexual rights in 2006 that is more focused on sexual health than reproductive health; it also highlighted the issue of women's consent, i.e. the right to have sex without coercion.[14] There is, therefore, a conflict between the IPPF, which is more focused on reproductive health, and the WHO, which is more focused on sexual health. This conflict and the conditions for the emergence of sexual rights have been well described by Alain Giami.[15]

In 2015 the WHO published a report aimed at governments and policymakers. The report sought to improve sexual health by mapping relevant laws and policies in the field of human rights, and by clarifying the links between sexual and reproductive health.[16] In March 2022 the WHO published a new report titled "Abortion care guidelines", which provides the latest empirical evidence on the clinical, legal and human rights aspects of pre- and post-abortion care services.[17] The report updates and replaces the recommendations that the organisation had previously issued. Considering reproductive rights to be human rights, this report highlights the specific rights they entail.

---

14 World Health Organization, 2006, "Defining sexual health: report of a technical consultation on sexual health, 28–31 January 2002". See in particular the list of sexual rights recognised by the WHO on page 5.

15 Giami, Alain, 2015, "Sexualité, santé et droits de l'homme : l'invention des droits sexuels", *Sexologies* 24(3), 105–113.

16 World Health Organization, 2015, *Sexual Health, Human Rights and the Law*, Geneva: WHO; World Health Organization, 2015, *Sexual Health and its Linkages to Reproductive Health: An Operational Approach*, Geneva: WHO. See also World Health Organization, 2017, *Selected Practice Recommendations for Contraceptive Use*, 3rd edition, Geneva: WHO.

17 World Health Organization, 2022, "Abortion care guidelines".

(1) The right to the highest attainable standard of physical and mental health, including sexual and reproductive health and rights.
(2) The right to life.
(3) The right to non-discrimination.
(4) The right to equality.
(5) The right to privacy.
(6) The right to be free from torture and cruel, inhuman or degrading treatment or punishment.
(7) The right to be free from violence.
(8) The right to decide freely and responsibly on the number, spacing and timing of children and to have the information and means to do so.
(9) The right to information.
(10) The right to education.
(11) The right to benefit from scientific progress and its realisation.

The report also highlights that safe abortion is a privilege reserved for the wealthy in countries where procured abortion is legally prohibited, highly restricted or inaccessible due to various procedures that impede it. In addition, the report draws attention to the fact that quality access to medical abortion has seen huge advances, and it recommends that it be expanded further. The report calls for the full decriminalisation of abortion and, in particular, for the removal of legal and procedural restrictions on gestational age limits and the mandatory waiting periods for abortion, as well as the removal of requirements for parental, institutional and third-party consent. Finally, the report recommends that the continuity of abortion care be protected from the limitations and obstacles created by conscientious objection.

2.2 Towards the political and legal inclusion of access to safe and legal abortion in the field of human rights

In the decades of the 2000s and 2010s, a series of texts drafted by the monitoring committees of human rights treaties (under the headings of "general comments", "general recommendations" and "concluding observations"), as well as resolutions passed by the Parliamentary Assembly of the Council of Europe and the European Parliament, were used by activists to legitimise or delegitimise the right to access abortion. Unsurprisingly, the votes in these resolutions were far from unanimous, and the recognition of subsidiarity (i.e. that abortion is the responsibility of individual states) was often reiterated in both the resolutions and the observations (see Appendix B). Against this backdrop, the general trend that has emerged in the EU is to recognise a right of access to abortion based on women's right to health but not one based on their right to self-determination.

Table 2.1. International political bases: conferences organised by the United Nations.

Protected human rights	Vienna 1993	Cairo 1994	Beijing 1995
Right to life		Principle 1 Paragraph 83.4	Paragraph 106 Paragraph 126
Right to be free of all cruel, inhuman and degrading treatment	Paragraph 56	Paragraph 4.10	
Right to equality and freedom from all forms of discrimination	Paragraph 18	Principle 1 Principle 4	Paragraph 214 Paragraph 216 Paragraph 232
Right to change discriminatory practices against women	Paragraph 18 Paragraph 38 Paragraph 49	Paragraph 4.4 Paragraph 5.5 Paragraph 9.2	Paragraph 107 Paragraph 224 Paragraph 230
Right to health, reproductive health and family planning	Paragraph 18 Paragraph 24 Paragraph 31 Paragraph 41	Principle 8 Paragraph 7.2 Paragraph 7.3 Paragraph 7.5	Paragraph 89 Paragraph 92 Paragraph 106 Paragraph 223
Right to privacy		Paragraph 7.2	Paragraph 106 Paragraph 107
Right to choose the number and spacing of births		Principle 8 Paragraph 7.3	Paragraph 223
Right to the benefits of scientific progress		Paragraph 7.3	
Right to freedom of thought, conscience and religion	Paragraph 22		

Source: Center for Reproductive Rights, 2011, "Safe and legal abortion is a woman's human right", p. 6 (www.reproductiverights.org).

Table 2.2. Main international and European legal instruments related to human rights.

Protected human rights	European Convention on Human Rights (1950)	International Covenant on Civil and Political Rights (1966)	International Covenant on Economic, Social and Cultural Rights (1966)	Convention on the Elimination of All Forms of Discrimination against Women (1979)	Convention on the Rights of the Child (1989)	Revised European Social Charter (1996)	Charter of Fundamental Rights of the European Union (2000)
Right to life	Art. 2.1 Art. 5.1	Art. 6.1			Art. 6		Art. 2
Right to be free of all cruel, inhuman and degrading treatment	Art. 3	Art. 7			Art. 37 (a)		Art. 4
Right to equality and freedom from all forms of discrimination	Art. 14	Art. 3	Art. 3	Art. 1 Art. 2 Art. 3	Art. 2		Art. 23
Right to change the practice of discrimination against women				Art. 2 Art. 3 Art. 5	Art. 24.3		
Right to health, reproductive health and family planning			Art. 12	Art. 11.1 (f) Art. 11.3 Art. 12 Art. 14.2 (b)	Art. 24	Art. 11	Art. 35

Among the main international and European legal instruments that may be taken into consideration by the European Court of Human Rights (ECHR) and the Court of Justice of the European Union (CJEU), it is important to cite the following: the Convention for the Protection of Human

Table 2.2. Continued.

Protected human rights	European Convention on Human Rights (1950)	International Covenant on Civil and Political Rights (1966)	International Covenant on Economic, Social and Cultural Rights (1966)	Convention on the Elimination of All Forms of Discrimination against Women (1979)	Convention on the Rights of the Child (1989)	Revised European Social Charter (1996)	Charter of Fundamental Rights of the European Union (2000)
Right to privacy	Art. 8	Art. 17			Art. 16		Art. 7
Right to choose the number and spacing of births				Art. 16.1 (e)			
Right to the benefits of scientific progress		Art. 15 (b)					
Right to freedom of thought, conscience and religion	Art. 35						Art. 10
Right to human dignity							Art. 1

Source: Center for Reproductive Rights, 2011, "Safe and legal abortion is a woman's human right", p. 6 (www.reproductiverights.org) (last two columns of the table completed by Bérengère Marques-Pereira).

Rights and Fundamental Freedoms (1950), commonly known as the European Convention on Human Rights; the International Covenant on Civil and Political Rights (1966); the International Covenant on Economic, Social and Cultural Rights (1966); the Convention on the Elimination of All Forms of Discrimination against Women (1979); the Convention against Torture and Other Cruel, Inhuman or Degrading Treatment or Punishment (1984); the Convention on the Rights of the Child (1989); the Revised

European Social Charter (1996); and the Charter of Fundamental Rights of the European Union (1999).

International treaties ratified by the states parties have binding force (*hard law*). In the European legal system, treaty-related court decisions are also binding between the parties. In the UN legal system, the work of treaty-monitoring committees is authoritative but not binding (*soft law*).[18] The questions of who decides the effective scope of a treaty (i.e. whether it is binding) and of how that decision is made form a central aspect of the complexity of the struggle around sexual and reproductive rights. States parties remain the lead voices in making these decisions. One element of the complexity of international and European legal instruments is the multitude of decision makers, which makes it difficult to determine legal standards for sexual and reproductive rights.[19]

The main international human rights treaties have monitoring committees whose primary duty is to assess the progress of states parties with regard to a treaty and its implementation. Committee members are appointed by the states parties but act independently. Their autonomy is nonetheless relative; without taking orders from the states parties, the committee members are attentive to their interests. The legitimacy of these committees is therefore based on this relative degree of autonomy. The committees receive periodic reports by the states parties setting out the various initiatives they have taken in order to respect, protect and ensure the various human rights provided for in the treaty. The committees draw up "concluding observations", which are summarised in a report to the UN General Assembly. In addition, committees may issue "general comments" or "general recommendations". These documents help states parties interpret the different human rights protected by the various treaties.

Some committees also have a mandate to examine individual complaints about human rights violations, which results in written decisions. The following treaties have either an optional additional protocol allowing their committees to hear individual complaints or a similar mechanism in the treaty itself: the International Covenant on Civil and Political Rights; the International Covenant on Economic, Social and Cultural Rights; the Convention on the Elimination of All Forms of Discrimination against

---

18   Chatzistavrou, Filippa, 2005, "L'usage du *soft law* dans le système juridique international et ses implications sémantiques et pratiques sur la notion de règle de droit", *Le Portique* (15), 1–12.

19   Miller, Alice, and Mindy Roseman, 2011, "Sexual and reproductive rights at the United Nations: frustration or fulfilment?", *Reproductive Health Matters* 19(38), 102–118.

Women; and the Convention against Torture and Other Cruel, Inhuman or Degrading Treatment or Punishment. These protocols give women who experience discrimination under national laws the option to bring a complaint against their state. They are also a valuable tool for many associations that work to change their national legislation.

The European Convention on Human Rights is binding on all EU countries. Ensuring the respect of human rights is first the responsibility of the European Court of Human Rights and then of the Committee of Ministers of the Council of Europe, whose follow-up was reserved by the signatory states to the decisions of the Court (see Appendix B, the section on European judicial bases). As for the Revised European Social Charter, compliance with the commitments entered into by the states is monitored by the European Committee of Social Rights (see Appendix B, same section). Controlling effective compliance with the Charter of Fundamental Rights of the European Union (which became binding in 2007) is the responsibility of the CJEU. In addition, the European Commission has developed its strategy for the implementation of the Charter in its communication titled "Strategy for the effective implementation of the Charter of Fundamental Rights by the European Union". In particular, it states: "The Union's accession to the European Convention on Human Rights was made obligatory by the Lisbon Treaty (Article 6(2) TEU) and will complement the system to protect fundamental rights by making the European Court of Human Rights competent to review Union acts."[20] The Charter is also the reference for the work of the European Agency for Fundamental Rights, which was set up in Vienna in February 2007. "Women's rights in turbulent times" was the theme of the 2017 Annual Colloquium on Fundamental Rights in the European Union. In this context, the Agency published a report in November 2017 titled "Challenges to women's human rights in the EU". The report only makes one reference to women's reproductive rights in its chapter on the decline in women's rights.[21] It should be mentioned that access to abortion is not recognised as a fundamental right in the Charter.

Since the adoption of the Cairo Programme of Action, the UN's legal discourse has been similar to the political discourse emanating from international conferences in its emphasis on how the link between restrictive

---

20 European Commission, 2010, "Strategy for the effective implementation of the Charter of Fundamental Rights by the European Union", COM (2010) 573 final, 19 October, p. 3.

21 European Union Agency for Fundamental Rights, 2017, "Challenges to women's human rights in the EU", p. 21.

laws and the high rate of unsafe abortions leads to maternal mortality and morbidity. It also underlines women's right to life and health, which is protected by international treaties on human rights. For their part, the treaty-monitoring committees go beyond the commitments made by states at international conferences, by issuing texts condemning restrictive abortion laws and calling on states to liberalise these laws in order to combat recourse not just to illegal and unsafe abortion but to all clandestine abortion. These texts recommend that states ensure access to abortion at least where a woman's life or physical and mental health are at risk, and in cases of foetal malformation, rape or incest. Recommendations relating to these criteria have been addressed to Northern Ireland, Malta and Poland (which does not apply its own law), as well as Cyprus until 2018 and the Republic of Ireland until 2019. Furthermore, these texts call for the decriminalisation of abortion and the elimination of criminal sanctions for women, doctors and health professionals, although the treaty-monitoring committees have not explicitly called on states to provide abortion on request or on socio-economic grounds. The texts also recommend that countries with laws liberalising abortion also remove non-legislative barriers to its access. Finally, the monitoring committees report that laws and practices that impede access to abortion can lead to violations of women's human rights, including the rights to life, to health, to non-discrimination and to protection from torture and inhuman, cruel and degrading treatment.

However, international and European judgements lag behind these legal discourses. When the UN Human Rights Committee received two applications concerning Ireland (see Appendix B), it highlighted, in its communications concerning the country, only the violation of the right to freedom from abuse and the right to privacy, and it did not uphold the right to non-discrimination. When the ECHR received applications lodged against Ireland and Poland, first and foremost it considered the right to privacy (Article 8).[22]

Although this Court has never clarified the extent to which the right to abortion is protected by the European Convention on Human Rights and has never considered any restriction on access to abortion a violation of the right to freedom from ill-treatment, the ECHR obliges states parties

---

22   Zampas, Christina, and Jaime M. Gher, 2008, "Abortion as a human right: international and regional standards", *Human Rights Law Review* 8(2), 249–294; Zampas, Christina, 2017, "Legal and political discourses on women's right to abortion", in *A Fragmented Landscape: Abortion Governance and Protest Logics in Europe*, edited by Silvia De Zordo, Joanna Mishtal and Lorena Anton, New York/Oxford: Berghahn, pp. 23–45.

to the Convention to effectively guarantee access to abortion where it is legal; the Court considers that they fail in their obligations in the absence of such guarantees (see Appendix B, ECHR, "R. R. v. Poland", "P. and S. v. Poland" and "Tysiąc v. Poland"). In the case "A, B and C v. Ireland" the ECHR found that the right to privacy had been violated because of the absence of a constitutional protection that would guarantee the pregnant woman's right to life (see Appendix B). However, in none of these cases did the Court consider a violation of the right to non-discrimination. Thus, European case law does not, to date, recognise the principles of non-discrimination and gender equality, which are at the heart of women's decision-making autonomy when faced with an abortion. In dealing with abortion applications, the ECHR has adopted a procedural paradigm that avoids a substantive approach.[23] As a result, European case law fails to grasp the scope and scale of women's experiences of abortion, and the gender stereotypes that reduce motherhood to maternalism.[24] The description of these cases in the following four boxes allows for an assessment of violence against women, both symbolically and in terms of physical health.

Case of Tysiąc v. Poland.
The applicant was born in 1971 and had suffered from severe myopia since the age of 6. She had two children, both born by caesarean section, and became pregnant again in February 2000. Concerned about the possible consequences of a pregnancy on her eyesight, she consulted three ophthalmologists, all of whom concluded that pregnancy and childbirth were a risk to her eyesight. Despite her requests, they all refused to issue a certificate authorising an abortion, as there was no certainty that the pregnancy would cause retinal detachment. On 20 April 2000, Dr O. R. G., a general practitioner, certified that a third pregnancy could cause a rupture of the uterus following the two previous deliveries by caesarean section. The doctor also pointed out that, given the condition of the patient's eyes, she would have to avoid

---

23   Erdman, Joanna, 2014, "The procedural turn: abortion at the European Court of Human Rights", in *Abortion Law in Transnational Perspective: Cases and Controversies*, edited by Rebecca J. Cook, Joanna Erdman and Bernard Dickens, Philadelphia (PA): University of Pennsylvania Press, pp. 121–142.

24   Oja, Liiri, and Alicia Ely Yamin, 2016, "'Woman' in the European human rights system: how is the reproductive rights jurisprudence of the European Court of Human Rights constructing narratives of women's citizenship?", *Columbia Journal of Gender and Law* 32(1), 62–95.

physical exertion, which would be difficult for her as she was already raising two small children alone.

On 26 April, convinced that the certificate would allow her to have a legal abortion, the applicant went to a gynaecology and obstetrics clinic in Warsaw, where she was seen by the head of the department, Dr R. D. After a very cursory examination and without consulting the patient's ophthalmological file, he noted on the back of the certificate issued by Dr O. R. G. that neither myopia nor caesarean section are grounds for therapeutic abortion. He then had this note countersigned by a colleague, Dr B., who did not even speak to the patient.

Unable to obtain a therapeutic abortion, the applicant gave birth by caesarean section in November 2000. After giving birth, her eyesight deteriorated dramatically, and on 2 January 2001 she was taken to the emergency room of the Warsaw eye clinic. On 14 March an ophthalmologist certified that, because of recent retinal haemorrhages, the deterioration of her sight was irreversible.

On 29 March 2001 the applicant lodged a complaint against Dr R. D. for having prevented her from obtaining a therapeutic abortion, despite the fact that it was permitted under the law on the prohibition of the termination of pregnancy. This had been detrimental to her physical health, as she had almost lost her sight as a result of the pregnancy and birth. During the investigation, neither of the two doctors who signed the note on 26 April 2000 was interviewed. Furthermore, an expert report drawn up by three doctors from the medical academy in Białystok (an ophthalmologist, a gynaecologist and a forensic pathologist) denied that the pregnancy had had any effect on her sight. On the basis of this report, the public prosecutor closed the case.

The applicant appealed against this decision, contesting the expert examination on the grounds that only the ophthalmologist had examined her, although the report had been signed by all three experts, and that the examination had lasted only ten minutes and no specialised ophthalmological equipment had been used during it. Pointing to other inconsistencies in the investigation, she added that her short-sightedness had prevented her from reading the documents in her file, some of which were handwritten, and that the prosecutor had refused to help her read them.

The decision to close the case was nevertheless upheld (and on 2 August 2002 it was confirmed by a court). The applicant also attempted to instigate disciplinary proceedings with the medical association against doctors R. D. and B., but without success. As of

2001 the applicant was in fear of going blind, no longer able to care for her children, and unemployed and in receipt of a small disability allowance.

In "Tysiąc v. Poland" (2007) it was argued that Articles 3, 8 and 14 of the European Convention on Human Rights had been violated. Only Article 8 was considered relevant and there was no reference to reproductive rights or any recognition that access to abortion could be a matter of gender equality.[25]

Case of A, B and C v. Ireland.
Ms A and Ms B were Irish nationals while Ms C was a Lithuanian national. All three believed that they did not qualify for a legal abortion in Ireland and all three travelled to England to terminate their pregnancies.

Ms A was single, alcoholic and unemployed. Her four children (the youngest was disabled) were in care. Having become pregnant again, and having previously suffered from postnatal depression, she feared that this new pregnancy would harm her efforts to stop drinking and regain custody of her children. She borrowed the €650 needed for her trip and her treatment in a private clinic. On 28 February 2005, nine and a half weeks pregnant, she travelled to England in secret and without the knowledge of her social workers. She returned to Ireland the day after the abortion so as not to miss any meetings with her children but had to undergo an emergency curettage and then suffered pain and bleeding for several weeks, though she did not dare seek medical attention.

Ms B also became pregnant "by accident". Unable to care for a child on her own, she took the morning-after pill. When it did not work, she decided to go to England for an abortion. She had to wait several weeks for information from a centre in Dublin and struggled to raise the money for her trip. On 17 January 2005, seven weeks pregnant, she travelled to London in secret, without the knowledge of her family and friends. There she was advised to tell the Irish doctors that she had had a miscarriage. Back in Ireland, she suffered from bleeding

---

25   Sanction: "The Court [...] 6. Holds unanimously (a) that the respondent State shall pay to the applicant, within three months from the date on which the judgement becomes final [...], the following sums [...]: EUR 25,000 [...] for non-material damage; EUR 14,000 [...] for costs and expenses."

and, fearing that she had committed an illegal act, she sought treatment at a clinic in Dublin that was affiliated to the English clinic.

Ms C had undergone chemotherapy for three years to treat a rare form of cancer. Her doctor informed her that the effects of pregnancy on cancer were uncertain and that chemotherapy could pose a danger to the foetus during the first three months of pregnancy. While in remission, she underwent a series of tests without knowing that she was pregnant. When she realised that she was pregnant, she consulted her general practitioner and several specialists, but she said that she did not get sufficient information about pregnancy's risks to health and life or the possible consequences that the tests she had undergone could have for the foetus. She attributed the inadequacy of the information she received to the dissuasive nature of the Irish legislative framework.

After having been forced to seek information about these risks on the internet, she travelled to England at an early stage in her pregnancy to have a medical abortion, but she was refused one on the grounds that she was not resident in England and could not be monitored there. She had to wait until the eighth week of pregnancy to undergo a surgical abortion on 3 March 2005. Back in Ireland she suffered complications from an incomplete abortion that led to bleeding and infection. She complained about the inadequacy of medical care in Ireland and pointed out that, when she saw her general practitioner several months after the abortion, they made no mention of her no longer being pregnant.

In the case "A, B and C v. Ireland" (2010) the ECHR again upheld Article 8. It did so only for applicant C, ruling that it had not been violated for applicants A and B since they could access safe and legal abortion in England. For her part, applicant C was at risk of death, a situation that allows for abortion under Irish law, and the Court found that in the case of applicant C the state had failed to put in place procedures for obtaining a therapeutic abortion and had not respected the right to privacy.[26] The Court overlooked the socio-economic exclusivity of obtaining an abortion abroad, and the compromised ability of some disadvantaged women to exercise reproductive autonomy.

---

26   Sanction: "The Court [...] 7. Holds unanimously (a) that the respondent State shall pay to the third applicant the sum of EUR 15,000 [...] plus any tax that may be chargeable to the applicants, for non-material damage."

Case of R. R. v. Poland.
Born in 1973, the applicant, Ms R. R., was married and had two children. In early December 2001 she consulted her family doctor at a hospital in T., Dr S. B., who diagnosed a pregnancy of six to seven weeks using ultrasound. On 23 January and 20 February she underwent further ultrasound scans, and after the second one Dr S. B. told her that the foetus may have a malformation. The applicant then expressed her wish to have an abortion if the malformation was confirmed.

A third ultrasound, performed in the same public hospital in T., confirmed the malformation. Dr O. recommended that the applicant undergo amniocentesis for genetic testing. On 28 February the applicant went to a clinic in Łódź where a fourth ultrasound scan confirmed the previous ones, and Dr K. Sz. invited her to undergo a genetic examination, which, for administrative reasons, required a referral from Dr S. B. The latter refused to issue this referral or perform an abortion, on the pretext that the pathology supposedly affecting the foetus did not justify recourse to an abortion under the law. Faced with this refusal, the applicant sought advice from the public hospital in T. The hospital informed her of the serious danger that an abortion would pose to her life, as well as the risks involved in a genetic examination, and it referred her to the University Hospital in Krakow for further diagnosis.

On 14 March, in Krakow, Dr K. R. criticised the applicant for considering an abortion, which he said the clinic refused to perform and had never performed in its 150-year history. He also refused to prescribe a genetic examination, believing it to be unnecessary. After further examinations, she left the hospital on 16 March with a certificate from Dr K. R. stating that the foetus had developmental abnormalities and that genetic testing was recommended. On 21 and 22 March she tried, unsuccessfully, to obtain a referral from Dr K. Sz. (Łódź), and then Dr K. R. (Krakow) and her family doctor, Dr S. B., in order to be admitted to the hospital in Łódź for a genetic examination. Without a referral, she was nevertheless admitted on 24 March and an amniocentesis was performed on 26 March (in the twenty-third week of pregnancy). It was only on 9 April that she received the results of the genetic examination in a certificate confirming that the karyotype revealed serious congenital anomalies (Turner's syndrome), and that "the application of the provisions of the 1993 law relating to termination of pregnancy could be considered in this case". However, the doctors at the hospital in T. refused to terminate her pregnancy on the grounds that the foetus was now viable. On 11 July 2002 the applicant gave birth to a daughter with Turner's syndrome.

As early as April the applicant and her husband lodged several complaints with various health bodies, including the hospital in T., about the way she had been treated. On 31 July 2002 she asked the public prosecutor's office to open an investigation against the doctors for having failed in their duty as public officials to safeguard her legally protected interests. At the end of 2002 the case was closed; it was reopened following an appeal, before finally being closed in February 2004. She then brought a civil action against three doctors, the hospital in Krakow and the hospital in T. for having unreasonably delayed the authorisation to undergo a genetic examination, and for having made a decision under conditions that violated her individual rights and dignity.

The decision on the civil suit led to only Dr S. B. being convicted – for having disclosed to the press information about his patient that was covered by medical confidentiality. At the end of 2005 the applicant submitted an appeal against this decision, but the court of appeal dismissed it. In July 2008 she appealed to the supreme court, which overturned the court of appeal's decision and ordered a case review.

On 30 October 2008 the Krakow court of appeal delivered its judgement, referring to the findings of the supreme court, namely, that the person concerned had not been given a referral for a genetic examination in a timely manner, and that she had been deprived of her right to make an informed decision. It thus ordered the protagonists of the case to pay the moral damages requested by the applicant.

In "R. R. v. Poland" (2011) the applicant claimed a violation of Articles 3 and 8 of the European Convention on Human Rights, having been unable to obtain a therapeutic abortion for a case of foetal malformation even though this is provided for under Polish law. The point at question for the ECHR was not the issue of access to abortion but the procrastination of health professionals in determining whether the pregnant woman was legally entitled to an abortion. Again, the Court emphasised the failure of the state to meet its obligations to implement enforcement measures.[27]

Case of P. and S. v. Poland.
The applicants – a mother and daughter – were born in 1974 and 1993 respectively and lived in Lublin. On 9 April 2008 the daughter

---

27   Sanction: "EUR 45,000 for non-material damage".

declared that she had been raped by a boy her age. The rape was confirmed by medical examination and in a police interview. On 20 May the applicant's pregnancy was recognised by a public prosecutor as resulting from an illegal sexual relationship between minors under 15 years of age, a fact that allowed abortion under the family planning act ("Protection of the human foetus and conditions for termination of pregnancy").

The mother applied to the relevant ministry to obtain permission for her daughter to have an abortion, but she was told that to obtain this she would have to contact a doctor. In a public hospital in Lublin the head gynaecologist suggested that the applicants meet a Catholic priest – the mother refused. The mother then met a doctor (and "regional consultant for gynaecology and obstetrics") who was empowered to issue the authorisation for the abortion, but he advised the mother to "get her daughter married" and sent the applicants back to the hospital, where the daughter was hospitalised and where, on 30 May, the same gynaecologist had the mother sign a statement to the effect that she agreed to the abortion procedure but that she was aware that it could cost her daughter her life. The daughter – when her mother was not present – was pressured by the gynaecologist and a priest to make a statement renouncing the abortion.

In the presence of her mother, the daughter withdrew her statement. However, the mother, understanding that her daughter would not get the legal abortion in Lublin to which she was entitled, contacted the family planning federation in Warsaw, where her daughter was then hospitalised with an authorisation to abort on the basis of the certificate issued by the Lublin prosecutor. From then on, not only did the Lublin hospital publicise its refusal to perform the abortion, but the girl was harassed via text messages as well as by the Lublin priest and an anti-abortion activist, who, again, were allowed by the hospital to meet the girl in her mother's absence.

When the parents and their daughter decided to leave the hospital, feeling manipulated, they were harassed by two anti-abortion activists who said the mother should be stripped of her parental rights; the parents called the police. During a six-hour interrogation, the police informed the mother that she had been deprived of her parental rights by a family court in Lublin, and that this judgement ordered her daughter to be placed in a shelter for adolescents. There, treated as a delinquent, the daughter was again pressurised by a priest, as well as a psychologist and an education specialist.

In June the family court in Lublin instigated a case to prove that the girl had not received the appropriate assistance from her family and had been forced by them to terminate her pregnancy. The court concluded that the girl should be separated from her family "in her own interests". Although the girl was still a minor during the proceedings, she was not entitled to any legal assistance or the presence of an adult. The mother appealed and her daughter was allowed to leave the shelter and return home. It was not until February 2009 that the court recognised that the withdrawal of the mother's parental rights had not been justified.

On 16 June 2008 the Ministry of Health decided that an abortion could be performed in Gdańsk, i.e. 500 km north of Lublin. Though legal, the abortion would be carried out in a clandestine manner – but this did not prevent the Catholic Information Agency from denouncing it on the internet.

There were several criminal proceedings in this case: against the girl for unlawful sexual intercourse (dropped in November 2008), against the rapist (dropped in 2011) and against several others, including the parents, who were suspected of forcing their daughter to have an abortion, but also against the anti-abortion activists, priests and doctors for trying to dissuade her. Actions were also brought against the police officers for illegally detaining the girl. Other actions were brought for disclosing her personal data and breaching her medical confidentiality. All of these proceedings would eventually be dismissed.

In the case "P. and S. v Poland" (2012) the applicant claimed a violation of Articles 3, 5 and 8 of the European Convention on Human Rights because she had not been able to obtain a therapeutic abortion in the case of rape, which is provided for under Polish law. The ECHR upheld a violation of Articles 3 and 8 but again focused on the procedural rules of law enforcement. The Court was reluctant to recognise that access to abortion services is necessary for women, and that barriers to it constitute an institutionalised form of gender violence.[28]

---

28 Sanction: "The Court [...] 7. Holds unanimously (a) that the respondent State shall pay to the applicants [...] the following amounts [...]: EUR 30,000 [...] to the first applicant, plus any tax that may be chargeable to the applicant, for non-material damage; EUR 15,000 [...] to the second applicant, plus any tax that may be chargeable to the applicant, for non-material damage; EUR 16,000 [...] plus any tax that may be chargeable to the applicants, for costs and expenses."

As can be seen in all four of these cases, European case law falls far short of the European political and legal basis for legitimising a right of access to safe and legal abortion. This case law is cautious in terms of content but nevertheless demonstrates a certain openness in terms of procedural considerations.

While laws on sexual and reproductive health are the responsibility of individual member states under the principle of subsidiarity, the EU does have powers on public health, gender equality and non-discrimination. In this context, the European Parliament adopted an initial resolution in 2002 (the Van Lancker report, submitted by a member of the social democrat group of MEPs) recommending that states organise access to safe and legal abortion based on the right to health, and that they refrain from punishing women who have been forced to have an illegal abortion (see Appendix B, section on European policy bases, point 3). It was at this point that the EU adopted the recommendations put forward in Cairo in 1994 and in Beijing in 1995. However, in 2013, when a report was submitted by Edite Estrela (an MEP from the social democrat group) on sexual and reproductive rights, with a view to updating the previous one (following successive waves of EU enlargement, with the accession of Malta and Cyprus and the countries of Central and Eastern Europe), it was rejected in favour of an alternative bill tabled by the conservative parliamentary group and voted on without any substantive debate in the plenary session of the parliament (see Appendix B, same section, point 5). The report submitted by Estrela was relatively similar to the first in that it recognised the disparities between European countries in their protection of sexual and reproductive health rights. The report identified barriers to the exercise of these rights, including misuse of the conscience clause, and it recommended that states recognise a right of access to safe and legal abortion. However, the European political context had changed over the previous ten years, which were marked by the economic and financial crisis of 2008 and the rise of conservatives and right-wing identity-based populism.

Despite these upheavals in Europe, the reports submitted by Marc Tarabella (an MEP from the social democrat group) in 2010 and Maria Noichl (also an MEP from the social democrat group) in 2015 on equality between women and men do mention – when referring to sexual and reproductive health rights – the importance of women's autonomy in deciding on abortion, access to reproductive health services and sex education (see Appendix B, same section, points 4, 6 and 7). The European Parliament's 2019 resolutions on the situation of fundamental rights in the EU in 2017 and on the decline of women's rights and gender equality in the Union recommend that member states ensure a right of access to abortion (see Appendix B, same section, points 9 and 10).

Furthermore, the Parliamentary Assembly of the Council of Europe enshrined the right of access to safe and legal abortion in its 2008 resolution (see Appendix B, same section, point 1). Two years later the same assembly called on member states of the Council of Europe to regulate the practice of conscientious objection (see Appendix B, same section, point 1). The Council of Europe Commissioner for Human Rights reaffirmed these principles in 2017.[29]

Finally, the report on reproductive and sexual rights presented by the Croatian social democrat Predrag Fred Matić in June 2021 (during the Covid-19 pandemic) was seen as a victory for abortion rights supporters.[30] With 378 votes in favour, 255 against and 42 abstentions, the positions upheld by this resolution were relatively similar to those proposed in the Estrela Report, which was rejected. In particular, it advocates that the right to health (and in particular sexual and reproductive rights) is a fundamental pillar of women's rights and gender equality, on the basis of the "Abortion care guidelines" report then being prepared by the WHO. It calls on all member states to ensure universal access to safe and legal abortion, and to respect the rights to freedom, privacy and the highest attainable standards of health. The Matić report also calls on member states to ensure safe and legal abortion early in pregnancy and, if necessary, beyond then if the woman's health is at risk. While recognising individual conscientious objection, the report regrets that its widespread use is abusive, as it has become institutionalised in hospitals and in entire gynaecology departments, thus leading to a denial of pre- and post-abortion care, which puts women's lives at risk.

Furthermore, the almost total ban on abortion in Poland has led to a series of significant reactions from different European bodies in favour of the right to access safe and legal abortion. The Federation for Women and Family Planning (see Appendix D, Table D.6) invited Polish women to bring a case to the ECHR to challenge Poland's 22 October 2020 judgement. On 1 July 2021 the Court informed the Polish government of its

---

29 Council of Europe, Commissioner for Human Rights, "Women's sexual and reproductive health and rights in Europe". See Appendix B, section on European policy bases, point 3.

30 European Parliament, 2021, "European Parliament Resolution on sexual and reproductive health and rights in the EU, in the frame of women's health", 2020/2215 (INI), 24 June, points 33–37.

decision to hear a series of twelve cases.[31] These cases invoked the right to be free from cruel, inhuman and degrading treatment and the right to privacy. The Commissioner for Human Rights acted as a third party before the Court in these new cases. She observed that the constitutional judgement added to the deteriorating situation around women's sexual and reproductive health and rights and concluded, in this context, that the judgement deviated from the obligations incumbent upon Poland under international human rights law, and that it ran counter to the principle of the non-regression of said human rights.[32]

In addition, the Council of Europe Committee, which is responsible for supervising the execution of the Court's judgements, refused to close the cases in which Poland had been convicted.[33] The Commissioner for Human Rights intervened to express regret that Poland had not taken steps to implement its own legislation of 1993 in this respect.[34]

Finally, the European Parliament's resolution on the right to abortion in Poland condemned the Polish Constitutional Court's ruling banning almost all abortions.[35] This condemnation was reiterated one year later: the European Parliament resolution issued on the first anniversary of the de facto ban condemned "the illegitimate decision of the Constitutional Tribunal of 22 October 2020".[36] The resolution reiterated the European Parliament's position on access to safe and legal abortion and expressed solidarity with the Polish women and activists who continue to help women access abortion-related health care.

---

31 European Court of Human Rights, 2021, "K. B. v. Poland and 3 other applications", Application no. 1819/21, 1 July; "K. C. v. Poland and 3 other applications", Application no. 3639/21, 1 July; "A. L.-B. v. Poland and 3 other applications", Application no. 3801/21, 1 July.

32 Council of Europe, Commissioner for Human Rights, 2021, "Third party intervention by the Council of Europe Commissioner for Human Rights under Article 36, paragraph 3, of the European Convention on Human Rights", Strasbourg, 10 November.

33 Council of Europe, Committee of Ministers, 2021, "Decisions, supervision of the execution of the European Court's judgements, concerning Tysiąc and R. R. (Application nos. 5410/03, 27617/04), P. and S. (Application no. 57375/08) v. Poland", CM/Del/Dec (2021) 1419/H46-25, 2 December.

34 Council of Europe, Commissioner for Human Rights, 2020, "Submission by the Council of Europe Commissioner for Human Rights", Strasbourg, 27 January.

35 European Parliament, 2020, "European Parliament Resolution on the de facto ban on the right to abortion in Poland", 20/2876 (RSP), 26 November.

36 European Parliament, 2021, "European Parliament Resolution on the first anniversary of the de facto abortion ban in Poland", 2021/2925 (RSP), 11 November, points 1–3.

Table 2.3. Resolutions of the Parliamentary Assembly of the Council of Europe and of the European Parliament directly or indirectly concerning the issue of abortion.

Issues addressed	EP 06/06/2002	PACE 16/04/2008	EP 10/02/2010	PACE 20/07/2010	EP 10/12/2013	EP 10/03/2015	EP 09/06/2015	EP 16/01/2019	EP 13/02/2019
Subsidiarity					Paragraph 1	Paragraph 46			
Right to equality							Paragraph 53	Paragraph 1	Paragraph 1
Right to autonomy		Paragraph 7.3	Paragraph 36			Paragraph 47		Paragraph 23	Paragraph 1
Safe and legal access to abortion	Paragraph 12 Paragraph 13	Paragraph 7.1 Paragraph 7.2 Paragraph 7.4						Paragraph 23	
Access to sexual and reproductive health services	Paragraph 11		Paragraph 36			Paragraph 47	Paragraph 52	Paragraph 23	Paragraph 27

Sex education	Paragraph 7.5 Paragraph 7.7			Paragraph 48	Paragraph 23
Conscience clause	Paragraph 11		Paragraph 1		
Access to non-objecting doctors	Paragraph 11		Paragraph 2		
Access to contraception	Paragraph 8	Paragraph 10			Paragraph 23
Unsafe abortion as a public health problem	Paragraph 9				
Dissemination of scientific and objective information and advice	Paragraph 10				

Source: Table designed by Bérengère Marques-Pereira.

The date of 22 October 2020 was also marked by another event concerning the issue of abortion at the international level: an online ceremony was broadcast from Washington and hosted by the governments of Brazil, Egypt, Hungary, Indonesia, Uganda and the United States, to present the Geneva Consensus Statement on Promoting Women's Health and Strengthening the Family. This declaration, however, which presented itself as a restrictive amendment to the Universal Declaration of Human Rights, asserted state sovereignty with regard to abortion and denied that it should be considered a human right.

*

Overall in Europe, there is consensus in two areas: the predominance of women's right to life over the right of the foetus, and the recognition of a right of access to safe and legal abortion. However, there is no consensus when it comes to the beginning of life, and this question is left to the discretion of individual states in accordance with the principle of subsidiarity. Supporters of a right of access to abortion therefore focus mainly on women's right to health. However, the right to health and public health social policies – rather than being linked to women's autonomy – are part of social citizenship as classically defined by T. H. Marshall.[37] Opponents of the right to abortion, on the other hand, focus on the right to life from conception, relaying the positions of the Holy See. They oppose the inclusion of reproductive health, and of sexual and reproductive rights, within the scope of human rights. While Chapter 3 examines this opposition in more detail, Chapter 4 analyses the discourse of both supporters and opponents of abortion rights at the European level.

---

37   According to Marshall in *Citizenship and Social Class* (1950, Cambridge University Press), the notion of citizenship was extended from civil and political rights to include social rights. These rights ensure the maintenance of individual life through benefits in money or in kind via the implementation of social policies by public authorities, including health care.

3 | The Holy See's opposition to the inclusion of sexual and reproductive health and sexual and reproductive rights in the field of human rights

The Catholic Church has consistently and repeatedly expressed its strong opposition to the inclusion of reproductive health and reproductive rights, and the right to abortion in particular, in the field of human rights. This is evident in the statements made by representatives of the Holy See at the major international conferences discussed in the previous chapter, as well as in encyclicals, in apostolic letters addressed to its ecclesiastical body, to the faithful and to women, and in its general audiences.

The Holy See – a sovereign state in a territory defined by the Lateran Treaty of 1929 – is a non-member permanent observer in several UN institutions. As an observer, the Holy See participates in all their activities and can take the floor and issue documents when it considers it necessary, but it cannot vote. In this sense, it holds a non-political role engaged in "ethical–political diplomacy",[1] which does not mean that it acts solely as an ethical player. As a state, the Holy See has no means of coercion over Catholics outside its borders, and it exercises its power only to impose norms and sanctions on its ecclesiastical body. But like any state, even a micro one, it defends its own interests. Its international policy is expressed in two areas: defending religious freedom, and promoting ethical choices through its social teachings.[2] Thus, representatives of the Holy See systematically reiterate that the primary human right is the right to life (i.e. from conception to natural death). This focus also entails a privileged position for the right to human dignity. Moreover,

---

1   Mabille, François, "Le Saint-Siège, *weak state* et *soft power*", in *Religion et politique*, p. 177.

2   For more details, see ibid.; Nouailhat, Yves-Henri, 2006, "Le Saint-Siège, l'ONU et la défense des droits de l'homme sous le pontificat de Jean-Paul II", *Relations internationales* (127), 95–110.

these representatives consider respect for religious freedom to be a fail-safe test for the observance of basic rights.

On the basis of this perspective, the Holy See denounces the concepts of "abortion rights", "sexual and reproductive health", "sexual and reproductive rights" and "gender". In the field of sexuality it lays down two norms that it considers to be immutable: that the sexual act is only licit within the confines of marriage between a man and a woman, a marriage supposed to be expressed in love and the gift of self as reflected in the willingness to procreate (thus only natural contraception methods are allowed); and that life must be protected from the moment of conception (which implies a ban on procured abortion and embryonic manipulation).

The Catholic Church has always been reluctant to accept individual free will that transforms nature and refutes the existence of a divine, natural and unchanging order. In this spirit, the Church's moral position on the family condemns abortion, the growing number of divorces, sterilisation and what it calls the "contraceptive mentality". Individual freedom is stigmatised and seen as an abuse: it is "conceived not as a capacity for realising the truth of God's plan for marriage and the family, but as an autonomous power of self-affirmation, often against others, for one's own selfish well-being".[3] Therefore, developing responsible parenthood based on individual free will contradicts the Church's stance on sexual and family morality, which is based entirely on the biological laws of procreation. This is why the Vatican particularly condemns contraception and abortion. The inalienable value it accords to embryonic life indicates that the Church is trying to resist the evolution of morals in order to codify sexual behaviour.

In 1965 Pope Paul VI's Pastoral Constitution titled *Gaudium et Spes* condemned "whatever is opposed to life itself, such as any type of murder, genocide or abortion".[4] In 1968 the Pope's encyclical titled *Humanae Vitae* condemned "artificial birth control" and promoted periodic abstinence.[5] Abortion is defined not only as a sin but as a crime, since the assumption is of immediate life at conception. In this perspective, the

---

3   *Apostolic Exhortation, Familiaris Consortio of His Holiness Pope John Paul II to the Episcopate, the Clergy and the Faithful of the Whole Catholic Church on the Role of the Christian Family in the Modern World*, 1981, Rome: Libreria Editrice Vaticana, point 6.

4   *Pastoral Constitution on the Church in the Modern World, Gaudium et Spes*, 1965, Rome: Libreria Editrice Vaticana.

5   *Humanae Vitae: Encyclical Letter of the Supreme Pontiff, Pope Paul VI, on the Regulation of Birth*, 1968, Rome: Libreria Editrice Vaticana.

right of the embryo to be recognised as a human person constitutes the limit to responsible parenthood. The Church's doctrine did not change in this respect under Pope John Paul II, Pope Benedict XVI or Pope Francis, despite the adoption of more modern communication strategies.[6] These modernised strategies reveal, beyond the language itself, an attempt at substantive coherence based on criticisms of the societal and ecological effects of current global capitalism, in order to justify a return to the natural order. By denying women their freedom in the name of protecting ecological balances, Pope Francis's discourse, under the guise of progressivism, distorts the criticism of consumerist capitalism in order to obscure the allocation of women to the rank desired by the Church. The Holy See is firmly opposed to women having control over their sexuality in the sense affirmed at the Fourth World Conference on Women, in Beijing in 1995 (see Chapter 2 and Appendix B).

The series of major international conferences organised by the United Nations in the 1990s dealing directly or indirectly with women's rights saw the emergence of anti-abortion factions in international organisations, generally involving conservative states – such as Russia and the Arab States of the Persian Gulf – that were influenced by the traditional values of the Vatican and the Orthodox Church and by Islamic fundamentalist teachings.[7] The discursive activism of religious fundamentalists stands in stark contrast to the international norms that have developed in the field of reproductive health and rights (see Chapter 2).

This chapter analyses two bodies of work: firstly, the encyclicals, apostolic letters and audiences related to the most basic rights in the eyes of the Holy See (i.e. the right to life, dignity and freedom of conscience and religion), which shed light on the Church's conception of the

---

6   See Schreiber, Jean-Philippe, 2017, "En conclusion : Église et sexualité", in *La Sainte Famille. Sexualité, filiation et parentalité dans l'Église catholique*, edited by Cécile Vanderpelen-Diagre and Caroline Sägesser, Brussels: Éditions de l'Université de Bruxelles, pp. 223–232.

7   Buss, Doris E., 1998, "Robes, relics and rights: the Vatican and the Beijing Conference on Women", *Social and Legal Studies* 7(3), 339–363. For the Orthodox Church and abortion, see Stoeckl, Kristina, 2016, "The Russian Orthodox Church as moral norm entrepreneur", *Religion, State and Society* 44(2), 132–151. For the various schools and trends in Islamic views on abortion at the Cairo Conference, see Chetouani, Lamria, 1995, "Procréation ou contraception ? De la bioéthique à la biopolitique", *Mots. Les langages du politique* (44), 73–98; Hessini, Leila, 2008, "Islam and abortion: the diversity of discourses and practices", *IDS Bulletin* 39(3), 18–27.

role of women and the family; and secondly, the reservations made by the Holy See at the conferences in Cairo in 1994 and Beijing in 1995 on contraception, abortion, and reproductive health and rights, as well as the positions expressed by the Holy See's representatives between 1994 and 2018 on the themes of population and development, and women's and human rights.

Thematic analysis of these documents highlights the values and devaluations that legitimise the norms defended by the Holy See with regard to sexuality and procreation. This system of values rejects any new human rights, and in particular entails unwavering opposition to any recognition of the right to abortion in the field of these rights – a field opened up by the international community and enriched by the notions of reproductive health and reproductive rights.

3.1 The Holy See's positions on human rights in its religious discourse

The encyclicals and apostolic letters relating to human rights demonstrate the founding importance for the Holy See of the rights to life, human dignity, and freedom of conscience and religion. The values implied by these rights are reflected in three themes: firstly, all abortion is a crime; secondly, the dignity of women lies first and foremost in their roles as wives and mothers within the family in the context of the natural and social complementarity of the sexes; and thirdly, freedom can only lead to a "culture of death" if it is not subject to the transcendence of natural law. These values are accompanied by a devaluation of the right to have rights (since the Church values duty and responsibility), of a lack of differentiation between the sexes and of their equality in law (as opposed to the natural complementarity of the sexes and their equality in dignity) and of individualism and utilitarianism (rejected in favour of organicism and a dogma of personalism).

In these matters the Church grants itself a monopoly on ethical statements through a series of rhetorical devices that shift the direction of the debate and obstruct discussion; these include amalgamation (of abortion with genocide), denigration (e.g. the accusations against the IPPF, or the anathema cast on the notion of gender), "common sense" (the naturalness of the division of the sexes), the naturalisation of social relations (the gendered division of labour between men and women), the essentialisation of the other through biological determinism (*woman* as a figure of otherness embodying femininity) and the inversion of the meaning of terms (a "new feminism"[8] that is anti-feminist). These statements made by the Vatican find their sole legitimacy in the Church's role as the depository of the faith, and not in any form of actual experience, as Church leaders are not permitted to have any sexual or family life.

Let us review some of the areas developed in Church doctrine and see how they apply to sexual and reproductive health and rights.

All abortion is a crime

The first theme – that all abortion is a crime – became the Holy See's hobby horse at the Cairo and Beijing conferences. It was this context that saw the publication of Pope John Paul II's *Letter to Families* (1994), the encyclical titled *Evangelium Vitae* (1995) (subtitled *On the Value and Inviolability of Human Life*) and the Pope's *Letter to Women* (1995).[9]

The first of these documents reiterates that the sacred value of life opposes any separation between sexuality and procreation, and it recommends a legislative and activist strategy to combat the "culture of death", as opposed to the "culture of life".

In relation to the legislative field, the document states:

> The truth of faith is likewise the truth about the human being. It clearly indicates the gravity of all attempts on the life of a child in the womb [...] *No human lawgiver can therefore assert: it is permissible for you to kill, you have the right to kill, or you should kill.*[10] Tragically, in the history of our century, this has actually occurred when certain political forces have come to power, even by democratic means, and have passed laws contrary to the right to life of every human being, in the name of eugenic,

---

8   In this regard, see Couture, Denise, 2012, "L'antiféminisme du 'nouveau féminisme' préconisé par le Saint-Siège", *Recherches féministes* 25(1), 15–35; Garbagnoli, Sara, 2015, "L'hérésie des 'féministes du genre' : genèse et enjeux de l'antiféminisme 'antigenre' du Vatican", in *Les antiféminismes. Analyse d'un discours réactionnaire*, edited by Diane Lamoureux and Francis Dupuis-Déri, Montreal: Éditions du remue-ménage, p. 107–127; Garbagnoli, Sara, "De quoi 'le gender' des campagnes 'anti-genre' est-il le nom? Sur une contre-révolution straight et ses succès", in *Antiféminismes et masculinismes d'hier et d'aujourd'hui*, pp. 241–270.

9   *1994: Year of the Family; Letter [of Pope John Paul II] to Families*, 1994, Rome: Libreria Editrice Vaticana; *Encyclical Letter, Evangelium Vitae of the Supreme Pontiff John Paul II to Bishops, Priests and Deacons, Religious Men and Women, Lay Faithful and All People of Good Will on the Value and Inviolability of Human Life*, 1995, Rome: Libreria Editrice Vaticana; 1995, *Letter [of Pope John Paul II] to Women*, Rome: Libreria Editrice Vaticana.

10   In italics in the text. Note that any italics in quotations are the work of the original authors.

ethnic or other reasons. A no less serious phenomenon, notably because it meets with widespread acquiescence or consensus in public opinion, is that of laws which fail to respect the right to life from the moment of conception. How can one morally accept laws that permit the killing of a human being not yet born, but already alive in the mother's womb? The right to life becomes an exclusive prerogative of adults who even manipulate legislatures in order to carry out their own plans and pursue their own interests. [...] We are facing an immense threat to life: not only to the life of individuals but also to that of civilization itself. The statement that civilization has become, in some areas, a "civilization of death" is being confirmed in disturbing ways.[11]

This Manichaean reasoning is bolstered by the amalgamation of abortion, eugenics and genocide in the context of the rejection of individualism and utilitarianism. Moreover, the Pope frames his arguments as truths, thus undermining the ability of opponents to express themselves on the subject: their *logos*[12] cannot access the expression of human truth, because they cannot hear the truth of faith.[13]

With regard to activism, the Pope notes:

Nevertheless, in the last few decades some consoling signs of a *reawakening of conscience* have appeared: both among intellectuals and in public opinion itself. There is a new and growing sense of respect for life from the first moment of conception particularly amongst young people; pro-life movements are spreading. This is a leaven of hope for the future of the family and of all humanity.[14]

In the encyclical titled *Evangelium Vitae* the sacred value of human life, including that of the "unborn child", and the criminal nature of all abortion is reaffirmed within a framework that postulates the inviolability of the human body, and that rejects any individualistic perspective based on the right to autonomy and self-determination. Furthermore, the encyclical calls for a "cultural change"; it values the commitment of the voluntary sector, those involved in education or legislation, intellectuals and mothers.

With regard to the right to life, abortion is presented as an "unspeakable crime":

---

11   *1994: Year of the Family*, pp. 47.

12   *Logos* is understood here in the sense of speech, discourse.

13   For a theoretical approach to this type of problem, see Rancière, Jacque, 1995, *La mésentente. Politique et philosophie*, Paris: Galilée.

14   Ibid., p. 47. The religious inspiration behind the activism of voluntary associations that oppose any right to abortion will be analysed in the next chapter.

Procured abortion is *the deliberate and direct killing, by whatever means it is carried out, of a human being in the initial phase of his or her existence, extending from conception to birth* [...] The one eliminated is a human being at the very beginning of life. No one more absolutely *innocent* could be imagined [...] He or she is *weak*, defenceless [...] The unborn child is *totally entrusted* to the protection and care of the woman carrying him or her in the womb.[15]

The prohibition of abortion is therefore absolute, regardless of the circumstances in which the pregnant woman – thought of as a mother – finds herself, both in terms of health and in psycho-medical and socio-economic terms (point 58). The Vatican also prohibits any dissociation between sexuality and procreation, such as contraception (point 13), the medical termination of pregnancy (point 13) and medically assisted procreation (point 63). These texts denounce a hedonistic, individualistic and utilitarian mentality, and they shift meanings by amalgamation: contraception leads to an "abortion mentality" (point 13) and medically assisted procreation leads to a "eugenic mentality", thus paving the way to legitimising infanticide and euthanasia (point 63).

With regard to initiatives to be taken in order to achieve a "cultural change" based on a "culture of life", the *Evangelium Vitae* encyclical reiterates the importance of having a "Day for Life" celebration (point 85), as well as a range of educational initiatives: these would create "centres for natural methods of regulating fertility" to promote "responsible parenthood"; they would favour "the Christian vision of the person" through the specific work of "marriage and family counselling agencies"; they would set up "centres for assistance to life" and "homes or centres where new life receives a welcome" (point 88); and they would reassert the role of hospitals, clinics and convalescent homes whose Christian identity is clearly displayed, and the role of health care personnel whose desire for "absolute respect for every innocent human life also requires *the exercise of conscientious objection* in relation to procured abortion and euthanasia" (point 89).

Similarly, the encyclical stresses the important role of voluntary organisations and politicians in developing and implementing cultural and social projects to "remove unjust laws", to combat attacks on the right to life through a family policy that is "central to all social policies" (point 90) and to fight against demographic policies that encourage birth control through "contraception, sterilization and abortion" (points 17 and 91). On this topic the text does not hesitate to resort to conspiracy theories,

---

15   *Encyclical Letter, Evangelium Vitae*, point 58, pp. 49–50.

notably targeting – albeit not explicitly – international organisations such as the WHO and the IPPF (point 17):

> Aside from intentions, which can be varied and perhaps can seem convincing at times, especially if presented in the name of solidarity, we are in fact faced by an objective "conspiracy against life", involving even international institutions, engaged in encouraging and carrying out actual campaigns to make contraception, sterilization and abortion widely available. Nor can it be denied that the mass media are often implicated in this conspiracy, by lending credit to that culture which presents recourse to contraception, sterilization, abortion and even euthanasia as a mark of progress and a victory of freedom, while depicting as enemies of freedom and progress those positions which are unreservedly pro-life.[16]

This struggle for cultural hegemony in favour of a "culture of life" feeds into a "new evangelization" (point 95), which does not hesitate to disregard the separation between the Church and politics. Furthermore, while the call for voluntary commitment within civil society is certainly addressed to voluntary organizations that consider themselves pro-life, it also addresses women promoting a "new feminism" (point 99).

In keeping with this new "commitment", in June 1995, on the eve of the international conference in Beijing, Pope John Paul II sent a letter to women reminding them that their dignity lies in their "vocation" and "mission" as wives and mothers – a theme that is addressed below.

The dignity of women: complementarity between the sexes, the rejection of gender and ideological colonisation

Pope John Paul II, in his 1994 letter to families and 1995 letter to women, focuses on the themes of the dignity of women and gender complementarity. For his part, Cardinal Joseph Ratzinger – prefect of the Congregation for the Doctrine of the Faith from 1981 prior to becoming Pope Benedict XVI on 19 April 2005 – rejects the notion of gender both in his letter to the bishops on the collaboration of men and women (July 2004) and in his address to the members of the Roman Curia (December 2008). Pope Francis took up this theme again his general audience on the family in April 2015, but this time with the notion of "ideological colonization".[17] Let us examine the two main themes in turn.

---

16 Ibid., point 17, p. 14.

17 Case, Mary Anne, 2016, "The role of the popes in the invention of complementarity and the Vatican's anathematization of gender", *Religion and Gender* 6(2), 155–172.

Complementarity between the sexes

Complementarity between the sexes is part of an essentialist, organicist and personalist conception. Here, essentialism attributes to a set of individuals traits considered inherent to their gender, i.e. it sees women as a homogeneous group – *woman* as a symbol of otherness – thus making men the norm of reference and reverence. Contemporary organicism has inherited the reactionary responses of thinkers such as Joseph de Maistre and Louis de Bonald to the universalist and individualist doctrines of the French Revolution.[18] These responses see society as an organic body, which justifies the pre-eminence of society over individuals and affirms that each individual should remain in his or her place so as to respect so-called natural hierarchies and traditional values. Personalism was developed between the 1920s and 1970s by Emmanuel Mounier in the journal *Esprit*, which he founded in 1932.[19] It asserts the primacy of persons and the community, opposing both liberal individualism and totalitarian collectivism. This intellectual stance had a significant influence on political thought in majority-Catholic countries, and on Karol Wojtyła, who became Pope John Paul II on 16 October 1978.

In his 1994 letter to families, and referring to his earlier apostolic exhortation *Familiaris Consortio,* Pope John Paul II considers the duality of the human race from the complementarian perspective of the masculine and feminine nature of individuals (point 6, p. 7 of his letter to families). This complementarity is expressed in marriage, which is entirely centred around the creation of a new family, the fundamental "unit" of society (point 13, p. 21). "The truth of the family" is being destroyed by the grip of positivism, utilitarianism and individualism:

> Positivism, as we know, results in agnosticism in theory and utilitarianism in practice and in ethics. In our own day, history is in a way repeating itself. *Utilitarianism* is a civilization of production and of enjoyment, a civilization of "things" and not of "persons", a civilization in which persons are used in the same way as things are used. In the context of a civilization of enjoyment, "*the woman*" can become an object for "*the*

---

18   De Maistre, Joseph, 1998, *Considérations sur la France*, Brussels: Complexe (original edition: 1796). De Bonald, Louis-Ambroise, 1965, *Théorie du pouvoir politique et religieux*, Paris: Union générale d'éditions (original edition: 1796).

19   Mounier, Emmanuel, 2016, *Le personnalisme*, Paris: Presses universitaires de France (original edition: 1950). As opposed to the individual (an isolated, abstract being), the person is "the real man", engaged from birth in a community. The person is oriented towards transcendence and is therefore capable of ethical commitment.

man", children a hindrance to parents, the family an institution obstructing the freedom of its members. To be convinced that this is the case, one need only look at *certain sexual education programmes* introduced into the schools, often notwithstanding the disagreement and even the protests of many parents; or *pro-abortion tendencies* which vainly try to hide behind the so-called "right to choose" ("pro-choice") on the part of both spouses, and in particular on the part of the woman.[20]

This disqualification of the right to autonomy and the right to individual free choice is part of an organicist conception in which freedom that does not submit to the transcendence of natural law can only be understood as an abuse of rights and a loss of the sense of responsibility and duty:

> The person realizes himself by the exercise of freedom in truth. Freedom cannot be understood as a license to do *absolutely anything*: it means a *gift of self*. Even more: it means an *interior discipline of the gift*. The idea of gift contains not only the free initiative of the subject, but also the aspect of *duty*. All this is made real in the "communion of persons". We find ourselves again at the very heart of each family.[21]

Classical and utilitarian liberalism is rejected under the label of individualism, which is seen as denying transcendence and setting up an opposition between the individual and the person:

> Individualism presupposes a use of freedom in which the subject does what he wants, in which he himself is the one to "establish the truth" of whatever he finds pleasing or useful. He does not tolerate the fact that someone else "wants" or demands something from him in the name of an objective truth[22] [...] Individualism thus remains egocentric and selfish. The real antithesis between individualism and personalism emerges not only on the level of theory, but even more on that of "ethos". The "ethos" of personalism is altruistic: it moves the person to become a gift for others and to discover joy in giving himself.[23]

In this framework, human rights are related more to the person and the family than to individuals (point 17 of the letter to families), as advocated

---

20   *1994: Year of the Family*, pp. 21–22.
21   Ibid., pp. 23–24.
22   Here, the Pope is alluding to natural law.
23   *1994: Year of the Family*, p. 24.

by the Holy See's 1983 Charter of the Rights of the Family[24] in a vision that unites family and nation. In this same perspective, the Holy See underlines "how important and burdensome is the work women do within the family unit" and that it "deserves economic recognition" in the form of what could be termed a maternal salary (point 17, p. 35). The maternal ideology of the 1930s is not far away. Maternalism, as a social representation and practice, reduces the female identity to that of a mother. The assimilation of women to mothers in the discourse of the Holy See takes on Marianist inflections. Marianism elevates the image of the Virgin Mary; it endows maternalism with elements of sacrifice, compassion and pain. Being a mother is therefore a vocation and a mission to fulfil one's duties towards the family, behind which the subject with rights disappears.

In his apostolic letter to women titled *Mulieris Dignitatem*,[25] Pope John Paul II develops this maternal vision by describing motherhood as a "vocation" and a "mission", which gives it less the status of domestic work than an essentialist endowment of something like a "feminine genius". The feminine genius would in some way be the spirit of *care,* i.e. caring for others is specific to the "character of the feminine being" and complements the "character of the masculine being" (point 6 in his letter to women). The identity of "*the woman*" is thus defined once and for all; actual women are assigned a transcendental dignity, with men and women equal in dignity but not in rights. The immanence of social relations and their vicissitudes – which are at work in the division between the masculine and the feminine, in the hierarchisation of the masculine over the feminine that runs through all spheres of society, and in the framework of a gendered division of labour that varies in time and space – is obscured in favour of a naturalisation of social relations between the sexes. It is no wonder that the notion of gender is firmly rejected.[26]

---

24   "Charter of the Rights of the Family presented by the Holy See to all persons, institutions and authorities concerned with the mission of the family in today's world", 22 October 1983 (www.vatican.va).

25   *Apostolic Letter, Mulieris Dignitatem of the Supreme Pontiff John Paul II on the Dignity and Vocation of Women on the Occasion of the Marian Year*, 1998, Rome: Libreria Editrice Vaticana.

26   Paternotte, David, 2015, "Introduction. Habemus Gender ! Autopsie d'une obsession vaticane", *Sextant* (31), 7–22.

The rejection of the notion of gender

In his 2004 "Letter to the bishops of the Catholic Church on the collaboration of men and women in the Church and in the world", Cardinal Ratzinger presented "the doctrinal data of biblical anthropology – indispensable for protecting the identity of the human person".[27] He denounces two trends within debates on "women's issues":

> A first tendency is to emphasize strongly conditions of subordination in order to give rise to antagonism: women, in order to be themselves, must make themselves the adversaries of men. Faced with the abuse of power, the answer for women is to seek power. This process leads to opposition between men and women, in which the identity and role of one are emphasized to the disadvantage of the other, leading to harmful confusion regarding the human person, which has its most immediate and lethal effects in the structure of the family.[28]

The essentialisation of women and men into two homogeneous groups ("*the woman*" and "*the man*") and the inversion of the feminist project[29] defined for Pope John Paul II a "new feminism". This is rooted in a naturalistic anthropology that excludes any attempt to submit the foundations of patriarchal domination and oppression to political and social deliberation.
The text of the letter continues:

> A second tendency emerges in the wake of the first. In order to avoid the domination of one sex or the other, their differences tend to be denied, viewed as mere effects of historical and cultural conditioning. In this perspective, physical difference, termed *sex*, is minimized, while the purely cultural element, termed *gender*, is emphasized to the maximum and held to be primary. The obscuring of the difference or duality of the sexes has enormous consequences on a variety of levels. This theory of the human person, intended to promote prospects for equality of women through liberation

---

27   "Letter to the bishops of the Catholic Church on the collaboration of men and women in the Church and in the world", 31 May 2004 (www.vatican.va).

28   Ibid., p. 1.

29   The inversion of the feminist project sees the denunciation of social relations that monopolise economic, social, cultural and political resources of power as a search for power by women; the denunciation of the naturalisation of social relations of sex is reduced to rivalry between the sexes; and the denunciation of patriarchal structures of power within the family is turned into the misguided attempt to make "*the woman*" and "*the man*" identical.

from biological determinism, has in reality inspired ideologies which, for example, call into question the family, in its natural two-parent structure of mother and father, and make homosexuality and heterosexuality virtually equivalent, in a new model of polymorphous sexuality.[30]

The notion of gender is rejected here as opening the door to a lack of differentiation between the sexes, to homosexuality and to the recognition of non-traditional families. The promotion of a naturalistic anthropology is part of a logic of embodiment (a biological determinism rooted in the body) in which recourse to common sense (the naturalness of female and male identities) leads to the idea of a complementarity of the sexes that obscures heterosexist norms.

Cardinal Ratzinger builds on the reasoning of Pope John Paul II, in particular by emphasising "feminine values" and promoting social policies centred on the reconciliation of family and professional work for women (not for men). This reconciliation is centred primarily on the "free choice" between one or the other type of work, assuming the recognition of the economic value of family work (which paves the way to the idea of granting a maternal salary, thus favouring the return of women to the home).

As Pope Benedict XVI, Joseph Ratzinger renewed his denunciation of the notion of gender as "man's attempt at self-emancipation from creation and the Creator. Man wants to be his own master, and alone – always and exclusively – to determine everything that concerns him. Yet in this way he lives in opposition to the truth, in opposition to the Creator Spirit."[31] It is true that the usefulness of the notion of gender in the human sciences is at the opposite end of the spectrum from theological thinking based on the pre-eminence of the transcendence of natural law.[32]

Once he became Pope Francis, on 13 March 2013, Jorge Bergoglio took up this doctrinal issue once more.[33] However, compared with his predecessors, his tone is more moderate, more modernist and above all

---

30   "Letter to the bishops of the Catholic Church on the collaboration of men and women in the Church and in the world", pp. 1–2.

31   Benedict XVI (Pope), 2008, "Address to the Roman Curia on the occasion of the traditional meeting for Christmas greetings", 22 December (www.v2.vatican.va).

32   See Scott, De l'utilité du genre, pp. 17–54.

33   See Apostolic Exhortation, Evangelii Gaudium of Pope Francis to Bishops, Priests and Deacons, Consecrated Persons and All the Lay Faithful on the Proclamation of the Gospel in Today's World, 2013, Rome: Libreria Editrice Vaticana, points 213–214, p. 173; Francis (Pope), 2015, General Audience: St. Peter's Square, Wednesday 15 April and Wednesday 22 April 2015, Rome: Libreria Editrice Vaticana.

more practical. He starts from the actual experience of the poor through the prism of what he calls the "ideological colonisation" that the notion of gender implies with regard to the situation of poor women in the Global South.[34] His encyclicals are not guided by the thematic focus of the earlier ones.

The transcendence of natural law

The encyclicals *Veritatis Splendor*[35] and *Evangelium Vitae* (respectively developed in the contexts of the 1993 World Conference on Human Rights in Vienna and the 1995 Fourth World Conference on Women in Beijing) frequently refer to the transcendence of natural law in order to justify freedom of conscience (which is largely confined to religious freedom), to establish the legitimacy of the universalism of moral norms reduced to religious convictions and to argue for the pre-eminence of moral law over civil law.

As early as 1965 the Catholic Church produced its own declaration on religious freedom, titled *Dignitatis Humanae*, which was adopted at the Second Vatican Council.[36] It affirms that the Catholic Church professes the only true religion and that human dignity requires respect for religious freedom for all, but it does not specify the freedom of belief for non-believers. Since these non-believers are incapable of convictional *logos* when they enter into this debate, they talk about what they do not know, i.e. what they are incapable of knowing as non-believers. Freedom of conscience is clearly equated with religious freedom in *Veritatis Splendor*:

> Certain currents of modern thought have gone so far as to *exalt freedom to such an extent that it becomes an absolute, which would then be the source of values*. This is the direction taken by doctrines which have lost the sense of the transcendent or which are explicitly atheist. The individual conscience is accorded the status of a supreme tribunal of moral judgement which hands down categorical and infallible decisions about good and evil. To the affirmation that one has a duty to follow one's

---

34 Francis (Pope), 2014, "Not just good, but beautiful", address to participants at the international colloquium on the complementarity between man and woman sponsored by the Congregation for the Doctrine of the Faith, 17 November (http://humanum.it); Francis (Pope), *General Audience*.

35 *Encyclical Letter, Veritatis Splendor of the Supreme Pontiff John Paul II to all the Bishops of the Catholic Church on Some Fundamental Questions of the Church's Moral Teaching*, 1993, Rome: Libreria Editrice Vaticana.

36 *Declaration on Religious Freedom, Dignitatis Humanae*, 1965, Rome: Libreria Editrice Vaticana.

conscience is unduly added the affirmation that one's moral judgement is true merely by the fact that it has its origin in the conscience. But in this way the inescapable claims of truth disappear, yielding their place to a criterion of sincerity, authenticity and "being at peace with oneself", so much so that some have come to adopt a radically subjectivistic conception of moral judgement.[37]

Thus, the objectivity of moral judgement cannot belong to agnostics or atheists. The non-believer is disqualified from taking part in the debate as he or she has no authority in this respect. The Catholic Church thus forbids political debate to the non-believer and, in the same spirit, denies non-believers any moral sense. The freedom of conscience of non-believers cannot attain the position of moral authority, because it is part of an individualistic ethic built on the pluralism of values. Yet "there is a tendency to grant to the individual conscience the prerogative of independently determining the criteria of good and evil and then acting accordingly. Such an outlook is quite congenial to an individualist ethic, wherein each individual is faced with his own truth, different from the truth of others. Taken to its extreme consequences, this individualism leads to a denial of the very idea of human nature."[38]

This rooting in anthropological naturalism therefore leads to the negation of the neutrality that is incumbent on the state. The neutrality of the state in ethical matters is not conceivable, because political deliberation is not subject to natural law. This rejection of Enlightenment philosophy is expressed in the denial of the autonomy of reason and of a common humanity that lies in the exercise of reason:

Nevertheless, the autonomy of reason cannot mean that reason itself creates values and moral norms. Were this autonomy to imply a denial of the participation of the practical reason in the wisdom of the divine Creator and Lawgiver, or were it to suggest a freedom which creates moral norms, on the basis of historical contingencies or the diversity of societies and cultures, this sort of alleged autonomy would contradict the Church's teaching on the truth about man. It would be the death of true freedom.[39]

---

37 *Encyclical Letter, Veritatis Splendor*, p. 22.
38 Ibid., p. 23.
39 Ibid., p. 27.

This is a failure to recognise the common sharing of the *logos*. Conversely, this recognition would imply the legitimacy of non-belief, and political debate would once again become possible.[40]

In this perspective, which rejects the immanence of social and power relations in favour of the transcendence of natural law, democratic political deliberation based on the pluralism of values has no legitimacy. The freedom and autonomy of the individual in ethical matters are not conceivable outside the logic of the biological incarnation of the human person (points 47–50 of *Veritatis Splendor*), and abortion, like homicide and genocide, is classed among "intrinsically evil acts" (point 80). Being of divine origin, moral norms are necessarily immutable (point 95) and cannot be subject to a process of deliberation shaped by political power relations.

Thus, unsurprisingly, civil law and the practice of citizenship through participation in political deliberation are delegitimised:[41] in this perspective, the notion of reproductive rights – the rights to safe and legal abortion and to free self-determination – cannot, of course, be given political–legal legitimacy, whereas respect for natural law gives full legitimacy to the conscience clause (points 68–73 of *Evangelium Vitae*). Here we are confronted with a political use of conscience that manifests itself in the questioning of common norms in the name of moral values derived from natural law.[42] We will come back to this in the next chapter when we examine the discourse of voluntary associations that are opposed to the right to abortion.

In short, three main arguments support the values and devaluations of the Holy See's religious discourse: perversity, futility and jeopardy.[43]

The argument from perverse effects refers to the idea that freedom in matters of sexuality leads to the moral decay of people trapped in a

---

40 This perspective is developed by the philosopher Jacques Rancière: "Politics does not exist because men, through the privilege of speech, place their interests in common. Politics exists because those who have no right to be counted as speaking beings make themselves of some account, setting up a community by the fact of placing in common a wrong that is nothing more than this very confrontation, the contradiction of two worlds in a single world: the world where they are and the world where they are not, the world where there is something 'between' them and those who do not acknowledge them as speaking beings who count and the world where there is nothing." (Rancière, *La mésentente*, p. 49.)

41 *Encyclical Letter, Evangelium Vitae*, pp. 58–64.

42 Proeschel, Claude, "La conscience en politique", in *Religion et politique*, p. 288.

43 Arguments largely highlighted in Hirschman, Albert O., 1995, *Deux siècles de rhétorique réactionnaire*, Paris: Fayard (1991, *The Rhetoric of Reaction: Perversity, Futility, Jeopardy*, Belknap Press of Harvard University Press).

hedonistic, individualistic and utilitarian mentality, which ultimately leads to a "culture of death". The argument is based on the affirmation of a natural order based on the transcendence of natural law (which is immutable due to its divine origin).

The futility argument highlights the pointlessness of social change programmes aimed at population reduction as a development tool, on the assumption that artificial contraception, family planning and sex education programmes would not reduce abortion or maternal mortality and morbidity.

The endangerment argument proscribes reforms (i.e. the decriminalisation and legalisation of abortion) because they endanger a greater good obtained at great cost, namely, the right to life and dignity. The endangerment of the "culture of life" in favour of a "culture of death" is expressed using Manichaean reasoning that draws a line between "us" (supporters of the "culture of life") and "them" (supporters of a "culture of death").

3.2 The Holy See's positions at the UN on sexual and reproductive health and sexual and reproductive rights

The positions taken by the Holy See at the United Nations on reproductive health, reproductive rights and abortion are rooted in a less doctrinal and more secular rhetoric that relies on a register of facts and legal interpretation in the field of human rights.[44] Naturally, the doctrinal religious discourse is not abandoned; rather, it is inserted into a discourse that is audible to the international bodies to which it is directed. The Holy See adopts an ethical discourse presented as supporting its "fundamental mission" of seeking the "common good" of humanity. It is in this context that it emphasises religious freedom as one of the most fundamental human rights and highlights its practical actions to eradicate poverty through its health, educational and charitable institutions, as well as its financial contributions.

As a non-member permanent observer to the UN, the Holy See can sign and ratify international treaties. However, it has not ratified the International Covenant on Civil and Political Rights, the International Covenant on Economic, Social and Cultural Rights or the Convention on the

---

44 For more details, see Buss, "Robes, relics and rights"; Coates, Amy L., Peter S. Hill, Simon Rushton and Julie Balen, 2014, "The Holy See on sexual and reproductive health rights: conservative in position, dynamic in response", *Reproductive Health Matters* 22(44), 114–124.

Elimination of All Forms of Discrimination against Women. In fact, it has only ratified three conventions, including the Convention on the Rights of the Child, to which it added reservations regarding family planning education and services, as well as defending the "unborn child".[45]

At the Cairo Conference, the Holy See reiterated its positions through the following reservations:

1. [...] The terms "sexual health" and "sexual rights" and "reproductive health" and "reproductive rights" are to be understood as a holistic concept of health, which embrace, each in their own way, the person in the entirety of his or her personality, mind and body, and which foster the achievement of personal maturity in sexuality and in the mutual love and decision-making that characterise the conjugal relationship in accordance with moral norms. The Holy See does not consider abortion or access to abortion as a dimension of these expressions.

2. With regard to the terms "contraception", "family planning", "sexual and reproductive health", "sexual and reproductive rights" and "women's power to control their own fertility" and "a full range of family planning services" and any other terms relating to the concepts of family planning services and birth control in the document, the Holy See's adherence to the consensus reached on this subject should in no way be interpreted as constituting a reversal of its well-known position concerning those family planning methods which the Catholic Church considers morally unacceptable [...]

4. With regard to the expression "couples and individuals", the Holy See reserves its position on the understanding that this expression is to be interpreted as meaning the married couple and the man and woman who constitute it.[46]

These reservations have been reiterated in the follow-up reviews of the Cairo Conference, every five years and to this day.

At the Beijing Conference, the Holy See opposed any revision to women's rights that would class them as human rights, and in particular any revision from the perspective of gender and equality. This time, however, in contrast to its stance at the Cairo Conference, the Holy See was at pains to protect its image by defining itself as progressive, professional

---

45   See https://treaties.un.org. See also UN Committee on the Rights of the Child, 2012, "Consideration of reports submitted by States parties under article 44 of the Convention", CRC/C/VAT/2, 22 October, paragraphs 10–11, p. 4.

46   United Nations, 1995, *Report of the International Conference on Population and Development: Cairo, 5–13 September 1994*, A/CONF.171/13/Rev.1, New York: UN, item 27, pp. 142–143.

and sensitive to the actual situations of women. In this context, a female Harvard law professor, Mary Ann Glendon, led the Holy See delegation.

However, the reservations made with regard to the Conference's Platform of Action echo the idea of the natural and anthropological complementarity of the sexes, while recognising that women can fulfil roles other than those of wives and mothers (paragraph 11).[47] The "basic unit of society" remains a family composed of a man and a woman, "full human realisation" is based on the duality of the human gender as male and female (paragraph 7), and in no case can women have control over their sexuality (paragraph 5). The Holy See reaffirmed its positions on equality, opposing any extension of the scope of human rights to include women's rights (paragraph 11), and it rejected the term "gender" to emphasise the complementarity of the sexes and thereby exclude any openness to homosexuality (ibid.). Two spectres clearly haunt the Holy See: reproductive autonomy (including the right to abortion and contraception) and homosexuality (including the right to express a sexual orientation and gender identity outside heterosexual norms). In fact, it is the fear of the lack of differentiation between the sexes that underpins these reservations. Like the previous ones, these reservations of the Holy See were reiterated in the follow-up to the Beijing Conference.

In contrast to the statements it made at the Cairo Conference, at the Beijing Conference the Holy See focused less on abortion and contraception and more on the traditional family, the rights of parents to give their children the sexual education of their choice, and heterosexual orientation.

Ten years after the Cairo and Beijing conferences, the Pontifical Council for the Family compiled all these views and statements in a publication titled *Lexicon: Ambiguous and Debatable Terms Regarding Family Life and Ethical Questions*.[48] In this document, the Holy See reiterates the positions it expressed at these conferences and UN bodies.[49] Of particular note are the speeches made at the UN General Assembly on the promotion and

---

47   United Nations, 1996, *Report of the Fourth World Conference on Women: Beijing, 4–15 September 1995*, A/CONF.177/20/Rev.1, New York: UN, item 12, pp. 168–173.

48   Published in Paris by Pierre Téqui in 2005. In this book, see in particular Cancio, Alfredo Peris, "Sexual and reproductive rights", pp. 263–273; Ossa, Francisco J. Errazuriz, "Women: discrimination and CEDAW", pp. 535–542; Revoredo, Oscar Alzamora, "'Gender': dangers and scope of this ideology", pp. 559–574; Le Méné, Jean-Marie, "Medical interruption of pregnancy (IMG)", pp. 657–667; Casini, Carlo, "Voluntary interruption of pregnancy", pp. 669–677; Meaney, Joseph, and Michael Meaney, "The free choice of life: the 'pro choice' option", pp. 701–710; Ciccone, Lino, "Reproductive health", pp. 899–903.

49   Coates et al., "The Holy See on sexual and reproductive health rights", pp. 114–124.

protection of human rights, the right to life, the right to dignity and the freedom of religion:

> The right to life as enshrined in natural law and protected by international human rights laws lies at the foundation of all human rights. The Holy See reaffirms that all life must be fully protected in all its stages from conception until natural death. [...] The Universal Declaration of Human Rights and international human rights instruments explicitly state that the right to freedom of religion or belief includes the right of all to practice their faith alone or in community, in public or private, and the right to change his or her religion or belief.[50]

Opposition to all forms of abortion and the rejection of the concepts of gender, sexual and reproductive health, and reproductive rights, as well as the reservations expressed in Cairo and Beijing, have been reiterated at various sessions of the UN Commission on the Status of Women. Thus, the Holy See reiterates that:

> 1. Regarding the terms "sexual and reproductive health", "sexual and reproductive health-care services", and "reproductive rights", the Holy See considers these terms as applying to a holistic concept of health. These terms embrace, each in their own way, the person in the entirety of his or her personality, mind and body. They should also be understood to foster the achievement of personal maturity in sexuality and in the mutual love and decision-making that characterise the conjugal-relationship between a man and a woman in accordance with moral norms. The Holy See does not consider abortion, access to abortion, or access to abortifacients as a dimension of these terms.

> 2. With reference to the terms "contraception", "commodities", "condom use" and any other terms regarding family-planning services and regulation of fertility concepts in the document, the Holy See reaffirms its well-known position concerning those family-planning methods which the Catholic Church considers morally acceptable and, on the other hand, family-planning services which do not respect the liberty of the spouses, human dignity and the human rights of those concerned.

> 3. In relation to paragraphs 1 and 2 of this Statement of Position, the Holy See reiterates its statement and reservations as set out clearly and more fully in the Report of the 1994 International Conference on Population and Development, and the Report

---

50 Permanent Observer Mission of the Holy See to the United Nations, 2014, "69th session of the United Nations General Assembly Third Committee, agenda item 68(b,c): 'Human rights'", New York, 29 October, pp. 1–2.

of the 1995 Fourth World Conference and their respective follow-up Conferences. In particular, my delegation understands, in accordance with the ICPD 1.15, that no new rights or human rights were created, that recourse to abortion may never to be had for purposes of family planning (7.24), that abortion is a matter to be determined in accordance with national legislation (8.25).

4. With reference to "gender", the Holy See understands the term to be grounded in the biological sexual identity and difference that is male or female. Regarding the concepts of "gender norms" and "gender stereotypes", the Holy See does not recognize the idea that gender is socially constructed, rather gender recognizes the objective identity of the human person as born male or female.[51]

These positions are reflected in other sessions of the commission.[52] The Holy See also repeatedly defended its views on the human dignity of women within the naturalistic and essentialist logic developed by Pope John Paul II and taken up by Pope Francis.[53]

In short, the positions upheld by the Holy See before the UN bodies on abortion, reproductive health and rights remain unchanged in their reflection of its doctrinal and religious discourse, even if it has adopted the secular and legal vocabulary of these bodies. Strategically, the Holy See relies on the legal interpretation of international norms, especially conventions it has not ratified, to legitimise its positions. This strategy reinforces the fundamental ambiguity of the Holy See within the UN. Indeed, it adopts both the posture of a spiritual guarantor, as the universal government of the Catholic Church, and the role of a state jurisdiction, as the government of Vatican City. This ambiguity allows the Holy See to

---

51   Permanent Observer Mission of the Holy See to the United Nations, 2016, "60th Commission on the Status of Women, explanation of the position of the Holy See on the resolution 'Women, the girl child and HIV and AIDS'", E.CN.6/2016/L.5, New York, p. 1.

52   Permanent Observer Mission of the Holy See to the United Nations, 2011, "55th Commission on the Status of Women, explanation of position of the Holy See on the agreed conclusions", E.CN.6/2011/L.6, New York, 14 March; Permanent Observer Mission of the Holy See to the United Nations, 2013, "57th Commission on the Status of Women, intervention of the Holy See", New York, 12 March.

53   See, for example, Permanent Observer Mission of the Holy See to the United Nations, 2014, "8th session of the Open Working Group on the Sustainable Development Goals: 'Promoting equality, including social equity, gender equality, and women's empowerment'", New York, 6 February; 2015, "Remarks of H.E. Archbishop Bernardito Auza, Permanent Observer of the Holy See to the United Nations, at the conference on 'Women promoting human dignity'", New York, 18 March; 2015, "Remarks of H.E. Archbishop Bernardito Auza, Permanent Observer of the Holy See to the United Nations, at the conference on 'Defending human dignity in reproductive health'", New York, 19 March.

build international alliances with conservative states in order to curb progress on sexual and reproductive health and rights as much as possible. These obstacles play a major role in hindering the social construction of this issue in the field of human rights (see Chapter 2 and Appendix B).

Thus, the considerations developed in this chapter and the previous one provide the necessary context for analysing the discourses used by voluntary associations fighting for the right to abortion and those opposing it within the European Union.

4 | How the language of human rights is used by both supporters and opponents of abortion rights

The main foundations of the right to abortion are women's rights to health, equality with men, self-determination and autonomy, and physical and psychological integrity. Confronted with these principles, opponents of abortion rights emphasise the right to life of the "unborn child", human dignity, and freedom of conscience and religion.

Supporters and opponents alike use the language of human rights, which both aims at consensus and engenders contention. It aims at consensus in that it is a principle of legitimisation for the actors and their demands. However, the different ways of framing these demands are largely contentious in terms of their content and their prioritisation of different human rights. This is hardly surprising, since the debate over human rights mostly focuses on the question of the absence or existence of foundations. If they exist, do they fall under natural law or positive law?[1] If, on the other hand, we consider there to be no foundations, then it is the democratic legitimacy of public and political deliberation that decides on the content of these rights and their linkages.

This chapter looks at the values, phobias and arguments developed in the discourses of voluntary associations active in the European Union. We will review the progressive discourse – a discourse based on the language of human rights – through the prism of the dissociation between sexuality and procreation. We will also examine the sometimes conservative, and even reactionary, discourse that reinterprets human rights from the perspective of safeguarding a natural order. It should be noted at the outset that, in this conservative and reactionary discourse, women's autonomy with regard to decision making is denied, while in the case of the progressive discourse, it is instrumentalised in the name of

---

1   Benhabib, Seyla, 2008, "The legitimacy of human rights", *Daedalus* 137(3), 94–104.

public health. As a result, women's self-determination in relation to their bodies remains largely overlooked.

Given the very large number of actors involved in the abortion debate at the EU level,[2] we will focus on just two transnational advocacy networks: the One of Us European Federation (see Appendix C, Table C.9) and the High Ground Alliance for Choice and Dignity in Europe (see Appendix D, Table D.10). The first brings together the associations that launched and supported the European Citizens' Initiative "One of us" in May 2012 and that formed a federation following the European Commission's refusal to take the petition into consideration in May 2014.[3] The second network, the High Ground Alliance for Choice and Dignity in Europe, was created in June 2016 as a reaction against the first. The period that saw these networks emerge also saw the rejection, in October 2013, of the Estrela Report, which was in favour of sexual and reproductive rights (see Chapter 2).

The associations linked to the "One of us" petition unabashedly relay the doctrinal positions of the Holy See (see Chapter 3). Major and representative documents testify to this activist doctrine opposing the right to abortion.

In the legal sphere, the book coordinated by Grégor Puppinck titled *Droit et prévention de l'avortement en Europe (Law and Prevention of Abortion in Europe)*[4] and his study on conscientious objection are essential reading. The book was the result of a seminar with participants from across Europe, hosted by the Commission of the Bishops' Conferences of the European Union (COMECE; see Appendix C, Table C.5) on 22 June 2017 and organised by the European Centre for Law and Justice (ECLJ) (see Appendix C, Table C.7), of which Puppinck is the director. Puppinck regularly represents the Holy See on various committees of the Council of Europe, including those related to the Council of Europe Convention for the Protection of Human Rights and Fundamental Freedoms. In addition, he has appeared before the European Court of Human Rights (ECHR)

---

2   The various actors involved in the debate are the member states and their legislative, executive and judicial bodies, political and social actors, health workers, lawyers, philosophers, political scientists, sociologists, the media, churches, international and supranational institutions, etc. Many of them have already been referred to in the previous chapters, on access to abortion in the EU (Chapter 1), the history of the concepts used to justify this access (Chapter 2) and its opposition by the Holy See (Chapter 3).

3   European Commission, 2014, "Communication from the Commission on the European Citizens' Initiative 'One of us'", COM(2014) 355 final, Brussels, 28 May.

4   Puppinck, Grégor (ed.), 2016, *Droit et prévention de l'avortement en Europe*, Bordeaux: LEH.

in cases concerning abortion and freedom of conscience and religion. He is also a member of the Agenda Europe network (see Appendix C, Table C.1) and the One of Us European Federation. Puppinck's association – the ECLJ – is also part of a network with Fondazione Novae Terrae (see Appendix C, Table C.12).

With regard to legal and religious matters, Jakob Cornides's study *Natural and Un-natural Law* supports the importance of natural law as a foundation for human rights.[5] Cornides is a European Commission official and one of the founders of Fundacja Instytut na rzecz Kultury Prawnej Ordo Iuris (the Ordo Iuris Institute for Legal Culture; see Appendix C, Table C.13), which was behind the 2016 Polish bill to abolish all abortion.

In terms of religious radicalism, the manifesto *Restoring the Natural Order* and Stéphane Mercier's *La Philosophie pour la vie* are illustrative reading.[6] Mercier was a visiting lecturer at the Université Catholique de Louvain but was dismissed by the university authorities following a course he taught on the issue of abortion (see Chapter 5). As for the manifesto, it seems to come from the Agenda Europe network, although the network denies this. Originally an unpublished internal document, it was made public in a study by Neil Datta, the executive director of the European Parliamentary Forum for Sexual and Reproductive Rights (EPF; see Appendix D, Table D.5).[7]

The High Ground Alliance for Choice and Dignity in Europe includes Catholics for Choice, the EPF, the European Humanist Federation (EHF), the International Planned Parenthood Federation European Network (IPPF EN), the European Women's Lobby (EWL) and the European chapter of the International Lesbian, Gay, Bisexual, Trans and Intersex Association (ILGA-Europe) (see Appendix D, Tables D.2, D.4, D.7, D.8 and D.9). The analysis of the normative framing of the associations that belong to the High Ground Alliance focuses on the most relevant documents published by some of the associations that make up this network: Datta's work for the EPF, and in particular his analysis of the manifesto *Restoring The*

---

5   Cornides, Jakob, 2010, *Natural and Un-natural Law*, New York: Catholic Family and Human Rights Institute.

6   *Restoring the Natural Order: An Agenda for Europe*, N.D. (https://agendaeurope.files. word-press.com). Mercier, Stéphane, 2017, *La philosophie pour la vie. Contre un prétendu "droit de choisir" l'avortement*, Roosdaal: Quentin Moreau.

7   Datta, Neil, 2018, "'Restoring the Natural Order': the religious extremists' vision to mobilize European societies against human rights on sexuality and reproduction", European Parliamentary Forum on Population and Development (EPF), Brussels. The EPF changed its name in 2019.

Natural Order;[8] the EPF fact sheet on sexual and reproductive health and rights;[9] the speech made by Giulio Ercolessi (then president of the EHF) on International Safe Abortion Day;[10] the EHF presentation on "Securing sexual and reproductive rights" on its website;[11] the essay by Jane Hurst on the history of abortion ideas in the Catholic Church, published by Catholics for Choice;[12] and the EWL's position paper on women's health in the EU.[13] To this is added an analysis of the normative framework of the Estrela Report on sexual and reproductive health and rights (which was adopted, and then presented to the European Parliament, by the European Parliament's Committee on Women's Rights and Gender Equality), since each of the associations in question adheres to the considerations developed in the report.[14] It should also be noted that the study titled "Women's sexual and reproductive health and rights in Europe",[15] published by the Commissioner for Human Rights at the Council of Europe, echoes the Estrela Report.

In addition, Appendices C and D of this book contain information obtained from the websites of the associations linked to the "One of us" petition and those belonging to the High Ground Alliance for Choice and Dignity in Europe, respectively: their date of creation, headquarters and legal status, website, mission and objectives, key members, member organisations (if any), recognition by international organisations, European political relays, and scope of action and networking. This information was cross-checked with data found in academic publications and studies commissioned by political groups in the European Parliament.

---

8   Ibid.

9   European Parliamentary Forum on Population and Development, 2013, "Sexual and reproductive health and rights: the basics", *Intelligence Brief* (1).

10   Ercolessi, Giulio, 2017, "International Safe Abortion Day: a personal contribution", 2 October (https://humanistfederation.eu).

11   European Humanist Federation, "Securing sexual and reproductive rights" (https://humanistfederation.eu).

12   Hurst, Jane, 1983, *The History of Abortion in the Catholic Church: The Untold Story*, Washington (DC): Catholics for a Free Choice.

13   European Women's Lobby, 2010, "European Women's Lobby position paper: women's health in the EU".

14   European Parliament, Committee on Women's Rights and Gender Equality, 2013, "Report on sexual and reproductive health and rights", 2013/2040(INI), Edite Estrela (rapporteur), Meeting Document A7-0426/2013, 2 December.

15   Council of Europe, Commissioner for Human Rights, "Women's sexual and reproductive health and rights in Europe".

4.1 The One of Us European Federation

Overall, the One of Us European Federation, and in particular its member network Agenda Europe, has three objectives:

- to ban abortion, sterilisation, the sale of pharmaceutical contraceptives and all prenatal diagnoses;
- to prepare bills and drafts of bills relating to the conscience clause (in order to give doctors and pharmacists the right to refuse to provide care), to prevent any recognition of a right to abortion by any jurisdiction (including international jurisdictions) and to participate in international conventions on the prohibition of the use of stem cells and euthanasia;
- to hinder the practice of abortion, to promote parental rights for underage girls and to prohibit the funding of associations that counsel women seeking to terminate their pregnancy.

The "One of us" petition was officially launched by seven people from seven EU member states. Its organising committee was composed of Puppinck (ECLJ, France – the chair), Filippo Vari (Movimento per la Vita, Italy), Manfred Libner (Stiftung Ja zum Leben, Germany), Alicia Latorre (Federación Española de Asociaciones Provida, Spain), Josephine Quintavalle (Comment on Reproductive Ethics, United Kingdom), Edit Frivaldszky (Together for Life Association, Hungary) and Jakub Bałtroszewicz (Polska Federacja Ruchów Obrony Życia, Poland). The petition was presented to the Vatican by the late Carlo Casini, the honorary president of the Vatican's Pontifical Academy for Life and president of the Per la Vita movement. It was supported by Pope Benedict XVI and, later, Pope Francis, by COMECE, by the Protestant Evangelical Committee for Human Dignity and by networks of anti-abortion organisations, namely, Agenda Europe, Citizen Go, the Dignitatis Humanae Institute, European Dignity Watch, the Federation of Catholic Family Associations in Europe, the Federation Pro Europa Christiana, Fondazione Novae Terrae, the Ordo Iuris Institute for Legal Culture, Hazte Oir and the European Institute of Bioethics (see the corresponding tables of Appendix C).

The aim of the petition was "to obtain a commitment from the European Union to prohibit and end the funding of actions which involve or result in the destruction of human embryos in all these areas [including the funding of research and development cooperation], and to provide appropriate monitoring tools to ensure that the funds allocated are never used to destroy human life".[16] The petition obtained over 1.72 million signatures – well over the million signatures required for it to be considered by the European Commission. Of the eighteen member states in which the signatures were collected, Italy collected the most (623,947), followed by Poland (235,964), Spain (144,827), Germany (137,874) and Romania (110,405).[17] As might be expected, the number of signatures in countries such as Belgium, Denmark, Finland, the United Kingdom and Sweden fell far short of the required per-country threshold. Surprisingly, Ireland did not reach this threshold either.[18]

The petition presented three types of demand:

- to ensure that "no EU funds are allocated to activities that destroy or presuppose the destruction of human embryos";
- to prohibit the funding of "research that destroys human embryos, including research to derive stem cells, and research involving the use of human embryonic stem cells in subsequent steps to derive them";
- to ensure that, in the context of development cooperation, "EU aid [is not used] to fund abortion directly or indirectly, or through organisations that encourage or promote it".[19]

This petition sees the right to life as coextensive with the entire continuum of life, i.e. from conception to natural death, while its concept of the right to dignity opposes anything it considers a dehumanisation of the human embryo, and abortion in particular. In its comments on the European Commission's rejection of the "One of us" petition, Agenda Europe targeted family planning organisations, such as the IPPF, which it described as an abortion industry. It challenged the scientific legitimacy

---

16   Draft legal act tabled by the European Citizens' Initiative "One of us", registered by the European Commission as ECI(2012)000005, 11 May 2012 (https://register.eci.ec.europa.eu/core/api/register/document/1499).

17   European Commission, 2014, "Appendices to the Communication from the Commission on the European Citizens' Initiative 'One of us'", Appendix 1, COM(2014) 355 final, Brussels, 28 May, pp. 2–3. The European Commission's rejection of the petition was confirmed by the Court of Justice of the European Union on 23 April 2018. For details of the procedures, thresholds and conditions for making a European Citizens' Initiative valid and its effects on European Institutions, see European Commission, 2015, *Guide to the European Citizens' Initiative*, Luxembourg: Publications Office of the European Union.

18   For example, in Belgium, 5,478 signatures were collected while 16,500 were required; in Ireland, 6,679 signatures were collected while 9,000 were required.

19   Draft legal act tabled by the European Citizens' Initiative "One of us".

of the WHO's positions on maternal mortality and morbidity, and the democratic legitimacy of the political resolutions of the Cairo Conference (1994) and its follow-up in 2014 (Cairo+20). It also denounced the arbitrary nature of the European Commission's governance.[20]

The rejection of the "One of us" petition was a setback for opponents of abortion rights. Nevertheless, the influence of these opponents was highlighted in the European Parliament's vote in December 2013 on an alternative proposal to the Estrela Report on sexual and reproductive rights.[21] Drafted by the European People's Party (EPP) and the European Conservatives and Reformists Group, the bill held that only member states had the power to act on sexual and reproductive health issues, under the principle of subsidiarity. Adopted by 334 votes to 327, with 35 abstentions, it thus called into question the political legitimacy that the European Parliament had acquired in this area (see Appendix B and Chapter 2). On this occasion, one of the advocates for the protection of embryonic life was Slovakian MEP Anna Záborská (EPP), a member of the Committee on Women's Rights and Gender Equality in the European Parliament and also a member of the European Institute of Bioethics, the One of Us European Federation and the Federation Pro Europa Christiana. The campaign against the Estrela Report took a new turn when MEPs received thousands of spam messages calling on the European Parliament to reject the report, which had been the subject of a transnational disinformation campaign.

Záborská's "minority opinion", which was issued in committee against the Estrela Report and incorporated into it, perfectly sums up the positions of those who oppose the right to safe and legal abortion:

This non-binding resolution violates the EU Treaty and cannot be used to introduce [a] right to abortion, or against the full implementation of ECI(2012)000005. No international legally binding treaty nor the ECHR nor customary international law can accurately be cited as establishing or recognizing such right. All EU institutions, bodies and agencies must remain neutral on the issue of abortion. The ECJ confirms (C-34/10) that any human ovum after fertilization constitutes a human embryo which must be protected. The UN Declaration of the Rights of the Child states that every child has the right to legal protection before as well [as] after birth. Union assistance should not be provided to any authority or organisation which promotes, supports or

---

20   Agenda Europe, N.D., "The European Commission's reply to One of Us", reaction to the European Commission's communication on the "One of us" petition, *Marginalia* (2) (https://agendaeurope.wordpress.com).

21   The analysis of the report filed by Edite Estrela is developed below.

participates in the management of any action which involves abortion. The human right of conscientious objection together with the responsibility of the state to ensure that patients are able to access medical care in particular in cases of emergency prenatal and maternal healthcare must be upheld. No person, hospital or institution shall be coerced, held liable or discriminated against in any manner because of a refusal to perform, accommodate, assist or submit to practices which could cause the death of a human embryo.[22]

The online platform Citizen Go and European Dignity Watch took up the arguments of Záborská and other critics, and in particular arguments that opposed any form of sex education in primary and secondary schools. Associations linked to the One of Us European Federation launched other initiatives. To date, all of those listed below have failed.

At the political level, a petition titled "For the rights of new-borns surviving their abortion", submitted to the Parliamentary Assembly of the Council of Europe, made the following demands:

1. To investigate and report on the situation of children born alive during their abortion.

2. To reaffirm that all human beings born alive have the same right to life guaranteed by Article 2 of the European Convention on Human Rights, and that all human beings must benefit from appropriate and necessary health care, without discrimination based on the circumstances of their birth, in accordance with Articles 3, 8 and 14 of the ECHR.

3. To recommend to Member States to take into account the threshold of viability of human foetuses in their legislation on termination of pregnancy.[23]

---

22   European Parliament, Committee on Women's Rights and Gender Equality, "Report on sexual and reproductive health and rights", p. 29.

23   Petition for the rights of newborns surviving their abortion, launched by the European Centre for Law and Justice and the Federation of Catholic Family Associations in Europe, as well as the International Catholic Child Bureau (BICE), submitted to the Parliamentary Assembly of the Council of Europe in January 2015 (available at https://eclj.org). See de La Hougue, Claire, and Grégor Puppinck, 2015, "Enfants survivant à l'avortement et infanticides en Europe", *Revue générale de droit médical* (57), 111–134. BICE is an international network of Catholic organisations created in 1948 to promote the protection of children's rights. The organisation is accredited with a special consultative status to the United Nations Economic and Social Council (ECOSOC), and participates in the work of the UN Human Rights Council and the UN Committee on the Rights of the Child. It is recognised by the Holy See.

In the judicial sphere, the Federation of Catholic Family Associations in Europe (FAFCE) launched an application to the European Committee of Social Rights against Sweden for the lack of specific legislation on the conscience clause in reproductive health matters (see Chapter 2 and Appendix B).[24] The FAFCE thus supported Agenda Europe's aim of undermining the right of access to safe and legal abortion by asserting the right of Christians to derogate from the law by virtue of their religious beliefs. However, the FAFCE failed to convince the European Committee of Social Rights that the absence of this legislation constituted a form of discrimination in relation to freedom of religion.

In an extremist extra-institutional register, in 2015 the Alliance Defending Freedom International (see Appendix C, Table C.2) launched a campaign to stigmatise abortion, accusing the IPPF of selling foetal tissue, posting messages on Twitter calling for an end to all funding for the IPPF and disrupting a meeting organised by the IPPF EN in the European Parliament.[25]

Finally, at the legislative level, Hazte Oir and the Ordo Iuris Institute for Legal Culture prepared a number of bills to increase barriers to abortion in Spain (in 2013–14) and to prohibit all abortion in Poland (in 2016) (see Chapter 1).

4.2 The High Ground Alliance for Choice and Dignity in Europe

The High Ground Alliance for Choice and Dignity in Europe[26] comprises Catholics for Choice, the European Humanist Federation (EHF), the European Parliamentary Forum for Sexual and Reproductive Rights (EPF), the International Planned Parenthood Federation European Network (IPPF EN), the European Women's Lobby (EWL) and the European chapter of the International Lesbian, Gay, Bisexual, Trans and Intersex Association (ILGA-Europe).

---

24 European Committee of Social Rights, 2015, "Federation of Catholic Family Associations in Europe (FAFCE) v. Sweden", Complaint no. 99/2013, decision on the merits of 17 March. See Appendix B.

25 See https://adfinternational.org/campaign/defund-ippf and https://adfmedia.org. See also Zacharenko, Elena, 2016, "Perspectives on anti-choice lobbying in Europe: study for policy makers on opposition to sexual and reproductive health and rights in Europe", The Greens/EFA in the European Parliament, Brussels, p. 53.

26 This alliance is sometimes referred to in activist texts as All of Us, in contrast to the One of Us European Federation.

Each of these associations focuses on a specific issue. Thus, Catholics for Choice works towards a progressive Catholicism that breaks with the doctrinal system developed by the Holy See and the ecclesiastical hierarchy. The EHF focuses on the promotion of secularism in Europe. The EPF focuses on improving sexual and reproductive health and rights from a population and development perspective. The IPPF EN promotes family planning from the perspective of free choice, and it has evolved from the IPPF into an independent entity. The EWL promotes women's rights from a feminist perspective. Finally, ILGA-Europe focuses on rights related to gender identity and sexual orientation.

Each of these associations essentially works within its own network, although their coming together in a transnational advocacy network (the High Ground Alliance for Choice and Dignity in Europe) reflects a common normative framework, even if the associations have conflicting views on some issues, such as prostitution and surrogacy. However, these associations are united when it comes to the freedom of individuals to decide for themselves, and with other consenting adults, on matters of sexuality and reproduction, free from coercion, violence and discrimination. We will come back to this later.

In this context, the Estrela Report has been an important issue for the European Parliament's Committee on Women's Rights and Gender Equality. In response to the transnational misinformation campaign against the report, it received support from the High Ground Alliance for Choice and Dignity in Europe, as well as from other prominent organisations, such as the Center for Reproductive Rights (see Appendix D, Table D.3), which reaffirmed that sexual and reproductive rights are human rights. (The Center for Reproductive Rights, a key player in the expansion of human rights to include sexual and reproductive rights, brings cases concerning the right to abortion to international courts.[27]) Support for the Estrela Report also came from Federacja na Rzecz Kobiet i Planowania Rodziny (the Federation for Women and Family Planning; see Appendix D, Table D.6), a member of ASTRA (Central and Eastern European Network for Sexual and Reproductive Health and Rights; see Appendix D, Table D.1).

4.3 The discourse of opponents of abortion rights

Opponents of abortion rights use the language of human rights to legitimise three central elements of their discourse: the protection of the

---

27   See in particular Zampas and Gher, "Abortion as a human right", pp. 249–294.

foetus, the protection of women's dignity, and freedom of conscience and religion.

Protection of the foetus

This argument is based on the pre-eminence of natural law over positive law. Thus, for Jakob Cornides, the foundation of human rights does not lie in the subjectivity of opinions and in political deliberation (i.e. in a democratic space open to the pluralism of values):

> Under Natural Law we understand a set of ethical precepts that exists outside positive law and to which positive legislation, if it is not to be called abusive, must conform. This Natural Law is supposed to correspond to human nature, and to be accessible to reason – provided, of course, that this reason is not obscured by the desire to manipulate the law in one's own interest.[28]

Under this doctrine of submission to the order of things, the rights to autonomy, privacy and equality are not conceivable because they are abstract rights with no reality other than the manipulative assertion of pro-choice advocates who transform women's right to life into a right to abortion.[29] The opposition erected between abstract and concrete rights is based on a Christian logic of incarnation, whereby natural law must be incarnated in positive law.

According to the manifesto *Restoring the Natural Order*, this reliance on the transcendence of natural law requires the obedience of every person to the order of things, and the immanence of political will is rejected as the pure subjectivism of opinions:

> There is a Natural Law, which human reason can discern and understand, but which human will cannot alter. This Natural Law remains the same at all times and in all places, and it is pre-existent to all written legislation. Indeed, it is the task and purpose of all positive legislation to transpose and enforce Natural Law in a way that adapts to the specific needs and circumstances of a given society at a given time. A positive law that stands in contradiction to the precepts of the Natural Law has no legitimacy, and nobody is morally bound by it.[30]

---

28   Cornides, *Natural and Un-natural Law*, p. 27.
29   Ibid., p. 47.
30   *Restoring the Natural Order*, p. 7.

The use of natural law as a basis for human rights allows opponents of abortion rights to mobilise four themes: the sanctity of the right to life from conception, the biological character of the foetus as a human being, abortion as genocide and femicide, and the rights of the foetus versus the rights of women.

The first theme is clearly inspired by religion. Thus, like the Holy See, Stéphane Mercier considers, for example, that "abortion consists of the deliberate killing of an innocent person, in this case a human being in the mother's womb".[31]

While conferring a sacred character on the right to life requires recourse to the transcendence of natural law, the fact remains that this religious inspiration goes hand in hand with a secularised discourse that appeals to both common sense and science in order to establish the biological character of the foetus as a human being, which is the second theme used. Thus, Mercier uses the idea of a continuum to consider the embryo and the foetus as an "unborn child": "Whatever the stage of development, the developing being does not suddenly change species. The different terms: 'embryo', 'foetus', 'infant', 'child', etc. refer to different stages of development of the same entity. The human adolescent becomes a human adult, not a full-grown snail. Well, in the same way, a human foetus becomes an infant and then a human child."[32] By relying on the obvious and using irony, Mercier's rhetorical amalgamation of the foetus and the child makes it possible to overlook the fact that, before birth, positive law does not confer the legal status of a person, i.e. a subject with rights.

Writing from the same perspective, Cornides emphasises the inno-cence of the "unborn child" in order to reject any abortion regardless of the circumstances of the unintended pregnancy, except for a risk to the life of the pregnant woman:

It is generally known that life must be the highest ranking right in any legal order (because, by taking a person's life, one negates all his other rights at the same time), so that in a conflict of values life will usually be given priority over other values, as long as that life is to be considered innocent, and killing is not an act of legitimate self-defence against illegal aggression. Who could be more innocent than an unborn child? It is therefore completely self-evident and requires no further explanation that, once the unborn child is understood to be a human being, no other circumstance than

31 Mercier, *La philosophie pour la vie*, p. 10.
32 Ibid., p. 11.

one in which a choice must be made between the life of the child and the life of the mother can ever justify abortion.[33]

Within the same framework of the pre-eminence of natural law over positive law, the manifesto *Restoring the Natural Order* puts the point in more radical terms:

> Abortion is the deliberate destruction of a child while still inside the womb of its mother. Given that life begins at conception, it is irrelevant whether the destruction of the embryo takes place at an early or late stage of the pregnancy, before or after implantation, before or after the foetus has reached the status of "viability". It is also irrelevant whether the pregnancy is confirmed or whether it is only suspected. [...]
>
> Abortion in all cases destroys the life of an innocent and defenceless human being. A directly willed abortion can in *no* case and under *no* circumstances be justified.
>
> Laws that "legalise" abortion or that fail to provide adequate legal protection for the life of the unborn child stand in clear contradiction to the natural law of morality. Such laws are injustice vested in a false appearance of legality. Nobody is obliged to obey them, but everyone is under a moral obligation to work towards their abolition.[34]

Thus, religious inspiration intersects with a universalist approach to human rights to conclude that every human being has the right to be born, including the foetus as an "unborn child", regardless of the circumstances in which it was conceived or the wishes of the pregnant woman. In this view, abortion is never legitimate, not even when the woman's life is in danger. Incest, rape, the malformation of the foetus or even a risk to the life of the pregnant woman cannot justify an abortion. In the latter case, it is permissible to consider medical treatment of which one of the side effects "may cause the loss of the child".[35]

The absolute pre-eminence given to the foetus as a subject with rights has never been recognised by international conventions; what predominates in the inclusion of women's reproductive rights in the field of human rights is, above all, women's right to health, and in particular the prevention of maternal mortality associated with clandestine abortions (see Chapter 2 and Appendix B).

---

33 Cornides, *Natural and Un-natural Law*, p. 28.

34 *Restoring the Natural Order*, pp. 66–67 (emphasis in the original).

35 Ibid., p. 69. Such a position echoes the Dublin Declaration on Maternal Health Care, adopted in 2012 by Irish self-identified pro-life activists. For more details, see Lynn N. Morgan, 2017, "The Dublin Declaration on Maternal Health Care and anti-abortion activism: examples from Latin America", *Health and Human Rights Journal* 19(1), 41–53.

In their fight, opponents of abortion rights use ultrasound and foetal imaging to show that the foetus is already a baby in the making, and to allow the public to understand its humanity. The use of the scientific register is also based on the fact that the threshold for viability of the foetus outside the womb, which is currently twenty-four weeks after conception, is likely to be lowered by developments in medical technology. In a tone that is more moderate, but no less unambiguous, Puppinck and Claire de La Hougue consider that, beyond twenty-two weeks, termination of a pregnancy "is no longer an abortion *stricto sensu*, but rather 'foeticide' or neonatal infanticide, even in the case of the malformation or illness of the child. If the pregnancy poses a serious risk to the mother or the foetus, the birth can be decided upon by assuming the risk of the child's death, which is already practiced."[36] Thus, the increasing ability of the medical profession to detect foetal anomalies should lead to the development of perinatal care rather than abortion: "All premature children should have the same right to life and access to health care services without discrimination. All possible care and medical assistance should be offered to all, regardless of the conditions of their birth. Even when they are not viable, these children should be accompanied humanely until their death."[37]

The amalgamation of abortion and genocide, by association with the Shoah, reinforces the idea that abortion is not only murder but a societal phenomenon linked to the moral decline of liberal and secular societies. This third theme, which has been reiterated since the first pro-life associations came about, is now accompanied by a denunciation of abortion as femicide, referring to certain practices in countries such as India or China, where there is clear preference for male offspring, resulting in a deficit of girls. De La Hougue points out that

> the option is now available to find out the sex of the baby in the first trimester of pregnancy, i.e. at a time when abortion is legal on request in many countries. No control is possible, even in countries where abortion on the basis of sex is prohibited, since the woman does not have to give a reason for requesting an abortion. The parents are, therefore, able to decide whether or not to let the baby live based on its gender.[38]

---

36   Translated from Puppinck, Grégor, and Claire de La Hougue, "Les enfants survivant à l'avortement et les infanticides néonatals", in *Droit et prévention de l'avortement en Europe*, p. 140.

37   Ibid., p. 161.

38   De La Hougue, Claire, "L'avortement en raison du sexe de l'enfant", in *Droit et prévention de l'avortement en Europe*, p. 164.

A typical feminist concern is thus twisted – a mechanism frequently employed by anti-feminists.[39]

Finally, the theme of foetal rights versus women's rights is developed from an anti-feminist perspective, anathematising notions of gender and equality between men and women in favour of valuing the traditional family and maternalism. In this respect, the manifesto *Restoring the Natural Order* is the epitome of a reactionary ideology. Reviewing political ideologies that destroy natural law, the manifesto focuses on feminism and so-called "gender theory" to denounce, among other things, the emancipation and autonomy of women, in favour of their dependence on men. It thus promotes the persistence of gender relations against which the social state has developed public policies favouring the individuation of women.[40]

Protecting women's dignity

From the 1990s onwards, a secular discourse within associations opposed to abortion rights began to accompany the discourse on a right to life centred on the foetus. Indeed, over this period, the development of human rights language in international politics has led to this language supplanting the rhetoric centred solely on the foetus's right to life. Thus, these associations now focus on women in the name of their right to health, stressing the importance of establishing and strengthening legal procedures that ensure their genuine consent to undergoing an abortion and their awareness of the emotional costs and medical risks of such a procedure. This is a reversal of the arguments developed in favour of the notion of reproductive health in the field of human rights (see Chapter 2).

Opponents of the right to abortion argue that the notion of "informed consent" should protect the pregnant woman from pressure to abort from her partner, the doctor and society. The pregnant woman is seen as all the more vulnerable because an unwanted pregnancy would necessarily put her in a state of distress, making her sensitive to pressure from those around her. From this perspective, Christophe Foltzenlogel, de La Hougue and Puppinck highlight the fight against forced abortions:

---

39 See Garbagnoli, "De quoi 'le gender' des campagnes 'anti-genre' est-il le nom ?", pp. 241–270.

40 *Restoring the Natural Order*, pp. 15–18.

Can a woman who undergoes an abortion under threat from her parents, employer or spouse be considered to have given informed consent? The same applies to a young woman who has an abortion in a panic, without knowing or understanding the development of the child *in utero*, or to a woman who has an abortion under pressure from society or the medical profession, without being informed of the support or prospects for her disabled child. The difference between forced and coerced abortion is very slight, even non-existent.[41]

The idea that abortion can be a choice for a woman is thus a deceit based on the false representation of what abortion is; the use of medical imaging should allow the pregnant woman to be truly informed of the reality of such an act. The same legal experts argue as follows:

Properly informing the woman considering an abortion requires that she be made aware of the seriousness of the act and its possible consequences. […] Several countries have incorporated ultrasound into the abortion decision-making process, allowing the woman to see the being she is carrying and to hear its heartbeat. […] This condition for abortion may seem cruel to the mother, but it allows for an informed decision and has encouraged many women to keep the child. […] Currently, when they know that an abortion is being considered, ultrasound technicians often do not show the image to the mother and turn off the sound. Even if this is done with the intention of protecting the woman, this approach based on concealment does not really respect her. In order not to make women feel guilty, we take away their responsibility. Denying reality by hiding the images and talking about clusters of cells is a lie that brings future suffering.[42]

The irresponsibility of fathers, often denounced by feminists, is invoked here at the cost of turning the feminist attitude against itself:

The irresponsibility of the father is one of the main causes of abortion […] He may abuse the woman, tell her to choose between him and the child, or simply say that he does not want the child, so that the woman does not feel strong enough to raise it alone. This irresponsibility is an attack on women's rights, equality and justice in the relationship between men and women.[43]

---

41 Translated from Foltzenlogel, Christophe, Claire de La Hougue and Grégor Puppinck, "La prévention de l'avortement : garantir le droit de ne pas avorter", in *Droit et prévention de l'avortement en Europe*, p. 93.

42 Ibid., pp. 90–91.

43 Ibid., p. 96.

And to counteract this irresponsibility, these lawyers recommend the intervention of a third person – the father – in the decision:

> Paradoxically, such irresponsibility is encouraged by the fact that men are not involved in the abortion procedure and are often even excluded. This exclusion removes the father's responsibility without completely protecting the woman from possible pressures. [...] An abortion performed against the father's will is also, in his respect, a forced abortion.[44]

Whether it is because the woman needs medical guidance or because she needs to be accompanied by the child's father, her autonomy to decide to have an abortion is not conceivable from the perspective of opponents of the right to abortion: this autonomy is a threat to the woman, and her body is reduced to its sole, procreative function.

The risks that would be incurred by an abortion, whether emotional (e.g. post-abortion syndrome, similar to post-traumatic stress disorder) or health-related (e.g. breast cancer), are put forward as scientific arguments, even though they are rejected by most members of the medical profession. These arguments are used as part of a compassionate view of women and their vulnerability.[45] This vulnerability is accentuated by a particular conception of women's dignity, which is understood in terms of the natural link between femininity and motherhood. For Mercier,

> the woman's interests are not threatened by those of the child [...] The plea for the dignity and protection of the unborn child is, therefore, in no way intended to take its side against that of the woman [...] It is here that it must be understood that the unborn child is not the enemy of anyone, and that its interest is never contrary to that of the woman, whatever the circumstances of the conception or the difficulties encountered in the course of the pregnancy.[46]

Therefore, the mother–child pairing cannot be destroyed before birth by an informed choice of the woman, as only pressure and coercion would explain her decision to abort.

This line of reasoning ignores the coercion and violence exercised over women's bodies. In this sense, Andrea Dworkin explains:

---

44 Ibid., p. 98.

45 Translated from Louissaint, Cherline, "Les conséquences médicales et sociales de l'avortement", in *Droit et prévention de l'avortement en Europe*, p. 52–53.

46 Translated from Mercier, Stéphane, *La philosophie pour la vie*, p. 56.

With respect to pregnancy, if a woman can be forced to bear a child conceived by force in marriage, there is no logic in differentiating pregnancy as a result of rape or incestuous rape. Force is the norm; pregnancy is the result; the woman has no claim to a respected identity not predicated on forced intercourse – that is, at best her dignity inheres in being a wife, subject to forced intercourse and therefore to forced pregnancy; why would any woman's body be entitled to more respect than the married woman's?[47]

Even though rape within marriage is criminally sanctioned, women's consent remains problematic in an androcentric society.[48] It is therefore unsurprising, in Dworkin's view, that women object to the ability to choose, insofar as they "acquiesce to male authority in the hope of some protection from male violence".[49]

The naturalistic and essentialist approach used by opponents of abortion rights disqualifies women's autonomy in making reproductive decisions by distorting what constitutes women's consent. Indeed, in this view, protecting women's dignity means having legislation, counselling, a period of reflection and waiting, and foetal viewing practices that are meant to free pregnant women from the weight of gender relations that undermine the possibility of "informed consent". From this perspective, the state, conceived as the protector of the most vulnerable beings – namely, the pregnant woman and the "unborn child" – has a duty to regulate the practice of abortion as much as possible by increasing the number of obstacles to its access. In fact, it is no longer a question of obtaining the "informed consent" of the woman but of removing from her all capacity to make decisions on the fate of the "unborn child", as its profound nature would be intimately linked to her own. This logic naturally leads to the "ideal" measure of banning all abortions. In the case of minors, requiring the permission of the partner or parents redirects the decision to within the family unit. In short, hijacked by the family and/or state institutions, the choice is never given to the pregnant woman herself.

While the right to life from the moment of conception, as a human right, is presented as a right to freedom (albeit freedom limited by the freedom of others, in this case that of the "unborn child"), a conservative, even reactionary, conception of the dignity of women deprives them of

---

47   Translated from Dworkin, Andrea, 2012, *Les femmes de droite*, Montreal: Éditions du remue-ménage, p. 91 (original edition: 1983).

48   On the ambiguities of consent, see Fraisse, Geneviève, 2007, *Du consentement*, Paris: Seuil.

49   Translated from Dworkin, *Les femmes de droite*, p. 24.

any autonomy in the area of reproductive rights. In general, such positions are rooted in the refusal of any dissociation between sexuality and procreation. Moreover, Mercier,[50] the manifesto *Restoring the Natural Order*,[51] and Puppinck and his co-authors[52] call for a ban on all but natural contraception, as it leads to an "abortive mentality" hostile to the "order of things" or natural law.

Protecting freedom of religion and conscience

In the area of abortion, the defence of religious freedom as a human right opposes the right of actors faced with practicing or preventing abortion not to act contrary to their conscience or religion (i.e. the right of doctors and health care personnel to refuse to perform abortions and provide post-abortion care) with the right of patients to access reproductive health services (see Chapter 1). Thus, de La Hougue notes that no instrument of international law recognises a right to abortion, and she considers freedom of conscience to be one of the major levers of fundamental rights that disallows the state from taking refuge behind the margin of appreciation granted by the European Convention on Human Rights (see Chapter 2 and Appendix B). De La Hougue continues:

> Nor can freedom of conscience or religion be balanced against the right to health, which does not include a right to abortion, as it has no therapeutic effect. Pregnancy is not an illness that can be cured by abortion. This balancing would only be relevant in the very rare cases where the pregnancy directly threatens the life of the mother, but in this case there is no right to object; all measures must be taken to save the life of the mother, even if the consequence may be the loss of the child.[53]

Institutions – namely, hospitals and clinics – have also claimed a right to invoke the conscience clause, and they could use it to avoid the application of the law. For opponents of abortion, it could even be used in order to refuse to pay contributions towards national health and disability insurance that reimburses procedures and treatments that their conscience disapproves of. It is also in the name of freedom of conscience

---

50   Mercier, *La philosophie pour la vie.*, pp. 62–64.
51   *Restoring the Natural Order*, pp. 54–61.
52   See in particular Foltzenlogel et al., "La prévention de l'avortement", pp. 84–88.
53   De La Hougue, Claire, N.D., "L'objection de conscience dans le domaine médical en droit européen et international", European Center for Law and Justice, p. 8.

and religion that aid for embryo research and development (in its family planning aspect) has been prevented from receiving national and European subsidies.

Thus, for Jean-Pierre Schouppe, any faith-based hospital that allows abortion

> abdicates its institutional integrity and responsibility towards patients of this faith whose intimate convictions will be unjustly trampled on. [...] Finally, the practice of abortion may pose ethical problems for some health care personnel who may be called upon to collaborate, against their conscience, in an act they consider unlawful. This example shows that individual conscientious objection must be complemented by an institutional component.[54]

While freedom of conscience and religion as a human right is a negative right (protecting the individual from state interference), for these authors the right to women's health would not in any way fall under the positive rights that imply financial intervention by the state or social security. Although they deny it, their approach endorses the fact that only women with economic, social and cultural resources have the option to access safe abortion. Their vision of human rights thus leads to the disconnection of the social question from social citizenship. Once again, such a religiously inspired conception gives precedence to the transcendence of natural law, "the true source of our personal autonomy".[55]

According to Puppinck,

> respect for this "transcendence" by the public authorities is an essential condition for the establishment of a society oriented towards the search for justice, because, in so doing, these authorities accept the criticism brought by individuals and recognise that the law cannot be the omega of justice, and that respect for the law does not result from its formalism, but must be deserved and aroused by its ordination to the good.[56]

In this doctrinal framework, individual autonomy is reduced to a subjective individualism in a liberal Western society that does not question the

---

54   Translated from Schouppe, Jean-Pierre, "La dimension institutionnelle de l'objection de conscience", in *Droit et prévention de l'avortement en Europe*, p. 253.

55   Translated from Puppinck, Grégor, 2016, "Objection de conscience et droits de l'homme. Essai d'analyse systématique", *Société, Droit et Religion* 1(6), 217.

56   Ibid.

meaning of the choices made by individuals.[57] On the other hand, taking into consideration "the right to autonomy of institutions based on moral or religious convictions" recognises the legitimacy of freedom of conscience and religion.

Puppinck implicitly challenges the recognition of value pluralism in a democratic society through the following line of argument: "When the legislator, when decriminalising abortion, instituted a conscience clause, it did so not out of respect for the diversity of individual opinions on abortion, but in order not to force anyone to participate in performing an evil objective that is alien to the normal practice of medicine, but nevertheless necessary from its point of view."[58] In this light, obliging an objecting doctor to provide the contact details of a colleague who performs abortions or an objecting pharmacist to supply a drug for the purpose of causing an abortion is not respecting freedom of conscience. In other words, from the perspective of a doctrinal system that places moral conscience under the protection of natural law, there is no abuse of the conscience clause as denounced by the supporters of the right to abortion.

4.4 The discourse of abortion rights supporters

Proponents of abortion rights use human rights to legitimise four central elements of their discourse: women's rights to health, to physical and psychological integrity, to self-determination/autonomy and to equality. These elements are based on an evolving and dynamic conception of human rights that leaves room for the social construction of the notions of reproductive health and reproductive rights (see Chapter 2 and Appendix B). By establishing norms and standards for countries to follow in order to respect, protect and fulfil these human rights, this perspective also grants international and supranational legal and judicial bodies a legitimacy and authority that is denied by opponents of abortion rights who follow the prescriptions of the Catholic Church and intend, as we have just seen, to incorporate them into positive law.[59]

The discursive activism in favour of abortion rights is at the crossroads of both secular and feminist thinking. It is also rooted in pragmatic

---

57   Ibid., p. 250.

58   Ibid., p. 256.

59   Yamin, Alicia Ely, Neil Datta and Ximena Andión, 2018, "Behind the drama: the roles of transnational actors in legal mobilization over sexual and reproductive rights", *Georgetown Journal of Gender and the Law* 19(3), 533–569.

arguments based both on family planning and on population and development. This raises the question of the neutrality of the state in ethical matters.

Women's rights to health and to physical and psychological integrity

Movements in favour of legalising and decriminalising abortion generally choose pragmatic arguments to support their claims.

Abortion happens whether it is prohibited or not, often as a last resort in the event of contraceptive failure, but in all cases it constitutes an experience that is either undergone or considered as an option by a large proportion of women of reproductive age.[60] Clandestine abortions have extremely serious consequences for women's health. Abortion should therefore be legalised or decriminalised for the sake of public health and humanitarian concerns. This position is shared by Catholics for Choice, the EHF, the EPF, the EWL and ILGA-Europe.

From the same perspective, the report presented by Edite Estrela to the European Parliament considers that,

> because of the potential public health consequences of prohibiting abortion, it seems evident that prohibiting abortion will not encourage decreasing its rate; rather it would be more efficient to focus on preventing unwanted pregnancies. Finally, [although] there is very little relationship between abortion legality and abortion incidence, there is a strong correlation between abortion legality and abortion safety.[61]

In the same spirit, the report

> recommends that, as a human rights and public health concern, high-quality abortion services should be made legal, safe, and accessible to all within the public health systems of the Member States, including non-resident women, who often seek these services in other countries because of restrictive abortion laws in their country of origin, and to avoid clandestine abortions that seriously endanger women's physical and mental health.[62]

---

60   Bajos, Nathalie, and Michèle Ferrand, 2011, "De l'interdiction au contrôle : les enjeux contemporains de la légalisation de l'avortement", *Revue française des affaires sociales* (1), 42–60.

61   European Parliament, Committee on Women's Rights and Gender Equality, "Report on sexual and reproductive health and rights", p. 26.

62   Ibid., p. 13.

The demand for abortion to be reimbursed as a medical procedure is then justified in the name of equality between women, i.e. on the basis of not discriminating against women from disadvantaged backgrounds. Thus, the report

> urges the Member States to take targeted action to meet the specific needs of vulnerable people who are at risk of marginalisation and social and economic exclusion, in particular young women in rural areas, who may find it difficult to gain access to modern means of contraception as a result of economic and social problems, in particular during the current economic crisis.[63]

This concern for equality between women facing an unwanted pregnancy is part of a framework that links abortion and contraception, and that considers abortion a last resort. For example, the Estrela Report stresses that "voluntary family planning contributes to preventing unintended and unwanted pregnancies and reduces the need for abortion", and that "in no case must abortion be promoted as a family planning method".[64]

Therefore, women's right to health goes hand in hand with their right to physical and psychological integrity. For the EWL:

> Sexual and reproductive rights include open access to legal and safe abortion, [and] reliable, safe, and affordable contraception, coupled with sexual education and information in relation to sexual and reproductive health, free choice and consent. It is vital that all women living in the European Union Member States must enjoy freely these rights and have full access to the related health services.[65]

From a gender perspective, the EWL emphasises the significance of male violence as an obstacle to women's health, integrity and exercise of their free choice:

> Male violence against women can have serious health consequences [...] Sexually transmitted diseases and unplanned pregnancy are other consequences that women victims can experience in cases of rape (including in marriage), incest, prostitution, pornography, etc. [...] A variety of factors contribute to the way different forms of male violence impact on women's health, including poverty, economic dependence, lack of

---

63 Ibid.
64 Ibid.
65 European Women's Lobby, "European Women's Lobby position paper", p. 7.

---

social support, different forms of discrimination based on age, migrant status, sexual orientation, disability, etc.[66]

From this perspective, this means that respect for women's rights to health and to physical and mental integrity requires that the conditions necessary for their autonomy be taken into account.

Women's rights to self-determination, autonomy and equality with men

Women's rights to self-determination, autonomy and equality with men in matters of sexuality and reproduction relate to a major demand put forward by feminist movements in the 1960s and '70s: reproductive freedom.[67]

During those two decades, the conquest of this freedom politicised what was previously seen as intimate, private or taboo. In other words, this struggle questioned the very perimeter of the political domain and expanded it. As soon as the abortion taboo was broken in the 1960s and '70s, the emerging public debate saw feminists demand self-determination and control over their bodies. The slogans of the time ("My body, my right" or "Our bodies, ourselves") reflect women's desire for self-determination, control over their bodies and freedom from men based on the model of habeas corpus.

In the classical sense of the term, habeas corpus is a fundamental freedom that guarantees that any person who is arrested will be informed of the reasons for his or her arrest and will be brought promptly before a judge who will rule on the arrest's validity to prevent, as far as possible, the risk of arbitrariness. Its liberal extension to contraceptive and abortion rights emphasises freedom of choice in how women conduct their personal lives.[68] The philosophical–political argument behind this freedom is not so much the idea of self-ownership (the body is not seen as a thing) as it is a person's right to freedom over the use of her body and the right to privacy (which was clearly expressed in the slogans

---

66   Ibid., p. 11.

67   See De Zordo et al. (eds), *A Fragmented Landscape*; Orr, Judith, 2017, *Abortion Wars: The Fight for Reproductive Rights*, Bristol: Policy Press; Outshoorn (ed.), *European Women's Movements and Body Politics*; Pavard, Bibia, Florence Rochefort and Michelle Zancarini-Fournal, 2012, *Les lois Veil*, Paris: Armand Colin.

68   In this respect, it can be seen as a legacy of John Stuart Mill, beyond his utilitarian perspective. See Mill, John Stuart, 1859, *On Liberty*, London: John W. Parker and Sons.

"*Maître de mon ventre*" and "*Baas in eigen buik*" in the demonstrations that took place in the 1970s for the legalisation of abortion in Belgium; see Chapter 5). Abortion, then, is conceived as an act of private life arising from the freedom of conscience (and not a freedom to possess or exchange).[69] However, while legalised abortion became a constitutional right in the United States in the name of the right to privacy (on the basis of the Roe v. Wade ruling, issued by the Supreme Court in 1973), in the EU, when it is legalised or decriminalised, this is done not in the name of a positive principle – the right to privacy – but in the name of practical arguments (e.g. as a last resort, as an expression of a state of distress or as a means of combating clandestine abortion). Attempts to justify abortion by invoking Article 8 of the European Convention on Human Rights, titled "Right to respect for private and family life", have so far been rejected by European judges (see Chapter 2 and Appendix B).

Feminism in the 1960s and '70s developed primarily under the banners of the *Mouvement de libération des femmes* in France and French-speaking countries and the Women's Liberation Movement in the United Kingdom and the United States. Certainly, the feminist tradition of fighting for equal civil, social and political rights with men is still very much alive today, and this equality is demanded in the name of full citizenship. However, at that time, the libertarian aspect of the women's liberation movement, which followed on from May '68, was dominant. The right to privacy refers to the bodily integrity of the woman facing the possibility of abortion, and her self-determination implies that she alone can decide on such an intimate matter. In this perspective, personal autonomy over decision making is seen as a positive freedom, instead of being only the negative freedom of a choice free from any constraint by a third party (father, husband, partner) or community (the state, a church, public opinion). This perspective guides liberal thinkers such as Ronald Dworkin to defend the right to privacy.[70] It is also in this sense that feminist writers in liberal political theory – such as Rosalind Petchesky, Susan Okin and Anne Phillips – argue in favour of maintaining the separation between the private and the public, emphasising the abuses, in their view, of the feminist slogans of the 1970s: the slogan "The personal is political" means that the problems experienced by individual women are part of

---

69   Sintomer, Yves, 2001, "Droit à l'avortement, propriété de soi et droit à la vie privée", *Les Temps modernes* (615–616), 206–239.

70   Dworkin, Ronald, 1993, *Life's Dominion: An Argument about Abortion, Euthanasia, and Individual Freedom*, New York: Knopf.

a social logic, not that women's private decisions should be subject to political control.[71]

The contestation of the distinction between these two spheres in order to define what is political has led to the politicisation of the private, the bodily and the intimate. However, unlike Carole Pateman, who calls for the eradication of this distinction,[72] and Catherine MacKinnon, who sees in the notions of privacy and personal choice a legitimisation of the exploitation of women by men (with men freed from their reproductive responsibilities rather than women having control over their own repro-ductive capacities),[73] Petchesky emphasises a politics of abortion rights that considers not so much the legal and moral subject with a right to privacy and freedom of conscience as the empirical and sociological subject facing gender, class and ethnic inequalities and discrimination. As such, the right to abortion is conceived as a social right, i.e. a right that the individual – in this case the woman – has over the state. Attempting to realise freedom and equality thus brings into play the issue of women's social citizenship, which maps out a discursive landscape that includes the empirical and sociological reality of social gender relations in their intertwining with class relations and ethnic relations.

Beyond the liberal and individualistic principle of privacy, which tends to ignore the weight and depth of social relationships, the issue becomes a question of women's autonomy in a male-centric society. What does women's independent decision making mean in light of the current limits on access to contraception, women's unequal relationship to sexuality, the number of unwanted pregnancies and the burden of childcare? All of these factors reinforce the inequalities experienced by women in public life, whether at work or in economic, social and political decision-making bodies. According to this approach, it is up to women, and not the male-dominated state, to decide on the exercise of their reproductive capacities. But this right to freedom goes hand in hand with the obliga-tions placed on the state by positive rights. Thus, social policies, such as sex education, reimbursing contraception and abortion, and access to

---

71   Petchesky, Rosalind Pollack, 1990, *Abortion and Woman's Choice: The State, Sexuality, and Reproductive Freedom*, Boston (MA): Northeastern University Press (original edition: 1984). Okin, Susan Moller, 1991, "Gender, the public and the private", in *Political Theory Today*, edited by David Held, Cambridge: Polity Press, pp. 67–90. Phillips, Anne, 1991, *Engendering Democracy*, Cambridge: Polity Press, 1991.

72   Pateman, Carole, 1988, *The Sexual Contract*, Cambridge: Polity Press.

73   MacKinnon, Catherine, 1987, *Feminism Unmodified: Discourses on Life and Law*, Cambridge (MA): Harvard University Press.

health services, are fundamental to offsetting the inequalities faced by women. The mass feminist activism that has unfolded since the 2010s in Europe and Latin America to combat violence against women and to promote abortion rights has emphasised the collective and political dimensions of these demands, which go beyond individual choice.[74]

The issue of women's social citizenship is raised by supporters of abortion rights to define the contours of the autonomy of personal choice. Social issues are central to women's sexual and reproductive rights, according to the Estrela Report, which

> stresses that the current austerity measures have a detrimental impact, particularly for women, in terms of quality, affordability and accessibility [of] public health services, information and programmes related to sexual and reproductive health, and in terms of quality and accessibility [of] family planning and support organisations, [of] NGO service providers, and [of] women's economic independence; [the report] points out that the Member States should take the necessary steps to ensure that access to sexual and reproductive health services is not jeopardised.[75]

At the international level, the EPF highlights the need to anchor social citizenship in human rights through the recognition of the importance of the social question (that is, the weight of social and political relations):

> Advancing the right to health (including sexual and reproductive health) necessitates its inclusion into all relevant policy-making processes including policies for poverty reduction and international development.
> Focussing on technical and medical interventions in isolation will not be sufficient to ensure access to sexual and reproductive health services [...], because [the] root-causes [of sexual and reproductive health issues] relate to the status of women in a society as well as economic, social, political and cultural determinants.[76]

The EPF considers gender equality and women's empowerment as key factors for social and economic development. However, this

---

74 See Arruzza, Cinzia, Tithi Bhattacharya and Nancy Fraser, 2019, *Feminism for the 99%: A Manifesto*, New York/London: Verso; Descarries, Francine, 1998, "Le projet féministe à l'aube du XXIe siècle : un projet de libération et de solidarité qui fait toujours sens", *Cahiers de recherche sociologique* (30), 179–210.

75 European Parliament, Committee on Women's Rights and Gender Equality, "Report on sexual and reproductive health and rights", p. 12.

76 European Parliamentary Forum on Population and Development, "Sexual and reproductive health and rights: the basics", p. 6.

instrumental vision of gender equality and women's autonomy as furthering development is accompanied by a depiction of women's vulnerability, rather than their agency (i.e. their capacity for action and resistance to relations of domination).[77] Thus, the EPF highlights the sociological observation of the disparities between women and men in sexual and reproductive health and rights without mentioning women's struggles in this area. This does not prevent it from denouncing the *Restoring the Natural Order* manifesto and the reactionary logic of opponents of the right to abortion, pointing to the increasing influence of lobbyists and activists calling themselves pro-life.[78]

The neutrality of the role of the state

The pragmatic arguments in favour of women's rights to health and physical and psychological integrity, as well as their right to autonomy as part of the freedom–equality relationship, raise the question of women's social citizenship. In this context, can supporters of women's reproductive freedom provide an answer to the question raised by opponents of the right to abortion, namely, whether the foetus is a legal (or moral) person? The answer they have to offer is both biological–medical and legal–political.

The specific scientific responses may change as advances in neonatal medicine push the frontier of foetal viability. But the fairly broad consensus in the medical community on the different stages of foetal development seems to have played an important role in allowing abortion.

In this spirit, Giulio Ercolessi (then chair of the EHF), in his speech on the status of the embryo and the foetus on International Safe Abortion Day in 2017, questioned the position of the ecclesiastical hierarchy and its political and voluntary association relays, which, according to him, confuse natural law with so-called scientific evidence based exclusively on common sense:

> Unfortunately for the hierarchy and for its frantic and servile political and media claque, this "scientific" evidence cannot be confirmed by scientists that, as scientists, can only say what a zygote, a morula, a blastocyst, an embryo, a foetus, an individual are, but of course cannot define what a "human person" is, as this is no scientific concept; neither is this pretence considered as an indisputable truth by the generality

---

77 Ibid., pp. 1–2.
78 Datta, "'Restoring the Natural Order': the religious extremists' vision", pp. 11–13.

of believers and non-believers, not even of Catholics; and it does not correspond even to the orientations by now prevalent in Europe among many Protestants.[79]

However, when we move from the medical and biological field to the legal, it is even less easy to speak of a consensus. European judges indicate that the setting of publicly protected boundaries for human life is arbitrary, and the ECHR considers, to date, that only the state has discretion in setting this boundary (see Chapter 2 and Appendix B), because the principle of subsidiarity within the EU affirms the sovereignty of states with regard to ethical matters. Thus, although most European legislation allows abortion (within more or less definitive or restrictive margins), states could still give the foetus a legal personality and even constitutionalise this status (as in Ireland between 1983 and 2018 or in Hungary since 2012; see Chapter 1 and Appendix A).

In the liberal view of John Rawls, the state cannot endorse a particular concept.[80] Therefore, in order to remain neutral and fair to all citizens, the state must refrain from legislating and deciding between opposing or even antagonistic definitions of life. Similarly, the state must protect freedom of conscience without allowing it to be reduced to a religious freedom in the manner of the Holy See and its so-called pro-life associations (see above and Chapter 3). On this basis, the EHF, in the text quoted below, considers that the state must ensure that

• an effective solution is available to address any refusal to procure an abortion;

• an obligation is imposed on every medical practitioner exercising his or her right to conscientious objection on grounds of religious duty to refer a woman seeking an abortion to another doctor who is willing to perform abortions;

• a qualified practitioner who undertakes abortions is available, including in rural areas and places far from urban centres;

• conscientious objection remains an individual right and not an institutional one, i.e., a hospital can not claim a right to conscientious objection in order to refuse to perform abortions where it is legal.[81]

---

79 Ercolessi, "International Safe Abortion Day".
80 Rawls, John. 1971. *A Theory of Justice*. Cambridge, MA: Harvard University Press.
81 European Humanist Federation, "Securing sexual and reproductive rights".

The position of the EHF is thus in line with the draft resolution on women's access to legal medical care adopted on 22 June 2010 by the Social, Health and Family Affairs Committee of the Parliamentary Assembly of the Council of Europe,[82] which led to an assembly resolution on the right to conscientious objection (see Chapter 2 and Appendix B).[83] The EHF also denounces the hold that monotheistic religions seek to exert on individuals, and the role of COMECE in ethical matters in the EU. In this sense, Pierre Galand, president of the EHF from 2012 to 2015, recalled that:

> Secularism differs from monotheistic religions in that it refuses any form of hegemony over the destiny of man and his thought. It seeks to make the individual ever more capable of emancipation through free thought and the practice of free examination. In this sense, it is liberating and cannot submit to any form of totalitarian power, be it political, economic, cultural or religious. Thus, secularism is a gathering of free people in a democratic society.
>
> However, no individual or group can claim to hold the pre-established and definitive model either of the gathering of free people or of the form of democratic society to which they aspire.[84]

The issue is therefore political and philosophical.[85] The equality of all is at stake – believers, atheists and agnostics. Moreover, from this perspective, secularism is not a particular spiritual option but rather an ideal that allows the public sphere to be a common world directly concerned with the common good, and not to be reduced to a common world that different communities only happen to share. In this sense, freedom of conscience cannot be restricted to freedom of religion.

Furthermore, Catholics for Choice is denied Catholic status by the Church because of its pro-abortion stance. Its search for the information

---

82   Parliamentary Assembly of the Council of Europe, Social, Health and Family Affairs Committee, 2010, "Women's access to legal medical care: the problem of unregulated use of conscientious objection", rapporteur Christine McCafferty, Doc. 12347, 20 July.

83   Parliamentary Assembly of the Council of Europe, 2010, "The right to conscientious objection in lawful medical care", Resolution no. 1763, 20 July.

84   Translated from Galand, Pierre, 2012, "Créer l'imaginaire de la laïcité", 16 March, p. 2 (https://pierregaland.be).

85   For the different approaches and issues related to secularism, see Baubérot, Jean, 2007, *Les laïcités dans le monde*, Paris: Presses universitaires de France; Haarscher, Guy, 2004, *La laïcité*, Paris: Presses universitaires de France; Peña-Ruiz, Henri, 2003, *Qu'est-ce que la laïcité ?*, Paris: Gallimard; Portier, Philippe, "Les régimes de laïcité en Europe", in *Religion et politique*, pp. 211–221.

necessary for an informed decision on abortion led it to research the Church's varying historical positions on the human personhood of the embryo and foetus. The research concluded that the Church has not always considered life to be sacred from conception.[86]

For supporters of abortion rights, the neutrality of the state's role in ethical matters thus means that the ethical or moral subject cannot be taken into consideration alone at the expense of the empirical and socio- logical subject. Therefore, the inclusion of sexual and reproductive rights, including the right to abortion, in the field of human rights requires that these rights be interwoven with social rights to ensure that the conditions necessary for the exercise of a real free choice for women are in place. This means that – from this perspective, and far from the logic of incar- nation at work in the positions of the Holy See (see Chapter 3) – women and men realise their capacities for individuation through the acquisition of social citizenship.

---

86   Hurst, *The History of Abortion in the Catholic Church*.

5 | The right to abortion in Belgium (1970–2020)

As we have seen, abortion laws can be very open, as in France and Luxembourg, or they can be far more restrictive, as in Ireland. However, we have also seen that these laws are changing. In particular, these changes are shaped by the struggle for influence between supporters and opponents of abortion rights, sometimes taking place in a confrontational manner and sometimes more indirectly. In this respect, the evolution of the situation in countries where the stance of the Catholic ecclesiastical hierarchy is still strong – such as Spain, Ireland and Poland – is particularly interesting. More broadly, the analysis of the situation so far in this book highlights that access to abortion remains not only variable but precarious in many countries of the European Union.

Within the EU, the case of Belgium is interesting for the country's particularly complex nature, both historically and recently. However, one constant emerges: a deep porosity between civil and political society. This porosity was first reflected in a 1990 law[1] that partially decriminalised abortion and provided the right to its access; this law came in the wake of two events: the failure to adopt an accommodation policy within government coalitions, and the use of civil disobedience as a means of political action within civil society. The same porosity led to the adoption of a new law in 2018.[2] Although this law removes abortion from the country's criminal code, it does not remove criminal sanctions for the doctor or the woman, and even provides for sanctions to be applied to any other person who allows an abortion to be performed outside the legal conditions. Considered by many to be a merely cosmetic

---

1   *Moniteur belge*, 1990, "Law of 3 April 1990 on the termination of pregnancy, amending Articles 348, 350, 351 and 352 of the Criminal Code and repealing Article 353 of the same Code", 5 April.

2   *Moniteur belge*, 2018, "Law of 15 October 2018 on the voluntary termination of pregnancy, repealing Articles 350 and 351 of the Criminal Code and amending Articles 352 and 383 of the same Code, and amending various legislative provisions", 29 October.

Table 5.1. Overview of the main political parties in Belgium.

Joint parties

Socialist pillar

PSB: *Parti socialiste Belge – Belgische Socialistische Partij*, active from 1945 until its linguistic split in 1978.

Christian pillar

PSC-CVP: *Parti Social Chrétien-Christelijke Volkspartij*, active from 1945 until its linguistic split in 1968.

Liberal pillar

PLP: *Parti de la Liberté et du Progrès*, which succeeded the Parti Libéral in 1961 and was active until its linguistic split in 1972.

Other

PTB-PVDA: *Parti du Travail de Belgique - Partij van de Arbeiders van Belgïe*, a communist (Maoist) party created in 1979.

PCB-KPB: *Parti Communiste de Belgique – Kommuistische Partij van Belgïe*, active from 1921 until its linguistic split in 1989.

French-speaking parties

Socialist pillar

PS: *Parti Socialiste* (French-speaking), active since 1978.

Christian pillar

PSC: *Parti Social Chrétien* (Christian democrats), active between 1968 and 2002.

CDH: *Centre Démocrate Humaniste*, which succeeded PSC in 2002. It became *Les Engagés* in 2022.

Liberal pillar

PRL: *Parti Réformateur Libéral*, resulting from the split, in 1972, of the joint party PLP. It took its name in 1979.

PRLW: *Parti des Réformes et de la Liberté de Wallonie*, resulting from the merger of PRL with RW (and active between 1976 and 1979).

MR: *Mouvement Réformateur*, a coalition formed in 2002 between PRL, FDF and a dissident section of PSC (FDF left the coalition in 2011).

Other

RW: *Rassemblement Wallon*, the Walloon federalist party (1968–1985).

FDF: *Front Démocratique des Francophones*, created in 1964 to defend the rights of French speakers.

DéFI: *Démocrate Fédéraliste Indépendant*, the new name of FDF since 2015.

Ecolo : *Ecologistes confédérés pour l'organisation de luttes originales*, an environmentalist party created in 1980.

PC: *Parti communiste*, the French-speaking communist Party, active since 1989.

Dutch-speaking parties

Socialist pillar

SP: *Socialistische Partij* (Dutch-speaking), active between 1978 and 2001.

SP.A: *Socialistische Partij Anders*, which succeeded SP in 2001 (and became Vooruit in 2021).

Christian pillar

CVP: *Christelijke Volkspartij*, active between 1968 and 2001.

CD&V: *Christen-Democratisch en Vlaams*, active since 2001.

Liberal pillar

PVV: *Partij voor Vrijheid en Vooruitgang*, born from the split in 1972 of the unitary PLP. It became VLD in 1992.

VLD: *Vlaamse Liberalen en Democraten*, active between 1992 and 2007.

Open VLD: *Open Vlaamse Liberalen en Democraten*, which succeeded VLD in 2007.

Other

VU : *Volksunie*, a Flemish nationalist party founded in 1954. It dissolved in 2001.

N-VA: *Nieuw-Vlaamse Alliantie*, a party formed from the right wing of VU after its dissolution in 2001.

Groen: formerly *Agalev* (*Anders Gaan Leven*, 1979–2003), a Flemish environmentalist party.

KP: *Kommunistische Partij*, the Dutch-speaking communist party, active between 1989 and its disappearance in 2009.

VB: *Vlaams Blok* (from 1978 to 2004) or *Vlaams Belang* (since 2004), Flemish nationalist parties of the extreme right.

exercise, this new law will probably not change the right to abortion in practice. However, it does mark a return to the accommodation policy by the government coalition (the Michel I government, N-VA/MR/CD&V/Open VLD, 11 October 2014 to 9 December 2018) and reflects the close vigilance of secularists, feminists and family planning centres. The result is twofold: the right of access to abortion remains, but it remains as a right to a medical procedure, not a right to self-determination for women.

5.1 The 1990 law: the result of an impossible accommodation policy and civil disobedience

In order to understand the processes of politicisation and decision making surrounding abortion rights as they emerged in the 1970s, it is important to consider the main characteristics of the Belgian consociational regime.[3] Belgian society is segmented into two or three different "worlds": the Christian world and the two divisions – liberal and socialist – of the secular world.[4] Since the nineteenth century these worlds have been built around networks of institutions (such as parties, trade unions, and cultural, women's and youth organisations) and services (such as mutual societies, cooperatives and hospitals), turning them into true

---

3   There is an extensive literature on Belgium's consociational regime and its evolution. See in particular Magnette, Paul, and Jean-Benoit Pilet, 2008, "La Belgique", in *Les démocraties européennes*, edited by Jean-Michel De Waele and Paul Magnette, Paris: Armand Colin, pp. 51–68; Deschouwer, Kris, *The Politics of Belgium: Governing a Divided Society*, 2nd edition, Basingstoke: Palgrave Macmillan, 2012.

4   Translation from the French expression *monde laïque*. According to CRISP, the term *laïcité* refers to the following elements: "A political principle of separation of Church and State which aims to ensure the equality of citizens of all convictions and to remove political decision-making from the influence of religions. [...] In Belgium, the term has a philosophical meaning. It is namely used to designate a group of organisations which not only campaign for the deepening of the secular character of the State [...] but also bring together atheists or agnostics around the same humanist ideal." (CRISP, 2022, *Vocabulaire politique/Laïcité et Laïcité organisée*, Brussels; see https://www.vocabulairepolitique.be/category/abecedaire/l, accessed 6 September 2022.)

"pillars" of Belgian society.[5] These pillars are the product of, and continue to be affected by, three major cleavages that have shaped Belgian society: the church–state or philosophical cleavage, the owner–worker or economic cleavage and the centre–periphery or linguistic cleavage. Thus, while these pillars uphold the visions, interests and demands of the groups within them, they are also the actors between whom the terms of the conflicts and compromises that arise from these rifts are decided.

The relative importance of each rift varies – sometimes very strongly – from one issue and conflict to the next. More often than not they intersect. This interweaving creates political stability, albeit precariously, by mitigating the disruptive effects of philosophical, economic and linguistic contrasts and avoiding polarisation. On the other hand, this stability is threatened when a particular conflict causes the cleavages to become superimposed, as with the Royal Question. However, stability is reinforced by the practice of mutual pledges made by political elites. This method of finding negotiated solutions to conflict is based on consensus rather than the strict application of majority rule; it aims for universal agreement, with each side obtaining satisfaction within the division of power (through, for instance, subsidies and appointments).

The adoption of the 1990 abortion law does not correspond to the decision-making process that has become typical of the consociational system.[6] Historically, ethical problems have been resolved through compromise between secular actors and the Christian democrats. The vote on the law on abortion resulted from the formation of an alternative majority to the governing one and thus went against the usual procedures associated with Belgium's consociational regime. This issue divided the Martens VIII coalition government (9 May 1988 to 29 September 1991) – formed by the Christian democrats (CVP and PSC), the socialists (PS

---

5   With regard to the theory of cleavages and pillars in Belgian society, see in particular the publications of CRISP, including Mabille, Xavier, 1986, *Histoire politique de la Belgique. Facteurs et acteurs de changement*, Brussels: CRISP; de Coorebyter, Vincent, 2008, "Clivages et partis en Belgique", *Courrier hebdomadaire* (2000), CRISP; Mabille, Xavier, 2011, *Nouvelle histoire politique de la Belgique*, Brussels: CRISP; Verleden, Frederik, 2019, *Aux sources de la particratie. Les relations entre les partis politiques belges et leurs parlementaires (1918–1970)*, Brussels: CRISP; Bruyère, Lynn, Anne-Sophie Crosetti, Jean Faniel and Caroline Sägesser, 2019, "Introduction. Sécularisation, déconfessionnalisation et pluralisme : les piliers résistent", in *Piliers, dépilarisation et clivage philosophique en Belgique*, edited by Lynn Bruyère, Anne-Sophie Crosetti, Jean Faniel and Caroline Sägesser, Brussels: CRISP, pp. 5–22.

6   Witte, Els, 1990, "Twintig jaar politieke strijd rond de abortuswetgeving in Belgë (1970–1990)", *Res Publica* 32(4), pp. 427–487.

and SP) and the Flemish nationalists (VU) – and the law was adopted thanks to the favourable vote of the liberal opposition. The desire of the socialist and liberal parties not to jeopardise the governmental coalition – together with the delaying tactics of the Christian democrats, who at the time were the linchpin of all governmental coalitions – explains the lengthy decision-making process affecting this issue.

Furthermore, faced by the political obstruction of the decision within the government, parliamentarians in favour of decriminalising abortion formed alliances with civil society organisations to combat the status quo around abortion. It is therefore the porosity between civil and political society[7] that made it possible to overcome the failure of the traditional accommodation policy on abortion. This porosity was expressed in the activism of secular and feminist organisations through the use of a "scope of actions"[8] that was both lawful and unlawful, institutional and extra-institutional. It included the tabling of bills, the use of the right of association, marches, demonstrations, networking, advocacy, lobbying and, in particular, civil disobedience.[9]

Civil disobedience organised by feminist women, secular doctors, and male and female health care professionals broke the abortion taboo, developed a process of politicisation and spurred political decision making. At all times and in all societies, people have broken the law. Some women have abortions, some people perform abortions, some people accompany women who wish to terminate their pregnancies, and some people provide those women with information and guidance. What made civil disobedience in support of the right to abortion distinct was that it was collective movement. It was about breaking the law publicly and

---

7   Faniel, Jean, Corinne Gobin, and David Paternotte, 2020, "Introduction. La Belgique des mouvements sociaux", in *Se mobiliser en Belgique. Raisons, cadres et formes de la contestation sociale contemporaine*, edited by Jean Faniel, Corinne Gobin and David Paternotte, Louvain-la-Neuve: Academia-L'Harmattan, pp. 5-42.

8   Tilly, Charles, 1984, "Les origines du répertoire de l'action collective contemporaine en France et en Grande-Bretagne", *Vingtième Siècle* (4), pp. 89–108; Tilly, Charles, 2006, *Regimes and Repertoires*, Chicago: University of Chicago Press; Tarrow, Sidney, and Charles Tilly, 2008, *Politique(s) du conflit. De la grève à la révolution*, Paris: Presses de Sciences Po.

9   Marques-Pereira, Bérengère, 1989, *L'avortement en Belgique. De la clandestinité au débat politique*, Brussels: Éditions de l'Université de Bruxelles (this book covers the period from 1970 to 1986). See also Celis, Karen, 2001, "The abortion debates in Belgium (1974–1990)", in *Abortion Politics, Women's Movements, and the Democratic State: A Comparative Study of State Feminism*, edited by Dorothy McBride Stetson, Oxford: Oxford University Press, pp. 39–61.

collectively in order to bring about change. The individuals involved readily accepted the legal consequences of their actions.

The issue of abortion rights is not a purely twenty-first-century issue. In fact, it had already arisen in the previous century within the feminist movement. In the 1960s and '70s, feminist groups such as Dolle Minas and Marie Mineur often staged playful actions in support of the rights to abortion and contraception. Their slogan "Master of your own belly" reflects the sexual liberation movement that started as part of May '68. The desire for self-determination concerns the personal sphere and the body in order to make them political issues. This is one of the meanings of a major feminist slogan from the 1970s onwards: "The personal is political."

January 1973 marked an important turning point. Dr Willy Peers was arrested on 18 January following an anonymous tip-off and was charged by the Namur public prosecutor's office for having performed nearly 300 abortions during the previous nine months. Peers was not unknown. A communist doctor from a free-thinking liberal background, his commitment took the form of a threefold battle, focused on the introduction (in Belgium) of painless childbirth methods, the prescription of modern contraception in hospitals and the medicalisation of abortion.[10] Even before the 1970s, Peers had been breaking the silence surrounding abortion. He performed abortions without undue publicity, but not in a clandestine manner either. His continued detention was seen as a symbolic retaliation against the breaking of the taboo. However, the moral stature of Peers was such that the reprisals looked like provocation and discredited the criminal law.

His arrest led to massive demonstrations, whose focus was effectively a court trial in the streets. More than 800 women and 200 doctors publicly declared that they had undergone or performed abortions, in the vein of the French "Manifesto of the 343", a petition signed by 343 women – most of whom were well-known figures – and published on 5 April 1971 in the magazine *Le Nouvel Observateur*. The "Manifesto of the 343" was followed two years later by a manifesto from 330 doctors who claimed they had performed abortions. These acts of civil disobedience were used to denounce a law that was considered unjust.[11]

---

10   Amy, Jean-Jacques, 2009, "Homage to Willy Peers", *European Journal of Contraception and Reproductive Health Care* 14(6), 383–384.

11   Chassagnard-Pinet, Sandrine, 2008, "La désobéissance civile face à la normativité du droit", in *La désobéissance civile. Approches politique et juridique*, edited by David Hiez and Bruno Villalba, Villeneuve d'Ascq: Presses universitaires du Septentrion, pp. 51–66.

Beyond these demonstrations, the whole of Belgium was riven by deep political divisions on the issue – between its majority Christian wing and its socialist wing but also between Dutch-speakers (among whom the Christian wing dominated) and French-speakers (who were more influenced by socialists). A political compromise was sought that would ease tensions, and the Peers affair led to three outcomes: Peers was released by the courts following a month in custody, information about contraception was decriminalised[12] and a de facto judicial truce began. (Permitting advertising around contraception actually allowed Christian democrats to better relay the ecclesiastical hierarchy's positions on abortion and thus maintain abortion's criminal ban.) The developments in the wake of the Peer's affair led to the setting up of a commission to examine the issue (lasting from 1974 to 1976) and then to the decision not to decide: the issue of abortion was removed from the terms of any agreement on the formation of government coalitions, for which CVP was the essential pivot at that time.

The division of the country into two opposing camps became threatening: on the one hand was the predominantly Catholic Flanders region, which was dominated by the Christian democrats, who were opposed to even partial decriminalisation of abortion; on the other was the predominantly secular and left-leaning Wallonia, which demanded the right to abortion. The superimposed cleavages in Belgian society threatened to destabilise the state.

Since 1974, Christian democrats had opposed the tabling of any bill on abortion and lumped the issue together with other related questions, such as adoption and the anonymity of the mother, which only served to delay a decision. At the same time, a National Commission on Ethical Issues was set up. The creation of commissions is often used to neutralise the politicisation of an issue that has entered the public realm. In this case, however, far from depoliticising the issue of abortion, the commission reopened the divide between the secularists and the Christians, resulting in the drafting of not one but two texts. The resulting philosophical tension prevented any government from using these texts. From 1977, when the Tindemans III government (CVP/PSC/PVV/PRLW) was formed in March and the Tindemans IV government (PSB-BSP/CVP/PSC/VU/FDF) was formed in June, the abortion issue remained a subject of government disagreement. Until the end of the 1980s, the legislative initiative left solely in the hands of parliamentarians proved powerless to change the balance of power that sustained the status quo. Faced

---

12 *Moniteur belge*, 1973, "Law of 9 July 1973 repealing the last three paragraphs of Article 383 of the Criminal Code", 9 August.

with the need to safeguard government coalitions, the political elites of the time considered the issue of abortion to be a political counter-priority.[13] Under these conditions, the decriminalisation of abortion could not become an inter-party fight for the liberals, who had been open to working with the Christians since 1961, or even for the socialists, who had remained in the secular tradition.

However, government inaction and the failure of the accommodation policy were radicalising civil society groups, and the upsurge in civil disobedience forced the debate to be reopened. Illegal yet non-clandestine abortions were performed under good medical and psychological conditions, as had been happening in the Netherlands. The practice was publicly advocated by the Université libre de Bruxelles (ULB) and the Vrije Universiteit Brussel (VUB), as well as by outpatient centres (Centres Extra Hospitaliers), which were far more accessible to women who were in a precarious situation and who did not dare to go to a hospital.

While this civil disobedience was gaining traction, several civil society organisations came into being: the Comités de dépénalisation de l'avortement (Committees for the Decriminalisation of Abortion), in 1976; the Groupe d'action des centres extrahospitaliers pratiquant l'avortement (GACEHPA; Action Group of Outpatient Abortion Centres), in 1978; and the Comité pour la suspension des poursuites (Committee for the Suspension of Legal Proceedings), also in 1978. The latter was created by Monique Rifflet and Monique Van Tichelen, two socialists who came from the free-thinking milieu and who had founded the family planning organisation La Famille Heureuse (The Happy Family) in 1962.

However, the authorities and the judiciary could not ignore the unlawful actions through which university hospitals and outpatient centres had created the de facto situation, especially as this strategy was coupled with a tactic of blocking any political decision that would jeopardise the development of outpatient abortion centres, a tactic that represented a win for public health.[14] The stakes were all the higher at this point

---

13   This counter-priority "results from the procedures of agreement between political elites that are based on a 'general interest', i.e. the safeguarding of government coalitions. This structural regulation of Belgium's political system is due to the preponderance of the executive in setting political priorities" (Marques-Pereira, L'avortement en Belgique, p. 96). See also Marques-Pereira, Bérengère, 1986, "L'interruption volontaire de grossesse", Courrier hebdomadaire (1127), CRISP, p. 5.

14   This is a public health achievement insofar as there has been a significant reduction in the number of clandestine abortions, as evidenced by the decrease in the number of hospital admissions due to their after-effects. See Marques-Pereira, L'avortement en Belgique, p. 43.

because the Dutch-speaking liberals sought a compromise that would satisfy the Christian democrats by proposing the legalisation of the medical termination of pregnancy, which accounted for barely 5% of cases of induced abortion and was already recognised by the courts. It was as part of this blocking tactic that, in January 1978, a bill was tabled by the member of parliament (MP) Leona Detiège (SP) and two of her colleagues; the bill radicalised the socialist positions of the time and took up the positions of the Centre d'action laïque (CAL; Lay Action Centre),[15] and it was supported by the Committees for the Decriminalisation of Abortion (which recognised the practice of abortion in outpatient centres).[16] This interweaving of lawful and unlawful actions once again highlighted the porosity of political and civil society, and it was type of politics far from the mutual pledges made between political elites, i.e. between the leaders and figureheads of Belgium's pillars (see above).

Faced with political paralysis and civil disobedience among large sections of left-wing, secular and/or feminist civil society, the judiciary decided to react. The obstruction of a political decision on abortion and the persistent public lawbreaking resulted in some public prosecutors breaking the de facto judicial truce as early as 1978, while avoiding a generalised crackdown, which would have been politically impracticable. From 1981 onwards the prosecution of doctors and paramedics in various judicial districts led to court trials. During this period, the criminal law

---

15   CAL represents non-confessional and philosophical organisations of the French-speaking community in Belgium.

16   House of Representatives, 1978, "Bill on the termination of pregnancy", tabled by Leona Detiège, Jeanne Adriaensens and Georgette Brenez (BSP-PSB), no. 240/1, 18 January; House of Representatives, 1979, "Bill on termination of pregnancy", tabled by Leona Detiège (BSP), Jeanne Adriaensens (BSP) and Georgette Brenez (PS), no. 106/1, 16 May. Another bill was tabled on 4 February 1982 by Detiège (SP), concerning the repeal of the articles in the criminal code criminalising abortion ("Bill on the termination of pregnancy", no. 52/1). The same representative and six of her colleagues (Basile-Jean Risopoulos, FDF; Anne-Marie Neyts-Uyttebroeck, PVV; Hervé Brouhon, PS; Édouard Klein, PRL; Olivier Deleuze, Ecolo; and Jacques Nagels, PCB) tabled on 15 December 1981 a "Bill on the termination of pregnancy with the aim of suspending Articles 350, 351, 352, 353 and 383, paragraph 5 and following, of the Criminal Code" (no. 20/1). On 11 March 1982 Detiège and nine other MPs (Basile-Jean Risopoulos, FDF; Robert Henrion, PRL; Edward Beysen, PVV; Hervé Brouhon, PS; Édouard Klein, PRL; Georgette Brenez, PS; Olivier Deleuze, Ecolo; Daniel Fedrigo, PCB; and Armand De Decker, PRL) tabled a "Bill authorising the termination of pregnancy on a trial basis for one year" (no. 195/1). Finally, Detiège and eight other representatives (Basile-Jean Risopoulos, FDF; Georges Mundeleer, PRL; Lucen Van de Velde, PVV; Georgette Brenez, PS; Edward Beysen, PVV; Daniel Fedrigo, PCB; Olivier Deleuze, Ecolo; and Édouard Klein, PRL) tabled a "Bill on the termination of pregnancy" on 17 February 1983 (no. 545/1).

was itself put on trial within the judiciary: doctors and health workers facing reprisals openly declared to trial judges their resistance, regardless of whether they would be sentenced to prison. Far from being marginalised, this resistance was supported by institutions who carried significant philosophical weight, such as the ULB and its Dutch-speaking counterpart the VUB; moreover, it did not encounter any political will to repress it.

As a result, judicial practice proved contradictory. A Belgian woman could escape prosecution if she had an abortion abroad, but she risked being convicted if she terminated her pregnancy in Belgium. After spending thirty-four days on remand, Dr Peers was never brought to trial. His case was not dismissed, nor was he acquitted or convicted, although another doctor was convicted in a case for which he, like Peers, claimed moral, functional and material responsibility. When the Brussels criminal court heard the testimony of two university professors discussing their abortion practice, one (a witness) was not prosecuted, while the other (a defendant) was sentenced to an eighteen-month suspended sentence. Some courts convicted defendants who pleaded a state of necessity,[17] while others acquitted defendants on the same grounds. The Brussels court of appeal, using the principle of invincible error, acquitted doctors who had broken the law in good conscience and who had acted in a non-clandestine manner.[18] The French- and Dutch-speaking wings of the Brussels court of appeal differed in their assessment of induced abortion, with the former invoking the evolution of the concept of a state of health and the latter refusing to do so.

As for the public prosecutors, they acted only on an ad hoc basis: they were content to prosecute abortions that were reported to them and they were consciously uninterested in others, refusing to take legal action against abortions for which doctors claimed responsibility. Public

---

17   The state of necessity is a compelling moral imperative. This argument was used in the Bobigny trial in France in 1972. "The state of necessity [...] makes it possible to escape punishment by eliminating the legal aspect of the offence: the violation of the legal obligation is justified in this case by the need to safeguard a value that is deemed, socially, to be greater than or equal to that protected by the strict law. [...] Only necessity in the most material sense of the term is [...] admissible" (Lochak, Danièle, 1998, "Désobéir à la loi", in *Pouvoir et liberté. Études offertes à Jacques Mourgeon*, Brussels: Bruylant, p. 195). See also Legros, Robert, 1983, "1830–1980. Droit pénal et société", *Revue belge d'histoire contemporaine* 14(1–2), 177–199.

18   The Belgian Court of Cassation defines invincible error as follows: "The error may, because of certain circumstances, be considered invincible provided that, based on these circumstances, it can be deduced that the person who relies on them acted as any reasonable and prudent person placed in the same situation would have done" (Court of Cassation, 2013, Judgement no. S.12.0076.F, 18 November, p. 11).

prosecutors also refrained from prosecuting institutions and individuals who provided women with the means to obtain abortions, such as the ULB and the VUB as well as parliamentarians who were members of outpatient centres' boards of directors.[19] These contradictions reflected the divisions in the judiciary and the disruptive nature of repression.

Finally, from 1986 onwards there was a rapprochement between the socialists and the liberals, which was reflected in the tabling of a Senate bill co-signed by the French-speaking socialist Roger Lallemand and the Flemish liberal Lucienne Herman-Michielsens.[20] Three elements played a key role in this rapprochement: (1) the persistent refusal of the Christian democrats to grasp the opportunity offered to them by the Dutch-speaking liberals; (2) GACEHPA's lobbying and arguments, which, among other things, convinced Herman-Michielsens of the public health benefits of the medical practice of abortion in outpatient centres; and (3) the safeguarding of the rule of law in the face of the legal and judicial uncertainty arising from the contradictory practices of the country's public prosecutors.

The combination of these three factors once again illustrates the porosity between Belgium's civil and political society. It also reflects the failure of the accommodation policy between political elites, as the vote on the Lallemand–Michielsens bill on 6 November 1989 in the Senate, and the subsequent vote on 29 March 1990 in the House of Representatives, was won by an alternative majority – rather than by an agreement reached within the government coalition (Martens VIII), which brought together Christian democrats, socialists and Flemish nationalists. In both

---

19   The book by the gynaecologist Jean-Jacques Amy, who was charged and convicted several times during this period, bears witness to the almost surreal way in which the legal system operated in these cases: Amy, Jean-Jacques, 2019, *"Anoniem" is een vrouw. De strijd voor gelijke rechten*, Brussels: VUB Press, pp. 83–97.

20   Senate, 1986, "Bill on the termination of pregnancy to amend Articles 348, 350 and 351 of the Criminal Code and to repeal Articles 352 and 353 of the same Code", tabled by Roger Lallemand (PS), Lucienne Herman-Michielsens (PVV), Jozef Wyninckx (SP), Robert Henrion (PRL), Jean-François Vaes (Ecolo), Magda Aelvoet (Agalev), Jacques Lepaffe (FDF), Paul Pataer (SP) and Monique Rifflet-Knauer (PS), no. 189/1, 6 March. This bill was re-tabled at the beginning of the next legislature period: Senate, 1988, "Bill on the termination of pregnancy to amend Articles 348, 350 and 351 of the Criminal Code and to repeal Articles 352 and 353 of the same Code", tabled by Lucienne Herman-Michielsens (PVV), France Truffaut-Denef (PS), Jozef Wyninckx (SP), Robert Henrion (PRL), Jean-François Vaes (Ecolo), Magda Aelvoet (Agalev) and Paul Pataer (SP), no. 247/1, 19 April; Lallemand was president of the Senate at the time (Mabille, Xavier, 1990, "Le débat politique d'avril 1990 sur la sanction et la promulgation de la loi", *Courrier hebdomadaire* (1275), CRISP, p. 5).

votes, all the socialist, Ecolo and FDF MPs approved the legal text, as did the Flemish liberals and the Flemish green party, with just a few abstentions. Conversely, all the CVP and VB representatives were opposed to it, as were the PSC MPs (with a few abstentions). The VU representatives also voted against the text, with two positive votes and many abstentions. While the majority of the French-speaking liberals approved the text, a few opposed it and a few abstained. Support was strong among the French-speaking members of both assemblies but weaker among the Dutch-speaking MPs, though there was slightly stronger rejection among Dutch-speaking senators.[21]

In the wake of this vote came another major and unprecedented political event, which reflected the extent of the reluctance to decriminalise abortion at the highest levels of government. The day after the vote in the House, King Baudouin, a fervent Catholic, wrote to the prime minister to raise the problem of conscience, as he was jointly responsible for the law adopted. To get around the king's refusal to sign the law, the Council of Ministers, invoking Article 82 of the Belgian Constitution, noted the "incapacity of the sovereign to reign" and took the king's place in sanctioning and promulgating the law, which was then published in the *Moniteur belge*.[22] This king's refusal caused a great stir and provoked much lively debate.[23]

The partial decriminalisation of abortion in Belgium came about in 1990, at the end of a particularly long period of activism first at the social level and then at the political level, but it would be hampered by deadlocks right until the very end.

Faced with this significant change, Christian democratic political elites wanted to be able to monitor and assess the new law. Opponents of decriminalisation hoped to reopen the debate, while supporters feared that the results of a commission's review could be used to roll back the clock.[24] Nevertheless, on 13 August 1990, a few months after the law

---

21   A very detailed analysis of the votes, broken down by party and language group in each of the two houses, is provided by Mabille, "Le débat politique d'avril 1990", pp. 4–13.

22   The official journal publishing the laws and other regulatory texts of the Belgian state.

23   For this topic, see Mabille, "Le débat politique d'avril 1990", pp. 4–13.

24   Swennen, Béatrice, 2001, "Évaluation de la politique d'interruption volontaire de grossesse", in *Évaluer les politiques publiques. Regards croisés sur la Belgique*, edited by Christian de Visscher and Frédéric Varone, Louvain-la-Neuve: Academia-Bruylant, pp. 103–114.

Table 5.2. Distribution by party of votes on the "Bill on the termination of pregnancy to amend Articles 348, 350 and 351 of the Criminal Code and to repeal Articles 352 and 353 of the same Code" (plenary sessions of the Senate and the House, 6 November 1989 and 29 March 1990).

	Yes		No		Abstentions		Total present		Absent	
	S	H	S	H	S	H	S	H	S	H
PS	36	39	–	–	–	–	36	39	–	1
SP	29	31	–	–	–	–	29	31	–	–
PRL	12	19	7	2	2	–	21	21	–	2
PVV	14	24	–	–	4	–	18	24	–	1
Agalev	5	5	–	–	–	1	5	6	–	–
Ecolo	3	3	–	–	–	–	3	3	–	–
FDF	2	3	–	–	–	–	2	3	–	–
CVP	–	–	39	42	–	–	39	42	–	1
PSC	–	–	15	14	1	4	16	18	–	–
VU	1	1	11	8	–	7	12	16	1	–
VB	–	–	1	2	–	–	1	2	–	–
Independent	–	1	–	1	–	–	–		–	–
Total	102	126	73	69	7	12	182	207	1	5

*One MP elected on the Flemish socialist list (voted "for") and the other MP (ex-UDRT) elected on the APB-PSC list (voted "against"). "S" denotes the Senate; "H" denotes the House.

Source: Mabille, Xavier, 1990, "Le débat politique d'avril 1990 sur la sanction et la promulgation de la loi", *Courrier hebdomadaire* (1275), CRISP, pp. 7, 11.

was passed, a National Evaluation Commission was set up to evaluate the application of the provisions regulating abortion.[25]

Since its creation, the National Evaluation Commission has produced a statistical report every two years "detailing and evaluating the application of the law", and, where appropriate, it makes "recommendations for

25 *Moniteur belge*, 1990, "Law of 13 August 1990 to create a commission to evaluate the law of 3 April 1990 on the termination of pregnancy amending Articles 348, 350, 351 and 352 of the Criminal Code and repealing Article 353 of the same Code", 20 October.

a possible legislative initiative and/or other measures likely to contribute to reducing the number of abortions and improve the guidance provided to women in distress".[26] The commission also draws up a document that must be completed by health care institutions that perform abortions; the document must include the number of abortion requests received, performed and refused, as well as the reasons given by women seeking abortion services. It should be noted that, before the law of 3 April 1990, the outpatient centres and hospitals that performed abortions illegally but openly were already keeping statistics on their activity and evaluating the number of abortions performed. This committee did not meet for the six years between 2012 and 2018 due to a lack of candidates.[27]

5.2 A legal exemption to the criminal prohibition: the 1990 law and its effectiveness

In 1990 Belgium adopted new abortion legislation that ended twenty years of hypocrisy. Until that point the situation had been paradoxical: on the one hand, repressive legislation coexisted with the de facto liberalisation of abortion; on the other, repression was carried out through an ad hoc and arbitrary application of the criminal law, although many cases were dismissed without follow-up by the public prosecutor's office (mainly in the French-speaking part of the country). Despite this paradoxical situation, and the fact that 15,000 abortions were performed every year, Belgium had not changed its criminal laws on abortion since the early 1970s. It was only after a long process of politicisation that new legislation was finally passed in 1990.

However, the law of 3 April 1990 did not fully authorise abortion, which was still listed in the criminal code (promulgated in 1867) under Title VII, "Crimes against family order and public morality". Instead, the law redefined the offence to exclude abortions performed under a precisely defined set of conditions. The law on the partial decriminalisation of abortion thus established a legal exemption from the criminal prohibition when a set of cumulative conditions were met:

---

26   Ibid., Article 1 §3.

27   *Moniteur belge*, 2018, "Royal Decree of 15 October 2018 appointing the members of the National Evaluation Commission responsible for evaluating the application of the provisions of the law of 3 April 1990 on the voluntary termination of pregnancy", 5 November.

- abortion must be performed by a doctor in a health care facility (a hospital or outpatient centre);
- the doctor must attest to the "state of distress" of the woman seeking abortion;
- the health care facility must arrange psychological counselling for the woman and inform her about contraceptive measures; existing social benefits for families, single and unmarried mothers, and children; and the possibility of having the unborn child adopted;
- the woman should be informed of the immediate and future medical risks that she may face if she has the abortion;
- the procedure must be performed at a maximum of twelve weeks of pregnancy (or fourteen weeks of amenorrhoea);
- beyond this period, only medical reasons linked to a serious threat to the woman's health or the certainty that the foetus is suffering from an incurable condition can be invoked to carry out a medical termination of pregnancy and, in this case, the opinion of two doctors is required;
- a six-day waiting period is required between the request for abortion and the actual procedure; and
- the woman's consent to having abortion must be given in writing.

Failure to comply with any one of these conditions could result in criminal penalties for the doctor or the woman. In addition, the law provided for use of the conscience clause by the doctor or any other qualified person in the health care institution, without any obligation for the doctor to refer the woman to another doctor.

Currently, most abortions are performed in outpatient centres.[28] The configuration of these centres is not the same everywhere; those in Brussels and Wallonia are family planning centres, whereas in Flanders these centres do not offer abortion, which is carried out in seven special centres covering the needs of the Flemish population. Five of them are part of the non-profit organisation Unie Nederlandstalige Abortus Centra (LUNA; Union of Dutch-Speaking Abortion Centres). Out of the 102 family planning centres in Wallonia and Brussels, only 31 perform abortions (15 of them in Brussels). Twenty-two of them operate under the umbrella of GACEHPA. French-speaking family planning centres are approved and subsidised either by the Walloon Region or, in Brussels,

---

28 House of Representatives, 2020, "Biennial reports of the National Evaluation Commission of the Law of 3 April 1990 on the voluntary termination of pregnancy: hearings", no. 1201/1, 28 April, p. 42.

by the Commission communautaire française (COCOF; French Community Commission). Four family planning centres in Brussels are also recognised as bi-community organisations – and therefore depend on the Commission communautaire commune (COCOM; Joint Community Commission) – but do not perform abortions. As they are not integrated into the family-planning-centre sector (financed in French-speaking Wallonia by the Region and on the Dutch-speaking side by the Flemish Community), these *abortus centra* had to finance themselves until 2003. Since then almost the entire cost of abortion has been covered at the federal level through agreements with the Institut national d'assurance maladie-invalidité (INAMI; National Institute for Health and Disability Insurance).

GACEHPA also works in a network with LUNA and regularly collaborates with CAL, the Fédération laïque des centres de planning familial (FLCPF; Lay Federation of Family Planning Centres), Femmes prévoyantes socialistes (FPS; Socialist Women's Forum) and the Abortion Right platform (see below). At the international level, GACEHPA regularly collaborates with the International Planned Parenthood Federation European Network (IPPF EN).

Although access to abortion has, to date, been effective and takes place in safe psycho-medical settings, the issue of the medical qualification of general practitioners was raised for a time, but training in abortion techniques provided by the ULB and GACEHPA seems to have mitigated this risk.

All these elements are part of a socio-economic context that is increasingly marked by the precariousness of material living conditions, particularly for women. The 2012 report of the National Commission for the Evaluation of the Law of 1990 highlights this precariousness for those women who go to outpatient centres.[29] Nearly 30% of the women seen by outpatient centres have no social security coverage, and only a minority of them receive urgent medical assistance free of charge. Moreover, the number of undocumented women, asylum seekers and women who are registered with a Centre public d'action sociale (CPAS; Public Centre for

---

29 Senate and House of Representatives, 2012, "Report of the National Commission for the Evaluation of the Law of 3 April 1990 on the termination of pregnancy: report to Parliament; 1 January 2010–31 December 2011", no. 1784/1 (Senate) and no. 2399/1 (House), 27 August, pp. 70–71, 74, 79, 90.

Social Welfare) is increasing.[30] One response to this increase has come from the non-governmental organisation Médecins du Monde Belgium, whose mission is to help the most vulnerable groups. Since 2002 the NGO has had a specific programme called Avec Elles (With Women), one of the aims of which is to reach out to the most disadvantaged women to offer them care and information, as well as education about sexual and reproductive health.

Under these conditions, the effectiveness of access to abortion and appropriate contraception is increasingly dependent on public policies aimed at achieving social citizenship.

5.3 Abortion rights activism and its opponents

This review of the conditions under which the law of 3 April 1990 came into being allows us to identify the strategies and arguments used in Belgium by the supporters and opponents of the right to abortion.

The secular and feminist framing of a right of access to abortion is based on a new common sense that emerged in the wake of the Peers affair: first, modern contraception is seen as the positive norm; second, any induced abortion is seen as a failure in terms of this norm; and third, the distinction is established between safe and unsafe abortion. The legal recognition of a right to information about contraception is based on this common sense and finds support in an objective shared by all philosophical trends: the reduction of recourse to induced abortion, whether clandestine or medical.

As for the individuation of women, supporters and opponents of decriminalising medical abortion legitimise their positions in an antagonistic way. Secularists and feminists joined forces to challenge the 1867 criminal law, considering abortion to be a private act and a matter for the personal conscience of each individual – and of each woman in particular – as well as a public health issue. As such, this issue must be regulated, and the inequalities that exist between women facing a termination of pregnancy must be addressed, while at the same time recognising their autonomy with regard to decision making in this area. The promotion of public health and respect for the woman's decision are intimately linked

---

30   Public Centres for Social Welfare are public organisations whose mission is to allow each person to be able to lead a life in accordance with human dignity. They are therefore responsible for providing social assistance to certain people, but they also provide other specific psychological, social, financial, medical and administrative support measures to enable these people to reintegrate into an active social life.

---

and must be effective if clandestine abortion is to be eliminated. Moreover, the secular demand for the right to abortion broadens the process of the secularisation of society, which has at stake the political recognition of philosophical pluralism. In this respect, feminism appears as a "new bastion of Belgian secularism".[31] Women's right to autonomous decision making is, in this context, an extension of a classical liberal individualist principle defining the human person by his or her capacity for self-determination, in the sense of habeas corpus. Secularists and feminists thus agree in rejecting any assignment of women to forced motherhood, which would lead to the instrumentalisation of the female body. This rejection reflects a position favourable to the individuation of women through a politicisation of the body. The body is indeed an essential determination of the individual and the subject.

Opposed to the framing put forward by the Christian democrats, the secular and feminist framing is clearly presented as an alternative to a religious traditionalism that sees the criminal law punishing abortion as the expression of a social order that opposes the dissociation between sexuality and procreation – a dissociation made increasingly effective by the development of contraception. The process of women's individuation challenges religious traditionalism. Indeed, the conception of the latter creates a radical limitation to the autonomy of every individual, since its principle of the respect for life, from the moment of conception, makes biological reproduction appear as the expression of the heteronomy with which every individual is confronted and which cannot be thought of in terms of choice.

For its part, the Belgian Catholic Church – led from 1961 to 1979 by Cardinal Archbishop of Malines–Brussels Léon-Joseph Suenens – was opposed to all abortion. Thus, Suenens did not hesitate to issue various statements to remind the orthodoxy of ecclesiastical norms in ethical matters. For example, his statement in April 1973, following the Peers case, emphasised the imprescriptible value of embryonic life and considered all abortion to be a crime.[32] Yet Suenens was also viewed by the Vatican as one of the main actors in the fight against Pope Paul VI's

---

31 Delgrange, Xavier, David Koussens, "Les nouveaux arcs-boutants de la laïcité belge pilarisée", in *Piliers, dépilarisation et clivage philosophique en Belgique,* pp. 83–99. Beyond the pillars, several new bastions have helped to build secularism in Belgium. Among these, the voice of women in their fight for the decriminalisation of abortion has been aided by, and has in turn strengthened, organised secularism.

32 Suenens, Léon-Joseph, et al., 1973, *Déclaration sur l'avortement,* Brussels: Licap (cited in Marques-Pereira, *L'avortement en Belgique,* p. 51).

---

encyclical *Humanae Vitae*. While the Church's position on birth control has not changed since that encyclical was published, Suenens stressed the need for some form of sex education. Moreover, as early as 1971, religious traditionalism was being challenged within the Catholic world. For example, Canon Pierre de Locht, the leader of the Centre d'éducation à la famille et à l'amour (CEFA; Centre for Education for Family and Love) was known for making statements that openly broke from the Catholic Church's official position. Moreover, Godfried Daneels, the Primate of Belgium from 1979 to 2010, tried through his interventions to not exacerbate the divisions within the Catholic world and to not be the cause of demonstrations against the 1990 law partially decriminalising abortion.[33]

The Church in Belgium has been far from eager to join the fierce anti-abortion battles. In Flanders only Vlaams Belang took up the anti-abortion cause of the most radical right, while in Wallonia this cause was supported by Civitas, a group that was historically linked to the extreme right.[34] However, after the appointment of André Léonard as archbishop of Malines–Brussels in 2010, the official discourse of the Belgian Church became more hard-line, particularly on the occasion of the twenty-fifth anniversary of the 1990 law.[35] In 2015 Jozef De Kesel succeeded Léonard as Primate of Belgium. Although he is often considered the heir of Daneels, this did not change the Church's position, which has remained traditionalist on issues of sexuality and bioethics.

It is therefore hardly surprising that the campaigns of opponents of abortion rights have based their legitimacy on the Church's doctrine.[36] While associations such as Pro Vita (founded in 1971) are in relative decline, others have taken over with renewed efficacy in their communication strategies by making extensive use of social media networks. A highly motivated generation of anti-abortion activists clearly wants the 1990 law abolished and does not hesitate to equate abortion with

---

33   See Marques-Pereira, *L'avortement en Belgique*, pp. 50–60; Bracke, Sarah, Wannes Dupont and David Paternotte, 2018, "'Personne n'est prophète en son pays' : le militantisme catholique anti-genre en Belgique", in *Campagnes anti-genre en Europe. Des mobilisations contre l'égalité*, edited by Roman Kuhar and David Paternotte, Lyon: Presses universitaires de Lyon, pp. 79–98.

34   See Brébant, Émilie, and Cécile Vanderpelen, 2015, "Pourquoi le ventre des femmes est-il sacré ? Quand les catholiques belges s'engagent contre l'IVG (de 1990 à aujourd'hui)", *Sextant* (31), pp. 223–238.

35   Ibid.

36   The following paragraphs are an updated version of Marques-Pereira, Bérengère, and Sophie Pereira, 2014, "Abortion in Belgium: a precarious right?", *About Gender: International Journal of Gender Studies* 3(5), 225–244.

murder, even in cases of incest or rape. These activists are careful, however, to use prudently worded rhetoric in order to avoid bringing religious considerations to the fore. Their main objective is to give the foetus a legal personality, thus playing into both emotional and legal–scientific registers. This discourse, which is widely shared on social media, aims to revive the debate on the partial decriminalisation of abortion and bring it back to the centre of the public arena. As part of this effort, family planning centres are occasionally targeted. Acting primarily on the internet, movements such as Souffle de Vie or Jongeren Info Life present themselves as voluntary associations seeking to help women faced with an unwanted pregnancy.[37] On its website, the voluntary association *Jeunes pour la vie* clearly presents itself as being opposed to abortion and claims links with pro-life lobbies at the European level, such as Alliance Vita, European Dignity Watch, the Federation of Catholic Family Associations in Europe, the Fondation Jérôme Lejeune and the European Institute of Bioethics (EIB) (see Chapter 4 and Appendix C).[38]

Every year since 2010, these activists have organised "Marches for Life" in Brussels as a festive and offbeat way to proclaim "a culture of life". The associations involved in these marches are not clearly identifiable, even at the EU level.[39] However, some personalities can be identified, such as the spokesperson for the March for Life, Constance du Bus (whose views are published on the CathoBel website),[40] and one of its organisers, Anne-Chantal André-Dumont (whose views are shared on the website of the Association Famille Chrétienne, or Christian Family Association).[41] The Croissance group, whose aim is to train and participate in Education à la vie relationnelle, affective et sexuelle (EVRAS; Education in Relationships, Emotional and Sexual Life in Schools), includes among its representatives Bénédicte De Wagter-Gillis – who is in favour of the French movement La Manif pour Tous, which is opposed to same-sex marriage and has links to the EIB.[42] André Léonard, the then newly appointed Archbishop of Malines–Brussels, participated in the first March for Life, held on 28 March 2010.

37   See www.souffledevie.be and www.jongereninfolife.be.

38   See www.jeunespourlavie.org.

39   See Zacharenko, "Perspectives on anti-choice lobbying in Europe"; Celis, Karen, and Gily Coene, "Still a woman's right? Feminist and other discourses in Belgium's abortion struggles", in *A Fragmented Landscape*, p. 130.

40   See the interview from 27 April 2018 on www.cathobel.be.

41   See the interview from 31 August 2017 on www.famillechretienne.fr.

42   See www.groupe-croissance.be.

During these marches, activists promote one of their main arguments, namely, the supposed increase in the number of abortions, a claim not backed up by official figures.[43] They also make other unsubstantiated claims – for example, that the number of abortions would decrease if the abortion law were repealed, that abortion can cause infertility and mental health problems, and that abortion can cause breast cancer.[44] They do not hesitate to use medical misinformation about abortion, or discourses that stigmatise abortion and make pregnant women feel guilty about requesting one.

In March 2017 this discursive activism against abortion became part of a philosophy course taught at the Université Catholique de Louvain by a visiting lecturer, Stéphane Mercier. Even though the university quickly distanced itself from Mercier's views and terminated his appointment, his reactionary remarks describing abortion as "murder paid for by the state health care system" and as "more serious than rape" quickly spread on the internet.[45] Mercier received a standing ovation at a March for Life in Brussels on 26 March 2017.

The theme of the 2018 March for Life was "Are they doomed to disappear?", amalgamating "abortion and euthanasia, the embryo, the foetus and the child". On the eve of the debate in the House Committee on Justice on the bill tabled by the government majority (see below), a statement by the Belgian bishops drew attention to the danger they saw in the total decriminalisation of abortion:

> It is taking the risk of making abortion a harmless medical procedure. Not only will abortion no longer be considered an offence in the cases provided for by the law. It will become a right. Anyone who asks questions or refuses an abortion will have

43 Although the latest reports of the National Commission for the Evaluation of the Law of 3 April 1990 show a clear increase in the absolute number of abortions (with an increase between 1998 and 2001, stabilisation in 2014–15, and then a decrease), this number must be weighted by various elements, in particular by taking into account the increase in Belgium's overall population since the law was passed. In addition, the number of deliveries also increased, so that the number of abortions per 100 births has remained stable, at around 14 to 15. See House of Representatives, 2020, "Biennial Reports of the National Commission for the Evaluation of the Law of 3 April 1990: hearings", no. 1201/1, 28 April, pp. 8–9.

44 These myths are exposed and deconstructed in a note from the Dutch-speaking outpatient abortion centres in Senate and House of Representatives, 2012, "Report of the National Commission for the Evaluation of the Law of 3 April 1990: report to Parliament; 1 January 2010–31 December 2011", no. 1784/1 (Senate) and no. 2399/1 (House), 27 August, pp. 63–67.

45 Mercier, La philosophie pour la vie, p. 55.

to justify themselves. This applies to both the doctor and the woman concerned. Even if the freedom of conscience clause is retained, it will be invoked less and less. For a medical procedure requires a medical decision, not so much a decision of conscience.[46]

Two petitions echoed this statement: the first from a citizens' group, dated 28 August 2018 and titled "Open letter to the members of the Belgian House of Representatives concerning the distress of women and girls faced with an unplanned pregnancy", and the second drafted by health care workers, invoking the threat that the total decriminalisation of abortion would pose to them.

Faced with such activism, the defence of the right to abortion entered a new phase marked by the coordination of national and transnational strategies to safeguard this right. Thus, some of the most recent campaigns of abortion rights defenders at the European level led to the constitution of a federation called the High Ground Alliance for Choice and Dignity in Europe, in order to counterbalance the One of Us European Federation (see Chapter 4 and Appendices C and D). In Belgium, supporters of the right to abortion – including feminists, secularists and federations of family planning centres – employed tried-and-tested tactics such as marches, petitions, lobbying and advocacy. These actions were not limited to the Belgian context, but were used to demand the right to abortion for all women living in Europe, targeting in particular those countries that upheld a criminal ban or that were seeking to revert to one. Thus, a march organised on 24 March 2012 in Brussels symbolically linked the embassies of Cyprus, Ireland, Malta and Poland by delivering to each a letter – signed by more than 360 associations, institutions, trade unions and political figures – that demanded the right to abortion for all women living in Europe. This action demonstrates the intertwining of the national and European struggles, with Brussels being a strategic centre for activists as it hosts the headquarters of several EU institutions.

In this context, the Fédération des Centres de Planning Familial des Femmes Prévoyantes Socialistes (FCPF-FPS; Federation of Planned Parenthood Centres of the Socialist Women's Forum) sounded the alarm for the first time at the end of 2005 by organising an international colloquium at the ULB titled "Abortion: freedoms in danger".[47] The following year, the

---

46   Belgian Bishops' Conference, 2018, "Supprimer l'avortement du Code pénal : une décision symboliquement lourde", Press Release, 15 June (http//info.catho.be).

47   See Femmes Prévoyantes Socialistes, N.D., "Avortement: libertés en danger", proceedings of the international colloquium of 12 December 2005, Brussels.

four federations of family planning centres in the French Community[48] officially launched their vigilance platform called Vive la Vie (Long Live Life), whose main objective was to defend the right to abortion and whose name was chosen to counter the monopolisation of the notion of the "right to life" by opponents of abortion rights. The initiative, which was quickly joined by around forty other organisations, was a reaction to calls to action from a collective called Papa, Maman et Moi (Mummy, Daddy and Me), which was opposed to same-sex marriage and adoption. These calls led to 25 July 2006 being declared the first European Anti-Abortion Day, with a national demonstration in Brussels.

The celebration of the twentieth anniversary of the law decriminalising abortion, in 2010, led to an increase in activism by supporters of abortion rights. As a first step, the FLCPF and the FCPF-FPS decided to join forces, in particular by updating a memorandum advocating improved access to abortion.[49] Subsequently, a communication campaign, a march and a symposium organised by CAL[50] helped to raise public awareness of the current issues surrounding abortion rights.

As the annual rallies against the 1990 law attracted more participants, abortion rights supporters continued their activism efforts and formed the Abortion Right platform in 2011. This pluralist platform for vigilance and action brought together CAL, the Cercle du libre examen, the Conseil des femmes francophones de Belgique (CFFB), deMens.nu, the four federations of French-speaking family planning centres, the Fédération générale du travail de Belgique (FGTB, a socialist trade union), GACEHPA, the feminist association Garance, LUNA, the Mouvement ouvrier chrétien (MOC), Mutualités socialistes, Nederlandstalige vrouwenraad, the Belgian committee of Ni putes ni soumises, RAPPEL (Réseau d'action pour la promotion d'un État laïque), the Séverine family planning centre, the Université des Femmes, Vlaamse Expertisecentrum voor Seksuele

---

48   The French-speaking family planning centres are grouped into four federations: the Fédération des centres de planning et de consultations (FCPC), the Fédération des centres de planning familial des Femmes prévoyantes socialistes (FCPF-FPS), the Fédération des centres pluralistes de planning familial (FCPPF) and the Fédération laïque des centres de planning familial (FLCPF).

49   Plateforme pour le droit à l'avortement, 2013, "Mémorandum 2014", (published in *Chronique féministe* (112), 63). The signatories are the same as those of the Abortion Right platform (see below).

50   Centre de documentation et d'information de la Fédération laïque des centres de planning familial, 2010, "Les 20 ans de la loi sur l'avortement: de la subversion au droit", proceedings of the colloquium of 1 April 2010, Brussels.

Gezondheid (SENSOA), VIVA-Socialistische Vrouwen Vereniging and Vrouwen Overleg Komitee (VOK).

Abortion Right aims to guarantee the right to abortion and free choice for women at the Belgian and European levels. To this end, the platform offers an alternative to the prohibitionist discourse of opponents in the public arena, developing various advocacy and public awareness initiatives. Abortion Right also challenged political parties in the run-up to the European, federal, regional and EU elections on 25 May 2014, by reviving one of the main slogans of feminist protesters from the 1970s and 1980s: "Abortion out of the criminal code!"

In preparation for the commemoration of the twenty-fifth anniversary of the Lallemand–Michielsens Act, several associations organised awareness-raising campaigns. LUNA, the IPPF EN and GACEHPA launched a campaign against the stigmatisation of abortion, lasting from 2014 to 2015 and resulting in a resolution on 3 April 2015;[51] this resolution was submitted to Maggie De Block (Open VLD), the Belgian minister of social affairs and public health. GACEHPA also created a campaign to give more visibility to outpatient centres and their practices by reaffirming on its website that "Abortion is possible," in order to counter the misinformation spread on the internet and social media by opponents of the right to abortion.[52] GACEHPA also denounced private clinics that perform abortions for profit, sometimes at exorbitant prices reaching up to €1,000.[53] With the same objective as GACEHPA and LUNA, the FCPF-FPS has been providing reliable information since April 2014 on the website www.jeveuxavorter.be, and in 2015 it published an analysis of the stigmatisation of abortion,[54] which was disseminated via the Abortion Right platform.[55]

In particular, these initiatives aim to compensate for the lack of official information published on the website of the SPF Santé publique, Sécurité de la chaîne alimentaire et Environnement (Federal Government Service

---

51   See Groupe d'action des centres extrahospitaliers pratiquant l'avortement, 2016, "Rapport d'activités 2015", pp. 6–7, 22–24.

52   See, for example, the following websites: www.ivg.net (launched in 2008), www.ecouteivg.org (launched in 2011) and www.afterbaiz.com (launched in 2016).

53   Groupe d'action des centres extrahospitaliers pratiquant l'avortement, 2014, "Campaign: Avorter c'est possible", Chronique féministe (114), 42.

54   Malcourant, Éloïse, 2015, La stigmatisation de l'avortement, Brussels: Femmes prévoyantes socialistes.

55   See Abortion Right, 2016, "Lutter contre la stigmatisation de l'avortement", Press Release, 1 April (published in Chronique féministe (117), 68).

for Public Health, Food Chain Safety and Environment), information that had been demanded since the celebration of the twenty-fifth anniversary of the 1990 law.[56] This information was made available on the SPF website in January 2016.[57]

CAL regularly creates political campaigns in favour of removing abortion from the criminal code.[58] However, the platform of the FLCPF (Lay Federation of Family Planning Centres) – which is, in principle, in favour of this removal – expresses doubts as to the relevance of the demand, fearing that it would be a step backwards in relation to the achievements of the 1990 law. The FLCPF is thus at odds with the positions of other organisations such as GACEHPA, the Fédération des centres pluralistes de planning familial (FCPPF; Federation of Pluralistic Family Planning Centres) and the FCPF-FPS. Flemish pro-abortion associations also fear that, in a political context in which N-VA has little or no chance of being overruled, a change in legislation will lead to a loss of rights rather than an expansion of them (see below). Therefore, LUNA, SENSOA and the FLCPF do not participate in the advocacy and awareness-raising work carried out by CAL and other members of the platform.

However, party lobbying for the removal of abortion from the criminal code continued in 2017. Thus, on the occasion of International Women's Rights Day on 8 March, the *Collectif des 350* distributed a manifesto on this topic.[59] The manifesto was drafted with reference to Article 350 of the criminal code, which considers abortion in Belgium to be an offence against the family and public morality, and also with reference to the 343 French women who, in 1971, publicly declared in an act of civil

---

56   See Abortion Right, 2015, Press Release, 28 March; Groupe d'action des centres extrahospitaliers pratiquant l'avortement, 2015, Resolution, 3 April (published in *Chronique féministe* (115), 54–56).

57   See www.health.belgium.be/fr/sante, under the heading "Début et fin de vie".

58   In this context, CAL published a brochure titled "L'avortement hors du Code pénal" (2015, Brussels; it was updated in the following years) and organised colloquiums on the same theme in Brussels on 30 September 2016, in Liège on 23 November 2016 and in the Senate on 27 January 2017 (see "Sortir l'avortement du Code pénal belge", N.D., proceedings of colloquiums in Brussels (20 September 2016), Liège (23 November 2016) and the Senate (27 January 2017), www.laicite.be). CAL also organised a meeting on 23 November 2017 titled "IVG hors du Code pénal. Six propositions de loi et puis quoi ?", with representatives of the DéFI, Ecolo, Groen, MR, Open VLD, PS, PTB and SP.A parties; CDH and CD&V declined the invitation.

59   This manifesto was published on the CAL website on 7 March 2017 and subsequently published as an open letter: *Le Soir*, 2018, "Appel à un débat parlementaire pour réellement légaliser l'IVG", 9 July. See www.manifestedes350.be.

disobedience that they had had an abortion despite the law. Furthermore, on 28 September 2017, on the occasion of International Safe Abortion Day, the World March of Women,[60] together with GACEHPA and the Abortion Right platform, organised a demonstration in Brussels demanding respect for the right to self-determination, the right to health for women in all European countries and the recognition of these rights as fundamental for equality in Europe.

The following year, 2018, saw several marches take place.[61] Among other noteworthy initiatives, we should highlight the publication of an opinion poll commissioned by CAL and deMens.nu on abortion in Belgium.[62] This survey, which was mainly intended to raise political awareness, showed that 75.4% of those polled thought that abortion should no longer be a crime, 75.3% that abortion should be regulated by a health law, 59.0% that denying safe and legal access to abortion constitutes violence against women and 76.8% that the final decision on whether to have an abortion belongs to the pregnant woman. We should also mention the international forum organised jointly by Belgium's French Community and CAL on 21 and 22 June titled "All united for the right to abortion", which resulted in the *Déclaration de Bruxelles*;[63] the document's foreword referred to the major international legal instruments that legitimise the right to abortion in the name of human rights.

---

60 The World March of Women brings together a large number of organisations in Belgium, such as feminist associations (Comité de liaison des femmes, CLF; Commission femmes et développement, CFD; the CFFB and its Dutch-language equivalent, Nederlandstalige Vrouwenraad; Garance; La voix des femmes; Le monde selon les femmes; Association 29 rue Blanche Mouvements de femmes; SOS Viol; Université des femmes; le Vrouwen Overleg Komitee, VOK; and, among the most important quantitatively speaking, FPS and Vie Féminine), family planning centres (FLCPF, Centre de planning et de consultations conjugales and La Famille Heureuse), trade unions (CSC and FGTB, including their women's sections), women's organisations from CDH, CD&V, Ecolo, MR, Open VLD and SP.A, and non-governmental organisations (including Amnesty International, Comité pour l'abolition des dettes illégitimes (CADTM), and Ligue des familles et Oxfam-Magasins du monde).

61 On the initiative of the *Collectif des 350*, a women's caravan was organised on 9 September 2018 and, a month later, the World March of Women organised another march in favour of removing abortion from the criminal code.

62 CAL, deMens.nu, Université libre de Bruxelles and Universiteit Hasselt, 2018, "Sondage d'opinion sur l'interruption volontaire de grossesse en Belgique". This survey was conducted among 1,000 Belgians aged 18 and over; the sample was representative in terms of language, gender, age, region, level of education, socio-professional categories and philosophical/religious beliefs.

63 See "Déclaration de Bruxelles. L'interruption volontaire de grossesse : un droit fondamental des femmes" (https://droitavortement.be).

5.4 The 2018 law: a return to a policy of accommodation within the government coalition

More than twenty-five years after the adoption of the law of 3 April 1990, the complete removal of abortion from the criminal code remains a major objective for Belgian supporters of the right to abortion. Permanently removing abortion from the criminal domain implies that it should no longer be seen as a criminal act, and as socially and morally reprehensible, but rather as a medical procedure and a matter of public health, with the discussion taking place in the context of a one-to-one meeting between a doctor and the pregnant woman, and respecting the woman's free choice to continue with her pregnancy or not. It also requires the abolition of the notion of the "state of distress" of the woman requesting an abortion. This notion was introduced into the abortion laws in France in 1975 and in Belgium in 1990 as a concession to opponents of the right to abortion in order to avoid trivialising the portrayal of abortion. In so doing, abortion was recognised not as a right to self-determination but as a right to access abortion in order to combat the risks from it being carried out in a clandestine manner. Another demand of Belgian supporters of the right to abortion is the extension of the time limit for abortion so as not to put some women in the position of having to travel abroad (a practice sometimes describe as "abortion tourism"), particularly to the Netherlands, where the time limit is twenty-two weeks from conception, compared with twelve weeks in Belgium.

From 2016 onwards these demands led to the tabling of a series of bills based on international human rights standards and the examples of France and Luxembourg, two neighbouring countries that had removed abortion from their criminal codes and abolished the notion of a state of distress (see Appendix E). These bills were initiated by opposition parties with one exception: Open VLD, a member of the Michel I government coalition (N-VA/MR/CD&V/Open VLD) also tabled a bill to remove abortion from the criminal code. These legislative initiatives came about following concern from abortion rights supporters over the shift to the right of the Belgian political landscape, especially in Flanders, where N-VA became the largest party in 2010 and entered a federal government for the first time in 2014.[64]

---

64   See Govaert, Serge, 2016, "La montée des nationalistes flamands au pouvoir dans les gouvernements fédéraux, 1977–2014", *Courrier hebdomadaire* (2313), CRISP.

CDH, which was part of the parliamentary opposition, also tabled a bill. This bill formally removed abortion from the criminal code but provided for criminal sanctions for doctors and women, as well as maintaining the notion of a state of distress. It amounted to safeguarding the content of the law of 3 April 1990, as we shall see later. In the context of increasing devolution to the federated entities, reinforced by Belgium's sixth institutional reform,[65] several bills were tabled from 2014 onwards – mainly by Flemish parties (some of which are in favour of extending the right to abortion) – with the aim of broadening the legal recognition of the existence of the stillborn foetus.[66] One of them, tabled by CD&V, appears to pose the most serious threat to the law of 3 April 1990 in the eyes of the defenders of the right to abortion.[67] This parliamentary activity is in fact part of a long-standing desire on the part of certain political representatives to clarify the procedure for "registering a lifeless child" in order to adapt it to advances in neonatology and to help parents grieve. For example, the coalition agreement of the Michel I government, finalised in October 2014, provides that "there will be legislation on the issue of the name and registration of stillborn children".[68]

All of these bills, which claim to meet the needs of parents of a "lifeless child", are intended to clarify the regulations regarding the name and registration of such children. The obligation to draw up a "lifeless birth certificate" when a child has died at birth is provided for in Article 80*bis* of the civil code (Title II, Chapter 4, on death certificates), which was introduced in 1999 but without mentioning at what point in the pregnancy this

---

65   See Blaise, Pierre, Jean Faniel, and Caroline Sägesser, 2022, *Introduction à la Belgique fédérale*, Brussels: CRISP.

66   See House of Representatives, 2014, "Bill on the law on lifeless children", tabled by Catherine Fonck, Francis Delpérée and Vanessa Matz (CDH), no. 506/1, 24 October; House of Representatives, 2015, "Bill amending the Civil Code with regard to stillborn children", tabled by Peter Vanvelthoven, Karin Jiroflée and Maya Detiège (SP.A), no. 801/1, 20 January; House of Representatives, 2015, "Bill to amend the Civil Code with regard to the registration of stillborn children", tabled by Carina Van Cauter and Sabien Lahaye-Battheu (Open VLD), no. 957/1, 12 March.

67   See House of Representatives, 2014, "Bill amending the regulation of stillborn children", tabled by Sonja Becq and Raf Terwingen (CD&V), no. 243/1, 10 September. This bill was substantially amended by Sonja Becq (CD&V), Raf Terwingen (CD&V) and Goedele Uyttersprot (N-VA): House of Representatives, 2017, "Bill amending the regulation of stillborn children: amendments", no. 243/5, 22 February.

68   Federal Government of Belgium, 2014, "Government agreement", 10 October, p. 126.

declaration must be made.[69] A threshold of 180 days is, however, spec-
ified by a 1999 circular that states that "a child who has left the womb
without life after the one-hundred-and-eightieth day (sixth months) of
gestation shall be considered stillborn".[70]

The bills in question, none of which were voted on in parliament,
were in one way or another intended to introduce this 180-day threshold into Article 80*bis* of the civil code and, in addition, to allow (possibly
on an optional basis) the procedure for recognising a lifeless child born
between 140 and 179 days of pregnancy. Another new element provided
for in some of these texts is the possibility (beyond the 180 days) of
giving not just a first name but also a surname to the child, and the possibility of granting benefits that are, in principle, reserved for living children
(such as a birth allowance, or the declaration of dependent children).
Within the framework of the declared grounds of "humanity" and adap-
tation to medical progress, the aim of all these bills is for the parents'
bereavement to be taken care of by the authorities, since, at the parents'
request, the funeral of a foetus stillborn before 180 days of gestation
could be arranged in accordance with the procedures specific to the federated entities competent in the matter of funerals, i.e. the Regions and
Belgium's German-speaking Community.

Secular and feminist circles, as well as GACEHPA and the federations
of family planning centres, are deeply concerned about this parliamentary activity, seeing it as an indirect challenge to the right to abortion in
a context of an increasing number of ethical debates that are not condu-
cive to women's rights.[71]

The adoption of one particular bill, this time tabled by the four parties
of the government majority, has prompted some feminist associations to
react.[72] The text adopted by the House on 9 February 2017 allows for the

---

69 *Moniteur belge*, 1999, "Law of 27 April 1999 introducing Article 80*bis* into the Civil
Code and repealing the decree of 4 July 1806 on the method of drawing up the certificate
in which the civil registrar notes that he/she is recording a lifeless child", 24 June.

70 The 180-day threshold appears in two articles of Title VII of the civil code ("On
parentage"); one on the "presumption of paternity" (Chapter 2, Section 1, Article 316bis),
and the other on the "time of conception" (Chapter 3, Section 1, Article 326). See *Moniteur
belge*, 1999, "Circular of the Minister of Justice of 10 June 1999 on the introduction into
the Civil Code of Article 80*bis* concerning the registration of a lifeless child", 1 July.

71 *Le Soir*, 15 April 2010. See also the open letter signed by Henri Bartholomeeusen,
then president of CAL, in *Le Soir*, 19 April 2016: "Le droit à l'avortement pourrait être mis
à mal".

72 See House of Representatives, 2016, "Bill amending the Civil Code with regard to the
prenatal recognition of a child by an unmarried parent", no. 1658/1, 17 February.

recognition of paternal filiation outside of marriage from the beginning of the pregnancy.[73] In the view of the CFFB, by allowing the recognition of early paternity, the legislator is in effect giving legal leverage to an abusive partner to prevent a pregnant woman from seeking abortion.[74] Such a measure risks legitimising reproductive coercion, i.e. men's interference with the contraception taken by women and women's family planning choices in order to force them into childbirth and tie them down with the indissoluble bond of paternity. More generally, the question of the effect of this prenatal recognition on women's reproductive rights arises: "Once a woman has accepted that the co-parent recognises the embryo she is carrying, from the moment of conception, does she still have the right to terminate the pregnancy? In other words, could the co-parent rely on subjective rights arising from the act of prenatal recognition?"[75]

A few months later, on 2 June 2017, two bills were rejected, one by the Ecolo-Groen party and the other by PS.[76] Both bills aimed at legalising a practice that has been in place for decades in family planning centres, namely, the accessibility of contraception at any time, including in emergencies. Family planning centres are allowed to distribute medication only to a very limited extent. Contraceptive pills, in particular, must be dispensed by a pharmacy, and on the basis of prescription by a doctor (which can be problematic in emergencies, given that the

---

73   *Moniteur belge*, 2017, "Law of 20 February 2017 amending the Civil Code with regard to the prenatal recognition of a child by an unmarried parent", 22 March. The PS, DéFI and PP representatives voted against this bill; the SP.A and PTB representatives abstained. See House of Representatives, 2017, *Full Report* (156 and 157), 9 February, pp. 83–95 and pp. 46–47 and 60–61, respectively.

74   Conseil des femmes francophones de Belgique, 2017, "Statut du fœtus, reconnaissance anté-natale", Press Release, 13 February (published in *Chronique féministe* (119), 68).

75   Bernard, Diane, Sahra Datoussaid, Eugénie d'Ursel and Valérie Eloy, 2019, "L'autonomie reproductive et les droits des femmes à l'aune de trois nouvelles lois 'symboliques' : du glissement au recul ?", *Journal des tribunaux* (6771), 4 May, p. 345.

76   House of Representatives, 2015, "Bill amending Royal Decree no. 78 of 10 November 1967 on the practice of the health care professions in order to allow the free distribution of contraceptives and the morning-after pill via family planning centres by means of a 'Contraception Pass'", tabled by Muriel Gerkens, Anne Dedry, Stefaan Van Hecke, Wouter De Vriendt, Benoit Hellings, Jean-Marc Nollet and Evita Willaert (Ecolo-Groen), no. 1456/1, 17 November; House of Representatives, 2016, "Bill amending the coordinated laws of 10 May 2015 on the practice of the health care professions in order to allow the distribution of emergency contraception and contraceptives that are not likely to present a danger to health by approved organisations", tabled by Fabienne Winckel, André Frédéric, Özlem Özen, Daniel Senesael, Karine Lalieux and Alain Mathot (PS), no. 1759/1, 13 April.

majority of doctors working in family planning are only part-time and are not permanently available). Family planning centres and the doctors who work there therefore act illegally if they distribute the pill to their patients directly and without a prescription. It is this type of situation that the two bills aim to regularise. The rejection[77] of the two bills was surprising, as the morning-after pill was available in pharmacies without a prescription, and therefore without medical consultation or follow-up.

A few days later, on 27 June 2017, the Committee on Justice agreed to a request from CD&V to adjourn *sine die* the examination of the bills to remove abortion from the criminal code (with representatives from the government majority outweighing those from the opposition in the decision).

Nearly a year later, on 23 May 2018, in the House Committee on Justice, discussion of the bills to remove abortion from the criminal code resumed under pressure from abortion rights supporters. They considered it undemocratic to restrict the debate, especially since the opinion poll on abortion in Belgium commissioned by CAL and deMens.nu (see above) clearly showed that, a few months before the elections (namely, the local elections on 14 October 2018 and the European and legislative elections on 26 May 2019), decriminalisation appeared to be widely accepted within Belgian society, and thus political parties would not offend their electorate by defending decriminalisation.

On 19 September 2018 this committee adopted a bill tabled by representatives from the government majority, which provided for the removal of abortion from the criminal code, as we will see later. On the same day, the government revoked the agreement on the registration of lifeless children, an issue that was considered a priority by CD&V in particular; the minister of justice, K. Geens (CD&V), then tabled a bill on this subject.[78] In other words, having failed to prevent the resumption and advancement

---

77   See House of Representatives, Committee on Public Health, Environment and Social Renewal, 2017, "Bill amending Royal Decree no. 78 of 10 November 1967 on the practice of the health care professions in order to allow the free distribution of contraceptives and the morning-after pill via family planning centres by means of a 'Contraception Pass'; bill amending the coordinated laws of 10 May 2015 on the practice of the health care professions in order to allow the distribution of emergency contraception and contraceptives that are not likely to present a danger to health by approved organisations: report", no. 1456/5, 2 June, pp. 19–20; House of Representatives, 2017, *Full Report* (172), 8 June, pp. 122–125, 138–141.

78   House of Representatives, 2018, "Bill amending Article 4 of the law of 18 June 2018 on various provisions in civil law and provisions to promote alternative forms of dispute resolution concerning the lifeless child act", no. 3271/1, 19 September.

of the parliamentary debate on the decriminalisation of abortion, the government was clearly engaged in a form of bartering over ethical issues.

In his overview, Minister Geens explained:

> The essence of this bill is to develop a legal framework that adequately addresses the existing needs of parents of a lifeless child in order to give that child a place in their lives and to help them grieve. [...] A balanced regulation has been adopted to allow the stillborn child to be given not only a first name but also a surname without this having any other legal effect, and also to extend the option of registering a lifeless child born after a pregnancy of at least 140 days from the date of conception.[79]

This bill essentially reflects the content of the various other bills mentioned above. The minister's statement refers to "a *lifeless child born* after a pregnancy of at least 140 days";[80] even if their registration is optional, they are already granted the status of a "lifeless child" – although, as we have seen, a duration of 140 days (or twenty weeks) of pregnancy is, in the current state of medicine, clearly below the "perinatal period".

Reacting a few days later in an open letter titled "Humaniser le deuil ou les fœtus" ("Humanising mourning or foetuses"), Henri Bartholomeeusen, then president of CAL, reminded us that this form of personification of the foetus is not without consequences, for both women and doctors, because "legally granting the status of child to a 140-day-old foetus will have, whether we like it or not, consequences for all those who – from near or far – are faced with problematic, risky or unwanted pregnancies".[81] An example of this is Hungary, which recognised the personhood of the foetus in its constitution in 2012 (see Chapter 1).

Minister Geens' bill was adopted by the House on 13 December 2018. The members of the parties of the government majority (N-VA, MR, CD&V and Open VLD), as well as those of CDH, Groen (except for one who abstained), PP, SP.A, and the independent members (elected on N-VA lists) Hendrik Vuye and Veerle Wouters voted in favour of this text; the

---

79 Translated from ibid., p. 4. Technically, this bill amended the law of 18 June 2018, which, among many other measures, concerned a "modernisation of the civil status" (Title 2) and a complete rewording of Articles 34–101 of the civil code. As a result of the law of 18 June 2018, which came into force in January 2019, the procedure for registering a "lifeless child" was set out in (new) Articles 58 and 59 of the Civil Code (Section 7, "Death certificates"; Subsection 3, "The lifeless child certificate"). However, in these articles, no mention is made of the 180-day (or 140-day) period.

80 Emphasis added.

81 Translated from *Le Soir*, 26 September 2018.

Table 5.3. Distribution by party of votes on the "Bill on the voluntary termination of pregnancy repealing Articles 350 and 351 of the Criminal Code, amending Articles 352 and 383 of the same Code, and amending various legislative provisions" (plenary session of the House, 4 October 2018).

	Yes	No	Abstentions	Total present	Absent
N-VA	29	–	–	29	2
MR	18	–	2	20	–
CD&V	14	–	–	14	4
Open VLD	14	–	–	14	–
CDH	7	–	–	7	2
Independent*	2	–	–	2	–
PS	–	17	–	17	6
SP.A	–	9	–	9	4
Ecolo	–	5	–	5	1
Groen	–	3	3	6	–
VB	–	2	–	2	1
DéFI	–	2	–	2	–
PTB	–	1	–	1	1
PP	–	–	–	–	1
Total	84	39	5	128	22

*The two independent MPs were Hendrik Vuye and Veerle Wouters, who were both elected on N-VA lists.

members of DéFI, Ecolo (except for two who abstained), PS and PTB voted against it; no VB member was present at the time of the vote.[82] In the opinion of some legal experts, the law of 19 December 2018 amending various provisions relating to the regulations on lifeless children[83] ratifies a shift in meaning that opens the door to rolling back women's rights, particularly with regard to abortion:

---

82   House of Representatives, 2018, *Full Report* (262), 13 December, p. 73.
83   *Moniteur belge,* 27 December 2018.

The lifeless child act [...] creates a dangerous confusion between the conception of an embryo and the birth of a child, and has implications for women's reproductive rights, some of which are exercised, without necessarily being considered as subjective rights under Belgian law, during the particular period of pregnancy, i.e. between conception and childbirth. According such a status (even a limited one) to foetuses conflicts with the very possibility of terminating a pregnancy, whether this is by choice or for medical reasons.[84]

The decriminalisation of abortion was not included in the government's coalition agreement; only the federal parliament could act in this matter. Between 10 May 2016 and 29 May 2018, bills on this topic were tabled in the House by members of seven different political groups or parties: DéFI,[85] PS,[86] Ecolo-Groen,[87] SP.A,[88] PTB,[89] Open VLC[90] and CDH.[91] A comparative analysis of these seven bills can be found in Appendix E (Table E.1).

---

84   Translated from Bernard et al., "L'autonomie reproductive et les droits des femmes à l'aune de trois nouvelles lois 'symboliques'", p. 344.

85   House of Representatives, 2016, "Bill amending the Criminal Code and the law of 22 August 2002 on the rights of the patient aimed at decriminalising the voluntary termination of pregnancy", tabled by Olivier Maingain and Véronique Caprasse, no. 1823/1, 10 May.

86   House of Representatives, 2016, "Bill to remove the voluntary termination of pregnancy from the Criminal Code and to introduce it into the law of 22 August 2002 on the rights of the patient", tabled by Karine Lalieux, Laurette Onkelinx and Fabienne Winkel, no. 1867/1, 31 May.

87   House of Representatives, 2017, "Bill on the voluntary termination of pregnancy", tabled by Muriel Gerkens, Evita Willaert, Georges Gilkinet, Anne Dedry, Benoit Hellings, Meyrem Almaci, Jean-Marc Nollet and Gilles Vanden Burre, no. 2271/1, 18 January. Members of the Ecolo-Groen group had already tabled a similarly titled bill on 1 July 2016 (no. 1947/1).

88   House of Representatives, 2018, "Bill on decriminalising the voluntary termination of pregnancy", tabled by Karin Jiroflée, Monica De Coninck, Annick Lambrecht and Karin Temmerman, no. 3059/1, 26 April. The same SP.A representatives had already tabled a "Bill on the voluntary termination of pregnancy" on 27 June 2017 (no. 2571/1).

89   House of Representatives, 2017, "Bill on decriminalising abortion and updating the law on the voluntary termination of pregnancy", tabled by Marco Van Hees and Raoul Hedebouw, no. 2518/1, 8 June.

90   House of Representatives, 2017, "Bill on abortion", tabled by Carina Van Cauter, no. 2527/1, 12 June.

91   House of Representatives, 2018, "Bill on the termination of pregnancy", tabled by Catherine Fonck, no. 3123/1, 29 May.

The government majority appeared divided. Open VLD was the only one of the four parties to table a bill. MR, the only French-speaking party in the coalition, was in favour of decriminalisation, although its members were not unanimous on the ethical issues. CD&V and N-VA were opposed to the decriminalisation of abortion. For Prime Minister Charles Michel the challenge was to keep the government coalition together, despite a divided liberal family and in the face of an N-VA that is conservative in ethical matters and a CD&V that did not intend to accept that, in this matter, parliamentarians should be free to vote as they choose, which would lead to an alternative majority, as happened to the Di Rupo government (PS/CD&V/MR/SP.A/Open VLD/CDH) with the February 2014 vote on the extension of euthanasia to minors.[92]

After the House Committee on Justice hearing involving some twenty experts, the positions were clarified and two new bills were tabled at the same time, on 4 July 2018 (see Appendix E, Table E.2): one brought together the four parties of the government majority,[93] while the other was supported by five of the six opposition groups that had tabled various bills;[94] only CDH did not support the latter, instead supporting the majority's bill. The possibility of forming an alternative majority for the removal of abortion from the criminal code was fading, while the cohesion of the government coalition was strengthened. On 19 September 2018, in the Committee on Justice, the majority's bill was adopted with the support of CDH despite the negative votes of the other opposition representatives (there were no abstentions). On 4 October this scenario was repeated in the plenary session. The two VB MPs present rejected the majority's bill (this party had only three seats and did not have a vote in the committee), there were two abstentions in the majority (both from MR) and three in the opposition (from the Groen MPs), and the only PP MP did not vote.[95] There was overwhelming support among the Dutch-speaking group in the

92   See Delfosse, Marie-Luce, 2019, "Vers la loi du 28 mai 2002 relative à l'euthanasie (II). Une approche des débats parlementaires et de leurs prolongements", *Courrier hebdomadaire* (2429–2430), CRISP, pp. 103–104.

93   House of Representatives, 2018, "Bill on the voluntary termination of pregnancy", tabled by David Clarinval (MR), Carina Van Cauter (Open VLD), Valérie Van Peel (N-VA) and Els Van Hoof (CD&V), no. 3216/1, 4 July.

94   House of Representatives, 2018, "Bill to remove the voluntary termination of pregnancy from the Criminal Code", tabled by Karine Lalieux (PS), Véronique Caprasse (DéFI), Muriel Gerkens (Ecolo-Groen), Karin Jiroflée (SP.A) and Marco Van Hees (PTB), no. 3215/1, 4 July.

95   House of Representatives, 2018, *Full Report* (246), 4 October, pp. 51–86, 94–99, 111–112.

House (59 out of 87 MPs, with 11 absent), while in the French-speaking group the number of "for" and "against" votes was the same (25, with two MR MPs abstaining and 11 absent).The decision-making process leading up to the vote on this law involved a twofold compromise: one between the bills tabled by the opposition parties (with the exception of CDH), which resulted in the joint bill of 19 September; and the other between the most conservative section of the majority (CD&V and N-VA) and its liberal section (MR and, above all, Open VLD, which had tabled its own decriminalisation bill at the same time), a compromise that was achieved by the bill tabled on the same date by the parties of the government majority.

The new law essentially replicated the terms of the law of 3 April 1990, but removed abortion from the criminal code and regulated its practice through a stand-alone law.[96] While it contained some meaningful changes, it fell far short of the changes contained in most of the bills that had been tabled in the House, including that of Open VLD, the government majority party. Thus, under the new law, abortion must always take place before the end of the twelfth week of conception – Open VLD proposed, for example, to increase this period to eighteen weeks, and PTB went as far as twenty (see Appendix E, Table E.1). The waiting period from the first appointment between the doctor and the pregnant woman to the procedure was kept at six days, "unless there is an urgent medical reason for the pregnant woman to bring forward the termination of pregnancy". The "urgent medical reason" was new compared with the 1990 law; however, the bills tabled by Ecolo-Groen, PTB and Open VLD reduced the waiting period from six days to forty-eight hours. As in the past, the doctor is obliged to inform the patient of "the current and future medical risks she runs" in the event of abortion and to remind her of the various alternatives to it. Furthermore, the doctor is obliged to assess the woman's determination and this assessment is "sovereign". On the other hand, the notion of a state of distress is removed (as in the DéFI, PS, Ecolo-Groen, PTB and Open VLD bills), as well as the articles criminalising the advertising of abortion (apart from the CDH bill, all the bills repealed the last two paragraphs of Article 383, but the Open VLD bill put them back into a specific law on abortion). The conditions for performing a medical abortion beyond twelve weeks of pregnancy are identical to the law of 3 April 1990, whereas several of the bills proposed extending this period (Open VLD beyond eighteen weeks and PTB bill beyond twenty weeks).

---

96 *Moniteur belge*, 2018, "Law of 15 October 2018 on the voluntary termination of pregnancy repealing Articles 350 and 351 of the Criminal Code and amending Articles 352 and 383 of the same Code and amending various legislative provisions", 29 October.

In the event of non-compliance with the conditions laid down by the law of 15 October 2018, the criminal penalties are those that the law of 3 April 1990 imposed on the woman (with some adaptations concerning the offence of obstruction; see below).[97] Moreover, penalties are now imposed on any person who has induced an abortion without respecting these conditions (and no longer only – as the 1990 law intended – if the abortion "caused the death" of the woman). On the other hand, the provisions of the 1990 law (or those of the Open VLD bill, for example) in the case of non-consensual abortion (especially in cases of violence) are not included. As in the 1990 law, "no doctor [or other health care provider] is obliged to assist in an abortion"; however, it is now obligatory for a doctor who invokes the "conscience clause" to refer the patient to another doctor, abortion centre, etc. to obtain an abortion; the doctor is also obliged to transfer the patent's medical file. Finally, the 2018 law now provides for an "offence of obstruction" against any person who attempts to prevent a woman from having an abortion;[98] this offence is punishable by the same penalty as that imposed on a woman who has an abortion outside the conditions provided for by the law.

Two of the most important measures brought the law of 15 October 2018 closer to the bill tabled in May 2018 by CDH than to the bill tabled by Open VLD in June 2017 (even though CDH was in the opposition and Open VLD was in the government majority): as the conditions for having an abortion, the maximum duration of the pregnancy remained at twelve weeks and the waiting period at six days. Furthermore, both the new law and the CDH bill ensured that abortion was not treated as a medical procedure like any other.[99] In contrast, the Open VLD bill and the one tabled jointly by several opposition parties (except CDH) associated abortion

---

97   See Appendix E, Table E.3.

98   This constitutes an offence within the meaning of the criminal code; the penalties provided for in Article 3 of the law are as follows: "Anyone who attempts to prevent a woman from having free access to a health care facility providing the voluntary termination of pregnancy shall be sentenced to a period of imprisonment of three months to one year, and a fine of one hundred euros to five hundred euros."

99   In the plenary session, Catherine Fonck (leader of CDH and author of the bill) said that making the right to abortion "an unconditional right of the woman without criminal sanctions would allow abortion at any time. We are not in favour of it because it is not a medical procedure like any other" (House of Representatives, 2018, *Summary Record* (246), 4 October, p. 46). See also the hearing of Professor Willem Lemmens, philosopher-ethicist at the Universiteit Antwerpen, in the Committee on Justice on 13 June 2018: House of Representatives, Committee on Justice, 2018, "Bill on the voluntary termination of pregnancy […] first reading of the report", no. 3216/3, 1 August, pp. 133–136, 143–144.

with a medical procedure and mentioned the context of a regression in women's rights that had been driven by movements opposed to the right to abortion.

On another level, the new law abolishes – as most of the opposition parties wished – the notion of a state of distress and introduces an "obstruction offence" penalising anyone who tries to prevent an abortion being performed on a consenting woman. Despite these few advances, this text led to strong reactions from institutions providing abortion,[100] secular organisations,[101] the ULB,[102] feminist organisations,[103] and crimi-

---

100   Groupe d'action des centres extrahospitaliers pratiquant l'avortement, Fédération laïque des centres de planning familial, Fédération des centres pluristes de planning familial, Fédération des centres de planning et de consultations and Fédération des centres de planning familial des Femmes prévoyantes socialistes, 2018, "Dépénalisation de l'IVG: la proposition de loi de la majorité fédérale votée en commission Justice. Tout ça pour ça ?", Press Release, 19 September. See also the hearings in the Committee on Justice on 23 May 2018 of Professor Jean-Jacques Amy (FLCPF representative), Katrien Vermeire (SENSOA representative) and Carine Vrancken (LUNA VZW coordinator), and the hearing on 13 June 2018 of Dominique Roynet (GACEHPA representative): House of Representatives, Committee on Justice, 2018, "Bill on the voluntary termination of pregnancy [...] first reading of the report", no. 3216/3, 1 August, pp. 52–59, 90–93, 131–133.

101   See Centre d'action laïque (CAL), 2018, "#IVGHorsDuCodePenal : une proposition symbolique dont on espère pouvoir réellement se réjouir !", Press Release, July 4 (www.laicite.be); Centre d'action laïque (CAL), 2018, "Où en est le projet de sortir l'IVG du Code pénal ?", Press Release, July 11 (www.laicite.be); Centre d'action laïque (CAL), 2018, "IVG : un vote sans surprise", Press Release, September 19 (www.laicite.be). See also deMens. nu, 2018, "Symbolische over-winning, geen perfect akkoordfect akkoord", Press Release, 4 July (www.demens.nu).

102   On 17 September 2018, the board of directors of the ULB adopted a motion on abortion calling "to reject any simulacrum of a law on the removal of abortion from the criminal code" (*Belga*, 18 September 2018). See also the hearing of Yvon Englert, chancellor of the ULB, in the Committee on Justice on 6 June 2018; that of Anne Verougstraete, gynaecologist at the VUB, on the same day; and that of VUB professor Jean-Jacques Amy, mentioned above: House of Representatives, Committee on Justice, 2018, "Bill on the voluntary termination of pregnancy [...] first reading of the report", no. 3216/3, 1 August 2018, pp. 52–55, 83–88, 93–96.

103   In addition to the FPS, see the letter sent by Vie Féminine to the presidents of the government coalition parties on 17 September 2018 (reproduced on the website www.viefeminine.be). See also the hearing of Cécile De Wandeler, representative of Vie Féminine, in the Committee on Justice on 23 May 2018, and that of Sylvie Lausberg, president of the CFFB, on 6 June 2018: House of Representatives, Committee on Justice, 2018, "Bill on the voluntary termination of pregnancy [...] first reading of the report", no. 3216/3, 1 August, pp. 59–62, 100–103.

nal lawyers,[104] for whom the new law is just a facade that will not change the practice of abortion that has developed in Belgium since 1990.

The 2018 law ultimately comes very close to maintaining the status quo insofar as the compromise reached within the government coalition (with the support of CDH) linked the abolition of the state of distress, the criminally sanctioned offence of obstruction and the removal of abortion from the criminal code to the recognition of a status for the foetus and to criminal sanctions for the doctor and the woman, refusing to recognise the right to abortion as a medical procedure and as an act of self-determination for women. This does not prevent abortion procedures from being reimbursed by INAMI (the Belgian Institute for Health and Disability Insurance), which makes it an *ipso facto* part of social citizenship.[105] Generally speaking, the paradox of the new Belgian abortion law was that it endorsed some progress in order to better maintain a de facto status quo and thus safeguard the cohesion of the government coalition.

However, this same coalition fell after N-VA refused to allow Belgium to sign the Global Compact for Safe, Orderly and Regular Migration (known as the Marrakech Compact), then under preparation at the United Nations; the party's federal ministers and secretaries resigned on 9 December 2018. Unable to find an alternative majority to support his coalition (MR/CD&V/Open VLD), which had become a minority, Prime Minister Michel presented the resignation of his government to the king on 18 December. The king accepted it on 21 December, instructing the team in place to expedite the transition process.

Since then, the abortion debate has come to the fore more than once. In April 2019 a de facto association called Citoyens pour la vie (Citizens for Life) lodged an appeal for the annulment of the law of 15 October 2018 before the Constitutional Court;[106] this appeal was rejected.[107]

Some months after the renewal of the House, during the multiple votes on 26 May 2019, bills aimed at relaxing the conditions under which

---

104   *Le Soir*, 2018, "Les sanctions pénales, pas une nécessité" and "Michèle Hirsch sur la proposition de loi IVG : Ne votez pas ce texte !", 6 and 10 July; *L'Écho*, 2018, "Vers une vraie fausse dépénalisation de l'avortement", 18 September; *L'Avenir*, 2018, "Avortement : ce n'est pas du tout une dépénalisation", 19 September.

105   See Marshall, Thomas H., 1950, *Citizenship and Social Class*, Cambridge: Cambridge University Press, Chapter 9, p. 97.

106   Action brought on 26 April 2019, received by the Court on 29 April 2019, registered under roll number 7168 and announced in the *Moniteur belge* on 4 June 2019.

107   Constitutional Court, judgment no. 122/220, dated 24 September 2020 and published in the *Moniteur belge* on 31 December 2020, p. 98,004.

abortion could be performed were successively tabled by members of several political groups and formations: PS, DéFI, PVDA-PTB, Ecolo-Groen, Open VLD, SP.A and MR.[108] At the same time, N-VA tabled a bill to lift the restrictions in the legislation on anonymous childbirth, while MR also tabled a bill to counteract Belgian case law that recognised that being born with a disability can constitute a prejudice (in the legal sense of a recognised loss or injury);[109] both bills were at odds with parliamentary initiatives on abortion.

The results of the 26 May 2019 elections rendered the formation of a new federal government very complicated. On 27 October 2019 the Michel II government was succeeded by a government of the same composition (MR/CD&V/Open VLD) led by Sophie Wilmès, who had been entrusted by the king with the task of expediting the transition. This minority government held 38 seats out of 150 in the House (compared with 52 for the Michel II government before the elections). In March

---

108   House of Representatives, 2019, "Bill to relax the conditions for the voluntary termination of pregnancy", tabled by Éliane Tillieux, Caroline Désir, Patrick Prévot, Özlem Özen, Laurence Zanchetta, Mélissa Hanus, Jean-Marc Delizée and Sophie Thémont (PS), no. 158/1, 16 July; House of Representatives, 2019, "Bill to decriminalise the voluntary termination of pregnancy and to relax the conditions for its use", tabled by Sophie Rohonyi and François De Smet (DéFI), no. 385/1, 17 September; House of Representatives, 2019, "Bill decriminalising abortion and updating the law on the voluntary termination of pregnancy", tabled by Marco Van Hees, Raoul Hedebouw, Maria Vindevoghel, Nadia Moscufo, Sofie Merckx and Greta Daems (PVDA-PTB), no. 458/1, 30 September; House of Representatives, 2019, "Bill to decriminalise the voluntary termination of pregnancy", tabled by Sarah Schlitz, Jessika Soors, Séverine de Laveleye, Evita Willaert, Cécile Thibaut, Barbara Creemers, Marie-Colline Leroy, Kim Buyst, Julie Chanson and Laurence Hennuy (Ecolo-Groen), no. 614/1, 16 October; House of Representatives, 2019, "Bill on abortion", tabled by Katja Gabriëls, Egbert Lachaert and Goedele Liekens (Open VLD), no. 652/1, 22 October; House of Representatives, 2019, "Bill relaxing the conditions for the termination of pregnancy", tabled by Karin Jiroflée (SP.A), no. 676/1, 23 October; House of Representatives, 2019, "Bill on the voluntary termination of pregnancy", tabled by Kattrin Jadin, David Clarinval, Philippe Goffin, Caroline Taquin, Florence Reuter, Daniel Bacquelaine, Emmanuel Burton and Michel De Maegd (MR), no. 740/1, 12 November. See also Appendix E, Table E.4.

109   House of Representatives, 2019, "Bill on amending the Civil Code and the Judicial Code in order to allow anonymous childbirth", tabled by Valérie Van Peel (N-VA), no. 183/1, 16 July; House of Representatives, 2019, "Bill on inserting Article 1383bis into the Civil Code specifying that there is no prejudice due to the sole fact of one's birth", tabled by Daniel Bacquelaine, Philippe Goffin, Emmanuel Burton, Caroline Taquin, Michel De Maegd and David Clarinval (MR), no. 531/1, 3 October. For the recent case law of the Court of Cassation in this regard, see De Saint-Moulin, Élise, 2019, "Les actions en grossesse et vie préjudiciables. État des lieux critique au regard de la jurisprudence récente de la Cour de cassation", *Journal des Tribunaux* (6759), 2 February, pp. 81–93.

2020 the health crisis caused by the Covid-19 pandemic and its socio-economic consequences resulted in nine political parties (MR, CD&V and Open VLD on the one hand, and PS, Ecolo, SP.A, Groen, CDH and DéFI on the other) putting their trust in a Wilmès II government with the same composition as the previous one and then, supported by N-VA, granting it special powers for three months (renewable once). The prime minister was committed to limiting the scope of her action to managing this crisis and seeking the confidence of the House no later than six months after her declaration of government on 17 March 2020.

Against this backdrop, and in the same of period of May 2019 to March 2020, numerous initiatives were underway that tried to establish a federal government with a majority in the House. In some cases, discussions on the evolution of abortion legislation seems to have been on the agenda of these meetings. These discussions were facilitated when the socialist, liberal and green parties were expected to form a coalition (as in November 2019), and they were complicated when the initiatives involved some of these parties together with N-VA, CD&V or CDH. The clear electoral progression of PTB (twelve seats, a gain of ten) and VB (eighteen seats, a loss of fifteen), whose positions on abortion are diametrically opposed, has somewhat changed the balance of power in the House on this issue compared with the previous legislature.

Partially freed from the classic game between majority and opposition, the parliamentary process of examining the tabled texts continued, though it was affected by the jolts of the government formation process. In November 2019, while the president of PS, Paul Magnette (who had been entrusted with a fact-finding mission by the king), was in talks to bring together socialists, liberals and greens in a coalition, the possibility emerged in the House Committee on Justice that a majority of representatives would adopt a joint text in the form of amendments to the bill tabled in July by PS and signed by SP.A, DéFI, PTB, MR, Groen, Ecolo and Open VLD (in addition to PS itself).[110] This legislation aimed to abolish the criminal sanctions relating to abortion and to make the conditions for having an abortion more flexible: an abortion could be carried out within eighteen weeks of conception and the waiting period would be reduced to forty-eight hours. The parties co-signing these amendments

---

110   House of Representatives, 2019, "Bill to relax the conditions for the voluntary termination of pregnancy: amendments", tabled by Éliane Tillieux (PS), Karin Jiroflée (SP.A), Sophie Rohonyi (DéFI), Sofie Merckx (PVDA-PTB), Kattrin Jadin (MR), Jessika Soors (Ecolo-Groen), Sarah Schlitz (Ecolo-Groen) and Katja Gabriëls (Open VLD), no. 158/3, 13 November. See Appendix E, Table E.4.

totalled ninety-two seats.[111] These legislative changes were adopted at the first reading in the Committee on Justice and then, after some new amendments,[112] at the second reading as well – with most articles being adopted by ten votes to six (with the ten votes coming from Ecolo-Groen, PS, MR, PTB, Open VLD and SP.A, with DéFI sitting in the committees in an advisory capacity, and the six coming from N-VA, VB and CD&V, with CDH sitting in the committees in an advisory capacity).[113]

The debates were held not only in institutional forums. Indeed, it was in this context that the Belgian bishops reiterated the positions of the Catholic Church on abortion.[114] Two weeks after this statement from the Church, and on the eve of a meeting of the House Committee on Justice, the newspaper *La Libre Belgique* published in its opinion section an article by 700 French-speaking health care workers denouncing "the breakdown of ethical guidelines in the bill that aims to broaden the conditions of access to abortion".[115] In response to this declaration, the newspaper *Le Soir*, some time later, published a petition ("IVG : respectons le choix

---

111   The exclusion of Emir Kir from the PS ranks in January 2020 reduced the PS party in the House from twenty to nineteen members.

112   House of Representatives, 2019, "Bill to relax the conditions for the voluntary termination of pregnancy: amendment submitted at the second reading", tabled by Katja Gabriëls (Open VLD), Sarah Schlitz (Ecolo-Groen), Jessika Soors (Ecolo-Groen), Sophie Rohonyi (DéFI), Sofie Merckx (PVDA-PTB), Kattrin Jadin (MR) and Éliane Tillieux (PS), no. 158/6, 16 December; House of Representatives, 2019, "Bill to relax the conditions for the voluntary termination of pregnancy: amendments submitted at the second reading", tabled by Éliane Tillieux (PS), Sophie Rohonyi (DéFI), Sofie Merckx (PVDA-PTB), Jessika Soors (Ecolo-Groen), Karin Jiroflée (SP.A), Sarah Schlitz (Ecolo-Groen), Kattrin Jadin (MR) and Katja Gabriëls (Open VLD), no. 158/7, 20 December.

113   House of Representatives, Committee on Justice, 2019, "Bill to relax the conditions for the voluntary termination of pregnancy: report of the first reading", no. 158/4, 6 December; House of Representatives, Committee on Justice, 2019, "Bill to relax the conditions for the voluntary termination of pregnancy: articles adopted in the first reading", no. 158/5, 6 December; House of Representatives, Committee on Justice, 2019, "Bill to relax the conditions for the voluntary termination of pregnancy: report of the second reading", no. 158/8, 30 December; House of Representatives, Committee on Justice, 2019, "Bill to relax the conditions for the voluntary termination of pregnancy: text adopted at the second reading", no. 158/9, 30 December. From this point on the title of the bill becomes "Bill to amend various legislative provisions in order to relax the conditions for the voluntary termination of pregnancy".

114   De Kesel, Joseph (Cardinal), et al., 2019, "Nouvel élargissement des conditions de l'avortement : déclaration des évêques de Belgique", 12 November (www.cathobel.be).

115   *La Libre Belgique*, 2019, "Nous, personnel soignant opposé à la proposition de loi sur l'avortement", 26 November.

---

des femmes et leur droit à la santé") signed by 1,500 health care staff and supporting the reform of the existing law.[116]

In mid-December 2019 it appeared that the formation of a new federal government involving the socialists, liberals and greens would be acceptable to all protagonists (and in particular to Open VLD) only if it included CD&V, so that the majority would be larger (88 seats instead of 76) and the Dutch-speaking wing of the government would not appear too small in the eyes of the Flemish public – although it would be a minority within its language group in the House. This coalition formula was nicknamed "Vivaldi", in reference to the composer of the *Four Seasons*, as it involved four political families. It also appeared that CD&V did not like the fact that the other six parties involved in these discussions seemed to have agreed to pass the reform aimed at relaxing the conditions under which an abortion could be performed; it seemed that the Flemish Christian democrats intended to block this legislative procedure by using it as a bargaining chip for their possible participation in a government coalition. Consequently, anticipating the request of N-VA, VB and CD&V, the president of the House, Patrick Dewael (Open VLD), requested (at the end of December) the opinion of the Council of State on the text adopted in committee before it was examined in the plenary session.[117]

On most of the points examined, the Council of State declared that it had no comment to make on the text adopted at the second reading by the Committee on Justice. In the months that followed, however, CD&V and CDH, and then N-VA and VB, repeatedly tabled a series of amendments in plenary sessions aimed at thwarting the approach of the eight parties who were in favour of relaxing the conditions for abortion.[118] On each occasion, the opinion of the Council of State was sought, as these four parties jointly held more than the fifty seats required to do so

---

116 *Le Soir*, 2019, "Avortement : 1 500 professionnels de la santé soutiennent la réforme", 16 December. See also *De Morgen*, 2019, "Abortus: laten we de keuze van vrouwen en hun recht op gezondheid respecteren", 16 December.

117 House of Representatives, 2020, "Bill to relax the conditions for the voluntary termination of pregnancy: Council of State opinion no. 66.881/AG of 24 February 2020", no. 158/10, 2 March.

118 House of Representatives, 2020, "Bill to relax the conditions for the voluntary termination of pregnancy: amendments tabled in the plenary session", no. 158/11, 12 March; House of Representatives, 2020, "Bill to amend various legislative provisions in order to relax the conditions for the voluntary termination of pregnancy: amendments tabled in the plenary session", no. 158/13, 30 June; House of Representatives, 2020, "Bill to amend various legislative provisions in order to relax the conditions for the voluntary termination of pregnancy: amendments tabled in the plenary session", no. 158/15, 15 July.

(they held fifty-nine).[119] For the eight other parties, the repeated tabling of amendments, a second reading in committee and the four referrals to the Council of State were seen as a tactic to delay a parliamentary decision, as well as an instrumentalisation of the Council of State and a disrespectful manipulation of the parliamentary process by making women's rights a political bargaining chip.[120] The Council of State did not give an opinion on most of the amendments, which it had already examined at earlier stages of the procedure; as for the others, the Council of State considered them to be within the freedom of the legislator.[121]

In the summer of 2020 – while the process of forming a federal government to succeed the Wilmès II government in September was undergoing new developments and various coalition options were being tested with or without N-VA, PS and CD&V – the two Flemish parties reiterated that their participation in a possible majority was conditional on the withdrawal of the abortion bill currently under discussion.[122] When, in September, the seven-party coalition (PS/MR/Ecolo/CD&V/Open VLD/ SP.A/Groen) led by the Flemish liberal Alexander De Croo was finally agreed on, it became clear that the referral of the debates on abortion to the Committee on Justice was a *sine qua non* condition for CD&V to participate in this coalition, and thus necessary condition for its creation.[123] In practice, and despite the activism of abortion rights supporters that continued during the final stages of the federal coalition process, the text of the government's coalition agreement foresaw a very uncertain future for the consideration of abortion-related bills:

---

119   House of Representatives, 2020, "Bill to amend various legislative provisions in order to relax the conditions for the voluntary termination of pregnancy: Council of State opinion no. 67.122/AG of 19 June 2020", no. 158/12, 22 June; House of Representatives, 2020, "Bill to amend various legislative provisions in order to relax the conditions for the voluntary termination of pregnancy: Council of State opinion no. 67.732/AV of 10 July 2020", no. 158/14, 10 July. See also House of Representatives, 2020, *Verbatim Report* (31; Appendix), 19 March, p. 7; House of Representatives, 2020, *Summary Record* (49), 2 July, pp. 26–30; House of Representatives, 2020, *Summary Record* (52), 15 July, pp. 2–23.

120   House of Representatives, 2020, *Summary Record* (49), 2 July, pp. 27–30.

121   House of Representatives, 2020, "Bill to amend various legislative provisions in order to relax the conditions for the voluntary termination of pregnancy: Council of State opinion no. 67.732/AV of 10 July 2020", no. 158/14, 10 July.

122   Sägesser, Caroline, 2020, "La formation du gouvernement De Croo (mai 2019 – octobre 2020)", *Courrier hebdomadaire* (2471–2472), CRISP, p. 47.

123   Ibid. pp. 53, 56.

With regard to the processing of the abortion bills pending in the House, it is appropriate to continue their examination in the House Committee on Justice, and – after a multi-disciplinary scientific committee (appointed by the parties in government) has conducted a study and evaluation of the practice and legislation – to continue the work in a constructive manner so that consensus can be reached between the parties in government and, in the meantime, not to proceed to a vote.[124]

After the elections on 26 May 2019, the debates conducted as part of the process of forming the federal government gave rise to several developments. A large majority of MPs[125] appeared ready to adopt the eight-party bill aimed at easing the conditions under which an abortion could be performed, including extending the limit from twelve to eighteen weeks of pregnancy and reducing the reflection period from six to two days. The other four parties represented in the House were fiercely opposed to the adoption of this text and decided, in the case of N-VA and CD&V, to make this issue a condition for their participation in a future government. At the same time, they used various means of parliamentary obstruction in order to postpone a vote in the plenary session for as long as possible, and to make the issue of abortion a matter of governmental stability.[126] The inclusion of this postponement of the vote in the government's coalition agreement compromised the possibility of any decision on the issue until the end of the current legislature. This episode once again illustrates that the abortion debate remains highly sensitive, and that women's rights in this area are never won once and for all.

---

124   Federal Government of Belgium, 2020, "Note de formation. Pour une Belgique prospère, solidaire et durable. Introduction par les deux formateurs", 30 September, item I, 6, 58.

125   The precise number of representatives in this case, however, cannot be determined, as MR announced that its representatives would be free to cast their vote as they saw fit, and some of them seemed reluctant to approve the text under discussion.

126   On this subject see El Berhoumi, Mathias, and John Pitseys, 2016, "L'obstruction parlementaire en Belgique", *Courrier hebdomadaire* (2289–2290), CRISP.

Conclusion: exploring the articulations and tensions between human rights and citizenship

Whether in the context of the European Union and its different member states or more specifically in the Belgian case, this book has attempted to put into perspective the legal rules governing abortion in its various national contexts, the practices that have developed in each and the discourse of the actors who clash in defence of or in opposition to access to abortion. On the basis of this examination, we can identify a dual problematisation of the demand for the right to abortion in the EU and Belgium, in terms of citizenship on the one hand and human rights on the other. The articulation of the dual problematisation proposed below is situated at the crossroads of political sociology and political theory.

Depending on their focus, researchers who consider the demand for access to abortion in terms of citizenship refer to feminist citizenship,[1] inclusive citizenship,[2] gendered citizenship,[3] sexual citizenship,[4] repro-

---

1   Lister, Ruth, 1997, *Citizenship: Feminist Perspectives*, Basingstoke: Palgrave Macmillan.

2   Lister, Ruth, 2007, "Inclusive citizenship: realizing the potential", *Citizenship Studies* 11(11), 49–61.

3   Siim, Birte, 2000, *Gender and Citizenship: Politics and Agency in France, Britain and Denmark*, Cambridge: Cambridge University Press; Lister, Ruth, et al., 2007, *Gendering Citizenship in Western Europe: New Challenges for Citizenship Research in a Cross-National Context*, Bristol: Policy Press; Halsaa, Beatrice, Sasha Roseneil and Sevil Sümer (eds), 2012, *Remaking Citizenship in Multicultural Europe: Women's Movements, Gender and Diversity*, Basingstoke: Palgrave Macmillan.

4   Evans, David, 1993, *Sexual Citizenship: The Material Construction of Sexualities*, London: Routledge; Lister, "Sexual citizenship", pp. 191–208; Richardson, Diane, 2017, "Rethinking sexual citizenship", *Sociology* 51(2), 208–224; Richardson, Diane, 2018, *Sexuality and Citizenship*, Cambridge: Polity Press.

ductive citizenship,[5] intimate citizenship,[6] bodily citizenship[7] and the concept of the citizenship regime.[8]

The historian and political scientist Joyce Outshoorn – a specialist in women's studies – notes that, outside the academic field, national feminist movements base their demand for abortion rights not on the idea of citizenship but rather on the idea of self-determination and autonomy for women.[9] Moreover, analysis of national and international movements supported by large sections of civil society in the EU since the 1970s shows that activists from women's associations, doctors, health workers and secular organisations support the right to abortion in the context of a number of different rights: women's health and public health, physical and psychological integrity, privacy, social equality between women, and equality between women and men. At the international and European levels since the 1990s, these activists have used the language of human rights to articulate these rights, while their opponents have used the very same language to legitimise the rights of foetal life, the right to human dignity and the right to religious freedom.

There is thus a gap between the language of activists and the language of researchers. This divergence highlights the tensions and the links between citizenship and human rights. By focusing on the articulations and conflicts between human rights and citizenship with regard to the right to abortion in the EU and Belgium, we will be able to shed light on a paradox: despite the fundamental conflict between citizenship

5   Richardson, Eileen, and Bryan Turner, 2001, "Sexual, intimate or reproductive citizenship?", *Citizenship Studies* 5(3), 329–338; Turner, Bryan, 2008, "Citizenship, reproduction and the state: international marriage and human rights", *Citizenship Studies* 12(1), 45–54; Roseneil, Sasha (ed.), 2013, *Beyond Citizenship? Feminism and the Transformation of Belonging*, Basingstoke: Palgrave Macmillan; Roseneil, Sasha, Isabel Crowhurst, Ana Cristina Santos and Mariya Stoilova, 2013, "Reproduction and citizenship/reproducing citizens: editorial introduction", *Citizenship Studies* 17(8), 901–911.

6   Plummer, Ken, 2001, "The square of intimate citizenship: some preliminary proposals", *Citizenship Studies* 5(3), 237–253; Plummer, Ken, 2003, *Intimate Citizenship: Private Decisions and Public Dialogues*, Seattle: University of Washington Press; Roseneil, Sasha, et al., 2011, "Intimate citizenship and gendered well-being: the claims and interventions of women's movements in Europe", in *Transforming Gendered Well-Being in Europe: The Impact of Social Movements*, edited by Alison Woodward, Jean-Michel Bonvin and Mercè Renom, Farnham: Ashgate, pp. 187–206; Roseneil, Sasha, et al., "Remaking intimate citizenship in multicultural Europe: experiences outside the conventional family", in *Remaking Citizenship in Multicultural Europe*, pp. 41–69.

7   Outshoorn, *European Women's Movements and Body Politics*.

8   Marques-Pereira, "Abortion rights", pp. 238–254.

9   Outshoorn, *European Women's Movements and Body Politics*, pp. 1–2.

(which is exclusive) and human rights (which are inclusive), both have the potential to play an emancipatory political role – a fact that precludes drawing a clear dividing line between the two. From this perspective, we can consider three major elements involved in articulating the demand for abortion rights: the processes of women's social and political sub-jectivation, institutional support for women's autonomy and equality with men, and the importance for women of having a status as citizens.[10]

The political and international-legal underpinnings of abortion rights allow pro-abortion activists to harness human rights for the purpose of a dual legitimisation. By using human rights they legitimise both their demands and their status as interlocutors in a process of political delib-eration against the opponents of these demands, a process that in recent years has been marked by setbacks – direct or insidious, achieved or attempted – for access to abortion (see Chapters 1 and 2).

The following reflections require us to clarify the approach to the con-cept of citizenship that will be adopted here; the choice to reason in terms of a citizenship regime rather than in terms of reproductive, sexual, inti-mate or bodily citizenship will therefore be explained. This choice avoids the pitfall of further expanding the polysemy of the notion of citizenship by adding new meanings to the term.

After having clarified our conceptual approach, we will analyse how the demand for abortion rights oscillates between citizenship and the human rights. This oscillation cannot be reduced solely to the process of dual legitimisation mentioned above. Indeed, the actors who voice this demand in the national and supranational public spheres invoke human rights to reinvent a new kind of citizenship, by shifting the borders between the private and the public, and between the individual and the universal.

The right to abortion: a question of the citizenship regime

The sociologist Bryan Turner is one of the few authors working outside the sociology of gender to have taken reproduction into account when thinking about the issue of citizenship, by developing the notion of repro-ductive citizenship alongside civil, social and political citizenship and by

10   This is a political approach to human rights, as taken by Lacroix, Justine, and Jean-Yves Pranchère, 2016, *Le procès des droits de l'homme. Généalogie du scepticisme démocratique*, Paris: Seuil.

linking it to social rights.[11] For Turner, reproductive citizenship concerns the question of who can reproduce with whom, and the legal and social conditions associated with this reproduction, especially the rights and duties related to parenting.

The full recognition of reproductive rights is an essential component of an effective form of citizenship for women that would put them on an equal footing with men, and it remains a goal on the path towards women's self-determination. This premise is shared by the sociologists and political scientists mentioned above who focus on citizenship in its many dimensions and variations (notes 5 to 7). The centrality of the politics of reproduction (such as the work of care by mothers and the work of the nation's reproduction through social and demographic policies) is a constant in the sociological, political, anthropological and historical literature on gender and social welfare regimes. In particular, this literature shows that the care work of citizen mothers has been and remains crucial for the production of civic identity, for a sense of belonging to the nation[12] and for social investment policies focused on the child as a future working citizen.[13]

Political scientists and sociologists who focus on sexual and intimate citizenship tend to focus on gender identities and sexual subjectivities. That is not the purpose of this book. However, the European FEMCIT research project – on the importance of women's movements in Europe for the defence of gendered citizenship – underlines the fundamental importance of the politics of reproduction, which cut across the different dimensions of citizenship: political, social, economic, multicultural, bodily and intimate.[14] In the context of this project, Outshoorn develops and clarifies the concept of bodily citizenship, notably by addressing the issue of abortion rights. With her co-authors,[15] Outshoorn points out that the literature on citizenship, with the exception of the sociology of gender, has overlooked the importance of the body, since the individual citizen is seen as an abstract subject going beyond his or her actual and contingent determinations. In contrast, bodily citizenship encompasses

---

11   Turner, "Citizenship, reproduction and the state".

12   Yuval-Davis, Nira, 1997, *Gender and Nation*, London: Sage.

13   Jenson, Jane, 2017, "The new maternalism: children first; women second", in *Reassembling Motherhood: Procreation and Care in a Globalized World*, edited by Yasmine Ergas, Jane Jenson and Sonya Michel, New York: Columbia University Press, pp. 269–286.

14   Halsaa et al., *Remaking Citizenship in Multicultural Europe*.

15   The book *European Women's Movements and Body Politics* contained contributions from Radka Dudová, Lenita Freidenvall and Ana Prata in addition to Outshoorn.

sexuality and the right to abortion, which has been a fundamental issue for feminist movements since the 1970s. Outshoorn and her colleagues analyse this issue by examining how feminist movements have challenged state governance and the dominant political discourses. This approach focuses on the state, governance and law, and it emphasises a sociological and discursive-institutionalist framework, as well as drawing on theories of social movements. From this perspective, it is the fight for women's bodily integrity, autonomy and self-determination that shapes the concept of bodily citizenship. These authors point out that demands for abortion rights are expressed in terms of autonomy and self-determination rather than in terms of citizenship rights. They also highlight the absence of bodily citizenship for women in abortion laws and abortion reforms that do not include significant feminist input and that, in the absence of this activism, leave control of decisions about abortion in the hands of doctors.

The concepts of reproductive and bodily citizenship – considered within a framework of the multiplicity of social relations, including gender and power relations – certainly make it possible to address the right to abortion. However, the extension of the concept of citizenship to new dimensions (sexual, reproductive, intimate and bodily) beyond those highlighted by the sociologist Thomas H. Marshall (civil, political and social)[16] hits a major stumbling block: it aggravates the polysemy of the concept of citizenship. Without fuelling this problem, there is, however, a need to embrace the pluralist demands associated with extending citizenship, including demands for the right to abortion. To do this, we will use the concept of a citizenship regime, as defined by the political scientist Jane Jenson.[17]

---

16   See in particular Marshall, Thomas H., 1963, *Class, Citizenship and Social Development*, Chicago: Chicago University Press.

17   Jenson, "Des frontières aux lisières de la citoyenneté". The concept of a citizenship regime has four dimensions. The first focuses on social citizenship beyond its state-centric character and raises the question of responsibility with regard to the social construction of collective well-being: what are the respective contributions of actors linked to the state, the private sector, the voluntary sector and families? The second dimension is statutory and relates to the rights and duties of citizenship. This raises the question of the extent to which rights and duties that are subjects of public and political debate are currently leading to a redefinition of citizenship. The third dimension concerns the channels of access to political decision making, particularly through new modes of governance that tend to favour the associative fabric of civil society and to overcome the crisis of representation; the challenge is that of the *practice* of citizenship. Finally, the fourth dimension – identity – raises the problem of the sense of belonging to the political community in the context of growing differences and inequalities.

Because new citizenship rights are not acquired in a linear manner or without a fight, citizenship will be considered here as an ongoing practice. In this sense, the fight for reproductive freedom also feeds into the process of political subjectivation that feminists are engaged in, namely, the affirmation of a new political subject struggling and negotiating for the recognition of a collective identity based on the visibility of gender relations. Therefore, citizenship must be understood here as a process of construction, not as a fixed set of rights. This approach highlights the richness of a citizenship linked to practices that are both conflictual and consensual: a conflictual practice of struggles to gain recognition for actors as legitimate bearers of demands, and for the legitimacy of the demands themselves; and a consensual practice linked to the actors' agreement over the rules of the game that define the common norms for conflict resolution.

What is at stake in these practices concerns the citizenship regime in two respects. On the one hand, the exercise and assertion of rights as democratic practices contribute to a sense of belonging to a political community and help construct collective identities. On the other, the rules of the democratic game that guide the modes of participation in civic life and public debate give legitimacy to the expression of demands and to the way in which they are achieved.

Both the dimension of identity and the dimension of access to political decision making therefore permeate these conflictual and consensual practices. Thus, at the heart of these practices lies the issue of participation in the development of new social norms that challenge the power relations and social relations that maintain the status quo. Understanding the right to abortion from the perspective of citizenship entails understanding how this right is acquired through the various stages of its politicisation and through the modes of politicisation employed by the actors who advocate for it in different national institutional contexts.

Philosophers and political scientists, such as Jürgen Habermas, David Held and Seyla Benhabib, have developed a more deliberative perspective, which focuses on human rights. In addition to a citizenship-based approach, this alternative perspective may be relevant for addressing the opposition that surrounds abortion rights. It gives primacy to the inclusive character of these rights – which are inherent to each person's shared humanity – to the detriment of the exclusive character of citizenship, which prescribes the rights and duties of citizens, as well as who can or cannot be a citizen in a given country. In line with the concepts of global citizenship[18] and cosmopolitan citizenship,[19] the deliberative approach attempts to ground citizenship rights in human rights. It develops a primarily procedural vision of the democratic regime based on a Habermasian perspective of global legalism.[20]

In this respect, it is interesting to contrast Habermas's views with those of another philosopher, Jacques Rancière, as the importance of conflict and value pluralism in democratic politics risks being neglected if procedural rationality is about consensus only. At the same time, it would be simplistic to say that Habermas ignores dissensus and value pluralism. Instead, Habermas brings this question back to the cognitive presuppositions that citizens – believers and non-believers alike – must hold in order to access "a public use of reason" that recognises the supremacy of positive law over natural law, and secular morality over religious conceptions.[21] Rancière, however, highlights the asymmetrical nature of the debate, since opponents of the right to abortion deny its supporters the status of interlocutors in a common space and "the common sharing of *logos*" (see Chapters 3 and 4).[22] The mere recognition of dissensus between social and political actors is not enough to account for this division.

Freedom and equality are, of course, two values that are a matter of dispute between social and political actors. For the political philosopher Chantal Mouffe, these values constitute a common grammar of citizenship as seen from the perspective of the Enlightenment; their interpretations are plural and immanent to the relations of force and power between actors. Thus, certain interpretations render the articulation between these values hegemonic, to the detriment of other interpretations.[23] Yet, if the groups fighting for the right to abortion link the values of reproductive freedom and self-determination to the values of gender equality, equality between women and women's autonomy by legitimising them as human rights, the groups that oppose the right to abortion cannot even conceive

18   Held, David, 1995, *Democracy and the Global Order: From the Modern State to Cosmopolitan Governance*, Cambridge: Polity Press.

19   Benhabib, Seyla, 2007, "Twilight of sovereignty or the emergence of cosmopolitan norms? Rethinking citizenship in volatile times", *Citizenship Studies* 11(1), 19–36.

20   Habermas, Jürgen, 1996, *Droit et démocratie. Entre faits et normes*, Paris: Gallimard.

21   Habermas, Jürgen, 2008, *Entre naturalisme et religion. Les défis de la démocratie*, Paris: Gallimard, pp. 170–211.

22   Rancière, *La mésentente*, p. 82.

23   Mouffe, Chantal, 2016, *Le paradoxe démocratique*, Paris: Beaux-Arts de Paris.

of these links, since, for them, human rights refer to natural law, which invalidates any "common sharing of the *logos*" (see Chapter 4).

In the perspective developed by Rancière, this asymmetry in the use of the legitimising function of human rights can be described as follows: supporters of the right to abortion use human rights as a form of subjectivation that can test the capacity of the demand for equality to produce conflict and litigation, while opponents of the right to abortion dissociate human rights from their "litigious capacity" and eliminate their "political capacity" for emancipation by making their rightful claimants victims whose language is shaped by complaint and suffering.[24] For the former group, political subjectivation undoes the perceived naturalness of social roles and functions, while for the latter, the possibilities of subjectivation are absent, so that the assignment to these roles and functions is anchored in a naturalised social order.

This means that political subjects do not emerge *ex nihilo*, but rather through a process of struggle, in particular through the dynamics of acquiring citizenship rights. It is in this sense that we refer to the concept of a citizenship regime.[25] This is done by situating it in a multi-level framework because, in the era of globalisation, conflicting and asymmetrical interpretations of the values of equality and freedom take place in a multiplicity of public spaces of debate, ranging from the national to the international, via the supranational and the transnational. Alongside this multi-level framework, the concept of the citizenship regime needs to be complemented by a reflection on the links between citizenship and human rights in the context of the demand for abortion rights.

The demand for abortion rights: between citizenship and human rights

Recognition of the right to abortion as a human right at the European level is, of course, one ambition of those who demand freedom of choice. However, the principle of subsidiarity that prevails in the EU is a major restriction to an EU-wide right of access to abortion; legal regimes for authorising or prohibiting abortion fall within the sole competence of member states. Further, only member states can submit reservations to articles in international legal instruments that they consider too liberal with regard to sexual and reproductive rights. Lastly, it is the states

---

24   Rancière, *La mésentente*, p. 172.
25   Marques-Pereira, "Abortion rights".

themselves that are the recipients of the recommendations issued by the monitoring committees of international and European conventions (see Chapters 1 and 2 and Appendix B).

The idea that access to abortion could be an element of global citizenship therefore seems difficult to support. Moreover, actors in the international arena are less concerned with changing the boundaries of the citizenship regime than in gaining recognition from UN agencies in order to put pressure on governments to enact their demands (see Chapter 4 and Appendices C and D). To this end, activists are using arguments that link reproductive freedom to human rights. However, the use of these arguments deserves consideration beyond the process of legitimising a demand and its actors. Indeed, the controversy over the emancipatory political roles of human rights and citizenship in relation to abortion is still ongoing. This is evidenced by the conflict between activists who support the demand for women's right to self-determination and those who oppose it.

The fight for the right to abortion consisted in overturning the taboo that was and still is imposed on the practice of abortion. Transforming a highly intimate practice into a public issue – a process of politicisation par excellence – required breaking the silence surrounding abortion. This was the purpose of the manifestos by French women in 1971 and Belgian women in 1973 who publicly declared that they had undergone an abortion, declarations that constituted an open transgression of the criminal law. Civil disobedience was necessary in these countries in order to transgress or circumvent laws that made abortion a criminal offence (see Chapters 1 and 5). It was an expression of public, non-clandestine, non-violent resistance by women who had undergone abortions, as well as doctors and health personnel who had performed or participated in safe abortions.

Civil disobedience has also been central to the practices of Dutch feminist organisations, such as Women on Waves, which was established in 1999. It carries out early medical abortions in international waters close to countries that prohibit, restrict or impede the right to abortion. The organisation has conducted national and international campaigns in Spain (2008), Ireland (2001), Poland (2003) and Portugal (2004). As Dutch law criminalises the practice of medical abortions in international waters, Women on Waves also set up telephone call centres to provide reliable information on early medical abortions in the home.

Activism in favour of freedom of choice has also emerged in the face of attempts at legislative regression, such as in Spain and Poland, and it has led to major legislative changes in countries such as France,

Luxembourg and Ireland (see Chapter 1). Up to now, however, Belgium has been characterised by a de facto status quo enshrined in the law adopted in 2018 (see Chapter 5).

Activists in favour of the right to abortion are also vigilant with regard to the discourse of the Holy See and its political and organisational relays, particularly in the European Parliament and the Council of Europe (see Chapters 3 and 4 and Appendices C and D). At the same time, these activists work to develop a strategy of coalition between organisations that demand freedom of choice, and a strategy of relaying this demand via left-wing political parties or those close to the secular community.

The steps taken by abortion rights supporters can be situated in a context of ever greater global interdependence, as illustrated by the way demands made by women's movements and organisations have been institutionalised at the global level since the 1990s. Indeed, new public forums for states (such as international conferences) and for social actors (in forums parallel to these conferences) have facilitated the emergence of the concept of sexual and reproductive rights on a global scale.

The challenge to the nation-state-based citizenship regime thus lies in the existence of new spaces and actors operating at international and transnational levels. One aim of supporters of the right to abortion is thus to involve new actors and to open up new spaces for the deployment of the issue of the citizenship regime at international and transnational levels. The aim of these new ways of expressing demands is not to create a new global order but rather to exert pressure on national governments from the international level, thus creating a "boomerang effect".[26] It is a matter of transforming the configuration of the national citizenship regime through one of its existing dimensions, i.e. the access route to political decision making.

The issue is therefore a new gender arrangement within the citizenship regime, an arrangement that would allow recognition of the right to abortion. This would question the state's sovereignty over reproductive bodies, challenging it via the statutory and identity dimensions of citizenship and on the basis of the guarantee of collective well-being.[27] Indeed, the recognition of women's individuation based on the dissociation between sexuality and procreation, and the recognition of the notion of sexual and reproductive rights within the unified perspective of women's autonomy and their equality with men, imply that the regulation of procreation is no

---

26   Keck and Sikking, *Activists Beyond Borders*, pp. 165–198.

27   Marques-Pereira, "Abortion rights".

longer the monopoly of the state but has transferred to the field of individual autonomy. Thus, the demand to remove abortion from the criminal code aims to ensure women's full sovereignty over their bodies at the expense of the state's sovereignty over reproductive bodies.

However, this aim is far from being realised at the EU level. There are still many obstacles to the right to abortion, particularly due to the systematic use of the conscience clause in countries such as Spain, Ireland, Italy and Poland (see Chapter 1). Across the EU, opponents of abortion rights continue to defend state sovereignty over reproductive bodies. They base their arguments on the rights to life, human dignity and freedom of conscience and religion, and ultimately on a doctrine of the transcendence of natural law – as demonstrated by the "One of us" petition (see Chapter 4). In this sense, the recognition of the right to abortion relates to the statutory dimension of the citizenship regime. This statutory dimension is thus a major issue for activists who pit women's rights against the right of the unborn child, which they see as a human right (see Chapter 4).

Moreover, women's individuation defies both natalist and anti-natalist demographic policies. This invites the state to define the boundaries of a new gender arrangement in a reconfigured citizenship regime. Henceforth, maternity as a duty of women's citizenship and as their role in the formation of the national community is called into question, as conscription was for men.[28] In this case, the new gender arrangement concerns the identity dimension of the citizenship regime.

Here too, conservative resistance vigorously opposes the various transformations of the dimension of status and identity. In Germany, for example, abortion remains *de jure* prohibited and the right to life is enshrined in the country's constitution, although there is a de facto regime of allowing abortion in the first twelve weeks of pregnancy.[29] Hungary, Poland and (until May 2018) Ireland are the clearest examples of identity-based resistance. Indeed, these countries explicitly consider the lifting of the criminal ban as an attack on their national identity.[30]

---

28   Yuval-Davis, Nira, 1996, "Women and the biological reproduction of 'the nation'", *Women's Studies International Forum* 19(1), 17–24.

29   Siegel, Reva, "The constitutionalization of abortion", in *Abortion Law in Transnational Perspective*, pp. 13–35.

30   Erdman, "The procedural turn", pp. 121–142; Mishtal, Joanna, "Quietly 'beating the system': the logics of protest and resistance under the Polish abortion ban", in *A Fragmented Landscape*, pp. 226–244; Whitaker, Robin, and Goretti Horgan, "Abortion governance in the new Northern Ireland", in *A Fragmented Landscape*, pp. 245–265.

Opponents of the right to access to abortion therefore see the inclusion of the right to life in the constitution as the inclusion of a right of the "unborn child" (see Chapter 4).

It must be emphasised that, in terms of human rights, the legitimisation of the demand for women's right to self-determination clashes head-on with a transcendental and naturalised doctrine of the right to life developed by groups that oppose access to abortion. Discourses about the abortion debate can only be constructed in an antagonistic way – that is, by national, international, supranational and transnational actors who draw the contours of public debate by separating "us" and "them", "friend" and "foe". Therefore, the recognition of a right to abortion cannot be a matter of women's subjectivation alone. It must go hand in hand with institutional support that guarantees women's autonomy and rights, especially for those who do not have citizenship status, such as migrant women, non-nationals, residents, undocumented women and underage girls (see Chapter 1).

Various institutional support mechanisms guarantee women's rights: international, European and national legal instruments, such as conventions and treaties; the obligation of states to report to UN and parliamentary bodies; the recommendations issued to states by treaty-monitoring committees; recourse to European judicial bodies; the institutional recognition of women's organisations, which ensure vigilance with regard to the international commitments made by states; and the implementation of public action tools. While these institutional instruments do not ensure recognition of the right to abortion, they can guarantee more or less effective access to abortion in states that do recognise the right (see Chapters 1 and 2).

However, as states remain the leading actors in providing effective access to abortion, citizenship remains the cornerstone of this provision. More precisely, if citizenship as a practice – which translates into a process of subjectivation and individuation for women – is essential, then institutional support for women's autonomy is no less so. In this respect, two elements seem to be particularly important: social citizenship and the possession of citizenship status.

Indeed, the fight against gender discrimination has gained international recognition and legitimacy, which has encouraged states to amend their legal provisions in this area. However, fiscal austerity policies and conservative political forces generally hinder the exercise of social rights, thus undermining public health policies. The emancipatory scope of the call for human rights therefore comes up against the limits imposed on social citizenship by the recent economic and financial crises, which have called into question the redistribution of resources for social welfare, as well as the power relations between the actors responsible for or dependent on social, budgetary and redistributive policies and networks of political power.

In Northern Europe and France, for example, abortion is free or inexpensive. On the other hand, in other EU countries, free access to abortion or its reimbursement is often subject to restrictive conditions (such as requiring the existence of a medical indication), or abortion is only available to women with social security rights (see Chapter 1 and Appendix A). In this respect, one may wonder whether legitimising a right to abortion in terms of human rights does not amount to disconnecting the social question from the citizenship question.

This conflict between human rights and social citizenship is all the more acute for women without citizenship status. Indeed, having the status of a citizen is key to effective access to the right to abortion. The legitimisation of reproductive freedom as a human right can certainly play an emancipatory political role for women, but it is statutory citizenship that will provide real guarantees of access to abortion. This is evidenced by the restrictions that states have imposed on access to health care for migrant women, undocumented women, non-nationals and non-residents (such as in Croatia, Germany, Ireland, Latvia, Lithuania, Poland, Portugal, Slovenia, Romania and Spain) and for underage girls in most EU countries (with the exception of Austria, Belgium, Finland, France, the Netherlands and Sweden) (see Chapter 1 and Appendix A).

*

The analysis that has just been outlined on the conflicts and links between citizenship and human rights with regard to the right to abortion offers a conceptual framework that makes it possible to problematise the use of the language of human rights within the citizenship regime, beyond that language's function of dual legitimisation – that is, of legitimising the actors as interlocutors of political decision makers while also legitimising their demands. This framing places this problematisation at the intersection of political subjectivation processes, institutional support for individual emancipation and the possession of citizenship status.

While the emancipatory scope of human rights refers the singularisation of human beings, making them bearers of an abstract and universal supreme value independent of any affiliation, that of citizenship rights inscribes individual autonomy in social, cultural, political, familial and other ties. As we have seen throughout this book, it is the autonomy of individuals, in this case women, that is at stake in the debates between supporters and opponents of the right to abortion, which have been particularly heated in Europe in recent decades. It also appears that restrictions of this right – whether through attempts at regression in more or less permissive legislation; blatant violations of even very restrictive laws, as in Poland; or radical prohibitions, as in Malta and until recently Cyprus, Northern Ireland and the Republic of Ireland – undermine the individuation of women.

APPENDICES

Appendix A. Legal regimes and effective access to abortion in EU member states

The information presented in the following five tables is that which was available in April 2022 and – for the recent legislative changes in Spain – in March 2023. In the "Cost to the woman" column of these tables, the following terminology is used: "very low" (<€60), "low" (€60 to €100), "rather expensive" (€100 to €200), "expensive" (€200 to €400) and "very expensive" (>€400). "Criminal sanctions" refers to sanctions for abortions performed outside the legal framework. "Medical abortion" involves taking abortion tablets in two doses 48 hours apart.

These tables were designed by the author, based on data published by the Mouvement français pour le planning familial (MFPF), 2019, "Tableau comparatif des législations sur l'avortement dans l'Union européenne". This source has been updated and supplemented by the documents listed in the section at the end of the appendix.

Table A.1. An authorisation regime that provides easy access to abortion on request with few restrictive conditions (e.g. time limits).

Country	Legislation	Time limit (from conception)	Cost to the woman	Conditions	Criminal sanctions
Denmark	Law of 1973 and law of 1995, consolidated in 2008. Health Act of 2014.	12 weeks on request. May be extended on medical or social grounds, and in cases of rape or other sexual crimes.	Free for residents. Since 2004, accessible to non-residents (but at their expense).	>12 weeks: consultation with a medical commission composed of gynaecologists, social workers and psychologists.	Yes, but not for the woman.
Finland	Laws of 1970, 1978, 1985 and 2001.	12 weeks on social grounds and in cases of rape. Can be extended on medical grounds.	Financial contribution (low) from the woman.	Agreement of two doctors, or only one doctor if patient is aged <17 or >40 or has four children. Mandatory contraceptive counselling.	Yes.
The Netherlands	Law of 1981. Decree of 1984. The criminal code defines killing a viable foetus as infanticide.	No time limit. In practice, 20 to 22 weeks on social grounds. The legal viability of the foetus is 24 weeks.	Reimbursed for residents; paid for by non-residents.	In hospitals and licensed clinics, and by a doctor only. Must ensure the woman's free choice.	Yes, but not for the woman.
Sweden	Abortion Act of 1974, amended in 2007 and 2013.	Up to 18 weeks on request. Beyond that, for "special reasons" (including the woman's physical and psychological health).	Financial contribution (very low) from the woman.	<18 weeks: interview. >18 weeks: National Health Board.	Yes.

Conscience clause	Parental consent	Waiting period	Medical abortion	Comments
Yes.	Yes, up to the age of 18.	No.	Since April 2000.	For minors, an ad hoc committee can override a parental refusal or decide that parental consent is not necessary. Local hospitals are obliged to receive women for abortion up to 12 weeks. After 12 weeks the abortion must be performed by a doctor in a regional hospital.
Not mentioned in the law.	No.	No.	Since May 2000.	Illegal abortions are rare. Abortion allowed up to 20 weeks for patients aged <17, up to 24 weeks if foetal malformation and with no limit if the woman's life is in danger.
Yes, with an obligation to inform the woman.	No.	Five days unless there is a serious risk to the woman.	Since January 2000.	The law is very freely interpreted. Almost no illegal abortions. Most abortions are performed in licensed clinics. The woman's state of distress must be established.
No (confirmed in January 2017).	No.	No.	Since 1992.	Foetal viability set at 22 weeks. This limit can be crossed if the woman's life is in danger. Since January 2008, abortion is allowed for non-nationals.

Table A.2. An authorisation regime that allows abortion with partial or total decriminalisation, subject to criteria, but where standards of access to abortion remain high.

Country	Legislation	Time limit (from conception)	Cost to the woman	Conditions	Criminal sanctions
Belgium	The 1990 law partially decriminalised abortion. The law of October 2018 removed abortion from the criminal code.	12 weeks on request. May be extended if there is danger to the health of the woman or malformation of the foetus.	Virtually free for women, as covered by social security. Otherwise, expensive.	Mandatory interview. Counselling and procedure must be in the same place. The abortion must be performed in an outpatient centre or in a hospital, and by a doctor.	Maintained despite its removal from the criminal code.
France	Laws of 1975 (the Veil Act) and 2001. In 2016, removed from the criminal code and introduced in the health code.	Since 2022, 14 weeks on request. Can be extended on medical grounds	Completely free for all women since March 2013.	>14 weeks: advisory opinion from a multidiscipli-nary team.	Yes, but not for the woman.
Luxembourg	Laws of 1978 and 2012. Law of 2014 removed abortion from the criminal code.	12 weeks on request. Can be extended on medical grounds.	Reimbursed for women covered by social security. Otherwise, rather expensive.	<12 weeks: consultation with a doctor. >12 weeks: opinion of two doctors.	Yes.
United Kingdom (excluding Northern Ireland)	The Abortion Act of 1967 legalises abortion under certain conditions. Amended in 1990.	24 weeks on social or medical indications. Can be extended on medical grounds.	Free of charge through the National Health Service. Very expensive in the private sector.	>24 weeks: certificate from two doctors.	Not since March 2017.

Conscience clause	Parental consent	Waiting period	Medical abortion	Comments
Yes. Obligation to refer the woman to a doctor who performs abortions.	Presence of a trusted person or interview.	6 days.	Since July 2000, but abolished since 2017 for family planning centres.	The law is interpreted quite freely. Has an offence of obstruction. Removed the notion of a state of distress. For abortion outside the legal time limit, abortion centres refer women to the Netherlands.
Yes, but obligation to refer the woman to another doctor.	No. Compulsory interview and support from an adult chosen by the minor.	Abolished since January 2016.	Since 1987. Up to seven weeks by a midwife, nine weeks in a hospital.	Removed of the notion of a state of distress in 2014. Since February 2017, has the offence of obstruction (sanctions for websites spreading disinformation). Abortion is not performed in many hospitals. Among the new generation of doctors, fewer and fewer are willing to perform abortions.
Yes, even for paramedics.	Yes, but possibility of secrecy if the minor is accompanied by an adult.	3 days.	Since January 2001. Since 2009, up to 7 weeks in a family planning centre.	Removed the state of distress condition. Compulsory psychological interview for minors. No time limit if the life of the woman or the foetus is threatened.
Yes. Its use is prohibited if the woman's life is in danger.	Yes. Doctors can override the authorisation.	No.	Since 1991.	Increasing use of the conscience clause among young obstetricians.

Table A.3. An authorisation regime in Southern and Central European countries where access to abortion is restricted and/or de facto obstructed.

Country	Legislation	Time limit (from conception)	Cost to the woman	Conditions	Criminal sanctions
Germany	Federal law prohibits abortion but, in practice, it is no longer punishable below 12 weeks of pregnancy since the 1995 law. Abortion falls under the criminal code.	12 weeks on request and in cases of rape and other sexual crimes. Can be extended on medical or social grounds.	Abortion on demand at the woman's expense (rather expensive to expensive) except for women with low incomes.	Interview (plus certificate) required except in cases of rape. Second medical opinion if >12 weeks.	Yes.
Austria	Federal law of 1974. Abortion falls under the criminal code.	3 months on request. In practice, up to 16 weeks. Can be extended on medical grounds and for patients aged <14.	Free of charge on medical grounds. Otherwise, very expensive.	<3 months: interview. >3 months: medical opinion. Abortion must be performed in a public hospital by a doctor.	Yes.
Cyprus	Abortion is allowed by law since March 2018.*	12 weeks on request. Extended to 19 weeks in the case of rape or incest.	Free of charge for patients receiving free medical care. Otherwise expensive (often performed in private clinics).	Mandatory medical and psychological consultation and written authorisation from two doctors.	Information not found.

* The 1974 law (amended in 1986 and 1995) tolerated abortion only in cases of rape or incest, or if the pregnancy posed a major health risk to the woman and the "unborn child".

Conscience clause	Parental consent	Waiting period	Medical abortion	Comments
Yes, but guaranteed right of access.	Yes, up to the age of 16.	Three days, even on medical grounds.	Since November 1999, up to nine weeks.	For a doctor, the mere fact of giving public information on abortion is punishable in criminal law. Since March 2022, Article 219 of the criminal code, which prohibited all advertising, has been repealed. In some *Länder*, there is no choice between counselling centres run by local or federal authorities and those linked to the Church.
Yes, but its use is prohibited if there is imminent danger of death to the woman.	Yes, up to the age of 13.	No.	Since December 1999.	In four *Länder*, there is no abortion in public hospitals. Difficult to obtain outside the main urban centres. Misuse of the conscience clause.
Information not found.	Yes.	Information not found.	Information not found.	The Orthodox Church is very influential and is opposed to abortion. The new situation created by the law of March 2018 remains to be analysed.*

* Information on the new Cypriot legislation seems to be difficult to find. The Cypriot family planning organisation's website could not be found at the address given by IPPF EN (www.cyfamplan.org).

Table A.3. Continued.

Country	Legislation	Time limit (from conception)	Cost to the woman	Conditions	Criminal sanctions
Spain	Law of March 2010 and law of September 2015.	14 weeks on request, 22 weeks in cases of foetal malformation or danger to the woman's health. Unlimited in serious cases.	Reimbursed for women covered by social security. Expensive to very expensive for others.	Prior interview if <14 weeks. Opinion of two doctors if there is foetal malformation or one if there is a risk to the woman's health.	Yes.
Greece	Law of 1986.	12 weeks on request, 19 in the case of rape, 24 in cases of foetal anomaly. Unlimited if there is a danger to the woman's physical or mental health.	Free of charge since 2013. Support for women without social security.	<12 weeks: must be performed by a doctor and an anaesthetist.	Yes.
Italy	Law of 1978.	13 weeks on social or medical indications. Can be extended on medical grounds. Rape and incest are not accepted grounds.	Free of charge.	Prior consultation with a doctor.	Yes.

Conscience clause	Parental consent	Waiting period	Medical abortion	Comments
Yes, but the new system introduced in 2023 establishes that public hospital doctors cannot be forced to carry out an abortion *provided* that they have already registered their objection in writing.	No, as of the 2023 law expanding abortion rights, which allows 16- and 17-year-olds to undergo abortion without parental consent. (Earlier provisions introduced in 2015 required parental consent up to the age of 18.)	Three days, unless the abortion is performed on medical grounds or in an emergency.	Since February 2000.	Use of the conscience clause is increasing in public hospitals, forcing many women to resort to abortion in private clinics. The new law adopted in 2023, however, enshrines the right to have an abortion in a public hospital. Judicial practice opens the door to complaints from ex-spouses and partners, as well as anti-abortion groups.
Yes, unless there is a danger to the woman.	Yes, up to the age of 18.	No.	Since 2001.	In practice, women resort to abortion in secret due to public moral disapproval.
Yes. Its use is prohibited if the woman's life is in danger.	Up to the age of 18, recourse to the guardianship judge is possible.	Seven days except in emergencies.	Since 2009 (in a hospital).	Increasing use of conscientious objection by doctors or hospitals. In some regions, no abortion is performed.

Table A.3. Continued.

Country	Legislation	Time limit (from conception)	Cost to the woman	Conditions	Criminal sanctions
Portugal	2007 law and 2015 law. Abortion falls under the criminal code.	10 weeks on request. May be extended on medical grounds and in the case of rape.	Free of charge before July 2015. Very low cost since then.	24 weeks for foetal malformation, unlimited if the woman's life is in danger, 16 weeks in the case of rape. Mandatory psychological interview since 2015.	Yes, but not for the woman.
Republic of Ireland	A law legalised abortion in December 2018.*	12 weeks on request. Can be extended on medical grounds.	Free for residents.	Up to 24 weeks in cases of danger to the life of the woman or serious abnormality of the foetus that could lead to its death *in utero*.	Yes, but not for the woman.

* Since 1983, the Eighth Amendment to the Constitution has protected the life of the embryo. In May 2018 this amendment was removed following a referendum.

Conscience clause	Parental consent	Waiting period	Medical abortion	Comments
Yes. The register of objecting doctors was discontinued in 2015.	Yes, up to the age of 16. But the doctor decides if it is urgent.	Three days, unless the legal time limit for performing an abortion has elapsed (in which case the waiting period is waived).	Since February 2006.	Difficult to access in public hospitals. The majority of abortions are performed privately and illegally. Accessible to women without a residence permit.
Yes. Obligation to refer the woman to a doctor who performs abortions.	Yes.	Three days.	Yes.	Abortion totally banned until 2018. The new situation created by the December 2018 law remains to be analysed.

Table A.4. An authorisation regime that permits abortion, but where access is hampered (sometimes severely) by restrictive procedures.

Country	Legislation	Time limit (from conception)	Cost to the woman	Conditions	Criminal sanctions
Bulgaria	A decree of February 1990 author- ises abortion. Amended in October 2000.	12 weeks on request. Can be extended on medical grounds.	Free of charge for patients aged <16 or >35, on medical grounds, in the case of rape or for women with social insurance. Low cost for others.	Authorisation from a medical commission for medical grounds.	No.
Croatia	Law of 1978. The law did not change at the time of independence in 1991.	10 weeks on request. May be extended on medical grounds and in the case of rape.	Free for wom- en with low incomes. Oth- erwise, rather expensive to expensive.	Abortion on request: in a hospital or approved facility with a gynaecology department. On medical grounds: agreement of a commission of two doctors (one of which is a gynaecol- ogist) and a social worker or nurse.	Yes.
Estonia	1998 law, amended in 2009 and 2015.	12 weeks on request. Can be extended on medical grounds.	Free on med- ical grounds. Otherwise, very low cost.	Written request of the woman and a mandatory interview. >12 weeks: agreement of two gynaecol- ogists and a health worker. Up to 22 weeks in cases of foetal malfor- mation or risk to the woman's health, or if patient is aged <15 or >45.	Yes.

Conscience clause	Parental consent	Waiting period	Medical abortion	Comments
Not mentioned.	Yes, up to the age of 18.	No.	Since 2013.	Irregular supply of contraceptives in planning centres.
Yes.	Yes, up to the age of 16.	6 days.	No.	The conscience clause is abused in hospitals. Many illegal, medically safe abortions in the private sector. In March 2017, the Constitutional Court reaffirmed the right to abortion. Abortion remains a contraceptive method due to a lack of access to contraception.
Yes.	Not since 2015.	No.	Since 2005, up to nine weeks.	Since independence, minor changes in the law. Improved contraception.

Table A.4. Continued.

Country	Legislation	Time limit (from conception)	Cost to the woman	Conditions	Criminal sanctions
Hungary	Law of 2000. Since 2012, the Orbán government has amended the constitution to "protect life from conception".	12 weeks in cases of "severe crisis" (as defined by the woman) or rape. May be extended on medical or social grounds.	Free on medical grounds, rather expensive if on demand. Exclusion of migrants and undocumented women from all but emergency health care.	<2 weeks: two mandatory interviews. >12 weeks: opinion of two doctors.	Yes.
Latvia	Law of 2002.	12 weeks on request or in the case of rape. Can be extended on medical grounds.	Free of charge on medical grounds, otherwise at the expense of the woman (rather expensive).	Mandatory interview (moral aspects, risks). Written statement by the woman. In an approved private or public centre.	Yes.
Lithuania	Law of 1955, ministerial regulation of 1987, decrees of 1990 and 1994.	12 weeks on request. Can be extended on medical grounds, or by court order in cases of rape or incest.	Reimbursed if medically indicated, otherwise at the woman's expense (very expensive).	Mandatory consultation. Written request. Husband's consent recommended.	Yes, but not for the woman.
Czech Republic	Law of 1986, ministerial regulation of 1992.	12 weeks on request. May be extended on medical grounds or in cases of rape or other sexual crimes.	Free on medical grounds, otherwise rather expensive.	Mandatory interview. At least six months between two abortions, except if patient is aged >35 or has two children, or in the case of rape.	Yes.

Conscience clause	Parental consent	Waiting period	Medical abortion	Comments
Yes.	Yes, up to the age of 18.	3 days.	Since May 2012, but strongly discouraged.	Right to life of the foetus enshrined in the constitution. Anti-abortion campaigns. Exclusion of migrants and undocumented women from all but emergency health care. Frequently used conscience clause.
Yes.	Yes, up to the age of 16; recourse to the Orphans' Court.	Three days.	Since 2008, up to nine weeks.	Deficient contraception. Lack of training for doctors in performing abortions. "For Life" birth campaigns.
Not mentioned.	Yes, up to the age of 16. In practice, up to the age of 18.	No, but in practice 10 to 12 days.	No.	Increasingly frequent use of the conscience clause. Limited access for adolescent girls and women without resources. Deficient contraception.
Yes, since 2011 (Medical Services Act).	Yes, up to the age of 16. Between the ages of 16 and 18, parents are informed.	No.	Since June 2014.	No access to abortion for non-resident women, unless there is a risk to the woman's life.

Table A.4. Continued.

Country	Legislation	Time limit (from conception)	Cost to the woman	Conditions	Criminal sanctions
Romania	Law of 1996, amended and supplemented by the criminal code in 2009.	14 weeks on request. May be extended if there is a risk to the life of the woman or a risk to the foetus.	At the woman's expense. Very low cost in the public sector to rather expensive in the private sector, free if in economic hardship.	Performed by obstetricians or gynaecologists.	Yes, but not for the woman.
Slovakia	Law of 1986. Abortion falls under the criminal code. In December 2007, abortion declared constitutional. Decree of 2009.	12 weeks on request. May be extended on medical grounds and in the case of rape.	Free of charge on medical grounds, otherwise at the expense of the woman (expensive).	Mandatory interview since 2009. At least six months between two abortions, except if patient is aged >35 or has two children, or in the case of rape.	Not mentioned.
Slovenia	Law of 1977, amended in 1992.	10 weeks on request. Can be extended on medical grounds.	At the woman's expense.	>10 weeks: multidisciplinary committee of two people.	Yes, but not for the woman.

Conscience clause	Parental consent	Waiting period	Medical abortion	Comments
Not mentioned in the law but practiced.	Yes, up to the age of 18.	No. In 2013, a proposal for a five-day period was rejected.	Since 2008 (rather expensive).	Abusive practice of the conscience clause without legal basis, according to a code adopted by an association of doctors. Common in rural areas. Deficient contraception.
Yes, in the constitution since 1993.	Yes, up to the age of 18.	Four days.	No. Was debated in April 2017.	Abuse of the conscience clause. Impossibility to procure an abortion in many districts. Lack of confidentiality.
Yes.	Yes, except for emancipated minors.	No.	Since 2013.	

Table A.5. A regime that prohibits abortion by imposing very restrictive conditions on its access and making it extremely difficult in practice.

Country	Legislation	Time limit (from conception)	Cost to the woman	Criminal sanctions
Northern Ireland	Law of 1861. Prohibition of abortion. In 2016, vote against abortion in cases of rape, incest or foetal malformation. As of 21 October 2019, the amendment passed by Westminster allows abortion.	Not applicable.	Not applicable.	Yes.
Malta	Prohibition of abortion in all cases except rape or foetal abnormalities (2003). Abortion falls under the criminal code.	Not applicable.	Not applicable.	Yes.
Poland	Since 1993, abortion has been prohibited. Since 1997, it is prohibited except in cases of rape or incest certified by a prosecutor, malformation of the foetus, or a health risk for the woman. Abortion falls under of the criminal code. The Constitutional Court's ruling of 22 October 2020 prohibits abortion for foetal malformation.	12 weeks in the case of rape certified by the public prosecutor. Can be extended on medical grounds (requiring the opinion of two doctors other than the one performing the procedure).	Free if legal (very rare cases).	

Conscience clause	Parental consent	Waiting period	Medical abortion	Comments
Not applicable.	Not applicable.	Not applicable.	Not applicable.	In 2015 the High Court of Justice in Northern Ireland found that the law violated the European Convention on Human Rights. The morning-after pill has been authorised since 2012. To date, abortion remains a taboo, despite Westminster passing an amendment allowing abortion on 21 October 2019. This allows abortion to be performed within 12 weeks of pregnancy and the limit can be extended for medical reasons, but services to access safe and legal abortion are not yet in place.
Not applicable.	Not applicable.	Not applicable.	Not applicable.	Protocol annexed to the Treaty of Accession to the European Union to ensure the absence of legislation. Morning-after pill allowed since 2016 without a doctor's prescription, but there is obstruction by pharmacists.
Yes. Its use is prohibited if the woman's life is in danger. Obligation to refer the woman to another professional.	Yes, up to the age of 18.	No.	Not applicable.	Extremely restrictive application of the law. Very frequent use of the conscience clause. The morning-after pill has not been authorised since June 2017, except on medical prescription. A bill was tabled to ban all abortions.

A.1 Sources

Avortement Info. 2013. Abortion clinics in Europe. URL: http://avortement.info.
Centre d'action laïque. 2020. État des lieux de l'avortement en Europe. URL: www.laicite.be.
Center for Reproductive Rights. 2019. The world's abortion laws. URL: http://worldabortionlaws.com.
Center for Reproductive Rights. 2022. European abortion laws: a comparative overview. Accessed 5 September 2022.
Council of Europe, Commissioner for Human Rights. 2017. Women's sexual and reproductive health and rights in Europe. Strasbourg.
Heinen, Jacqueline. 2015. Assauts tous azimuts contre le droit à l'avortement. La Pologne fait-elle école ? In *Genre et religion : des rapports épineux. Illustration à partir des débats sur l'avortement,* edited by Ana Amuchástegui, Edith Flores, Evelyn Aldaz, Jacqueline Heinen and Christine Verschuur, pp. 55–90. Paris: L'Harmattan.
Heino, Anna, Mika Gissler, Dan Pater and Christian Fiala. 2013. Conscientious objection and induced abortion in Europe. *European Journal of Contraception and Reproductive Health Care* 18(4), 231–233.
IPPF EN. 2019. The IPPF EN partner survey: abortion legislation and its implementation in Europe and Central Asia; threats to women's and girls' reproductive health. December.
Law Library of Congress, Global Legal Center. 2015. Abortion legislation in Europe. URL: www.law.gov.
Library of Congress. 2013. Abortion law of jurisdictions around the world. URL: www.loc.gov.
Mouvement français pour le planning familial. 2019. Tableau comparatif des législations sur l'avortement dans l'Union européenne.
Séhier, Véronique. 2019. *Droits sexuels et reproductifs en Europe : entre menaces et progrès*. Paris: Conseil économique, social et environnemental.
United Nations. 2017. Global abortion policies database. URL: https://abortion-policies.srhr.org.

Appendix B. International and European political and legal bases, and European case law, related to women's sexual and reproductive health

The extracts presented in this appendix contain the international and European political and legal bases for women's sexual and reproductive health in the European Union, as well as presenting European case law related to the European Convention on Human Rights and the revised European Social Charter.

B.1 International political bases

United Nations, International Conference on Population and Development, Cairo, 5–13 September 1994, Programme of Action (A/CONF.171/13/Rev.1)

Principle 8.

Everyone has the right to the enjoyment of the highest attainable standard of physical and mental health. States should take all appropriate measures to ensure, on a basis of equality of men and women, universal access to health-care services, including those related to reproductive health care, which includes family planning and sexual health. Reproductive health-care programmes should provide the widest range of services without any form of coercion. All couples and individuals have the basic right to decide freely and responsibly the number and spacing of their children and to have the information, education and means to do so.

In Chapter VII, on "Reproductive rights and reproductive health", and Chapter VIII, on "Health, morbidity and mortality" (which notes that the Holy See made a reservation), the following measures and principles of action can be highlighted:

7.2. Reproductive health is a state of complete physical, mental and social well-being and not merely the absence of disease or infirmity, in all matters relating to the reproductive system and to its functions and processes. Reproductive health therefore implies that people are able to have a satisfying and safe sex life and that they have the capability to reproduce and the freedom to decide if, when and how often to do so. Implicit in this last condition are the right of men and women to be informed and to have access to safe, effective, affordable and acceptable methods of family planning of their choice, as well as other methods of their choice for regulation of fertility which are not against the law, and the right of access to appropriate health-care services that will enable women to go safely through pregnancy and childbirth and provide couples with the best chance of having a healthy infant. [...]

7.3. Bearing in mind the above definition, reproductive rights embrace certain human rights that are already recognized in national laws, international human rights documents and other consensus documents. These rights rest on the recognition of the basic right of all couples and individuals to decide freely and responsibly the number, spacing and timing of their children and to have the information and means to do so, and the right to attain the highest standard of sexual and reproductive health. It also includes their right to make decisions concerning reproduction free of discrimination, coercion and violence [...]

[...]

8.25. In no case should abortion be promoted as a method of family planning. All Governments and relevant intergovernmental and non-governmental organizations are urged to strengthen their commitment to women's health, to deal with the health impact of unsafe abortion as a major public health concern and to reduce the recourse to abortion through expanded and improved family-planning services. Prevention of unwanted pregnancies must always be given the highest priority and every attempt should be made to eliminate the need for abortion. [...] In all cases, women should have access to quality services for the management of complications arising from abortion. Post-abortion counselling, education and family-planning services should be offered promptly, which will also help to avoid repeat abortions.

United Nations, Fourth World Conference on Women, Beijing, 4–15 September 1995, Programme of Action (A/CONF.177/20/Rev.1)

In Chapter IV, "Strategic objectives and actions", in the section "Women and health" (for which the Holy See submitted a reservation), points 89,

90, 94 and 95 were largely inspired by the principles of the Cairo Pro-gramme of Action (points 7.2 and 7.3) and measure 106(k) reiterates the terms of measure 8.25 (quoted above) of the previous programme.

Furthermore, the Beijing Programme of Action reaffirms the dissociation between sexuality and procreation:

> 96. The human rights of women include their right to have control over and decide freely and responsibly on matters related to their sexuality, including sexual and reproductive health, free of coercion, discrimination and violence. Equal relationships between women and men in matters of sexual relations and reproduction, including full respect for the integrity of the person, require mutual respect, consent and shared responsibility for sexual behaviour and its consequences.

United Nations, General Assembly, "Transforming our world: the 2030 agenda for sustainable development", Resolution no. 11 688, 25 September 2015 (A.RES/70/1)

> Goal 3. Ensure healthy lives and promote well-being for all at all ages. […]

> 3.1. By 2030, reduce the global maternal mortality ratio to less than 70 per 100,000 live births. […]

> 3.7. By 2030, ensure universal access to sexual and reproductive health-care services, including for family planning, information and education, and the integration of reproductive health into national strategies and programmes. […]

> Goal 5. Achieve gender equality and empower all women and girls. […]

> 5.6. Ensure universal access to sexual and reproductive health and reproductive rights as agreed in accordance with the Programme of Action of the International Conference on Population and Development and the Beijing Platform for Action and the outcome documents of their review conferences.

B.2 European policy bases

Council of Europe

*Council of Europe, Parliamentary Assembly,
"Access to safe and legal abortion in Europe",
Resolution no. 1607, 16 April 2008*

7. The Assembly invites the member states of the Council of Europe to:

7.1. decriminalise abortion within reasonable gestational limits, if they have not already done so;

7.2. guarantee women's effective exercise of their right of access to a safe and legal abortion;

7.3. allow women freedom of choice and offer the conditions for a free and enlightened choice without specifically promoting abortion;

7.4. lift restrictions which hinder, de jure or de facto, access to safe abortion, and, in particular, take the necessary steps to create the appropriate conditions for health, medical and psychological care and offer suitable financial cover;

7.5. adopt evidence-based appropriate sexual and reproductive health and rights strategies and policies, ensuring continued improvements and expansion of non-judgmental sex and relationships information and education, as well as contraceptive services, through increased investments from the national budgets into improving health systems, reproductive health supplies and information;

7.6. ensure that women and men have access to contraception and advice on contraception at a reasonable cost, of a suitable nature for them and chosen by them;

7.7. introduce compulsory age-appropriate, gender-sensitive sex and relationships education for young people (inter alia, in schools) to avoid unwanted pregnancies (and therefore abortions);

7.8. promote a more pro-family attitude in public information campaigns and provide counselling and practical support to help women where the reason for wanting an abortion is family or financial pressure.

Voting: 102 votes in favour, 69 against and 14 abstentions.

Parliamentary Assembly of the Council of Europe, "The right to conscientious objection in lawful medical care", Resolution no. 1763, 20 July 2010

1. No person, hospital or institution shall be coerced, held liable or discriminated against in any manner because of a refusal to perform, accommodate, assist or submit to an abortion, the performance of a human miscarriage, or euthanasia or any act which could cause the death of a human foetus or embryo, for any reason.

2. The Parliamentary Assembly emphasises the need to affirm the right of conscientious objection together with the responsibility of the state to ensure that patients are able to access lawful medical care in a timely manner. The Assembly is concerned that the unregulated use of conscientious objection may disproportionately affect women, notably those with low incomes or living in rural areas.

Voting: 56 votes in favour, 51 against and 4 abstentions.

Council of Europe, Commissioner for Human Rights, "Women's sexual and reproductive health and rights in Europe", 2017: "The Commissioner's recommendations" (pp. 9–14)

In order to ensure the human rights of all women and girls across Europe, the Commissioner for Human Rights calls on Council of Europe member states to:

I. Reaffirm commitments to women's human rights and gender equality and guard against retrogressive measures that undermine women's sexual and reproductive health and rights [...]

II. Invest in women's sexual and reproductive health and establish a health system designed to advance women's sexual and reproductive health and rights [...]

III. Ensure the provision of comprehensive sexuality education [...]

IV. Guarantee the affordability, availability and accessibility of modern contraception [...]

V. Ensure all women's access to safe and legal abortion care [...]

VI. Ensure that refusals of care by health care workers do not jeopardise women's timely access to sexual and reproductive health care [...]

VII. Respect and safeguard women's human rights in childbirth and guarantee all women's access to quality maternal healthcare [...]

VIII. Eliminate coercive practices and guarantee women's informed consent and decision making in sexual and reproductive health care contexts [...]

IX. Ensure all women's access to effective remedies for violations of their sexual and reproductive health and rights [...]

X. Eliminate discrimination in law and practice including intersectional and multiple forms of discrimination and guarantee equality for all women in the enjoyment of sexual and reproductive health and rights [...]

European Union

European Parliament, "Sexual and reproductive health and rights" (2001/2128 (INI)), Resolution, 3 July 2002

The European Parliament [...]

8. Underlines that abortion should not be promoted as a family planning method;

9. Recommends the governments of the Member States and the candidate countries to strive to implement a health and social policy which will lead to a lower incidence of abortion, in particular through the provision of family planning counselling and services and the offering of material and financial support for pregnant women in difficulties, and to regard unsafe abortion as an issue of major public health concern;

10. Recommends the governments of the Member States and the candidate countries to ensure the provision of unbiased, scientific and readily understandable information and counselling on sexual and reproductive health, including the prevention of unwanted pregnancies and the risks involved in unsafe abortions carried out under unsuitable conditions;

11. Calls upon the governments of the Member States and the candidate countries to provide specialised sexual and reproductive health services which include high quality and professional advice and counselling adapted to the needs of specific groups

(e.g. immigrants), provided by a trained, multidisciplinary staff; underlines that advice and counselling must be confidential and non-judgmental and that in the event of legitimate conscientious objection of the provider, referral to other service providers must take place; where advice on abortion is provided, attention must be drawn to the physical and psychological health risks associated with abortion, and alternative solutions (adoption, availability of support in the event of a decision to keep the child) must be discussed;

12. Recommends that, in order to safeguard women's reproductive health and rights, abortion should be made legal, safe and accessible to all;

13. Calls upon the governments of the Member States and the candidate countries to refrain in any case from prosecuting women who have undergone illegal abortions.

Voting: 280 votes in favour, 240 against and 28 abstentions.

European Parliament, "Equality between women and men in the European Union" (2009/2101 (INI)), Resolution, 10 February 2010

The European Parliament [...]

36. Emphasises that women must have control over their sexual and reproductive rights, notably through easy access to contraception and abortion; emphasises that women must have access free of charge to consultation on abortion; supports, therefore – as it did in its above-mentioned resolution of 3 September 2008 – measures and actions to improve women's access to sexual and reproductive health services and to raise their awareness of their rights and of available services; invites the Member States and the Commission to implement measures and actions to make men more aware of their responsibilities in relation to sexual and reproductive matters.

Voting: 381 votes in favour, 253 against and 31 abstentions.

European Parliament, "Sexual and reproductive health and rights" (2013/2040 (INI)), Resolution, 10 December 2013

The European Parliament [...]

1. Notes that the formulation and implementation of policies on SRHR [sexual and reproductive health and rights] and on sexual education in schools is a competence of the Member States;

2. Notes that, even though it is a competence of the Member States to formulate and implement policies on health and on education, the EU can contribute to the promotion of best practices among Member States.

The European People's Party and the European Conservatives and Reformists group presented this resolution as an alternative to Edite Estrela's report on sexual and reproductive rights.
Voting: 334 votes in favour, 327 against and 35 abstentions.

European Parliament, "Progress made in equality between women and men in the EU in 2013" (2014/2217(INI)), Resolution, 10 March 2015

The European Parliament [...]

45. Points out that various studies show that abortion rates in countries in which abortion is legal are similar to those in countries in which it is banned, and are often even higher in the latter (World Health Organization, 2014);

46. Notes that the formulation and implementation of policies on sexual and reproductive health and rights and on sexual education is a competence of the Member States; emphasises, nevertheless, that the EU can contribute to the promotion of best practice among Member States;

47. Maintains that women must have control over their sexual and reproductive health and rights, not least by having ready access to contraception and abortion; supports, accordingly, measures and actions to improve women's access to sexual and reproductive health services and inform them more fully about their rights and the services available; calls on the Member States and the Commission to implement measures and actions to make men aware of their responsibilities for sexual and reproductive matters;

48. Emphasises the importance of active prevention, education and information policies aimed at teenagers, young people and adults to ensure that sexual and reproductive health among the public is good, thereby preventing sexually transmitted diseases and unwanted pregnancies.

Voting: 441 votes in favour, 205 against and 52 abstentions.

European Parliament, "The EU strategy for equality between women and men post-2015" (2014/2152 (INI)), Resolution, 9 June 2015

The European Parliament [...]

52. Calls on the Commission to assist Member States in ensuring high-quality, geographically appropriate and readily accessible services in the areas of sexual and reproductive health and rights and safe and legal abortion and contraception, as well as general healthcare;

53. Urges the Commission to include sexual and reproductive health and rights (SRHRs) in its next EU Health Strategy, in order to ensure equality between women and men and complement national SRHR policies.

Voting: 341 votes in favour, 281 against and 81 abstentions.

European Parliament, "The situation of female refugees and asylum seekers in the European Union" (2015/2325 (INI)), Resolution, 8 March 2016

The European Parliament [...]

29. Urges the Commission and the Member States to guarantee full access to sexual and reproductive health and rights, including access to safe abortion, and to allocate additional resources to healthcare provision as a matter of urgency.

Voting: 388 votes in favour, 150 against and 159 abstentions.

European Parliament, "Situation of fundamental rights in the European Union in 2017" (2018/2103 (INI)), Resolution, 16 January 2019

The European Parliament [...]

23. Expresses its support for the demonstrations that took place in several Member States in 2017, following retrogressions related to sexual and reproductive health rights, and extensive media coverage of sexual harassment cases; strongly affirms

that the denial of services related to sexual and reproductive health and rights, including safe and legal abortion, is a form of violence against women and girls; reiterates that women and girls must have control over their bodies and sexualities; encourages EU Member States to take effective steps to respect and protect women's sexual and reproductive rights in relation to a range of civil, political, economic, social and cultural rights, including the rights to physical integrity, to health, to be free from torture and ill-treatment, to privacy, to equality and to non-discrimination [...]

Voting: 390 votes in favour, 153 against and 63 abstentions.

European Parliament, "Backward steps for women's rights and gender equality in the EU" (2018/2684 (RSP)), Resolution, 13 February 2019

The European Parliament [...]

26. Calls on the Commission to include the promotion and improvement of sexual and reproductive health and rights in the next Public Health Strategy;

27. Calls on the Member States to end and reverse cutbacks that apply to gender equality programming, public services and, in particular, the provision of sexual and reproductive healthcare.

Voting: 395 for, 157 against and 62 abstentions.

European Parliament, "European Parliament Resolution on sexual and reproductive health and rights in the EU, in the frame of women's health" (2020/2215 (INI)), 24 June 2021

The European Parliament [...]

33. Reaffirms that abortion must always be a voluntary decision based on a person's request, given of their own free will, in accordance with medical standards and availability, accessibility, affordability and safety based on WHO guidelines and calls on the Member States to ensure universal access to safe and legal abortion, and respect for the right to freedom, privacy and the best attainable health care;

34. Urges the Member States to decriminalise abortion, as well as to remove and combat obstacles to legal abortion, and recalls that they have a responsibility to ensure that women have access to the rights conferred on them by law […]

35. Invites the Member States to review their national legal provisions on abortion and bring them into line with international human rights standards and regional best practices by ensuring that abortion at request is legal in early pregnancy and, when needed, beyond if the pregnant person's health or life is in danger; recalls that a total ban on abortion care or denial of abortion care is a form of gendered-based violence and urges Member States to promote best practices in healthcare by establishing available SRH [sexual and reproductive health] services at primary-care level, with referral systems in place for all required higher-level care;

36. Recognises that for personal reasons, individual medical practitioners may invoke a conscience clause; stresses, however, that an individual's conscience clause may not interfere with a patient's right to full access to healthcare and services; calls on the Member States and healthcare providers to take such circumstances into account in their geographical provision of healthcare services;

37. Regrets that sometimes common practice in Member States allows for medical practitioners, and on some occasions entire medical institutions, to refuse to provide health services on the basis of the so-called conscience clause, which leads to the denial of abortion care on grounds of religion or conscience, and which endangers women's lives and rights; notes that this clause is also used in situations where any delay could endanger the patient's life or health.

Voting: 378 votes in favour, 255 against and 42 abstentions.

European Parliament, "European Parliament Resolution on the first anniversary of the de facto abortion ban in Poland" (2021/2925 (RSP)), 11 November 2021

The European Parliament […]

1. Reiterates its strong condemnation of the illegitimate Constitutional Tribunal's ruling of 22 October 2020 that imposes a near-total ban on abortion and of this blatant attack on SRHR in Poland […]

2. Strongly regrets the absence during the year that has elapsed of any initiative or proposal aimed at lifting the de facto abortion ban and the numerous restrictions

on access to SRHR in the country; reiterates that the de facto abortion ban is putting women's health and lives at risk and has already led to the death of at least one woman; recalls that universal access to healthcare and SRHR are fundamental human rights;

3. Stands in solidarity with Polish women, activists and with the brave individuals and organisations who continue to help women to access abortion care when they need it, as it is their body, their choice [...]

Voting: 373 votes in favour, 124 against and 55 abstentions.

B.3 International legal bases

United Nations, International Covenant on Civil and Political Rights, 16 December 1966

The equality of rights between men and women (Article 3)

The States Parties to the present Covenant undertake to ensure the equal right of men and women to the enjoyment of all civil and political rights set forth in the present Covenant.

Right to life (Article 6)

1. Every human being has the inherent right to life. This right shall be protected by law.

For the UN Human Rights Committee (commonly referred to as the CCPR), the right to life "is the foundation of all human rights" (CCPR, General Comment no. 14, 9 November 1984, paragraph 1).

In the committee's report on the right to life, it requires that "States parties should give information on any measures taken by the State to help women prevent unwanted pregnancies, and to ensure that they do not have to undergo life-threatening clandestine abortions" (CCPR, General Comment no. 28, 29 March 2000, paragraph 10). The Committee also needs to know "whether the State party gives access to safe abortion to women who have become pregnant as a result of rape" (CCPR, General Comment no. 28, 29 March 2000, paragraph 11).

Under the obligations of states parties, the committee considers that:

Although States parties may adopt measures designed to regulate voluntary terminations of pregnancy, such measures must not result in violation of the right to life of a pregnant woman or girl, or her other rights under the Covenant. Thus, restrictions on the ability of women or girls to seek abortion must not, inter alia, jeopardize their lives, subject them to physical or mental pain or suffering which violates article 7, discriminate against them or arbitrarily interfere with their privacy. States parties must provide safe, legal and effective access to abortion where the life and health of the pregnant woman or girl is at risk, or where carrying a pregnancy to term would cause the pregnant woman or girl substantial pain or suffering, most notably where the pregnancy is the result of rape or incest or is not viable. In addition, States parties may not regulate pregnancy or abortion in all other cases in a manner that runs contrary to their duty to ensure that women and girls do not have to undertake unsafe abortions, and they should revise their abortion laws accordingly. For example, they should not take measures such as criminalizing pregnancies by unmarried women or apply criminal sanctions against women and girls undergoing abortion or against medical service providers assisting them in doing so, since taking such measures compels women and girls to resort to unsafe abortion. States parties should not introduce new barriers and should remove existing barriers that deny effective access by women and girls to safe and legal abortion, including barriers caused as a result of the exercise of conscientious objection by individual medical providers. States parties should also effectively protect the lives of women and girls against the mental and physical health risks associated with unsafe abortions. In particular, they should ensure access for women and men, and, especially, girls and boys, to quality and evidence-based information and education about sexual and reproductive health and to a wide range of affordable contraceptive methods, and prevent the stigmatization of women and girls seeking abortion. States parties should ensure the availability of, and effective access to, quality prenatal and post-abortion health care for women and girls, in all circumstances, and on a confidential basis. [CCPR, General Comment no. 36, 30 October 2018, paragraph 8.]

Right not to be subjected to torture (Article 7)

No one shall be subjected to torture or to cruel, inhuman or degrading treatment or punishment.

The Committee reaffirms that the "text of article 7 allows of no limitation [...] and likewise observes that no justification or extenuating circumstances may be invoked to excuse a violation of article 7 for any reasons, including those based on an order from a superior officer or public authority" (CCPR, General Comment no. 20, 10 March 1992, paragraph 3). The prohibition of torture and ill-treatment is absolute and the rights of women not to be subjected to it cannot be balanced against other rights or interests of the state (CCPR, General Comment no. 31, 26 May 2004, paragraph 6).

Right to privacy (Article 17)

> 1. No one shall be subjected to arbitrary or unlawful interference with his privacy.

Unlike the prohibition of torture and ill-treatment, the protection afforded to the right to privacy is not absolute. The room for manoeuvre granted to state sovereignty can be more or less broad. In some cases, for example, the European Court of Human Rights has accorded a wide margin of appreciation to the state in restricting women's sexual and reproductive rights (see below, section on European case law). For its part, the UN Human Rights Committee has recognised the autonomy and power of women, while also restricting them and maintaining the power of the state over reproductive bodies in the case of sterilisation (the husband's consent may be required) or abortion (in states where doctors and health personnel must report it to the public authorities):

> Another area where States may fail to respect women's privacy relates to their reproductive functions, for example, where there is a requirement for the husband's authorization to make a decision in regard to sterilization; where general requirements are imposed for the sterilization of women, such as having a certain number of children or being of a certain age, or where States impose a legal duty upon doctors and other health personnel to report cases of women who have undergone abortion. [CCPR, General Comment no. 28, 29 March 2000, paragraph 20.]

Right to freedom of thought, conscience and religion (Article 18)

> 1. Everyone has the right to freedom of thought, conscience and religion; this right includes freedom to change his religion or belief and freedom, either alone or in community with others and in public or private, to manifest his religion or belief, in worship, teaching, practice and observance [...]

> 3. Freedom to manifest one's religion or beliefs shall be subject only to such limitations as are prescribed by law and are necessary in a democratic society in the interests of public safety, for the protection of public order, health or morals, or for the protection of the rights and freedoms of others.

The Committee considers that this article "may not be relied upon to justify discrimination against women by reference to freedom of thought, conscience and religion" (CCPR, General Comment no. 28, 29 March 2000, paragraph 21).

Concluding observations of the CCPR on abortion made to Poland, Ireland, Malta and Slovakia

Poland, CCPR/C/POL/CO/6, 15 November 2010

12. The Committee is concerned that, in practice, many women are denied access to reproductive health services, including contraception counselling, prenatal testing and lawful interruption of pregnancy. It notes with concern that procedural safeguards contained in article 39 of the Act of 5 December 1996 on the Medical Profession ("conscience clause") are often inappropriately applied. It also notes with concern that illegal abortions are reportedly very common (with estimates of 150,000 illegal abortions per year), that unsafe abortions have, in some cases, caused women's deaths and that those aiding or abetting abortions (such as husbands or parents) have been convicted. It finally notes with concern that a medical commission's decision on a complaint relating to a dissenting medical opinion about an abortion can be unduly delayed because of the 30-day response deadline.

The State party should urgently review the effects of the restrictive anti-abortion law on women.

Ireland, CCPR/C/IRL/CO/4, 19 August 2014

9. The Committee reiterates its previous concern regarding the highly restrictive circumstances under which women can lawfully have an abortion in the State party owing to article 40.3.3 of the Constitution and its strict interpretation by the State party. In particular, it is concerned at: (a) the criminalization of abortion under section 22 of the Protection of Life During Pregnancy Act 2013, including in cases of rape, incest, fatal foetal abnormality and serious risks to the health of the mother, which may lead to up to 14 years of imprisonment, except in cases that constitute a "real and substantive risk" to the life of a pregnant woman; (b) the lack of legal and procedural clarity concerning what constitutes "real and substantive risk" to the life, as opposed to the health, of the pregnant woman; (c) the requirement of [an] excessive degree of scrutiny by medical professionals for pregnant and suicidal women leading to further mental distress; (d) the discriminatory impact of the Act on women who are unable to travel abroad to seek abortions; (e) the strict restrictions on the channels via which information on crisis pregnancy options may be provided

to women and the imposition of criminal sanctions on health-care providers who refer women to abortion services outside the State party under the Regulation of Information (Services Outside the State For Termination of Pregnancies) Act, 1995; and (f) the severe mental suffering caused by the denial of abortion services to women seeking abortions due to rape, incest, fatal foetal abnormality or serious risks to health [...]

The State Party should:

(a) Revise its legislation on abortion, including its Constitution, to provide for additional exceptions in cases of rape, incest, serious risks to the health of the mother, or fatal foetal abnormality.

Malta, CCPR/C/MLT/CO/2, 21 November 2014

13. The Committee is concerned about the general criminalization of abortion, which forces pregnant women to seek clandestine abortion services which put their lives and health at risk. The Committee is concerned that no exception is admitted when a woman's life is in danger or for cases of pregnancy resulting from rape or incest [...]

The State party should revise its legislation on abortion by making exceptions to the general ban on abortion for therapeutic purposes and when the pregnancy is the result of rape or incest.

Slovakia, CCPR/C/SVK/CO/3-5, 20 July 2016

41. The Committee recommends that the State party: [...]

f. Amend legislation to explicitly prohibit institutions from adopting institutional conscience-based refusal policies or practices and establish effective monitoring systems and mechanisms to enable the collection of comprehensive data on the extent of conscience-based refusals of care and the impact of the practice on girls' access to legal reproductive health service.

Findings adopted by the CCPR on relevant communications

Findings on the communication submitted by Amanda Jane Mellet (represented by the Center for Reproductive Rights) v. Ireland, CCPR/116/D/2324/2013, 17 November 2016, paragraph 9

> To that end, the State party should amend its law on the voluntary termination of pregnancy, including if necessary its Constitution, to ensure compliance with the Covenant, ensuring effective, timely and accessible procedures for pregnancy termination in Ireland, and take measures to ensure that health-care providers are in a position to supply full information on safe abortion services without fearing they will be subjected to criminal sanctions.

Findings on the communication submitted by Siobhán Whelan (represented by the Center for Reproductive Rights) v. Ireland, CCPR/C/119/D/2425/2014, 11 July 2017, paragraph 9

The CCPR reiterates the same findings as it did for "Mellet v. Ireland".

United Nations, International Covenant on Economic, Social and Cultural Rights, 16 December 1966

The equality of rights between men and women (Article 3)

> The States Parties to the present Covenant undertake to ensure the equal right of men and women to the enjoyment of all economic, social and cultural rights set forth in the present Covenant.

To ensure gender equality and non-discrimination, the Committee on Economic, Social and Cultural Rights (CESCR) considers that states must respect women's right to make autonomous decisions regarding their sexual and reproductive health (CESCR, General Comment no. 22, 2 May 2016, paragraphs 10, 29 and 34). From this perspective, in order to enjoy sexual and reproductive health and rights, women must be empowered (CESCR, General Comment no. 16, 11 August 2005 and no. 20, 2 July 2009) and states must remove all legal, practical, financial, social and other barriers that undermine, threaten or impair women's sexual and reproductive health and rights (CESCR, General Comment no. 14, 11 August 2000, paragraph 21; General Comment no. 16, 11 August 2005, paragraph 29; General Comment no. 22, 2 May 2016, paragraphs 2, 9, 25–29, 34, 57, 59). The Committee points out that "there exists a wide range of laws, policies and practices that undermine autonomy and [the] right to equality and non-discrimination in the full enjoyment of the right to sexual and reproductive health, for example criminalization of abortion or restrictive abortion laws" (CESCR, General Comment no. 22, 2 May 2016, paragraph 34).

Right to health (Article 12)

1. The States Parties to the present Covenant recognize the right of everyone to the enjoyment of the highest attainable standard of physical and mental health.

The definition of health contained in the preamble to the Constitution of the World Health Organization – that "health is a state of complete physical, mental and social well-being and not merely the absence of disease or infirmity" – is not reflected in Article 12 of the 1966 International Covenant on Economic, Social and Cultural Rights. However, the wording of the latter is not limited to the right to health care: "The right to health embraces a wide range of socio-economic factors that promote conditions in which people can lead a healthy life, and extends to the underlying determinants of health" (CESCR, General Comment no. 14, 11 August 2000, paragraph 4). Further, when the CESCR addresses the right to sexual and reproductive health, it refers to the WHO's definition of sexual health, and also to Programme of Action of the International Conference on Population and Development, for which reproductive health "concerns the capability to reproduce and the freedom to make informed, free and responsible decisions. It also includes access to a range of reproductive health information, goods, facilities and services to enable individuals to make informed, free and responsible decisions about their reproductive behaviour" (CESCR, General Comment no. 22, 2 May 2016, paragraph 6).

The CESCR has defined the content of the right to health, which

entails a set of freedoms and entitlements. The freedoms include the right to make free and responsible decisions and choices, free of violence, coercion and discrimination, regarding matters concerning one's body and sexual and reproductive health. The entitlements include unhindered access to a whole range of health facilities, goods, services and information, which ensure all people full enjoyment of the right to sexual

and reproductive health. [CESCR, General Comment no. 22, 2 May 2016, paragraph 5.]
[...]

Retrogressive measures should be avoided and, if such measures are applied, the State party has the burden of proving their necessity. This applies equally in the context of sexual and reproductive health. Examples of retrogressive measures include the removal of sexual and reproductive health medications from national drug registries; laws or policies revoking public health funding for sexual and reproductive health services; imposition of barriers to information, goods and services relating to sexual and reproductive health; enacting laws criminalizing certain sexual and reproductive health conduct and decisions; and legal and policy changes that reduce oversight by States of the obligation of private actors to respect the right of individuals to access sexual and reproductive health services. [Ibid., paragraph 38.]

The Committee also sets out the obligations of states in relation to the right to health in its General Comment no. 14:

12. The right to health in all its forms and at all levels contains the following interrelated and essential elements, the precise application of which will depend on the conditions prevailing in a particular State party:

(a) Availability [...]

(b) Accessibility [...] [which] has four mutually overlapping dimensions:

(i) non-discrimination [...]

(ii) physical accessibility [...]

(iii) economic accessibility (affordability) [...]

(iv) information accessibility [...]

[...]

33. The right to health, like all human rights, imposes three types or levels of obligations on States parties: the obligations to *respect*, *protect* and *fulfil*. The obligation to fulfil contains obligations to facilitate, provide and promote. [...] The obligation to *fulfil* requires States to adopt appropriate legislative, administrative, budgetary, judicial, promotional and other measures towards the full realization of the right to health.

In this context, the committee stresses in its General Comment no. 22 that:

40. The obligation to *respect* [emphasis added] requires States to refrain from directly or indirectly interfering with the exercise by individuals of the right to sexual and reproductive health. States must not limit or deny anyone access to sexual and reproductive health, including through laws criminalizing sexual and reproductive health services and information, while confidentiality of health data should be maintained. States must reform laws that impede the exercise of the right to sexual and reproductive health. Examples include laws criminalizing abortion [...]

41. The obligation to respect also requires States to repeal, and refrain from enacting, laws and policies that create barriers in access to sexual and reproductive health services. This includes third-party authorization requirements, such as parental, spousal and judicial authorization requirements for access to sexual and reproductive health services and information, including for abortion and contraception; biased counselling and mandatory waiting periods [...] to access to abortion services [...] The dissemination of misinformation and the imposition of restrictions on the right of individuals to access information about sexual and reproductive health also violates the duty to respect human rights. National and donor States must refrain from censoring, withholding, misrepresenting or criminalizing the provision of information on sexual and reproductive health, both to the public and to individuals. Such restrictions impede access to information and services, and can fuel stigma and discrimination.

With regard to the obligation to *protect*, states must:

42. [...] take measures to prevent third parties from directly or indirectly interfering with the enjoyment of the right to sexual and reproductive health. [This obligation] requires States to put in place and implement laws and policies prohibiting conduct by third parties that causes harm to physical and mental integrity or undermines the full enjoyment of the right to sexual and reproductive health, including the conduct of private health-care facilities, insurance and pharmaceutical companies, and manufacturers of health-related goods and equipment. This includes the prohibition of violence and discriminatory practices, such as the exclusion of particular individuals or groups from the provision of sexual and reproductive health services.

43. States must prohibit and prevent private actors from imposing practical or procedural barriers to health services, such as physical obstruction of facilities, dissemination of misinformation, informal fees and third-party authorization

requirements. Where health-care providers are allowed to invoke conscientious objection, States must appropriately regulate this practice to ensure that it does not inhibit anyone's access to sexual and reproductive health care, including by requiring referrals to an accessible provider capable of and willing to provide the services being sought, and that it does not inhibit the performance of services in urgent or emergency situations.

[...]

45. The obligation to *fulfil* [emphasis added] requires States to adopt appropriate legislative, administrative, budgetary, judicial, promotional and other measures to ensure the full realization of the right to sexual and reproductive health. States should aim to ensure universal access without discrimination for all individuals, including those from disadvantaged and marginalized groups, to a full range of quality sexual and reproductive health care, including maternal health care; contraceptive information and services; safe abortion care [...] States must guarantee physical and mental health care for survivors of sexual and domestic violence in all situations, including access to post-exposure prevention, emergency contraception and safe abortion services.

46. The obligation to fulfil also requires States to take measures to eradicate practical barriers to the full realization of the right to sexual and reproductive health, such as disproportionate costs and lack of physical or geographical access to sexual and reproductive health care. States must ensure that health-care providers are adequately trained on the provision of quality and respectful sexual and reproductive health services and ensure that such providers are equitably distributed throughout the State.

47. [...] At the same time, States are required to provide age-appropriate, evidence-based, scientifically accurate comprehensive education for all on sexual and reproductive health.

48. States must also take affirmative measures to eradicate social barriers in terms of norms or beliefs that inhibit individuals of different ages and genders, women, girls and adolescents from autonomously exercising their right to sexual and reproductive health [...]

Concluding observations of the CESCR on abortion made to Poland, E/C.12/POL/CO/5, 2 December 2009

27. [...] The Committee recommends that the State party guarantee adequate access to basic sexual and reproductive health services. The Committee reiterates its recommendation that the State party provide family planning services through the public health-care system, including the provision of affordable contraception.

28. [...] The Committee calls upon the State party to take all appropriate measures to enable women to exercise their right to sexual and reproductive health, including through the enforcement of legislation on abortion and the establishment of a mechanism for the timely and systematic reporting of cases where conscientious objection is opposed. It also asks it to inform the medical profession about the provisions of the Polish legislation on legal termination of pregnancy [...]

United Nations, Convention on the Elimination of all Form of Discrimination Against Women, 18 December 1979

This UN convention explicitly elaborated the concept of reproductive health and reproductive rights. The preamble provides for the prohibition of discrimination based on women's reproductive roles. Article 4 provides for the protection of maternity. Article 10(h) provides for access to family planning education. Article 12, paragraphs 1 and 2, provide for access to reproductive health services:

1. States Parties shall take all appropriate measures to eliminate discrimination against women in the field of health care in order to ensure, on a basis of equality of men and women, access to health care services, including those related to family planning.

2. Notwithstanding the provisions of paragraph I of this article, States Parties shall ensure to women appropriate services in connection with pregnancy, confinement and the post-natal period, granting free services where necessary, as well as adequate nutrition during pregnancy and lactation.

Article 16 provides that women have the same rights as men, including:

1. [...] (e) The same rights to decide freely and responsibly on the number and spacing of their children and to have access to the information, education and means to enable them to exercise these rights.

These articles do not offer an explicit recognition of a right to abortion. This is evidenced by the reservations made by some states to Article 16 (which some states considered could pave the way for such recognition). However, a set of general recommendations issued by the Committee on the Elimination of Discrimination against Women (CEDAW) do recognise two points.

First, they recognize a definition of the right to health that corresponds to the one given by the CESCR and expressed, most notably, at the international conferences in Cairo in 1994 and Beijing in 1995 (CEDAW, General Recommendation no. 24, twentieth session (1999), paragraph 3). To respect this right, the state should adopt and implement a well-budgeted national strategy and plan of action on sexual and reproductive health that prioritises women's sexual and reproductive health (Ibid., paragraphs 29 and 30). It must also ensure access to quality health services that guarantee women respect for their informed consent and confidentiality and that do not allow any form of coercion (Ibid., paragraph 22), and that are also free from all forms of violence (CEDAW, General Recommendation no. 35, 26 July 2017, paragraph 18).

Second, these recommendations recognise that the right to gender equality goes hand in hand with women's autonomy in sexual and reproductive health. In this sense, states are obliged to "require all health services to be consistent with the human rights of women, including the rights to autonomy, privacy, confidentiality, informed consent and choice" (CEDAW, General Recommendation no. 24, twentieth session (1999), paragraph 31). In addition, states must address the disadvantages women face in the enjoyment of their sexual and reproductive rights (CEDAW, General Recommendation no. 24, twentieth session (1999), paragraph 12, and no. 25, thirtieth session (2004), paragraphs 8 and 11). States are also obliged to ensure that women have timely access to the full range of sexual and reproductive health services, goods, infrastructure and information they need. In doing so, they must address relevant shortcomings in regulation and implementation, including by ensuring that denials of care do not compromise women's access to services. The Committee considers that: "It is discriminatory for a State party to refuse to provide legally for the performance of certain reproductive health services for women. For instance, if health service providers refuse to perform such services based on conscientious objection, measures should be introduced to ensure that women are referred to alternative health providers" (CEDAW, General Recommendation no. 24, twentieth session (1999), paragraph 11). The Committee views the right to equality from an intersectional perspective:

The discrimination of women based on sex and gender is inextricably linked with other factors that affect women, such as race, ethnicity, religion or belief, health, status, age, class, caste and sexual orientation and gender identity. Discrimination on the basis of sex or gender may affect women belonging to such groups to a different degree or in different ways to men. States parties must legally recognize such intersecting forms of discrimination and their compounded negative impact on the women concerned and prohibit them. [CEDAW, General Recommendation no. 28, 16 December 2010, paragraph 18.]

CEDAW's concluding observations on abortion made to Greece, Hungary, Poland, Croatia, Slovakia and Germany

Greece, CEDAW/C/GRC/CO/7, 26 March 2013

31. The Committee urges the State Party to:

(a) Improve and increase access [to] as well as use of effective and affordable methods of contraception, including by subsidizing them, in order to starkly reduce the practice of abortion as a method of family planning.

Hungary, CEDAW/C/HUN/CO/7-8, 26 March 2013

30. The Committee notes the State party's statement that the new article in the Fundamental Law protecting life from the moment of conception will not be used to restrict the present legislation and the access of women to abortion. The Committee is concerned about campaigns, including a recent poster campaign, supported by the State party that stigmatize abortion and seek to negatively influence the public view on abortion and contraception; the limited access to emergency contraceptives; the subjection of women who want surgical abortion to biased mandatory counselling and a three-day medically unnecessary waiting period; and at the increasing resort to conscientious objection by health professionals in the absence of an adequate regulatory framework. [...]

31. The Committee urges the State party to:

(a) Cease all negative interference with women's sexual and reproductive rights, including by ending campaigns that stigmatize abortion and seek to negatively influence the public view on abortion and contraception;

(b) Provide adequate access to family planning services and affordable contraceptives, including emergency contraception […], by covering the costs of range of modern contraceptives under the public health insurance and eliminating the prescription requirement for emergency contraception;

(c) Ensure access to safe abortion without subjecting women to mandatory counselling and a medically unnecessary waiting period as recommended by the World Health Organization;

(d) Establish an adequate regulatory framework and a mechanism for monitoring of the practice of conscientious objection by health professionals and ensure that conscientious objection is accompanied by information to women about existing alternatives and that it remains a personal decision rather than an institutionalized practice.

Poland, CEDAW/C/POL/CO/7-8, 14 November 2014

36. The Committee reiterates its concern about the high prevalence of abortions, most of which are illegal as a result of the strict legal requirements contained in the 1993 Act on family planning, human foetus protection and preconditions for the admissibility of abortion. The Committee is also concerned about the restrictive application of this law and the extensive use, or abuse, by medical personnel of the conscientious objection clause. It is further concerned about the lack of official data and research on the prevalence of illegal and unsafe abortions in Poland. The Committee notes the efforts to improve the Act on Patient Rights […] but considers that this will not solve the obstacles that women face when confronted with an unwanted pregnancy. The Committee is also concerned about the limited access to modern contraceptives, including the barriers adolescent girls that may face in accessing information and reproductive health services, including contraception.

37. The Committee recommends that the State party:

(a) Enhance women's access to health care, in particular to sexual and reproductive health services, including by amending the 1993 Act on family planning, human foetus protection and preconditions for the admissibility of abortion, to make the conditions for abortion less restrictive;

(b) Establish clear standards for a uniform and non-restrictive interpretation of the conditions for legal abortion so that women may access it without limitations owing to the excessive use of the so-called conscientious objection clause by doctors and health institutions and ensure effective remedies for contesting refusals of abortion, within the revision of the Act on Patient Rights.

Croatia, CEDAW/C/HRV/CO/4-5, 28 July 2015

30. The Committee notes with concern:

(a) That the right to abortion is being denied by hospitals on the ground of conscientious objection, even though only individual doctors are recognized as having that "right" and hospitals are legally required to ensure the provision of abortions;

(b) The lack of inclusion of abortion and modern contraception in the Croatian Health Insurance Fund, thus discriminating against women because such services are required by them; [...]

31. The Committee urges the State party to:

(a) Ensure that the exercise of conscientious objection does not impede women's effective access to reproductive health-care services, especially abortion and post-abortion care and contraceptives;

(b) Ensure universal coverage of abortion and modern contraception within the Croatian Health Insurance Fund.

Slovakia, CEDAW/C/SVK/CO/5-6, 25 November 2015

30. The Committee notes with concern:

(a) That the adoption of a comprehensive programme on sexual and reproductive health and rights has long been pending, even though rates of teenage pregnancy and infant mortality are high [...]

(b) That the costs of modern forms of contraception for the purpose of preventing unintended pregnancies and abortion on request are not covered by public health insurance;

(c) That an amendment to the Healthcare Act in 2009 introduced a mandatory 48-hour waiting period, compulsory counselling and, in the case of girls under 18 years of age, parental consent before abortion, as well as the duty of doctors to report each case of a woman seeking abortion to the National Health Information Centre with personal details;

(d) That, in more than one third of districts, legal abortion is unavailable and in four of those districts as a result of the conscientious objections of health-care institutions; [...]

31. The Committee urges the State party to: [...]

(b) Revise relevant legislation and ensure universal coverage by public health insurance of all costs relating to legal abortion, including abortion on request, and modern contraceptives for the prevention of unwanted pregnancies;

(c) Revise the Healthcare Act, as amended in 2009, to ensure access to safe abortion and remove the requirement for mandatory counselling, medically unnecessary waiting periods and third-party authorization, in line with the recommendations of the World Health Organization;

(d) Ensure unimpeded and effective access to legal abortion and post-abortion services to all women in the State party, including by ensuring mandatory referrals in cases of conscientious objections by institutions, while respecting individual conscientious objections;

(e) Ensure that information provided by health-care professionals to women seeking abortion is based on science and evidence and covers the risks of having or not having an abortion, to ensure that women are fully informed and can take autonomous decisions;

(f) Ensure the confidentiality of the personal data of women and girls seeking abortion, including by abolishing the requirement to report the personal details of such women and girls to the National Health Information Centre.

Germany, CEDAW/C/DEU/CO/7-8, 9 March 2017

37. The Committee [...] remains concerned about:

(a) The disparities among federal states in the access to affordable contraceptives of women living in poverty;

(b) In accordance with section 218a (1) of the Criminal Code, the subjection of women who wish to have an abortion on request to mandatory counselling and a mandatory three-day waiting period (which the World Health Organization has declared to be medically unnecessary), and the fact that abortion in such cases is not paid for by health insurance [...];

38. In line with its general recommendation no. 24 (1999) on women and health, the Committee recommends that the State party:

(a) Ensure that modern contraceptives are accessible, affordable and available throughout the territory of the State party to all women and girls, in particular those living in poverty and/or in remote areas;

(b) Ensure access to safe abortion without subjecting women to mandatory counselling and a three-day waiting period [...] and ensure that such procedures are reimbursed through health insurance.

United Nations, Convention against Torture and Other Cruel, Inhuman or Degrading Treatment or Punishment, 10 December 1984

Article 2

1. Each State Party shall take effective legislative, administrative, judicial or other measures to prevent acts of torture in any territory under its jurisdiction.

2. No exceptional circumstances whatsoever [...] may be invoked as a justification of torture.

Article 16

1. Each State Party shall undertake to prevent in any territory under its jurisdiction other acts of cruel, inhuman or degrading treatment or punishment which do not amount to torture.

The Committee against Torture (CAT) has issued a general comment stating that the right of women not to be subjected to ill-treatment or torture must always prevail and no attempt should be made to compromise these rights in favour of other rights or the interests of the state (CAT, General Comment no. 2, paragraph 6).

United Nations, Convention on the Rights of the Child, 20 November 1989

Article 6

1. States Parties recognize that every child has the inherent right to life.

2. States Parties shall ensure to the maximum extent possible the survival and development of the child.

Article 24

1. States Parties recognize the right of the child to the enjoyment of the highest attainable standard of health and to facilities for the treatment of illness and rehabilitation of health. [...]

2. States Parties [...] shall take appropriate measures: [...]

(d) To ensure appropriate pre-natal and post-natal health care for mothers; [...]

(f) To develop preventive health care, guidance for parents and family planning education and services.

Concluding observations of the Committee on the Rights of the Child made to Slovakia, CRC/C/SVK/CO/3-5, 25 November 2015

41. The Committee recommends that the State party: [...]

(b) Take effective measures to expand adolescent girls' practical access to affordable contraception, including through training and information programmes designed to improve public and health-care providers' levels of knowledge and evidence-based information on contraception;

(c) Repeal the 2011 prohibition on the public health insurance coverage of contraception, ensure the universal coverage of modern contraception and abortion services under public health insurance and remove the parental consent requirement for abortions and contraceptives requested by adolescent girls above the age of sexual consent;

(d) Take effective measures to ensure adolescent girls' access to safe and legal abortion services, including by repealing legislative provisions which subject them to a mandatory waiting period;

(e) Ensure that health-care professionals provide medically accurate and non-stigmatizing information on abortion and guarantee adolescent girls' confidentiality;

(f) Amend legislation to explicitly prohibit institutions from adopting institutional conscience-based refusal policies or practices and establish effective monitoring systems and mechanisms to enable the collection of comprehensive data on the extent of conscience-based refusals of care and the impact of the practice on girls' access to legal reproductive health services.

B.4 European legal bases

Council of Europe, Convention for the Protection of Human Rights and Fundamental Freedoms, 4 November 1950

Right to life (Article 2)

1. Everyone's right to life shall be protected by law.

Prohibition of torture (Article 3)

No one shall be subjected to torture or to inhuman or degrading treatment or punishment.

Right to respect for private and family life (Article 8)

1. Everyone has the right to respect for his private and family life, his home and his correspondence.

2. There shall be no interference by a public authority with the exercise of this right except such as is in accordance with the law and is necessary in a democratic society in the interests of national security, public safety or the economic well-being of the country, for the prevention of disorder or crime, for the protection of health or morals, or for the protection of the rights and freedoms of others.

Freedom of thought, conscience and religion (Article 9)

1. Everyone has the right to freedom of thought, conscience and religion; this right includes freedom to change his religion or belief and freedom, either alone or in community with others and in public or private [...]

2. Freedom to manifest one's religion or beliefs shall be subject only to such limitations as are prescribed by law and are necessary in a democratic society in the interests of public safety, for the protection of public order, health or morals, or for the protection of the rights and freedoms of others.

Council of Europe, European Social Charter, 18 October 1961 (revised 3 May 1996)

Right to health protection (Article 11)

Part I. Everyone has the right to benefit from any measures enabling him to enjoy the highest possible standard of health attainable.

Part II. With a view to ensuring the effective exercise of the right to protection of health, the Parties undertake, either directly or in cooperation with public or private organisations, to take appropriate measures designed *inter alia*:

1. to remove as far as possible the causes of ill-health;

2. to provide advisory and educational facilities for the promotion of health and the encouragement of individual responsibility in matters of health;

3. to prevent as far as possible epidemic, endemic and other diseases, as well as accidents.

Non-discrimination (part V, Article E)

The enjoyment of the rights set forth in this Charter shall be secured without discrimination on any ground such as race, colour, sex, language, religion, political or other opinion, national extraction or social origin, health, association with a national minority, birth or other status.

A differential treatment based on an objective and reasonable justification shall not be deemed discriminatory.

Council of Europe, Convention on Preventing and Combating Violence against Women and Domestic Violence, 11 May 2011 (better known as the Istanbul Convention)

General support services (Article 20)

2. Parties shall take the necessary legislative or other measures to ensure that victims have access to services facilitating their recovery from violence. These measures should include, when necessary, services such as legal and psychological counselling, financial assistance, housing, education, training and assistance in finding employment.

Support for victims of sexual violence (Article 25)

Parties shall take the necessary legislative or other measures to provide for the setting up of appropriate, easily accessible rape crisis or sexual violence referral centres for victims in sufficient numbers to provide for medical and forensic examination, trauma support and counselling for victims.

Forced abortion and forced sterilisation (Article 39)

Parties shall take the necessary legislative or other measures to ensure that the following intentional conducts are criminalised:

a. performing an abortion on a woman without her prior and informed consent.

European Union, Charter of Fundamental Rights of the European Union, December 2000 (which became binding following the entry into force of the Lisbon Treaty in December 2009)

Human dignity (Article 1)

Human dignity is inviolable. It must be respected and protected.

Right to life (Article 2)

1. Everyone has the right to life.

Right to integrity of the person (Article 3)

1. Everyone has the right to respect for his or her physical and mental integrity.

2. In the fields of medicine and biology, the following must be respected in particular:

a. the free and informed consent of the person concerned, according to the procedures laid down by law;

b. the prohibition of eugenic practices, in particular those aiming at the selection of persons.

Freedom of thought, conscience and religion (Article 10)

2. The right to conscientious objection is recognised, in accordance with the national laws governing the exercise of this right.

Equality between women and men (Article 23)

Equality between women and men must be ensured in all areas, including employment, work and pay.
The principle of equality shall not prevent the maintenance or adoption of measures providing for specific advantages in favour of the under-represented sex.

Health care (Article 35)

Everyone has the right of access to preventive health care and the right to benefit from medical treatment under the conditions established by national laws and practices.

B.5 Bases of European case law

Case law linked to the European Convention on Human Rights

The human right to life does not apply before birth

European Court of Human Rights, "Case of Vo v. France", Application no. 53924/00, decision of 8 July 2004

75. Unlike Article 4 of the American Convention on Human Rights, which provides that the right to life must be protected "in general, from the moment of conception", Article 2 of the Convention is silent as to the temporal limitations of the right to life and, in particular, does not define "everyone" whose "life" is protected by the Convention. The Court has yet to determine the issue of the "beginning" of "everyone's right to life" within the meaning of this provision and whether the unborn child has such a right.

[...]

82. [...] the issue of when the right to life begins comes within the margin of appreciation which the Court generally considers that States should enjoy in this sphere, notwithstanding an evolutive interpretation of the Convention [...] The reasons for that conclusion are, firstly, that the issue of such protection has not been resolved within the majority of the Contracting States [...] and, secondly, that there is no European consensus on the scientific and legal definition of the beginning of life.

Specific forms of torture and ill-treatment related to women's sexuality and reproductive capacity in sexual and reproductive health care

European Court of Human Rights, "Case of V. C. v. Slovakia", Application no. 18968/07, judgement of 8 November 2011

154. [...] Accordingly, the absence at the relevant time of safeguards giving special consideration to the reproductive health of the applicant as a Roma woman resulted in a failure by the respondent State to comply with its positive obligation to secure to her a sufficient measure of protection enabling her to effectively enjoy her right to respect for her private and family life.

*European Court of Human Rights, "Case of I. G.
and Others v. Slovakia", Application no. 15966/04,
judgement of 13 November 2012*

143. [...] In addition, the Court has previously held, with reference to both international and domestic documents, that at the relevant time an issue had arisen in Slovakia as regards sterilisations and their improper use, including disregard for the informed consent required by the international standards by which Slovakia was bound. Such practice was found to affect vulnerable individuals belonging to various ethnic groups. [...]

144. [...] the Court finds that the respondent State failed to comply with its positive obligation under Article 8 to secure through its legal system the rights guaranteed by that Article, by putting in place effective legal safeguards to protect the reproductive health of, in particular, women of Roma origin.

Violation of the prohibition of ill-treatment

*European Court of Human Rights, "Case of R. R. v. Poland",
Application no. 27617/04, judgement of 26 May 2011*

148. According to the Court's well-established case-law, ill-treatment must attain a minimum level of severity if it is to fall within the scope of Article 3. The assessment of this minimum level of severity is relative; it depends on all the circumstances of the case, such as the duration of the treatment, its physical and mental effects and, in some cases, the sex, age and state of health of the victim [...]

149. Treatment has been held by the Court to be "inhuman" because, inter alia, it was premeditated, was applied for hours at a stretch and caused either actual bodily injury or intense physical and mental suffering [...]

150. Treatment has been considered "degrading" when it was such as to arouse in its victims feelings of fear, anguish and inferiority capable of humiliating and debasing them [...]

151. Although the purpose of such treatment is a factor to be taken into account, in particular whether it was intended to humiliate or debase the victim, the absence of any such purpose does not inevitably lead to a finding that there has been no violation of Article 3. [...]

152. Moreover, it cannot be excluded that the acts and omissions of the authorities in the field of health care policy may in certain circumstances engage their responsibility under Article 3 by reason of their failure to provide appropriate medical treatment.

[...]

186. The Court has already held that the issue of when the right to life begins comes within the margin of appreciation which the Court generally considers that States should enjoy in this sphere, notwithstanding an evolutive interpretation of the Convention [...] The reasons for that conclusion are that the issue of such protection has not been resolved within the majority of the Contracting States themselves and that there is no European consensus on the scientific and legal definition of the beginning of life [...] However, the Court considers that there is indeed a consensus amongst a substantial majority of the Contracting States of the Council of Europe towards allowing abortion and that most Contracting Parties have in their legislation resolved the conflicting rights of the foetus and the mother in favour of greater access to abortion. [...] Since the rights claimed on behalf of the foetus and those of the mother are inextricably interconnected, the margin of appreciation accorded to a State's protection of the unborn necessarily translates into a margin of appreciation for that State as to how it balances the conflicting rights of the mother. In the absence of such common approach regarding the beginning of life, the examination of national legal solutions as applied to the circumstances of individual cases is of particular importance also for the assessment of whether a fair balance between individual rights and the public interest has been maintained [...]

187. [...] While a broad margin of appreciation is accorded to the State as regards the circumstances in which an abortion will be permitted in a State, once that decision is taken the legal framework devised for this purpose should be "shaped in a coherent manner which allows the different legitimate interests involved to be taken into account [...]" [...]

[...]

193. The Court has already found that the legal restrictions on abortion in Poland, taken together with the risk of their incurring criminal responsibility under Article 156 § 1 of the Criminal Code, can well have a chilling effect on doctors when deciding whether the requirements of legal abortion are met in an individual case [...]

[...]

197. [...] In the same vein, in the context of pregnancy, the effective access to relevant information on the mother's and foetus' health, where legislation allows for abortion in certain situations, is directly relevant for the exercise of personal autonomy.

[...]

206. [...] For the Court, States are obliged to organise the health services system in such a way as to ensure that an effective exercise of the freedom of conscience of health professionals in the professional context does not prevent patients from obtaining access to services to which they are entitled under the applicable legislation.

European Court of Human Rights, "Case of P. and S. v. Poland", Application no. 57375/08, judgement of 30 October 2012

96. [...] While the Court has held that Article 8 cannot be interpreted as conferring a right to abortion, it has found that the prohibition of abortion when sought for reasons of health and/or well-being falls within the scope of the right to respect for one's private life [...] In particular, the Court held in this context that the State's obligations include both the provision of a regulatory framework of adjudicatory and enforcement machinery [...]

97. The Court has already found that there is indeed a consensus amongst a substantial majority of the Contracting States on the Council of Europe towards allowing abortion and that most Contracting Parties have in their legislation resolved the conflicting rights of the foetus and the mother in favour of greater access to abortion. [...] In the absence of such a common approach regarding the beginning of life, the examination of national legal solutions as applied to the circumstances of individual cases is of particular importance for the assessment of whether a fair balance between individual rights and the public interest has been maintained. [...]

[...]

99. [...] The Court has already found in the context of similar cases against Poland that once the State, acting within its limits of appreciation, adopts statutory regulations allowing abortion in some situations, it must not structure its legal framework in a way which would limit real possibilities to obtain an abortion. In particular, the State is under a positive obligation to create a procedural framework enabling a pregnant woman to effectively exercise her right of access to lawful abortion [...] The Court has already held that in the context of access to abortion the relevant procedure should guarantee to a pregnant woman at least the possibility to be heard in person and to

have her views considered. The competent body or person should also issue written grounds for its decision [...]

Women's lack of access to legal abortion services

European Court of Human Rights, "Case of Tysiąc v. Poland", Application no. 5410/03, judgement of 20 March 2007

116. [...] The Court further notes that the legal prohibition on abortion, taken together with the risk of their incurring criminal responsibility under Article 156 § 1 of the Criminal Code, can well have a chilling effect on doctors when deciding whether the requirements of legal abortion are met in an individual case. [...] Once the legislature decides to allow abortion, it must not structure its legal framework in a way which would limit real possibilities to obtain it.

117. [...] In circumstances such as those in issue in the instant case such a procedure should guarantee to a pregnant woman at least a possibility to be heard in person and to have her views considered. The competent body should also issue written grounds for its decision.

118. In this connection the Court observes that the very nature of the issues involved in decisions to terminate a pregnancy is such that the time factor is of critical importance. The procedures in place should therefore ensure that such decisions are timely so as to limit or prevent damage to a woman's health which might be occasioned by a late abortion. Procedures in which decisions concerning the availability of lawful abortion are reviewed *post factum* cannot fulfil such a function. In the Court's view, the absence of such preventive procedures in the domestic law can be said to amount to the failure of the State to comply with its positive obligations under Article 8 of the Convention.

The margin of appreciation for state discretion over restrictions on women's sexual and reproductive health

European Court of Human Rights, "Case of A, B and C v. Ireland", Application no. 25579/05, judgement of 16 December 2010

212. The Court notes that the notion of "private life" within the meaning of Article 8 of the Convention is a broad concept which encompasses, inter alia, the right to personal autonomy and personal development [...] It concerns subjects such as gender identification, sexual orientation and sexual life [...], a person's physical and

psychological integrity […], as well as decisions both to have and not to have a child or to become genetic parents […]

213. […] The Court has also previously found, citing with approval the case-law of the former Commission, that legislation regulating the interruption of pregnancy touches upon the sphere of the private life of the woman. […] The Court emphasising that Article 8 cannot be interpreted as meaning that pregnancy and its termination pertain uniquely to the woman's private life as, whenever a woman is pregnant, her private life becomes closely connected with the developing foetus. The woman's right to respect for her private life must be weighed against other competing rights and freedoms invoked including those of the unborn child […]

214. For the Court, […] while Article 8 cannot, accordingly, be interpreted as conferring a right to abortion […]

[…]

235. […] The Court considers that there is indeed a consensus amongst a substantial majority of the Contracting States of the Council of Europe towards allowing abortion on broader grounds than accorded under Irish law. […] Ireland is the only State which allows abortion solely where there is a risk to the life (including self-destruction) of the expectant mother. […]

236. However, the Court does not consider that this consensus decisively narrows the broad margin of appreciation of the State.

237. […] Because there was no European consensus on the scientific and legal definition of the beginning of life, so that it was impossible to answer the question whether the unborn was a person to be protected for the purposes of Article 2 of the Convention. […]

238. It is indeed the case that this margin of appreciation is not unlimited. […] A prohibition of abortion to protect unborn life is not therefore automatically justified under the Convention on the basis of unqualified deference to the protection of pre-natal life or on the basis that the expectant mother's right to respect for her private life is of a lesser stature. […] Nor is the regulation of abortion rights solely a matter for the Contracting States. […] The Court must determine whether the Irish State's prohibition of abortion on grounds of health or welfare is compatible with Article 8 of the Convention on the basis of the criterion […] of a fair balance […] [between the right to protection of the life of the unborn child and the right to health of the pregnant woman].

Case law linked to the revised European Social Charter

European Committee of Social Rights, "International Planned Parenthood Federation for Family Planning – European Network (IPPF EN) v. Italy", Complaint no. 87/2012, decision on the merits of 10 September 2013

The European Committee of Social Rights (ECSR) concluded by thirteen votes to one that there was a violation of Article 11, paragraph 1, of the Charter:

> 163. [...] The provision of abortion services must be organised so as to ensure that the needs of patients wishing to access these services are met. This means that adequate measures must be taken to ensure the availability of non-objecting medical practitioners and other health personnel when and where they are required to provide abortion services, taking into account the fact that the number and timing of requests for abortion cannot be predicted in advance.

> [...]

> 168. [...] The high number of objecting health personnel in Italy does not per se constitute evidence that the domestic legal provisions at stake are being implemented in an ineffective manner.

> [...]

> 174. [...] Women seeking access to abortion services can face substantial difficulties in obtaining access to such services in practice, notwithstanding the provisions of the relevant legislation. [...] The aforesaid health facilities do not adopt the necessary measures in order to compensate for the deficiencies in service provision caused by health personnel who decide to invoke their right of conscientious objection [...] The competent regional supervisory authorities do not ensure a satisfactory implementation of Section 9§4 within the territory under their jurisdiction.

The Committee also concluded by thirteen votes to one that there was a violation of Article E in conjunction with Article 11 of the Charter:

> 191. [...] As a result of the lack of non-objecting medical practitioners and other health personnel in a number of health facilities in Italy, women are forced in some cases to move from one hospital to another within the country or to travel abroad [...] in some

cases, this is detrimental to the health of the women concerned. [...] Women concerned are treated differently than other persons in the same situation with respect to access to health care, without justification.

[...]

193. [...] Women denied access to abortion facilities may have to incur substantial economic costs if they are forced to travel to another region or abroad to seek treatment.

European Committee of Social Rights, "Confederazione Generale Italiana del Lavoro (CGIL) v. Italy", Complaint no. 91/2013, decision on admissibility and merits of 12 October 2015

The Committee, bearing in mind the assessment it made in its decision on the merits of the IPPF EN's complaint against Italy, makes the same findings and similarly concludes that there has been a violation of Article 11, paragraph 1, of the Charter. The Committee also notes in paragraph 204 "that the allegations made by CGIL concerning Article E in conjunction with Article 11 [of the Charter] are almost identical to those examined in the IPPF EN v. Italy complaint" and concludes that there has been a violation of those articles.

European Committee of Social Rights, "Federation of Catholic Family Associations in Europe (FAFCE) v. Sweden", Complaint no. 99/2013, decision on the merits of 17 March 2015

69. The Committee notes that the essence of FAFCE's allegations relating to a violation of Article 11 of the Charter is Sweden's failure to establish a legal framework governing the practice of conscientious objection by healthcare providers. The complainant organisation also alleges that, as a result of the lack of such a legal framework, both healthcare providers and medical students are discriminated against in the exercise of their functions or their academic duties whereas this is prohibited by Article E of the Charter.

70. The Committee considers that Article 11 of the Charter does not impose on states a positive obligation to provide a right to conscientious objection for healthcare workers. [...]

71. Consequently, the Committee holds that Article 11 of the Charter does not as such confer a right to conscientious objection on the staff of the health system of a State Party. Therefore, Article 11 is not applicable.

72. [...] Since [...] Article 11 is not applicable, no question of discrimination under Article E can arise. [...]

73. [...] The Committee has consistently held that it is not called upon to address issues of a medical or ethical nature but to interpret the provisions of the Charter from the legal standpoint. The Committee finds that, in the context relating to FAFCE's above-mentioned allegations, States Parties enjoy a wide margin of appreciation in deciding when life begins and it is therefore for each State Party to determine, within this margin of appreciation, the extent to which a foetus has a right to health.

74. The Committee considers that the Government has not exceeded its margin of appreciation as the legislation strikes an appropriate balance between the rights of the woman and the right to health of the foetus.

Appendix C. The main European organisations opposed to abortion rights

C.1 Sources

Datta, Neil. 2013. Keeping it all in the family: Europe's antichoice movement. *Conscience* 34(2), 22–27.

Datta, Neil. 2018. "Restoring the Natural Order": the religious extremists' vision to mobilize European societies against human rights on sexuality and reproduction. European Parliamentary Forum on Population and Development, Brussels.

Ely Yamin, Alicia, Neil Datta and Ximena Andión. 2018. Behind the drama: the roles of transnational actors in legal mobilization over sexual and reproductive rights. *Georgetown Journal of Gender and the Law* 19(3), 533–569.

Kuhar, Roman, and David Paternotte (eds). 2018. *Campagnes anti-genre en Europe. Des mobilisations contre l'égalité.* Lyon: Presses universitaires de Lyon.

Zacharenko, Elena. 2016. Perspectives on anti-choice lobbying in Europe: study for policy makers on opposition to sexual and reproductive health and rights in Europe. The Greens/EFA in the European Parliament, Brussels.

Also consulted were the European Union Transparency Register (last checked in July 2020), LobbyFacts.eu and the websites of the individual organisations.

Table C.1. Agenda Europe.

Date of creation	2013
Headquarters	None
Legal status	De facto association
Website	www.agendaeurope.wordpress.com
Purpose/ objectives	To disseminate a political discourse in line with Vatican directives related to the Church's teachings on issues of public life (the organisation is opposed to sexual and reproductive rights, and lesbian, gay, bisexual and transgender (LGBT) rights, at the EU level)
Key members	• Founder and former director: Sophia Kuby • Grégor Puppinck (European Centre for Law and Justice) • Luca Volontè (president of the Dignitatis Humanae Institute, co-founder of Fondazione Novae Terrae, former president of the European People's Party group in the Parliamentary Assembly of the Council of Europe)
Recognition	• Not listed in the EU Transparency Register • Provides representation for the Holy See at the UN (via Terrence McKeegan), the Council of Europe (via Grégor Puppinck) and the Parliamentary Assembly of the Council of Europe (formerly via Luca Volontè)*
European political relays	• European People's Party • European Christian Political Movement† • Leo van Doesburg (European Christian Political Movement) • Ján Figel (former European Commissioner, appointed in 2016 as special envoy for the promotion of freedom of religion and belief outside the EU)
Scope of actions	• Organising seminars and conferences • Participating in the European Citizens' Initiative (ECI) "One of us" with Citizen GO
Networking	Alliance Defending Freedom International, Citizen GO, European Centre for Law and Justice, Federation of Catholic Family Associations in Europe, Hazte Oir, Ordo Iuris

* Luca Volontè was accused of corruption in the Parliamentary Assembly of the Council of Europe and was barred from entering the Council of Europe for life. See Council of Europe, 2018, "Independent investigation body on the allegations of corruption within the Parliamentary Assembly",15 April.

† Founded in 2002, the European Christian Political Movement is an ecumenical traditionalist political party bringing together Catholic and Protestant fundamentalists and networking with Vatican-inspired organisations, such as the Dignitatis Humanae Institute and Agenda Europe. It has set up a research foundation called the Christian Political Foundation for Europe.

Table C.2. Alliance Defending Freedom International.

Date of creation	1994
Headquarters	Vienna; office in Brussels
Legal status	Status not found.
Website	www.adfinternational.org
Purpose/ objectives	To defend religious freedom; the sanctity of life, marriage and family; freedom of conscience; and the conscience clause with regard to abortion
Key members	Director of strategic relations and training: Sophia Kuby (founder and former director of Agenda Europe, and founder and former executive director of European Dignity Watch)
Recognition	• Listed in the EU Transparency Register under no. 69403354038-78 since 20 August 2010 • Accredited with the EU, the United Nations Economic and Social Council (ECOSOC) and the Organization of American States • Participates in the European Union Agency for Fundamental Rights (based in Vienna) • Active in the Organization for Security and Co-operation in Europe
European political relays	Works with the European People's Party (within its Working Group on Bioethics and Human Dignity)
Scope of actions	• Organising training courses • Drafting documents, such as the "Declaration on the importance of strengthening the fundamental right to freedom of conscience" (April 2016), signed by 21 MEPs from different conservative political groups • Advocating at the legal level before the European Court of Human Rights (see the case "A, B and C v. Ireland") • Participating in the international campaigns against the funding of the International Planned Parenthood Federation and MSI Reproductive Choices* and against the Estrela Report
Networking	European Dignity Watch

* MSI Reproductive Choices, known as Marie Stopes International until 2020, is an international non-governmental organisation (INGO) established in London in 1976. It promotes sexual and reproductive health, including access to safe and legal contraception and abortion. See www .msichoices.org.uk.

Table C.3. Citizen GO.

Date of creation	2013
Headquarters	Platform created by Hazte Oir (Madrid)
Legal status	De facto association
Website	www.citizengo.org
Purpose/ objectives	To fight abortion and euthanasia
Key members	• President: Ignacio Arsuaga • Director: Luca Volontè (president of the Dignitatis Humanae Institute, former president of the European People's Party group in the Parliamentary Assembly of the Council of Europe)
Recognition	Not listed in the EU Transparency Register
European political relays	European People's Party
Scope of actions	• Launching online anti-abortion petitions, including one against the Estrela Report • Participating in the ECI "One of us"
Networking	• Links to the Dignitatis Humanae Institute, Fondazione Novae Terrae and Hazte Oir • Member of the One of Us European Federation

Table C.4. Protestant Evangelical Committee for Human Dignity (CPDH).

Date of creation	1999
Headquarters	Strasbourg
Legal status	Status not found
Website	https://cpdh.org
Purpose/ objectives	To respect human dignity and defend the right to life from conception
Key members	President: Frank Meyer
Recognition	• Formerly listed (as of 6 September 2011) in the EU Transparency Register under no. 13577216582-32 • Partner of European institutions in dialogue with religious and non-confessional organisations (in line with Article 17.3 of the Treaty on the Functioning of the European Union (TFEU))
European political relays	Not documented
Scope of actions	Participating in the ECI "One of us"
Networking	Alliance Vita,* European Centre for Law and Justice, European Dignity Watch

* Alliance Vita is an association founded in France in 1993, at the time of the first laws on bioethics. It fights against abortion and euthanasia rights. See www.alliancevita.org.

Table C.5. Commission of the Bishops' Conferences of the European Union (COMECE).

Date of creation	1980
Headquarters	Ixelles
Legal status	AISBL under Belgian law, registered in the *Moniteur belge* under no. 12505/80 on 27 November 1980 under the name *Association des Episcopats de la Communauté européenne* (company no. 0420 688 307)
Website	www.comece.eu
Purpose/ objectives	To support the policies and legislative initiatives of the EU in every area of interest to the Catholic Church in the context of its social doctrine
Key members	• Bishops delegated by the Catholic bishops' conferences of the 27 EU member states • Secretary general: Father Manuel Enrique Barrios Prieto
Recognition	• AISBL, listed under the the name Secretariat of COMECE (Commission of the Episcopates of the European Union) in the EU Transparency Register under no. 47350036909-69 since 7 October 2011 • Accredited with the European Parliament • Partner of European institutions in dialogue with religious and non-confessional organisations (Article 17.3 TFEU)
European political relays	Not documented
Scope of actions	• Producing expert reports and studies • Informing European institutions of the positions of the bishops' conferences of the EU • Communicating the positions of the Catholic Church to EU policymakers, MEPs and senior officials of EU institutions • Monitoring European policies
Networking	See "Key members" and "Recognition"

Table C.6. Dignitatis Humanae Institute.

Date of creation	2008
Headquarters	Collepardo (Italy)
Legal status	Status not found
Website	www.dignitatishumanae.com
Purpose/objectives	• "To promote human dignity based on the anthropological truth that man is born in the image of God" • To promote a Universal Declaration of Human Dignity based on the sanctity of life from conception to natural death, open for signature by European and national members of parliament
Key members	• Founder and first president: Benjamin Harnwell (former parliamentary attaché to Nirj Deva) • Honorary president (2010–19): Cardinal Renato Raffaele Martino (honorary president of the Pontifical Council for Justice and Peace) • President: Luca Volontè (former president of the European People's Party group in the Parliamentary Assembly of the Council of Europe) • Rocco Buttiglione (European Commissioner candidate for justice, freedom and security, rejected by the European Parliament in 2004) • Nirj Deva (European Conservatives and Reformists MEP, 2009–19; co-founder in 2009 of the Working Group on Human Dignity in the European Parliament) • Leo van Doesburg (European Christian Political Movement)
Recognition	Not listed in the EU Transparency Register
European political relays	European Christian Political Movement
Scope of actions	• Organising international seminars and colloquiums, including at the Pontifical Academy of Social Sciences • Producing research and publications • Participating in the ECI "One of us"
Networking	Fondazione Novae Terrae, European Christian Political Movement

Table C.7. European Centre for Law and Justice.

Date of creation	1998
Headquarters	Strasbourg
Legal status	INGO
Website	https://eclj.org
Purpose/ objectives	"The ECLJ bases its action on 'the spiritual and moral values which are the common heritage of the [European] peoples and the source of the principles of individual freedom, political liberty and the rule of law, on which all genuine democracy is founded' (Preamble to the Statute of the Council of Europe)"
Key members	Director: Grégor Puppinck
Recognition	• Registered as an INGO with the Strasbourg district court • Not listed in the EU Transparency Register • Accredited with the EU • Has special consultative status with the United Nations Economic and Social Council (ECOSOC) • Active in the Organization for Security and Co-operation in Europe • Accredited with the Holy See for its delegation to the Council of Europe
European political relays	Luca Volontè (president of the Dignitatis Humanae Institute, former president of the European People's Party group in the Parliamentary Assembly of the Council of Europe)
Scope of actions	• Providing legal expertise, including on abortion prevention, conscientious objection, religious freedom, and human life and dignity • Engaging in legal advocacy • Representing clients at the European Court of Human Rights, Council of Europe, Organization for Security and Co-operation in Europe, UN and EU with regard to conscientious objection and other sexual and reproductive rights issues • Acting as legal representative of the ECI "One of us"
Networking	Member of the One of Us European Federation

Table C.8. European Dignity Watch.

Date of creation	2010
Headquarters	Etterbeek
Legal status	AISBL under Belgian law, registered in the *Moniteur belge* on 9 April 2010 under company no. 0824 846 032
Website	www.europeandignitywatch.org
Purpose/ objectives	To protect the family on the basis of the complementarity of men and women in stable relationships as the foundation of family life
Key members	• Founder and director: Jorge Soley Climent • Founder, director and former executive director (2010–14): Sophia Kuby • Executive director: Roxana Stanciu
Recognition	AISBL, formerly listed (as of 1 September 2016) in the EU Transparency Register under no. 734182823220-08
European political relays	Not documented
Scope of actions	• Producing policy analysis and research on bioethical issues • Establishing a network of NGOs and experts who meet with MEPs and EU officials to communicate views opposed to freedom of choice • Playing a central role in supporting the ECI "One of us" • Coordinating letters to be sent to MEPs to protest against abortion rights initiatives
Networking	Alliance Defending Freedom International, One of Us European Federation, Ordo Iuris

Table C.9. One of Us European Federation.

Date of creation	2014
Headquarters	Ixelles
Legal status	AISBL under Belgian law, registered in the *Moniteur belge* on 15 October 2014 under the name ONE OF US European Federation for Life and Human Dignity under company no. 0564 729 644
Website	www.oneofus.eu
Purpose/ objectives	To call for an end to EU funding of actions that involve or result in the destruction of human embryos (in relation to the EU budget, development aid and research)
Key members	• President: Jaime Mayor Oreja • President of the ECI "One of us": Grégor Puppinck (European Centre for Law and Justice)
Member organisations	40 Days for Life, Actie voor het gezin-family/Action pour la famille, AESVIDA (Árbol de Esperanza de Vida), ANDOC-Asociación Nacional para la Defensa al Derecho a la Objeción de Conciencia, Asociación de bioetica Universidad Católica De Valencia, Associazione Comunità Papa Giovanni XXIII, Associazione Diffendere la Vita con Maria, Associazione Medici Cattolici Italiani (AMCI), Bundesverleben, Cidevida, Ciencia, vida y cultura (CIVICA), Citizen GO, Diaconia, Donum-vitae, European Center for Law and Justice, Familia y Dignidad Humana, Federação Portuguesa Pela Vida, Federación Española de Asociaciones Provida, Fondation Jérôme Lejeune, Foro Español de la Familia, Foro Universitario SYNTHESIS, Forum vitae, Fórum života, Fundação AJB (A Junção do Bem), Fundación Jérôme Lejeune, Fundación Más Vida, Fundación Red madre, Guido de Brès-Stichting, Hazte Oir, Hnutí Pro život ČR, Izbor za zhivot, Life Network Foundation Malta, Movimento italiano per la vita, Œuvre pour la protection de la vie naissante, Polska Federacja Ruchów Obrony Życia i Rodziny/Fundacji "Jeden z nas", Polskie Stowarzyszenie Obrońców Życia Człowieka, Precious Life, Profesionales por la Ética, Rally for Life, Respekt, Retten til Liv, Right To Life, Schreeuw om Leven, Stiftung Ja Zum Leben, Valores y Sociedad, Zavod za pravico do življenja (ŽIV!M)
Recognition	AISBL, listed in the EU Transparency Register under no. 478454716012-16 since 11 February 2015
European political relays	• European Conservatives and Reformists: Tobbias Teuscher (deputy secretary general of the group in the European Parliament) • European People's Party: Carlo Casini (deceased) (MEP, 1984–99 and 2006–14; member of the Pontifical Academy for Life and honorary president of Movimento per la Vita), Dana Rosemary Scallon (MEP, 1999–2004), Anna Záborská (MEP, 2004–19) • European Christian Political Movement

Table C.9. Continued.

Scope of actions	• Lobbying and launching petitions • Participating in pleadings before the European Court of Human Rights • Organising the ECI "One of us" (1.7 million signatures), supported by Pope Francis
Networking	• Links to the European Centre for Law and Justice • Connections through the ECI "One of us"

Table C.10. Federation of Catholic Family Associations in Europe (FAFCE).

Date of creation	1997
Headquarters	Ixelles
Legal status	NGO
Website	www.fafce.org
Purpose/ objectives	"To promote the interests of the family at the political level. To adopt a Christian approach based on the social and family teachings of the Catholic Church [and] explicitly to refer to the Social Doctrine of the Catholic Church."
Key members	• President: Vincenzo Bassi • Secretary general: Nicola Speranza • Former president (2009–19): Antoine Renard (*Confédération nationale des associations familiales catholiques*, France; a candidate on the "*Force vie*" list – submitted by former minister Christine Boutin – in the 2014 European elections)
Member organisations	Asociaţia Familiilor Catolice "Vladimir Ghika", Cana Movement Catholic Institute, Confédération nationale des associations familiales catholiques (CNAFC), Familienbund der Katholiken, Family Solidarity Ely House, Federazione Italiana Scuole Materne (FISM), Forum delle associazioni familiari (FORUM), Fundação AJB (A Junção do Bem), Hnutie kresťanských rodín na Slovensku (HKR), Katholischer Familienverband Österreich, Katholischer Familienverband Südtirol (KFS), Klub Mnohodetných Rodín, Lietuvos šeimos centras, Magyar Katolikus Családegyesület, Polska Federacja Ruchów Obrony Życia i Rodziny/Fundacji "Jeden z nas", Rodinný svaz ČR, Stowarzyszenie Przymierze Rodzin, Unión familiar española
Recognition	• NGO registered with the Strasbourg district court, with participatory status in the Council of Europe and listed in the EU Transparency Register under no. 509209111889-44 since 17 September 2013 • Represents 18 Catholic family associations before the Council of Europe (participatory status) and the European Parliament (accreditation) • Member of the European Union Agency for Fundamental Rights
European political relays	Not documented

Table C.10. Continued.

Scope of actions	• Producing anti-abortion publications • Lobbying • Participating in the ECI "One of us", as well as protesting against the directive on the principle of equal treatment between persons irrespective of their religion, belief, age, disability or sexual orientation • During the 2014 European elections, launching the "Vote for family 2014 manifesto", a call to vote for a pro-family pledge, which would include respect for life from conception
Networking	European Dignity Watch, Hazte Oir, La Manif pour Tous*

* Founded in 2012, La Manif pour Tous is a collective of French organisations that led to the largest of the demonstrations against the law on same-sex marriage in France, and that fought against the demand for the right to homoparentality (same-sex parenting via adoption, medically assisted reproduction and surrogate motherhood). This collective brings together associations such as Alliance Vita, the *Confédération nationale des associations familiales catholiques*, the *Fédération nationale des associations familiales protestantes*, and the Fondation Jérôme Lejeune.

Table C.11. Pro Europa Christiana Federation.

Date of creation	2002
Headquarters	Creutzwald
Legal status	Local law association (Alsace–Lorraine)
Website	www.federation-pro-europa-christiana.org
Purpose/ objectives	• To act as an umbrella organisation of national associations in order influence the social and moral development of Europe from a Christian perspective with an ultramontane vision • To defend life from conception to natural death
Key members	Director of the Brussels office: Duke Paul von Oldenburg
Member organisations	Acção Família; Avenir de la culture; Deutsche Vereinigung für eine Christliche Kultur (DVCK) eV; Droit de naître; Instytut Edukacji Społecznej i Religijnej im. Księdza Piotra Skargi; Luci sull'Est; Österreichische Jugend für eine christlich-kulturelle Gesellschaft im deutschsprachigen Raum (ÖJ – CGDR); Tradición y Acción; Tradition, Family, Property*
Recognition	Local law association (Alsace–Lorraine), formerly listed (as of 19 September 2011) in the EU Transparency Register under no. 65395896737-91
European political relays	Beatrix von Storch (MEP, 2014–17; member of the European Conservatives and Reformists group, then of the Europe of Freedom and Direct Democracy group), Anna Záborská (European People's Party MEP, 2004–19)
Scope of actions	• Producing political papers • Organising seminars, retreats for male youths and training courses from a perspective radically opposed to freedom of choice • Organising Walks for Life • Updating the *L'Ultramontain* blog
Networking	One of Us European Federation, Zivile Koalition eV (a Christian fundamentalist wing of Alternative für Deutschland)

* Tradition, Family, Property is an international organisation of militant conservative Catholics founded in 1960 in Brazil by landowner Plinio Corrêa de Oliveira, with the aim of fighting against the "external enemy" of communism and the "internal enemy" of liberation theology. The organisation has spread to other parts of Latin America as well as the United States and Europe.

Table C.12. Fondazione Novae Terrae.

Date of creation	2008
Headquarters	Milan
Legal status	Foundation registered in the Register of Legal Entities of the Prefecture of Milan
Website	www.novaeterrae.eu
Purpose/ objectives	To oppose freedom of choice in sexual and reproductive rights issues
Key members	• Co-founder and president: Emanuele Fusi • Co-founder: Luca Volontè (president of the Dignitatis Humanae Institute, former president of the European People's Party group in the Parliamentary Assembly of the Council of Europe)
Recognition	• Not listed in the EU Transparency Register • No EU accreditation
European political relays	European People's Party
Scope of actions	• Organising conferences • Formulating policy guidelines • Producing research on issues such as the defence of the family and the right to life • During the 2014 European elections, calling for future elected representatives to demand a European roadmap on family rights
Networking	Agenda Europe, Citizen GO, Dignitatis Humanae Institute, European Centre for Law and Justice, Fondation Jérôme Lejeune*

* The Fondation Jerôme Lejeune is a French foundation created in 1996 and is recognised as an association of public utility. It supports research on Down's syndrome, and it is one of the main French associations fighting against abortion and euthanasia rights. See www.manifestedes350.be.

Table C.13. Fundacja Instytut na rzecz Kultury Prawnej Ordo Iuris (Ordo Iuris Institute for Legal Culture).

Date of creation	2013
Headquarters	Warsaw; office in Brussels
Legal status	Foundation
Website	www.ordoiuris.pl
Purpose/ objectives	To promote the values of the natural order
Key members	• President: Jerzy Kwaśniewski • Co-founder and first president: Aleksander Stępkowski (former secretary of state for foreign affairs, appointed in 2019 to the Polish Supreme Court) • Partner: Jakob Cornides (European Commission official)
Recognition	• Foundation, listed in the EU Transparency Register under no. 206499215012-94 since 25 November 2014 • Representative of the Organization for Security and Co-operation in Europe
European political relays	Marek Jurek (European Conservatives and Reformists MEP, 2009–19; president of the Polish Sejm, 2005–7)
Scope of actions	• Organising seminars and hearings, and training young lawyers in a perspective opposed to freedom of choice • Drafting the 2016 Polish bill to abolish all abortion rights and generally providing legal expertise • Monitoring European policies • Participating in the ECI "One of us"
Networking	Alliance Defending Freedom International; European Centre for Law and Justice; European Dignity Watch; One of Us European Federation; Tradition, Family, Property – Poland

Table C.14. Hazte Oir.

Date of creation	2001
Headquarters	Madrid
Legal status	NGO under Spanish law
Website	hazteoir.org
Purpose/ objectives	To act as a platform for campaigns against freedom of choice
Key members	Founder, president and CEO: Ignacio Arsuaga
Recognition	• Not listed in the EU Transparency Register • No EU accreditation • Recognised as an association of public utility by Spanish Minister of the Interior Jorge Fernández Díaz (Partido Popular) in 2013
European political relays	Not documented
Scope of actions	• Calling for the "*Vota Valores*" commitment in the 2014 European elections • Producing information about the positions of different candidates on sexual and reproductive rights • Sending letters and emails opposing the Estrela Report to national and European parliamentarians • Creating the Derecho a Vivir association (in 2008) and the Citizen GO platform (in 2013)
Networking	• Links to Citizen GO • Member of the One of Us European Federation

Table C.15. European Institute of Bioethics.

Date of creation	2001
Headquarters	Etterbeek
Legal status	ASBL under Belgian law, registered in the *Moniteur belge* under company no. 0476 616 329
Website	www.ieb-eib.org
Purpose/ objectives	• To develop "critical vigilance with regard to scientific and technical advances – particularly in the field of biomedicine – and the legislation that accompanies them". • "To contribute to the development of bioethics based on the respect for and promotion of the human person from conception to natural death."
Key members	President: Éléonore Delwaide Members of the honorary committee: Albert Guigui (chief rabbi of Brussels), Prince Nikolaus of Liechtenstein, Miroslav Mikolášik (European People's Party MEP, 2004–19), Anna Záborská (European People's Party MEP, 2004–19)
Recognition	ASBL, listed in the EU Transparency Register under no. 93555467379-80 since 8 December 2011
European political relays	European People's Party
Scope of actions	• Organising seminars and conferences • Writing publications and open letters from a perspective that rejects freedom of choice
Networking	Alliance Vita, Fondation Jérôme Lejeune

Appendix D. The main European organisations supporting abortion rights

D.1 Sources

Ayoub, Philip M., and David Paternotte. 2016. L'International Lesbian and Gay Association (ILGA) et l'expansion du militantisme LGBT dans une Europe unifiée. *Critique internationale* (70), 55–70.

Jacquot, Sophie. 2011. Le lobby européen des femmes : de l'exception à la marginalisation ? Conference paper, Fourth International Congress of Francophone Political Science Associations, Brussels, April.

Jacquot, Sophie. 2017. "Nous étions des militantes, maintenant ce sont des fonctionnaires ma chère" : la professionnalisation de la politique européenne d'égalité entre les femmes et les hommes. In *La professionnalisation des luttes pour l'égalité : genre et féminisme*, edited by Petra Meier and David Paternotte, pp. 47–66. Louvain-la-Neuve: Academia-L'Harmattan.

Also consulted were the *Encyclopédie d'histoire numérique de l'Europe* (https://ehne.fr), the European Union Transparency Register (last checked in July 2020), LobbyFacts.eu and the websites of the individual organisations.

Table D.1. ASTRA (Central and Eastern European Network for Sexual and Reproductive Health and Rights).

Date of creation	1999
Headquarters	Warsaw
Legal status	Informal network of organisations
Website	https://astra.org.pl
Purpose/ objectives	• An informal network of 44 women's rights organisations from Central and Eastern European countries • Aims to empower women and girls through the transformation of gender relations, particularly around reproductive and sexual rights
Key members	Members of the advisory board: Daniela Draghici, Krystyna Kacpura (secretary), Medea Khmelidze and Iatamze Verulashvili
Member organisations	AnA Society for Feminist Analysis; Asociaţia pentru Libertate şi Egalitate de Gen (ALEG); Association HERA XXI; BaBe (Budi aktivna, Budi emancipiran); BOCS Alapítványt; Bulgarian Family Planning and Sexual Health Association (BFPA); Bulgarian Gender Research Foundation (BGRF); Center "Women and Modern World" (CW&MW); Center for Reproductive Rights; CESI (Centar za edukaciju, savjetovanje i istraživanje); CIDSR (Centrul de Instruire în Domeniul Sănătăţii Reproductive); DEMETRA Association; East Europe and Central Asia Union of People Living with HIV (ECUO); East European Institute for Reproductive Health; ESE (Association for Emancipation, Solidarity and Equality of Women); Euroregional Center for Public Initiatives; Family Planning Association of Moldova; Federacja na Rzecz Kobiet i Planowania Rodziny; Gender Alternatives Foundation; Gender and Development Tadjikistan; Gender Education, Research and Technologies Foundation (GERT); Grupa Ponton Edukacja Seksualna; Health Education and Research Association (HERA) – Macedonia; Istiqbolli Avlod; Macedonian Women's Rights Center – Shelter Center (MWRC); Možnosť voľby; Novgorod Gender Center; Papardes zieds; PATENT (Patriarchátust Ellenzők Társasága); Qendra Shqiptare për Popullsinë dhe Zhvillimin (QShPZh); Russian Association for Population and Development; SALUS Charitable Foundation; Sana Sezim; Sarajevski Otvoreni Centar; Šeimos planavimo ir seksualinės sveikatos asociacija; SEXUL vs BARZA; Society Without Violence; UDRUGA PARiTER; Union Women's Center; Women's Health and Family Planning; Women's Independent Democratic Movement (PA "WIDM"); Women's Resource Center of Armenia; Women's Rights Center; Ženska soba
Recognition	Not listed in the EU Transparency Register
European political relays	Not documented

Table D.1. Continued.

Scope of actions	• Providing expertise and advocacy at international and regional conferences on women's rights, in particular sexual and reproductive rights • Training NGO leaders and young lawyers • Drafting open letters to representatives of the EU and the UN
Networking	International Women's Health Coalition

Table D.2. Catholics for Choice.

Date of creation	1973
Headquarters	Washington
Legal status	NGO
Website	www.catholicsforchoice.org
Purpose/ objectives	• To obtain freedom of choice • To make the voice of Catholic supporters of women's free choice in sexual and reproductive rights heard
Key members	• President: Jamie Manson • Chair of the board of directors: Victor Reyes
Recognition	• Accredited with special consultative status with the United Nations Economic and Social Council (ECOSOC) and with participation in UN conference forums • Not listed in the EU Transparency Register
European political relays	Not documented
Scope of actions	• Producing publications, including the *Conscience* magazine • Corresponding with European parliamentarians on sexual and reproductive rights • Organising a global public education campaign called Condoms for Life (www.condoms4Life.org)
Networking	• Links to the International Planned Parenthood Federation European Network, the Planned Parenthood Federation of America and the Religious Coalition for Reproductive Choice • Member of ASTRA and the High Ground Alliance for Choice and Dignity in Europe

Table D.3. Center for Reproductive Rights.

Date of creation	1992
Headquarters	New York
Legal status	NGO
Website	www.reproductiverights.org
Purpose/ objectives	To fight for women's autonomy in matters of reproductive and sexual rights, from an emancipatory perspective and through the use of legislation and judicial procedures
Key members	• Chair of the board of directors: Amy Metzler Ritter • Vice-president: Joseph Stern • President and CEO: Nancy Northup
Recognition	• NGO, with participatory status in the Council of Europe and listed in the EU Transparency Register under no. 200145833328-59 since 26 November 2018 • Collaborates with various UN agencies, such as the United Nations Population Fund and the World Health Organization
European political relays	Not documented
Scope of actions	• Using human rights legal instruments • Organising legal advocacy for reproductive rights • Providing expertise on legislative proposals and bills • Lobbying policymakers on reproductive rights • Acting as a representative for applicants before the monitoring committees of international and European conventions and before the European Court of Human Rights • Monitoring state obligations and producing alternative reports to those of states for the monitoring committees of international conventions • Organising national and international campaigns
Networking	• Links to the Africa Reproductive Rights Initiative (ARRI), the Coalición de Derechos Humanos de las Américas and the South Asia Reproductive Justice and Accountability Initiative (SARJAI) • Co-founder of the International Initiative on Maternal Mortality and Human Rights, which brings together some 1,000 organisations in 192 countries to fight for sexual and reproductive rights and maternal health, and on behalf of premature babies, children and adolescents (www.righttomaternalhealth.org)

Table D.4. European Humanist Federation.

Date of creation	1992
Headquarters	Ixelles
Legal status	AISBL under Belgian law, registered in the *Moniteur belge* under no. 19057/92 on 29 October 1992 (company no. 0448 534 037)
Website	www.humanistfederation.eu
Purpose/ objectives	• An umbrella organisation for 55 non-religious organisations, including humanists, freethinkers, agnostics, atheists, rationalists and non-believers • Aims to promote secularism in Europe and at the EU level
Key members	• President: Michael Bauer • Director: Hervé Parmentier
Member organisations	Allianz vun Humanisten, Atheisten an Agnostiker Lëtzebuerg, Asociaţia Secular-Umanistă din România (ASUR), Asociaţia Umanistă Română, Associação Cívica República e Laicidade (R&L), Associació per a l'humanisme, Associazione Luca Coscioni per la libertà di ricerca scientifica, Ateistisk Selskab, Atheist Union of Greece, Bund Freireligiöser Gemeinden Deutschlands, Centar za građansku hrabrost, Central London Humanist Group, Centre d'action laïque (CAL), Centrum voor Academische en Vrijzinnige Archieven (CAVA)/ Centrum voor Vrijzinnig Humanistische Erfgoed (CVHE), Conway Hall Ethical Society, Cyprus Humanist Association, Dachverband Freier Weltanschauungsgemeinschaften (DFW), deMens.nu, Égalité Laïcité Europe (ÉGALE), ETHOS-Etika Tolerancia Humanizmus Občianstvo Sekularizmus, Europa Laica, European Humanist Professionals (EHP), Freidenker-Vereinigung der Schweiz/Association suisse de la libre pensée (FVS/ASLP), Fundació Ferrer i Guàrdia, Giordano Bruno Stiftung (GBS), Good Sense, Human-Etisk Forbund, Humanismo Secular Portugal, Humanist Association of Ireland, Humanist Society Scotland, Humanist Union of Greece, Humanisterna, Humanistisch Verbond, Humanistische Vereinigung, Humanistischer Verband Deutschlands, Humanistischer Verband Österreich, Humanistisk Samfund, Humanists UK, La Ligue de l'enseignement, Malta Humanist Association, National Secular Society, North East Humanists, Polskie Stowarzyszenie Racjonalistów, RIKZ.Z (Raad voor Inspectie en Kwaliteitszorg niet-confessionele Zedenleer), Russian Humanist Society, Siðmennt, South West London Humanists, Spoločnosť Prometheus, Stichting HSHB, Suomen Humanistiliitto, Towarzystwo Humanistyczne, Union des familles laïques (UFAL), Union rationaliste (UR), Unione degli Atei e degli Agnostici Razionalisti, Vapaa-ajattelijain liitto ry

Table D.4. Continued.

Recognition	AISBL, with participatory status in the Council of Europe and listed under the name European Humanist Federation in the EU Transparency Register under no. 84310943110-81 since 24 January 2010
European political relays	Not documented
Scope of actions	• Providing ethical, legal, political and scientific expertise on European and international public policies around freedom of conscience, freedom of expression, the rule of law and non-discrimination • Proposing European regulations that facilitate the development and promotion of its members' activities • Sharing information and experiences to contribute to the development of secular and humanist values in Europe • Issuing public statements to European institutions
Networking	• Links to Catholics for Choice; the Center for Inquiry (CFI); Civil Society Europe; the European Parliamentary Forum for Sexual and Reproductive Rights; the European Parliament Platform for Secularism in Politics; Humanists International; the International Planned Parenthood Federation European Network (IPPF EN); the European Women's Lobby; the European Region of the International Lesbian, Gay, Bisexual, Trans and Intersex Association (ILGA-Europe); and Young Humanists International • Member of the High Ground Alliance for Choice and Dignity in Europe

Table D.5. European Parliamentary Forum for Sexual and Reproductive Rights (EPF).

Date of creation	2004 (originally a project of the International Planned Parenthood Federation European Network (IPPF EN); until 2019 the organisation was known as the European Parliamentary Forum on Population and Development)
Headquarters	Brussels
Legal status	INGO
Website	www.epfweb.org
Purpose/ objectives	A network that serves as a platform for cooperation and coordination among parliamentarians from all over Europe who are committed to improving the sexual and reproductive health and rights of the world's most vulnerable people at home and abroad
Key members	• President: Petra Bayr • Secretary general: Neil Datta
Recognition	INGO, with participatory status in the Council of Europe and listed in the EU Transparency Register under no. 96700978173-62 since 28 February 2012
European political relays	• All political parties committed to the issue of sexual and reproductive health and rights from a pro-choice perspective • European Parliament Working Group on Reproductive Health, HIV/AIDS and Development (EPWG), with which it collaborates
Scope of actions	Providing services to parliamentarians: • offering expertise by organising conferences, seminars and training sessions on issues related to sexual and reproductive health and rights; • acting as a framework for building consensus and collaborating on strategies to mobilise resources for sexual and reproductive health and rights; • acting as a framework for field visits to developing countries centred on sexual and reproductive health and rights activities
Networking	• Member of the High Ground Alliance for Choice and Dignity in Europe • Works with UN agencies, NGOs and intergovernmental organisations at the national, regional and international levels that have an interest in working with parliamentarians

Table D.6. Federacja na Rzecz Kobiet i Planowania Rodziny (Federation for Women and Family Planning).

Date of creation	1991
Headquarters	Warsaw
Legal status	NGO
Website	https://federa.org.pl
Purpose/ objectives	"To defend basic human rights, in particular the right of women to decide freely if and when to have children" (for women, enjoying this right is seen as "a condition for self-determination" and a condition for achieving equal opportunities between women and men)
Key members	• President: Małgorzata Księżopolska • Executive director: Krystyna Kacpura
Member organisations	Federation created by five organisations: Ligii Kobiet Polskich; Neutrum – Stowarzyszenia na rzecz Państwa Neutralnego Światopoglądowo; Polskiego Stowarzyszenia Feministycznego; Stowarzyszenia Dziewcząt i Kobiet Chrześcijańskich Polska YWCA; Stowarzyszenia Pro Femina
Recognition	• Not listed in the EU Transparency Register • Accredited with special consultative status with the United Nations Economic and Social Council (ECOSOC)
European political relays	Not documented
Scope of actions	• Reporting on women's sexual and reproductive health and rights • Intervening in favour of women denied access to medical services in the context of sexual and reproductive rights • Advocating for the right to abortion • Organising media campaigns
Networking	Member of ASTRA

Table D.7. International Planned Parenthood Federation European Network (IPPF EN).

Date of creation	1952 (creation of the international federation)
Headquarters	Brussels
Legal status	AISBL under Belgian law, registered in the *Moniteur belge* under company no. 0840 619 519 on 29 August 2011
Website	www.ippfen.org
Purpose/ objectives	• A federation of 31 national organisations working on sexual and reproductive health and rights as fundamental rights • The mission of the international federation is "to contribute to the improvement of the quality of life of women and men by taking action for sexual health and rights at the political level and on the ground with populations. It is about giving people, especially the poor and vulnerable, the opportunity and the means to make free and informed choices about their sexual, emotional and reproductive lives and to have access to appropriate and quality services."
Key members	• Chair of the board of directors: Gabriel Bianchi • Regional Director: Caroline Hickson
Member organisations	Asocijacija XY; Asocijacija za seksualno i reproduktivno zdravlje Srbije (SRH Srbija); Associação Para o Planeamento da Família (APF); Association HERA XXI; Bulgarian Family Planning and Sexual Health Association (BFPA); Confédération nationale du Planning Familial; Cyprus Family Planning Association; Eesti Seksuaaltervise Liit; Federación de Planificación Familiar de España (FPFE); Fédération laïque de centres de planning familial (FLCPF); Health Education and Research Association (HERA) – Macedonia; Irish Family Planning Association (IFPA); Israel Family Planning Association (IFPA); Kazakhstan Association on Sexual and Reproductive Health (KMPA); Österreichische Gesellschaft für Familienplanung; Papardes zieds; Pro Familia Bundesverband; Qendra Shqiptare për Popullsinë dhe Zhvillimin (QShPZh); Reproductive Health Alliance of Kyrgyzstan; Riksförbundet för Sexuell Upplysning (RFSU); Rutgers; Santé sexuelle Suisse; Šeimos planavimo ir seksualinės sveikatos asociacija; Sensoa; Sex & Samfund; Sex og Politikk; Societatea de Educație Contraceptivă și Sexuală (SECS); Spoločnosť pre plánované rodičovstvo; Tajik Family Planning Alliance; Väestöliitto; Women's Health and Family Planning

Table D.7. Continued.

Recognition	• AISBL, with participatory status with the Council of Europe and listed under the name International Planned Parenthood Federation European Network in the EU Transparency Register under no. 49806329193-46 since 20 July 2012 • The international federation is accredited with special consultative status with the United Nations Economic and Social Council (ECOSOC) and works with various UN agencies, such as the United Nations Population Fund, the World Health Organization and the United Nations Children's Fund
European political relays	Not documented
Scope of actions	• Providing medical expertise • Advocating for sexual and reproductive health and rights • Producing recommendations on good practice in sexual and reproductive health care and family planning
Networking	Member of the High Ground Alliance for Choice and Dignity in Europe

Table D.8. European Women's Lobby.

Date of creation	1990
Headquarters	Saint-Josse-ten-Noode
Legal status	AISBL under Belgian law, registered in the *Moniteur belge* under company no. 0446 526 137
Website	www.womenlobby.org
Purpose/ objectives	• Umbrella organisation of 32 national women's networks, 17 European organisations and 4 support organisations • Acts as a relay between these organisations and European institutions • Works in various economic, cultural, political and social fields related to women's rights at the national and European levels, with a view to building a feminist Europe • Since 2002 it has adopted pro-choice positions despite disagreements among Polish feminists
Key members	Secretary general: Konstantina Vardaramatou
Member organisations	National networks: Avrupa Kadın Lobisi Türkiye Koordinasyonu; Bulgarian Platform of the European Women's Lobby; Česká ženská lobby; Conseil des femmes francophones de Belgique (CFFB); Conseil national des femmes du Luxembourg (CNFL); Coordinamento Italiano della Lobby Europea delle Donne; Coordination française pour le Lobby européen des femmes (CLEF); Coordination of Greek Women's NGOs for the EWL; Cyprus Women's Lobby; Deutscher Frauenrat; Eesti Naisteühenduste Ümarlaud; Fundacja NEWW; Kvenréttindafélag Íslands; Kvinderaadet; Latvijas Sieviesu Organizaciju Sadarbibas tikls; Lietuvos Moterų Lobistinė Organizacija; Lobby Europeo de Mujeres en España (LEM España); Macedonian Women's Lobby (MWL); Magyar Nöi Erdekérvényesitö Szövetség; Malta Women's Lobby; Mreža za Evropski Ženski Lobi; Naisjärjestöt Yhteistyössä – Kvinnoorganisationer i Samarbete (NYTKIS); National Women's Council of Ireland (NWCI)/Comhairle Náisiúnta na mBan in Érinn; Nederlandse Vrouwen Raad (NVR); Österreichischer Frauenring (OFR); Plataforma Portuguesa para os Direitos das Mulheres (PPDM); Romanian Women's Lobby (ROWL); Sveriges Kvinnolobby; UK Joint Committee on Women (UKJCW); Vrouwenraad; Ženská Loby Slovenska; Ženska mreža Hrvatske; Ženski lobi Slovenije

Table D.8. Continued.

Member organisations (continued)	European member organisations: Alliance internationale des femmes (AIF)/International Alliance of Women (IAW); Business and Professional Women Europe (BPWE); Centre européen du Conseil international des femmes (CECIF)/European Centre of the International Council of Women (ECICW); Confédération européenne des syndicats (CES); Confédération européenne des syndicats indépendants (CESI); Conseil européen des fédérations WIZO (CEFW); European Disability Forum (EDF); European Network of Migrant Women; European YWCA (European Young Women's Christian Association); Fédération européenne des femmes actives en famille (FEFAF); Fédération internationale des femmes des carrières juridiques (FIFCJ)/International Federation of Women in Legal Careers (IFWLC); International Council of Jewish Women (ICJW); Medical Women's International Association (MWIA); Soroptimist International of Europe; University Women of Europe; Women's International League for Peace and Freedom (WILPF); World Association of Girl Guides and Girl Scouts (WAGGGS) Supporting member organisations: Centre d'information et de documentation Femmes/Fraen an Gender; European Blind Union (EBU); National Council of Women of Malta; Rrjeti i Fuqizimit të Gruas në Shqipëri (AWEN)
Recognition	• AISBL, with participatory status with the Council of Europe and listed under the name European's Women Lobby in the EU Transparency Register under no. 85686156700-13 since 16 September 2011 • Accredited with special consultative status with the United Nations Economic and Social Council (ECOSOC)
European political relays	Not documented
Scope of actions	• Producing expert reports, publications and reports in fields related to women's rights and gender equality • Monitoring gender mainstreaming in national and European policies • Following up on states' commitments at the Beijing Conference, and the directives of the European Parliament and the Council of Europe • Participating in national and international campaigns
Networking	Member of the High Ground Alliance for Choice and Dignity in Europe

Table D.9. European Region of the International Lesbian, Gay, Bisexual, Trans and Intersex Association (ILGA-Europe).

Date of creation	1996 (ILGA was created in 1978)
Headquarters	Ixelles
Legal status	AISBL under Belgian law, registered in the *Moniteur belge* under the name Région Europe de l'International Lesbian and Gay Association (ILGA-Europe) under company no. 0476 617 319
Website	www.ilga-europa.org
Purpose/ objectives	To defend lesbian, gay, bisexual, trans and intersex (LGBTI) rights, fight discrimination on the basis of gender identity and sexual orientation, and strengthen human rights organisations
Key members	• Executive director: Evelyne Paradis • Co-president: Darienne Flemington
Member organisations	Over 600 organisations in 54 countries in Europe and Central Asia
Recognition	• AISBL, with participatory status in the Council of Europe and listed in the EU Transparency Register under no. 11977456675-84 since 14 September 2011 • Accredited with special consultative status with the United Nations Economic and Social Council (ECOSOC)
European political relays	Not documented
Scope of actions	• Producing publications and reports • Organising annual seminars and conferences • Lobbying and advocacy • Working on European legislative bills, actions and awareness-raising on LGBTI rights • Organising meetings and marches • Participating in international forums
Networking	Member of the High Ground Alliance for Choice and Dignity

Table D.10. High Ground Alliance for Choice and Dignity in Europe.

Date of creation	2016
Headquarters	Brussels
Legal status	Alliance of six NGOs active in Europe
Website	None
Purpose/ objectives	To inform, educate and support policymakers at the EU level as well as journalists and civil society actors who consider freedom of choice in the conduct of individual lives to be essential for a more just society
Key members	See "Member organisations"
Member organisations	Catholics for Choice; European Humanist Federation; European Parliamentary Forum for Sexual and Reproductive Rights; International Planned Parenthood Federation European Network (IPPF EN); European Women's Lobby; European Region of the International Lesbian, Gay, Bisexual, Trans and Intersex Association (ILGA-Europe)
Recognition	Not listed in the EU Transparency Register
European political relays	See "Member organisations"
Scope of actions	Providing expertise and advocacy at the EU level on secularism, sexual and reproductive health, and women's and LGBTI people's rights
Networking	See "Member organisations"

Appendix E. Bills on the removal of abortion from the Belgian criminal code

Table E.1. The seven bills introduced in the House of Representatives between 10 May 2016 and 29 May 2018.

Party	Défi	PS	Ecolo-Groen	PTB
Reference	House of Representatives, 2016, "Bill amending the Criminal Code and the law of 22 August 2002 on the rights of the patient aimed at decriminalising the voluntary termination of pregnancy", tabled by Olivier Maingain and Véronique Caprasse, no. 1823/1, 10 May	House of Representatives, 2016, "Bill to remove the voluntary termination of pregnancy from the Criminal Code and to introduce it into the law of 22 August 2002 on the rights of the patient", tabled by Karine Lalieux, Laurette Onkelinx and Fabienne Winkel, no. 1867/1, 31 May	House of Representatives, 2017, "Bill on the voluntary termination of pregnancy", tabled by Muriel Gerkens, Evita Willaert, Georges Gilkinet, Anne Dedry, Benoit Hellings, Meyrem Almaci, Jean-Marc Nollet and Gilles Vanden Burre, no. 2271/1, 18 January	House of Representatives, 2017, "Bill on decriminalising abortion and updating the law on the voluntary termination of pregnancy", tabled by Marco Van Hees and Raoul Hedebouw, no. 2518/1, 8 June
Time limit for obtaining an abortion (from conception)	12 weeks	14 weeks (reference to abortion tourism)	16 weeks	20 weeks
Waiting period between the request and the procedure	Six days	Six days	48 hours	48 hours
Doctor required to check the woman's resolve	No	No	Yes	No
Written agreement required from the woman	Yes	Yes	No	No
Mention of a state of distress	No	No	No	No
Criminal sanctions for non-compliance with the legal requirements for a consensual abortion	No	No	Yes, for the doctor	No
Ban on the promotion of and information about abortion (Article 383 of the criminal code)	Repeal of the last two paragraphs of Article 383	Repeal of the last two paragraphs of Article 383	Repeal of the last two paragraphs of Article 383	Repeal of the last two paragraphs of Article 383

Conscience clause: addition to the 1990 law	None	Mandatory referral to a doctor/centre performing abortion	Mandatory referral (under good conditions) to a doctor/centre performing abortion; transfer of the medical file with the woman's consent; a prohibition on preventing abortion on the basis of an institution-wide convention	Mandatory referral (under good conditions) to a doctor/centre performing abortion; transfer of the medical file with the woman's consent; a prohibition on preventing abortion on the basis of an institution-wide convention
Medical termination of pregnancy: amendment to the 1990 law (Article 350(4) of the criminal code)	None	>14 weeks of pregnancy; no six-day waiting period (if a "justified emergency")	>16 weeks of pregnancy, if there are serious psychosocial factors	>20 weeks of pregnancy, if there are serious psychosocial factors
Legal framework	Law of 22 August 2002 on patients' rights	Law of 22 August 2002 on patients' rights	Specific law, and amendment of the law of 22 August 2002 on patients' rights	Specific law, and amendment of the law of 22 August 2002 on patients' rights (references Royal Decree no. 78, of 10 November 1967, on the practice of healing, nursing, paramedical professions and medical commissions)
International references in preamble	Internationally recognised basic rights, CEDAW, ECHR, UN Human Rights Committee, Council of Europe, WHO, neighbouring countries	CEDAW, ECHR, CJEU, Council of Europe, WHO, UN, neighbouring countries	WHO, neighbouring countries	No
Comments	References the context of the challenges surrounding women's right to abortion and control over their own bodies, and the government's desire to legislate on the registration of stillborn children.	References the context of "pressure from anti-abortion lobbies [...] on parliamentary bodies throughout Europe" and "attacks on the practice of abortion". References the creation of a "European Federation for Embryo Rights" (One of Us).	Describes the need "to recognise the right to abortion as a public health duty of care in its own right. [...] The right to abortion has become a symbol of gender equality policy."	Abortion is a medical procedure. "The right to abortion is a fundamental right of women based on women's right to self-determination and, as such, must be protected." Described as the result of a long struggle by the women's movement. Mentions rights undermined (Poland, USA).

Table E.1. Continued.

Party	Open VLD	SP.A	CDH
Reference	House of Representatives, 2017, "Bill on abortion", tabled by Carina Van Cauter, no. 2527/1, 12 June	House of Representatives, 2018, "Bill decriminalising the voluntary termination of pregnancy", tabled by Karin Jiroflée, Monica De Coninck, Annick Lambrecht and Karin Temmerman, no. 3059/1, 26 April	House of Representatives, 2018, "Bill on the termination of pregnancy", tabled by Catherine Fonck, no. 3123/1, 29 May
Time limit for obtaining an abortion (from conception)	18 weeks	12 weeks	12 weeks
Waiting period between the request and the procedure	48 hours	Six days	Six days
Doctor required to check the woman's resolve	Yes	Yes	Yes
Written agreement required from the woman	Yes	Yes	Yes
Mention of a state of distress	No	Yes	Yes
Criminal sanctions for non-compliance with the legal conditions for a consensual abortion	Yes, for the doctor and the woman	No	Yes, for the doctor and the woman
Ban on the promotion of and information about abortion (Article 383 of the criminal code)	Paragraphs of Article 383 repealed, but reinstated in the text of the new specific law	Repeal of the last two paragraphs of Article 383	Not mentioned (maintained in the criminal code)
Conscience clause: addition to the 1990 law	Mandatory referral to a doctor/centre performing abortion, and transfer of the medical file	Mandatory referral to a doctor/centre performing abortion, and transfer of the medical file	Mandatory referral to a doctor/centre performing abortion
Medical termination of pregnancy: amendment to the 1990 law (Article 350(4) of the criminal code)	>18 weeks of pregnancy and if there are serious psychosocial factors	No	Removal of the six-day period

	Special law	Law of 22 August 2002 on patients' rights	Special law
Legal framework			
International references in preamble	CEDAW, ECHR, Council of Europe, WHO, neighbouring countries	Neighbouring countries	WHO
Comments	Abortion is a medical procedure. Describes the need "for abortion to be clearly defined as a right, for the taboo surrounding it to be eroded even further and for an end to the stigmatisation to which women who have recourse to it are still too often subjected".	"The choice of abortion must be defined more explicitly as a woman's right, and no longer as a partially and conditionally decriminalised privilege."	Abortion "cannot be reduced to a medical procedure like any other, to which every woman has an unconditional right. Abortion involves an ethical choice between a woman's freedom and the life she carries within her." "For CDH, it is essential to avoid both any form of trivialisation of abortion [...] and any shaming of women who have recourse to it."

E.1 Comments: similarities and differences between the seven bills in Table E.1

The maximum duration of pregnancy for obtaining an abortion varies between twelve weeks, as in the 1990 law (Défi, SP.A and CDH), and twenty weeks (PTB) (it is fourteen for PS, sixteen for Ecolo-Groen and eighteen for Open VLD). The waiting period between the first consultation and the procedure is either, as in the 1990 law, six days (Défi, PS, SP.A and CDH) or forty-eight hours (Ecolo-Groen, PTB and Open VLD).

The woman's written consent is not required in some bills (PTB and Ecolo-Groen), and in some the doctor does not have to check the woman's resolve (Défi, PS and PTB).

None of the parties mention an "offence of obstruction", which means that none of them enshrine a real right of access to abortion (Ecolo-Groen and PTB limit conscientious objection by prohibiting the prevention of abortion on the basis of an institution-wide convention).

The only parties not to delete the notion of a "state of distress" mentioned in Article 350 of the criminal code were SP.A and CDH. The other parties enshrine access to abortion not as a dispensation granted conditionally to women but as a right. However, this right of access does not go as far as recognising self-determination, as no offence of obstruction is mentioned or, *a fortiori*, criminally sanctioned.

The conscience clause from the 1990 law is retained by Défi, while the other parties oblige the doctor who invokes it to refer the woman to another doctor or centre performing abortion, and to send the woman's medical file to the centre (except for PS, and subject to the woman's agreement for Ecolo-Groen and PTB).

Non-consensual abortion (as a result of coercion or violence) remains criminally sanctioned by all parties.

Articles 351 and 352 of the criminal code, which provide for criminal sanctions in the event of non-compliance with the conditions laid down for abortion, are repealed in the bills of Défi, PS, PTB and SP.A; this repeal effectively removes abortion from the criminal code. The other parties remove sanctions from the criminal code and reintroduce them in a specific law; these sanctions are aimed at either the doctor alone (Ecolo-Groen) or both the doctor and the woman (Open VLD and CDH). It should be noted that Article 351 of the criminal code does not refer to the doctor but only the woman.

A medical termination of pregnancy beyond the maximum duration of pregnancy for on-request abortion is possible in all parties' bills under the same conditions as in the 1990 law. Ecolo-Groen, PTB and Open VLD add "serious psychosocial factors" to the conditions that allow it. SP and CDH, which provide for a six-day waiting period, remove this period in the case of an emergency situation requiring a medical abortion.

The two paragraphs of Article 383 of the criminal code that prohibit any form of promotion of or information about abortion are repealed, except by CDH, which maintains them, and Open VLD, which repeals them and puts them back in its new specific law.

The legal framework for abortion in the Défi, PS and SP.A bills is the law of 22 August 2002 on the rights of the patient. Abortion is the subject of a special law for Open VLD and CDH, as well as Ecolo-Groen and PTB. For the latter two parties, this special law also implies amendments to the law of 22 August 2002 and, for PTB, to Royal Decree no. 78, of 10 November 1967, on the exercise of "the art of healing", "the art of nursing", the paramedical professions and the medical commissions.

Finally, the Abortion Evaluation Commission, set up in 1990, is not considered in these various bills or in their preambles, but it should be noted that SP.A had tabled a bill (in July 2016) for a resolution "to update the legislation on the termination of pregnancy and to prevent unplanned and unwanted pregnancies".[1]

---

1   House of Representatives, 2016, "Motion for a resolution to update the legislation on termination of pregnancy and to prevent unplanned and unwanted pregnancies", tabled by Karin Jiroflée and Monica De Coninck (SP.A), no. 1989/001, 18 July.

Table E.2. The bill tabled by opposition parties and the bill tabled by government majority parties on 4 July 2018.

Parties	Opposition (except CDH)	Government majority
Reference	House of Representatives, 2018, "Bill to remove the voluntary termination of pregnancy from the Criminal Code", tabled by Karine Lalieux (PS), Véronique Caprasse (Défi), Muriel Gerkens (Ecolo-Groen), Karin Jiroflée (SP.A) and Marco Van Hees (PTB), no. 3215/1, 4 July	House of Representatives, 2018, "Bill on the voluntary termination of pregnancy", tabled by David Clarinval (MR), Carina Van Cauter (Open VLD), Valérie Van Peel (N-VA) and Els Van Hoof (CD&V), no. 3216/1, 4 July
Time limit for obtaining an abortion (from conception)	18 weeks (reference to neighbouring countries and abortion tourism)	12 weeks
Waiting period between the request and the procedure	48 hours, except for medical emergencies	Six days, except for urgent medical reasons
Doctor required to check the woman's resolve	No	Yes
Written agreement required from the woman	Yes	Yes
Mention of a state of distress	No	No
Criminal sanctions for non-compliance with the legal conditions for a consensual abortion	Yes, for the doctor and anyone who prevents a woman from accessing abortion	Yes, for the woman, the doctor and anyone who prevents a woman from accessing abortion

Ban on the promotion of and information about abortion (Article 383 of the criminal code)	Repeal of the last two paragraphs of Article 383	Repeal of the last two paragraphs of Article 383
Offence of obstruction with regard to abortion	Yes, including impeding abortion on the basis of an institution-wide convention	Yes, criminally sanctioned
Crimes and offences in cases of coercion or violence resulting in non-consensual abortion	Articles moved within the criminal code and some slightly amended	Retention of the existing articles of the criminal code
Conscience clause: addition to the 1990 law	Indication of two practitioners likely to carry out abortion, and the transfer of the medical file within a maximum of 24 hours, under good conditions and with the patient's consent	Mandatory referral to a doctor or a centre performing abortion, and transfer of the medical file
Medical termination of pregnancy: amendment to the 1990 law (Article 350(4) of the criminal code)	>18 weeks of pregnancy, if there are serious psychosocial factors	No change
Legal framework	Law of 22 August 2002 on patients' rights	Special law on abortion
International references in preamble	CEDAW, ECHR, CJEU, Council of Europe, WHO, UN, neighbouring countries	CEDAW, Council of Europe, WHO, UN
Comments	References the context of regression driven by anti-abortion activists. References the One of Us Federation. Abortion is considered in the context of the right to health. Entails almost total decriminalisation.	In practice, largely similar to the 1990 law; decriminalisation remains partial. Criminal prosecution for the doctor and the woman remains possible.

Table E.3. "Law of 15 October 2018 on the voluntary termination of pregnancy repealing Articles 350 and 351 of the Criminal Code and amending Articles 352 and 383 of the same Code and amending various legislative provisions" (*Moniteur belge*, 29 October 2018).

	Conditions	Comments
Time limit for obtaining an abortion (from conception)	12 weeks	Many actors working in the field argue for an extension to 16 weeks.
Waiting period between the request and the procedure	Six days except for urgent medical reasons	Urgent medical reasons are not defined in the law, but according to related parliamentary papers they can be physical or psychological. According to the experts heard in the Committee on Justice, in the vast majority of cases the decision is taken by the woman as soon as she becomes aware of her pregnancy.
Doctor required to check the woman's resolve	Yes	No change from the 1990 law.
Written agreement required from the woman	Yes	No change from the 1990 law.
Mention of a state of distress	Deleted	Notion deemed insufficiently objective by the Council of State as early as 1989. The deletion responds to the request of many actors working in the field.
Criminal sanctions for non-compliance with the legal conditions for a consensual abortion	Yes, for the doctor and anyone else	In the 1990 law, criminal sanctions were provided only for the doctor and the woman.

Ban on the promotion of and information about abortion	Repealed	The repeal responds to the demand of many actors working in the field.
Offence of obstruction with regard to abortion	Yes, criminally sanctioned	The importance of the inclusion of this offence lies in how it could curtail the activism of groups opposed to the right to abortion.
Conscience clause: addition to the 1990 law	Mandatory referral to another doctor; obligation to transfer the medical file	It is not specified that the doctor who refuses to perform an abortion must refer the woman to another doctor who does. No penalty for non-compliance. No reference to institutional use of the clause.
Medical termination of pregnancy	Possibility of extending the deadline with the opinion of a second doctor (attached to the medical file) if there is a serious risk to the mother's health or if there is a certainty of a serious condition for the foetus recognised at the time of diagnosis	Several experts heard in the Committee on Justice proposed extending the conditions.
		General comments. No reference is made to the law on patients' rights and health care. There is no recognition of abortion as a medical procedure.

Table E.4. Bills tabled to relax the conditions of the October 2018 law.

Party	PS	Défi	PTB	Ecolo-Groen
Reference	House of Representatives, 2019, "Bill to relax the conditions for the voluntary termination of pregnancy", tabled by Éliane Tillieux, Caroline Désir, Patrick Prévot, Özlem Özen, Laurence Zanchetta, Mélissa Hanus, Jean-Marc Delizée and Sophie Thémont, no. 158/1, 16 July	House of Representatives, 2019, "Bill decriminalising the voluntary termination of pregnancy and to relax the conditions for its use", tabled by Sophie Rohonyi and François De Smet, no. 385/1, 17 September	House of Representatives, 2019, "Bill decriminalising abortion and updating the law on the voluntary termination of pregnancy", tabled by Marco Van Hees, Raoul Hedebouw, Maria Vindevoghel, Nadia Moscufo, Sophie Merckx, Greta Daems and Nabil Boukili, no. 458/1, 30 September	House of Representatives, 2019, "Bill decriminalising the voluntary termination of pregnancy", tabled by Sarah Schlitz, Jessika Soors, Séverine de Laveleye, Evita Willaert, Cécile Thibaut, Barbara Creemers, Marie-Colline Leroy, Kim Buyst, Julie Chanson and Laurence Hennuy, no. 614/1, 16 October
Time limit for obtaining an abortion (from conception)	18 weeks (of amenorrhoea, according to the preamble of the bill)	18 weeks	20 weeks	18 weeks of amenorrhoea or 16 weeks from conception
Waiting period between the request and the procedure	48 hours	48 hours	None	48 hours
Removal of infantilising conditions for women (see comments below)	Yes	Yes	Yes	Yes, but the woman must be made aware of the alternatives to abortion
Doctor required to check the woman's resolve	Yes	Yes	No	Yes
Written agreement required from the woman	Yes	Yes	No	Yes
Criminal sanctions for non-compliance with the legal conditions for a consensual abortion	No, unless the woman dies, even if she consents (2018 law)	No, unless the woman dies, even if she consents (2018 law)	No	Yes, except for the woman
Offence of obstruction	2018 law	Repealed in Chapter 3 of the 2018 law, but the notion of obstruction is reintroduced in Chapter 2 (becoming a fault rather than an offence)	No (deleted following the repeal of Article 3 of the 2018 law)	Yes

Conscience clause	2018 law	Referral to at least two doctors performing abortion; transfer of the medical file with the woman's consent; prohibition of preventing abortion on the basis of an institution-wide convention.	2018 law + prohibition of preventing abortion on the basis of an institution-wide convention + transfer of the medical file with the woman's consent	Referral to a doctor who performs abortion; transfer of the medical file with the woman's consent; prohibition of preventing abortion on the basis of an institution-wide convention.
Medical termination of pregnancy	>18 weeks of pregnancy (2018 law)	>18 weeks of pregnancy; 2018 law + psychosocial situation of the woman (rape, violence, drug addiction) + accredited centre + "certainty" of a serious condition for the foetus replaced by "high risk"	>20 weeks of pregnancy; 2018 law + cases where the woman's psychosocial situation is a serious obstacle to her pregnancy	>18 weeks of pregnancy; 2018 law + cases where the woman's psychosocial situation is a serious obstacle to her pregnancy
Legal framework (in addition to the law of 15 October 2018)	Law of 22 August 2002 on patients' rights.	Law of 22 August 2002 on patients' rights and the Coordinated Law of 10 May 2015 on the practice of the health care professions	Royal Decree no. 78, of 10 November 1967, on the practice of healing, nursing, paramedical professions and medical commissions; law of 22 August 2002 on patients' rights	Law of 22 August 2002 on patients' rights
International references in preamble	Legislation from Austria, the UK, the Netherlands and Sweden	CEDAW, ECHR, Council of Europe, European Parliament, WHO, UN, neighbouring countries (UK, French, Luxembourg, Dutch and Swedish legislation)	WHO, Polish situation and US situation under Trump	ECHR, Council of Europe, WHO, UN, neighbouring countries (reference to French and Luxembourg legislation).
Comments	References the survey conducted by the Université libre de Bruxelles and the University of Hasselt on behalf of the CAL. References the demonstrations by actors in the field in favour of full decriminalisation. Abortion is considered a medical procedure.	References actors heard in the Committee on Justice (prior to the 2018 law), the CAL survey and the global trend of declining women's rights. Abortion is considered a medical procedure, which falls under women's right to autonomy.	Abortion is a medical procedure and part of women's fundamental right to self-determination. References the feminist struggles that started in 1973.	Abortion is part of a woman's right to health, and a choice protected by the law of 22 August 2002 on patients' rights.

Where minor changes (additions or replacements) have been made to the text of the 2018 law, they are noted as "2018 law + [...]".

Table E.4. Continued.

Party	Open VLD	SP.A	MR	PS, SP.A, Défi, PTB, MR, Ecolo-Groen, Open VLD
Reference	House of Representatives, 2019, "Bill on abortion", tabled by Katja Gabriëls, Egbert Lachaert and Goedele Liekens, no. 652/1, 22 October	House of Representatives, 2019, "Bill on easing the conditions for terminating pregnancy", tabled by Karin Jiroflée, no. 676/1, 23 October	House of Representatives, 2019, "Bill on the voluntary termination of pregnancy", tabled by Kattrin Jadin, David Clarinval, Philippe Goffin, Caroline Taquin, Florence Reuter, Daniel Bacquelaine, Emmanuel Burton and Michel De Maegd, no. 740/1, 12 November	House of Representatives, "Amendments of 13 November 2019, no. 158/3, replacing and supplementing the bill to relax the conditions for the voluntary termination of pregnancy of 16 July 2019 (no. 158/1)", tabled by É. Tillieux (PS), K. Jiroflée (SPA), S. Rohonyi (Défi), S. Merckx (PVDA-PTB), K. Jadin (MR), J. Soors and S. Schlitz (Ecolo-Groen), and K. Gabriëls (Open VLD)*
Time limit for obtaining an abortion (from conception)	18 weeks	20 weeks in a centre approved by Royal Decree, otherwise 12 weeks	18 weeks	18 weeks
Waiting period between the request and the procedure	48 hours	48 hours	48 hours	48 hours
Removal of infantilising conditions for women (see comments below)	No	No	Yes, but referral to a psycho-social support service	Yes, but obligation to offer medical and psychosocial support (replaces the duty to provide "information to the woman about contraception")
Doctor required to check the woman's resolve	Yes	Yes	No	Yes
Written agreement required from the woman	Yes	Yes	No	Yes
Criminal sanctions for non-compliance with the legal conditions for a consensual abortion	Yes	Yes, except for the woman	Yes, except for the woman	No

Offence of obstruction	2018 law + clarification: preventing "physically or in any other way" (e.g. through false information)	Yes, also inserted in Chapter 2 of the 2018 law ("Conditions and procedure")	Yes, very broad (preventing the dissemination of information on abortion, exerting moral pressure or intimidating women and their relatives)	2018 law + clarification: preventing "physically or in any other way" (e.g. by withholding information or providing false information)
Conscience clause	2018 law + clause extended to all health professionals	2018 law + mandatory referral to at least two doctors + transfer of the medical file within 24 hours and under the best possible conditions	Applicable to anyone assisting in abortion; cannot be imposed by a care institution	2018 law + extension to all "health care professionals" + prohibits preventing abortion on the basis of an institution-wide convention
Medical termination of pregnancy	>18 weeks; 2018 law + "certainty" of a serious foetal condition replaced by "serious risk"	>20 weeks; 2018 law + performed in a centre approved by Royal Decree	>18 weeks; 2018 law + "certainty" of a serious foetal condition replaced by "serious risk"	>18 weeks; 2018 law + "certainty" of a serious foetal condition replaced by "high risk"
Legal framework (in addition to the law of 15 October 2018)	No other framework	Law of 22 August 2002 on patients' rights and the Coordinated Law of 10 May 2015 on the practice of the health care professions	New law	Law of 22 August 2002 on patients' rights
International references in preamble	CEDAW, ECHR, Council of Europe, WHO, neighbouring countries (French, Luxembourg and Swedish legislation)	French and Luxembourg legislation	Swedish legislation	Attacks on abortion rights in Poland and the USA and activism against these attacks
Comments	Abortion should be a medical procedure. Mentions relatively low abortion rate in Belgium.	Abortion should be a medical procedure. It is a women's right and should be distinguished from an offence implying guilt.	Contains analysis of the 2018 law. Alludes to women's autonomy and control over their own bodies.	Mentions women's right to self-determination. Abortion is a medical procedure in its own right. Recalls the struggles in Belgium. Analyses contributions and limitations of the 2018 law. Bill is based on findings on the ground and from hearings held in the Committee on Justice.

Where minor changes (additions or replacements) have been made to the text of the 2018 law, they are noted as "2018 law + [...]".

* Amendment no. 3, on sanctions against doctors, was not co-signed by Jessika Soors (Ecolo-Groen).

E.2 Comments: similarities and differences between the eight bills in Table E.4

The maximum duration of pregnancy for obtaining abortion varies between eighteen weeks (PS, Défi, Ecolo-Groen, Open VLD and MR) and twenty weeks (PTB and SP.A; for SP.A, this is providing that the abortion is performed in an approved centre – otherwise the limit is twelve weeks). The waiting period between the first consultation and the procedure is reduced from six days (in the 2018 law) to forty-eight hours, and less in the case of an emergency (except for PTB, which does not impose any waiting period). The joint bill specifies eighteen weeks and forty-eight hours. In all the bills this extension of the legal conditions for abortion is motivated by the existence of abortion tourism and the situation that faces women who are unable to comply with the existing legal conditions.

The woman's written consent is still required by all the parties except MR and PTB. For these two parties, the doctor is also no longer required to "determine the woman's resolve". These two conditions are maintained in the joint bill.

The list of information to be provided to women requesting abortion (Article 2, 1(b), of the 2018 law), which is considered infantilising, has been deleted from all the bills except those of Open VLD and SP.A. The joint bill also specifies that the health care facility where the procedure was performed "must offer medical, psychological and social support to the woman".

The "offence of obstruction", introduced by the 2018 law, is retained and often clarified or extended (in particular by MR). Défi, however, takes it out of the "Criminal provisions" (Chapter 3 of the 2018 law) and no longer mentions a criminal sanction (it is considered in the preamble as "a denial of care that is not acceptable", and becomes a fault rather than an offence). For its part, PTB repeals Article 3 of the 2018 law without reintroducing an "offence of obstruction" elsewhere, while in the joint bill the offence of obstruction is maintained as a criminal provision (Article 3 of the 2018 law), and the bill specifies that a woman cannot be prevented from having an abortion "physically or in any other way".

Following the removal of the notion of a "state of distress" in the 2018 law, access to abortion is no longer considered a dispensation conditionally granted to women, but neither has it become a medical procedure falling under the right to health, even if the law punishes an offence of obstruction. Moreover, this right of access, reinforced by these various bills, does not go as far as to give women the right to control their bodies, even if this is sometimes mentioned in the preambles of the bills, and in particular in the justifications for the amendments that now take the place of the joint bill, which state: "The right to abortion is a fundamental right of women based on women's right to self-determination and, as such, must be protected." However, it is the PTB bill that comes closest to this recognition, by specifying in Article 2 that "abortion is a medical procedure".

The criminal sanctions for an abortion that is consensual but performed outside the legal conditions are completely removed by PTB, while PS and Défi maintain them only in the case of the woman's death. They are maintained by Open VLD, while Ecolo-Groen, SP.A and MR abolish them only for the woman. They are deleted from the joint bill.

Non-consensual abortion (as a result of coercion or violence) remains penalised in all the bills.

The conscience clause is carried over from the 2018 law with some adjustments. For Défi, PTB, Ecolo-Groen and MR this clause is personal and cannot be imposed by a health care institution. For Défi, PTB and Ecolo-Groen the transfer the women's medical file to another doctor or centre performing abortions must be done with the woman's consent. For Défi and SP.A the woman should be referred to two doctors, not one (for MR, the plural form "doctors" is used, without precision). Open VLD specifies that the conscience clause should be extended to all health care professionals; for MR it should be extended to anyone who "assists" in an abortion. The joint bill reiterates the terms of the 2018 law (which does not require the woman's consent to transfer her medical file) and extends the conscience clause to any "health care professional" as well as adding a paragraph stating that "no doctor may be prevented from performing an abortion by virtue of a convention".

The medical termination of pregnancy (that is, abortion beyond the legal time limit) is permitted under the same conditions as in the 2018 law. However, Défi, PTB and Ecolo-Groen add to these conditions cases where the psychosocial situation of the woman represents a serious obstacle to her pregnancy. For Défi, Open VLD and MR the "certainty" of a serious foetal condition should be replaced by "a high risk" or "a serious risk". The joint bill refers to a "high risk" but does not refer to the psychosocial situation of the woman.

It should be added that, in the joint bill, one of the conditions for abortion is that "the doctor or any other qualified person [...] must offer the woman medical and social support", an idea that is taken from other bills and that, in the joint bill, replaces the condition that the woman must be provided "with information about contraception". This change is justified by the fact that "this medical obligation is guilt-inducing for women who, in the vast majority of cases, [...] do not take their contraception lightly".

List of abbreviations

ADF: Alliance Defending Freedom International
AfD: Alternative für Deutschland
Agalev: Anders gaan leven (Belgium)
AISBL: Belgian international non-profit association
APB: Action pour Bruxelles
ASBL: Belgian non-profit association
ASTRA: Central and Eastern European Network for Sexual and Reproductive Health and Rights
BICE: International Catholic Child Bureau
BSP: Belgische Socialistische Partij
CADTM: Committee for the Abolition of Illegitimate Debt
CAL: Centre d'action laïque (Belgium)
CAT: United Nations Committee Against Torture
CCPR: committee monitoring the implementation of the International **Covenant** on Civil and Political Rights
CDH: Centre Démocrate Humaniste (Belgium)
CDU: Christlich Demokratische Union Deutschlands
CD&V: Christen-Democratisch en Vlaams (Belgium)
CEDAW: United Nations Committee on the Elimination of Discrimination against Women, or the Convention on the Elimination of All Forms of **Discrimination** against Women
CEDIF: documentation and information centre of the Fédération laïque **des** centres de planning familial (Belgium)
CEFA: Centre d'éducation à la famille et à l'amour (Belgium)
CESCR: committee monitoring the implementation of the International **Covenant** on Economic, Social and Cultural Rights
CFD: Commission femmes et développement (Belgium)
CFFB: Conseil des femmes francophones de Belgique (Belgium)
CGIL: Confederazione Generale Italiana del Lavoro
CJEU: Court of Justice of the European Union
CLF: Comité de liaison des femmes (Belgium)

CNAFC: Confédération nationale des associations familiales catholiques (France)

COCOF: Commission communautaire française (Belgium)

COCOM: Commission communautaire commune (Belgium)

COMECE: Commission of the Bishops' Conferences of the European Union

CPAS: Centre public d'action sociale (Belgium)

CPDH: Comité protestant évangélique pour la dignité humaine (Protestant Evangelical Committee for Human Dignity)

CRC: United Nations Committee on the Rights of the Child

CRR: Center for Reproductive Rights

CSC: Confédération des syndicats chrétiens de Belgique (Belgium)

CSU: Christlisch-Soziale Union (Germany)

CVP: Christelijke Volkspartij (Belgium)

DAWN: Development Alternatives with Women for a New Era

Défi: Démocrate, fédéraliste, indépendant (Belgium)

ECHR: European Court of Human Rights

ECI: European Citizen's Initiative

ECLJ: European Centre for Law and Justice

Ecolo: Écologistes confédérés pour l'organisation de luttes originales (Belgium)

ECOSOC: United Nations Economic and Social Council

ECSR: European Committee of Social Rights (Council of Europe)

EHF: European Humanist Federation

EIB: European Institute of Bioethics

EP: European Parliament

EPF: European Parliamentary Forum for Sexual and Reproductive Rights (formerly the European Parliamentary Forum on Population and Development)

EPP: European People's Party

EPWG: European Parliament Working Group on Reproductive Health, **HIV/AIDS** and Development

ESC: European Society of Contraception

EU: European Union

EVRAS: Education à la vie relationnelle, affective et sexuelle (Belgium)

EWL: European Women's Lobby

FAFCE: Fédération des associations familiales catholiques en Europe (Federation of Catholic Family Associations in Europe)

FCPC: Fédération des centres de planning et de consultations (Belgium)

FCPF-FPS: Fédération des centres de planning familial des Femmes pré-voyantes socialistes (Belgium)

FCPPF: Fédération des centres pluralistes de planning familial (Belgium)

FDF: Front démocratique des francophones (Belgium)

FDP: Freie Demokratische Partei

FGTB: Fédération générale du travail de Belgique (Belgium)

FLCPF: Fédération laïque des centres de planning familial (Belgium)

FPS: Femmes prévoyantes socialistes (Belgium)

GACEHPA: Groupe d'action des centres extrahospitaliers pratiquant l'avortement (Belgium)

ICPD: International Conference on Population and Development (Cairo, 1994)

ILGA: International Lesbian, Gay, Bisexual, Trans and Intersex Association

ILGA-Europe: European Region of the International Lesbian, Gay, Bisexual, Trans and Intersex Association

INAMI: Institut national d'assurance maladie-invalidité (Belgium)

INGO: international non-governmental organisation

IPPF EN: International Planned Parenthood Federation European Network

IPPF: International Planned Parenthood Federation

LGBT: lesbian, gay, bisexual and transgender

LUNA: Unie Nederlandstalige Abortus Centra (Belgium)

MEP: member of the European Parliament

MFPF: Mouvement français pour le planning familial

MOC: Mouvement ouvrier chrétien (Belgium)

MR: Mouvement réformateur (Belgium)

NGO: non-governmental organisation

N-VA: Nieuw-Vlaamse Alliantie (Belgium)

Open VLD: Open Vlaamse Liberalen en Democraten (Belgium)

PACE: Parliamentary Assembly of the Council of Europe

PCB: Parti communiste de Belgique

PRL: Parti réformateur libéral (Belgium)

PRLW: Parti des réformes et de la liberté de Wallonie (Belgium)

PS: Parti socialiste (Belgium)

PSB: Parti socialiste belge

PSC: Parti social-chrétien (Belgium)

PTB: Parti du travail de Belgique

PVDA: Partij van de Arbeid van België

PVV: Partij voor Vrijheid en Vooruitgang (Belgium)

RAPPEL: Réseau d'action pour la promotion d'un État laïque (Belgium)

SENSOA: Vlaamse Expertisecentrum voor Seksuele Gezondheid (Belgium)
SP: Socialistische Partij (Belgium)
SP.A: Socialistische Partij Anders (Belgium)
SPD: Sozialdemokratische Partei Deutschlands
SPF: Service Public Fédéral (Belgium)
TFEU: Treaty on the Functioning of the European Union
UDRT: Union démocratique pour le respect du travail (Belgium)
ULB: Université libre de Bruxelles (Belgium)
UN: United Nations
VB: Vlaams Belang, or Vlaams Blok (Belgium)
VIVA: Socialistische Vrouwen Vereniging (Belgium)
VOK: Vrouwen Overleg Komitee (Belgium)
VU: Volksunie (Belgium)
VUB: Vrije Universiteit Brussel (Belgium)
WGNRR: Women's Global Network for Reproductive Rights
WHO: World Health Organization

Bibliography

Documents of Belgian voluntary associations

Abortion Right. 2015. Press Release, 28 March. Published in *Chronique féministe* (115), 54–56.

Abortion Right. 2016. Lutter contre la stigmatisation de l'avortement. Press Release, 1 April. Published in *Chronique féministe* (117), 68.

Centre d'action laïque. N.D. Sortir l'avortement du Code pénal belge. Proceedings of colloquiums in Brussels (30 September, 2016), Liège (23 November 2016) and the Senate (27 January 2017). URL: www.laicite.be.

Centre d'action laïque. 2015. L'avortement hors du Code pénal. Brussels.

Centre d'action laïque. 2018. #IVGHorsDuCodePenal : une proposition symbolique dont on espère pouvoir réellement se réjouir ! Press Release, 4 July.

Centre d'action laïque. 2018. IVG : un vote sans surprise. Press Release, 19 September. URL: www.laicite.be.

Centre d'action laïque. 2018. Où en est le projet de sortir l'IVG du Code pénal ? Press Release, 11 July.

Centre d'action laïque. 2019. État des lieux de l'avortement en Europe. URL: www.laicite.be.

Centre d'action laïque, deMens.nu, Université libre de Bruxelles and Universiteit Hasselt. 2018. Sondage d'opinion sur l'interruption volontaire de grossesse en Belgique.

Centre de documentation et d'information de la Fédération laïque des centres de planning familial. 2010. Les 20 ans de la loi sur l'avortement : de la subversion au droit. Proceedings of the colloquium of 1 April 2010, Brussels.

Conseil des femmes francophones de Belgique. 2017. Statut du foetus, reconnaissance anté-natale. Press Release, 13 February. Published in *Chronique féministe* (119), 68.

Déclaration de Bruxelles. N.D. L'interruption volontaire de grossesse : un droit fondamental des femmes. URL: https://droitavortement.be.

DeMens.nu. 2018. Symbolische overwinning, geen perfect akkoord. Press Release, 4 July. URL: www.demens.nu.

Femmes prévoyantes socialistes. N.D. Avortement : libertés en danger. Proceedings of the international colloquium of 12 December 2005, Brussels.

Groupe d'action des centres extrahospitaliers pratiquant l'avortement. 2014. Campagne "Avorter c'est possible". *Chronique féministe* (114), 42.

Groupe d'action des centres extrahospitaliers pratiquant l'avortement. 2015. Résolution, 3 April. Published in *Chronique féministe* (115), 54–56.

Groupe d'action des centres extrahospitaliers pratiquant l'avortement. 2016. Rapport d'activités 2015.

Groupe d'action des centres extrahospitaliers pratiquant l'avortement, Fédération laïque des centres de planning familial, Fédération des centres pluralistes de planning familial, Fédération des centres de planning et de consultations and Fédération des centres de planning familial des Femmes prévoyantes socialistes. 2018. Dépénalisation de l'IVG : la proposition de loi de la majorité fédérale votée en commission Justice. Tout ça pour ça ? Press Release, 19 September.

Malcourant, Éloïse. 2015. La stigmatisation de l'avortement. Brussels: Femmes prévoyantes socialistes.

Plateforme pour le droit à l'avortement. 2013. Mémorandum 2014. Published in *Chronique féministe* (112), 63.

Documents of European associations

Agenda Europe. N.D. The European Commission's reply to One of Us. Reaction to the communication of the European Commission on the One of Us petition. *Marginalia* (2). URL: https://agendaeurope.wordpress.com.

Avortement Info. 2013. Abortion clinics in Europe. URL: http://avortement.info.

Datta, Neil. 2013. Keeping it all in the family: Europe's antichoice movement. *Conscience* 34(2), 22–27.

Datta, Neil. 2018. "Restoring the Natural Order": the religious extremists' vision to mobilize European societies against human rights on sexuality and reproduction. European Parliamentary Forum on Population and Development, Brussels.

de La Hougue, Claire. N.D. L'objection de conscience dans le domaine médical en droit européen et international. European Centre for Law and Justice.

Ercolessi Giulio. 2017. International safe abortion day: a personal contribution. 2 October. URL: https://humanistfederation.eu.

European Humanist Federation. N.D. Securing sexual and reproductive rights. URL: https://humanistfederation.eu.

European Parliamentary Forum on Population and Development. 2013. Sexual and reproductive health and rights: the basics. *Intelligence Brief* (1).

European Parliamentary Forum on Population and Development. 2022. European contraception policy atlas.

European Women's Lobby. 2010. European Women's Lobby position paper: women's health in the European Union.

Galand Pierre. 2012. Créer l'imaginaire de la laïcité. 16 March. URL: https://pierregaland.be.

Hickson, Caroline, and Neil Datta. 2020. Sexual and reproductive rights during the COVID-19 pandemic. European Parliamentary Forum for Sexual and

Reproductive Rights and International Planned Parenthood Federation – European Network, 22 April.

Hurst, Jane. 1983. *The History of Abortion in the Catholic Church: The Untold Story*. Washington, DC: Catholics for a Free Choice.

Hurst Jane. 1992. *La Historia de las Ideas sobre el Aborto en la Iglesia Católica (lo que no fue contado)*. México: Encuadernación Técnica Editorial and Católicas por el derecho a decidir.

Mouvement français pour le planning familial. 2019. Tableau comparatif des législations sur l'avortement dans l'Union européenne. URL: http://avorte-menteurope.org.

Restoring the Natural Order: An Agenda for Europe. N.D. URL: https://agendae-urope.files.wordpress.com.

Documents of international associations and non-European institutions

Center for Reproductive Rights. 2011. Safe and legal abortion is a woman's human right. URL: www.reproductiverights.org.

Center for Reproductive Rights. 2017. The world's abortion laws. URL: http://worldabortionlaws.com.

Cornides, Jakob. 2010. *Natural and Un-natural Law*. New York: Catholic Family and Human Rights Institute.

International Planned Parenthood Federation. 2008. Revised charter on sexual and reproductive rights.

International Planned Parenthood Federation. 2009. Sexual rights: an IPPF declaration.

Law Library of Congress, Global Legal Center. 2015. Abortion legislation in Europe. URL: www.law.gov.

Library of Congress. 2013. Abortion law of jurisdictions around the world. URL: www.loc.gov.

Singh, Susheela, Lisa Remez, Gilda Sedgh, Lorraine Kwok and Tsuyoshi Onda. 2018. Abortion worldwide 2017: uneven progress and unequal access. Guttmacher Institute. URL: www.guttmacher.org.

Belgian legislative documents

Moniteur belge. 1973. Law of 9 July 1973 repealing the last three paragraphs of Article 383 of the Criminal Code. 9 August.

Moniteur belge. 1990. Law of 3 April 1990 on the termination of pregnancy, amending Articles 348, 350, 351 and 352 of the Criminal Code and repealing Article 353 of the same Code. 5 April.

Moniteur belge. 1990. Law of 13 August 1990 to create a commission to evaluate the law of 3 April 1990 on the termination of pregnancy, amending Articles

348, 350, 351 and 352 of the Criminal Code and repealing Article 353 of the same Code. 20 October.

Moniteur belge. 1999. Circular of the Minister of Justice of 10 June 1999 on the introduction into the Civil Code of Article 80bis concerning the registration of a lifeless child. 1 July.

Moniteur belge. 1999. Law of 27 April 1999 introducing Article 80bis into the Civil Code and repealing the decree of 4 July 1806 on the method of drawing up the certificate in which the registrar notes that he/she is recording a lifeless child. 24 June.

Moniteur belge. 2017. Law of 20 February 2017 amending the Civil Code with regard to the prenatal recognition of a child by an unmarried parent. 22 March.

Moniteur belge. 2018. Law of 18 June 2018 containing various provisions on civil law and provisions to promote alternative forms of dispute resolution. 2 July.

Moniteur belge. 2018. Law of 15 October 2018 on the voluntary termination of pregnancy repealing Articles 350 and 351 of the Criminal Code and amending Articles 352 and 383 of the same Code and amending various legislative provisions. 29 October.

Moniteur belge. 2018. Law of 19 December 2018 amending various provisions relating to the regulation of lifeless children. 27 December.

Moniteur belge. 2018. Royal Decree of 15 October 2018 appointing the members of the National Evaluation Commission responsible for evaluating the application of the provisions of the law of 3 April 1990 on the voluntary termination of pregnancy. 5 November.

Belgian parliamentary documents

House of Representatives. 1978. Bill on the termination of pregnancy. Tabled by Leona Detiège, Jeanne Adriaensens and Georgette Brenez (BSP-PSB), no. 240/1, 18 January. (Chambre des représentants. 1978. Proposition de loi sur l'interruption de la grossesse. Déposée par Leona Detiège, Jeanne Adriaensens et Georgette Brenez (BSP-PSB), no. 240/1, 18 janvier.)

House of Representatives. 1979. Bill on the termination of pregnancy. Tabled by Leona Detiège (BSP), Jeanne Adriaensens (BSP) and Georgette Brenez (PS), no. 106/1, 16 May. (Chambre des représentants. 1979. Proposition de loi sur l'interruption de la grossesse. Déposée par Leona Detiège (BSP), Jeanne Adriaensens (BSP) et Georgette Brenez (PS), no. 106/1, 16 mai 1979.)

House of Representatives. 1981. Bill on the termination of pregnancy with the aim of suspending Articles 350, 351, 352, 353 and 383, paragraph 5 and following of the Criminal Code. Tabled by Leona Detiège (SP), Basile-Jean Risopoulos (FDF), Anne-Marie Neyts-Uyttebroeck (PVV), Hervé Brouhon (PS), Édouard Klein (PRL), Olivier Deleuze (Ecolo) and Jacques Nagels (PCB), no. 20/1, 15 December. (Chambre des représentants. 2018. Proposition de loi sur l'interruption de grossesse et tendant à suspendre les articles 350, 351, 352, 353 et 383, alinéa 5 et suivants, du Code pénal. Déposée par Leona

Detiège (SP), Basile-Jean Risopoulos (FDF), Anne-Marie Neyts-Uyttebroeck (PVV), Hervé Brouhon (PS), Édouard Klein (PRL), Olivier Deleuze (Écolo) et Jacques Nagels (PCB), no. 20/1, 15 décembre.)

House of Representatives. 1982. Bill on the termination or pregnancy. Tabled by Leona Detiège, no. 52/1, 4 February. (Chambre des représentants. 1982. Proposition de loi sur l'interruption de grossesse. Déposée par Leona Detiège (SP), no. 52/1, 4 février.)

House of Representatives. 1982. Bill authorising the termination of pregnancy on a trial basis for one year. Tabled by Leona Detiège (SP), Basile-Jean Risopoulos (FDF), Robert Henrion (PRL), Edward Beysen (PVV), Hervé Brouhon (PS), Édouard Klein (PRL), Georgette Brenez (PS), Olivier Deleuze (Ecolo), Daniel Fedrigo (PCB) and Armand De Decker (PRL), no. 195/1, 11 March. (Chambre des représentants. 1982. Proposition de loi autorisant l'interruption de grossesse, à titre expérimental, pendant un an. Déposée par Leona Detiège (SP), Basile-Jean Risopoulos (FDF), Robert Henrion (PRL), Edward Beysen (PVV), Hervé Brouhon (PS), Édouard Klein (PRL), Georgette Brenez (PS), Olivier Deleuze (Écolo), Daniel Fedrigo (PCB) et Armand De Decker (PRL), no. 195/1, 11 mars.)

House of Representatives. 1983. Bill on the termination of pregnancy. Tabled by Leona Detiège (SP), Basile-Jean Risopoulos (FDF), Georges Mundeleer (PRL), Lucen Van de Velde (PVV), Georgette Brenez (PS), Edward Beysen (PVV), Daniel Fedrigo (PCB), Olivier Deleuze (Ecolo) and Édouard Klein (PRL), no. 545/1, 17 February. (Chambre des représentants. 1983. Proposition de loi sur l'interruption de grossesse. Déposée par Leona Detiège (SP), Basile-Jean Risopoulos (FDF), Georges Mundeleer (PRL), Lucen Van de Velde (PVV), Georgette Brenez (PS), Edward Beysen (PVV), Daniel Fedrigo (PCB), Olivier Deleuze (Écolo) et Édouard Klein (PRL), no. 545/1, 17 février.)

House of Representatives. 2014. Bill amending the regulation of stillborn children. Tabled by Sonja Becq and Raf Terwingen (CD&V), no. 243/1, 10 September. (Chambre des représentants. 2014. Proposition de loi modifiant la réglementation concernant les enfants nés sans vie. Déposée par Sonja Becq et Raf Terwingen (CD&V), no. 243/1, 10 septembre.)

House of Representatives. 2014. Bill on the law on lifeless children. Tabled by Catherine Fonck, Francis Delpérée and Vanessa Matz (CDH), no. 506/1, 24 October. (Chambre des représentants. 2014. Proposition de loi relative aux enfants nés sans vie. Déposée par Catherine Fonck, Francis Delpérée et Vanessa Matz (CDH), no. 506/1, 24 octobre.)

House of Representatives. 2015. Bill amending Royal Decree no. 78 of 10 November 1967 on the practice of the health care professions in order to allow the free distribution of contraceptives and the morning-after pill via family planning centres by means of a "Contraception Pass". Tabled by Muriel Gerkens, Anne Dedry, Stefaan Van Hecke, Wouter De Vriendt, Benoit Hellings, Jean-Marc Nollet and Evita Willaert (Ecolo-Groen), no. 1456/1, 17 November. (Chambre des représentants. 2015. Proposition de loi modifiant l'arrêté royal no. 78 du 10 novembre 1967 relatif à l'exercice des professions des soins de santé, afin de permettre la distribution gratuite de moyens contraceptifs et de la pilule du lendemain via les Centres de planning familial au moyen d'un "Pass contraception". Déposée par Muriel Gerkens, Anne Dedry, Stefaan Van Hecke, Wouter De Vriendt, Benoit Hellings, Jean-Marc Nollet et Evita Willaert (Écolo-Groen), no. 1456/1, 17 novembre.)

House of Representatives. 2015. Bill amending the Civil Code with regard to stillborn children. Tabled by Peter Vanvelthoven, Karin Jiroflée and Maya Detège (SP.A), no. 801/1, 20 January. (Chambre des représentants. 2015. Proposition de loi modifiant le Code civil en ce qui concerne les enfants nés sans vie. Déposée par Peter Vanvelthoven, Karin Jiroflée et Maya Detiège (sp.a.), no. 801/1, 20 janvier.)

House of Representatives. 2015. Bill amending the Civil Code with regard to the registration of stillborn children. Tabled by Carina Van Cauter and Sabien Lahaye-Battheu (Open VLD), no. 957/1, 12 March. (Chambre des représentants. 2015. Proposition de loi modifiant le Code civil en ce qui concerne la déclaration d'enfant né sans vie. Déposée par Carina Van Cauter et Sabien Lahaye-Battheu (Open Vld), no. 957/1, 12 mars.)

House of Representatives. 2016. Bill amending the Civil Code with regard to the prenatal recognition of a child by an unmarried parent. No. 1658/1, 17 February. (Chambre des représentants. 2016. Projet de loi modifiant le Code civil en ce qui concerne la reconnaissance prénatale d'un enfant par un parent non marié. No. 1658/1, 17 février.)

House of Representatives. 2016. Bill amending the coordinated laws of 10 May 2015 on the practice of the health care professions in order to allow the distribution of emergency contraception and contraceptives that are not likely to present a danger to health by approved organisations. Tabled by Fabienne Winckel, André Frédéric, Özlem Özen, Daniel Senesael, Karine Lalieux and Alain Mathot (PS), no. 1759/1, 13 April. (Chambre des représentants. 2016. Proposition de loi modifiant les lois coordonnées du 10 mai 2015 relatives à l'exercice des professions des soins de santé, afin de permettre la distribution de moyens de contraception d'urgence et non susceptibles de présenter un danger pour la santé par des organismes agréés. Déposée par Fabienne Winckel, André Frédéric, Özlem Özen, Daniel Senesael, Karine Lalieux et Alain Mathot (PS), no. 1759/1, 13 avril.)

House of Representatives. 2016. Bill amending the Criminal Code and the law of 22 August 2002 on the rights of the patient aimed at decriminalising the voluntary termination of pregnancy. Tabled by Olivier Maingain and Véronique Caprasse (Défi), no. 1823/1, 10 May. (Chambre des représentants. 2016. Proposition de loi modifiant le Code pénal et la loi du 22 août 2002 relative aux droits du patient, visant à dépénaliser l'interruption volontaire de grossesse. Déposée par Olivier Maingain et Véronique Caprasse (Défi), no. 1823/1, 10 mai.)

House of Representatives. 2016. Bill on the voluntary termination of pregnancy. Tabled by Muriel Gerkens, Evita Willaert, Marcel Cheron, Georges Gilkinet, Anne Dedry, Benoit Hellings, Meyrem Almaci, Jean-Marc Nollet and Gilles

Vanden Burre (Ecolo-Groen), no. 1947/1, 1 July. (Chambre des représentants. 2016. Proposition de loi relative à l'interruption volontaire de grossesse. Déposée par Muriel Gerkens, Evita Willaert, Marcel Cheron, Georges Gilkinet, Anne Dedry, Benoit Hellings, Meyrem Almaci, Jean-Marc Nollet et Gilles Vanden Burre (Écolo-Groen), no. 1947/1, 1 juillet.)

House of Representatives. 2016. Bill to remove the voluntary termination of pregnancy from the Criminal Code and to introduce it into the law of 22 August 2002 on the rights of the patient. Tabled by Karine Lalieux, Laurette Onkelinx and Fabienne Winkel (PS), no. 1867/1, 31 May. (Chambre des représentants. 2016. Proposition de loi visant à sortir l'interruption volontaire de grossesse du Code pénal et à l'introduire au sein de la loi du 22 août 2002 relative aux droits du patient. Déposée par Karine Lalieux, Laurette Onkelinx et Fabienne Winkel (PS), no. 1867/1, 31 mai.)

House of Representatives. 2017. Bill amending the regulation of stillborn children: amendments. Tabled by Sonja Becq (CD&V), Raf Terwingen (CD&V) and Goedele Uyttersprot (N-VA), no. 243/5, 22 February. (Chambre des représentants. 2017. Proposition de loi modifiant la réglementation concernant les enfants nés sans vie. Amendements. Déposés par Sonja Becq (CD&V), Raf Terwingen (CD&V) et Goedele Uyttersprot (N-VA), no. 243/5, 22 février 2017.)

House of Representatives. 2017. Bill decriminalising abortion and updating the law on the voluntary termination of pregnancy. Tabled by Marco Van Hees and Raoul Hedebouw (PTB-GO!), no. 2518/1, 8 June 2017. (Chambre des représentants. 2017. Proposition de loi dépénalisant l'avortement et actualisant la loi relative à l'interruption volontaire de grossesse. Déposée par Marco Van Hees et Raoul Hedebouw (PTB-GO!), no. 2518/1, 8 juin.)

House of Representatives. 2017. Bill decriminalising the voluntary termination of pregnancy. Tabled by Karin Jiroflée, Monica De Coninck, Annick Lambrecht and Karin Temmerman (SP.A), no. 2571/1, 27 June. (Chambre des représentants. 2017. Proposition de loi relative à l'interruption volontaire de grossesse. Déposée par Karin Jiroflée, Monica De Coninck, Annick Lambrecht et Karin Temmerman (sp.a.), no. 2571/1, 27 juin.)

House of Representatives. 2017. Bill on abortion. Tabled by Carina Van Cauter (Open VLD), no. 2527/1, 12 June. (Chambre des représentants. 2017. Proposition de loi relative à l'avortement. Déposée par Carina Van Cauter (Open Vld), no. 2527/1, 12 juin.)

House of Representatives. 2017. Bill on the voluntary termination of pregnancy. Tabled by Muriel Gerkens, Evita Willaert, Georges Gilkinet, Anne Dedry, Benoit Hellings, Meyrem Almaci, Jean-Marc Nollet and Gilles Vanden Burre (Ecolo-Groen), no. 2271/1, 18 January. (Chambre des représentants. 2017. Proposition de loi relative à l'interruption volontaire de grossesse. Déposée par Muriel Gerkens, Evita Willaert, Georges Gilkinet, Anne Dedry, Benoit Hellings, Meyrem Almaci, Jean-Marc Nollet et Gilles Vanden Burre (Écolo-Groen), no. 2271/1, 18 janvier.)

House of Representatives. 2017. *Full Report* (156 and 157), 9 February. (Chambre des représentants. 2017. *Compte rendu intégral* (156 et 157), 9 février.)

House of Representatives. 2017. *Full Report* (172), 8 June. (Chambre des représentants. 2017. *Compte rendu intégral* (172), 8 juin.)

House of Representatives. 2018. Bill amending Article 4 of the law of 18 June 2018 on various provisions in civil law and provisions to promote alternative forms of dispute resolution concerning the lifeless child act. No. 3271/1, 19 September. (Chambre des représentants. 2018. Projet de loi modifiant l'article 4 de la loi du 18 juin 2018 portant dispositions diverses en matière de droit civil et des dispositions en vue de promouvoir des formes alternatives de résolution des litiges, concernant l'acte d'enfant sans vie. No. 3271/1, 19 septembre.)

House of Representatives. 2018. Bill decriminalising the voluntary termination of pregnancy. Tabled by Karin Jiroflée, Monica De Coninck, Annick Lambrecht and Karin Temmerman (SP.A), no. 3059/1, 26 April. (Chambre des représentants. 2018. Proposition de loi dépénalisant l'interruption volontaire de grossesse. Déposée par Karin Jiroflée, Monica De Coninck, Annick Lambrecht et Karin Temmerman (sp.a.), no. 3059/1, 26 avril.)

House of Representatives. 2018. Bill on the termination of pregnancy. Tabled by Catherine Fonck (CDH), no. 3123/1, 29 May. (Chambre des représentants. 2018. Proposition de loi relative à l'interruption de grossesse. Déposée par Catherine Fonck (CDH), no. 3123/1, 29 mai.)

House of Representatives. 2018. Bill on the voluntary termination of pregnancy. Tabled by David Clarinval (MR), Carina Van Cauter (Open VLD), Valérie Van Peel (N-VA) and Els Van Hoof (CD&V), no. 3216/1, 4 July. (Chambre des représentants. 2018. Proposition de loi relative à l'interruption volontaire de grossesse. Déposée par David Clarinval (MR), Carina Van Cauter (Open Vld), Valérie Van Peel (N-VA) et Els Van Hoof (CD&V), no. 3216/1, 4 juillet.)

House of Representatives. 2018. Bill to remove the voluntary termination of pregnancy from the Criminal Code. Tabled by Karine Lalieux (PS), Véronique Caprasse (Défi), Muriel Gerkens (Ecolo-Groen), Karin Jiroflée (SP.A) and Marco Van Hees (PTB), no. 3215/1, 4 July. (Chambre des représentants. 2018. Proposition de loi visant à sortir l'interruption volontaire de grossesse du Code pénal. Déposée par Karine Lalieux (PS), Véronique Caprasse (Défi), Muriel Gerkens (Écolo-Groen), Karin Jiroflée (sp.a.) et Marco Van Hees (PTB-GO!), no. 3215/1, 4 juillet.)

House of Representatives. 2018. *Full Report* (246), 4 October. (Chambre des représentants. 2018. *Compte rendu intégral* (246), 4 octobre.)

House of Representatives. 2018. *Full Report* (262), 13 December. (Chambre des représentants. 2018. *Compte rendu intégral* (262), 13 décembre.)

House of Representatives. 2018. *Summary Record* (246), 4 October. (Chambre des représentants. 2018. *Compte rendu analytique* (246), 4 octobre.)

House of Representatives. 2019. Bill amending the Civil Code and the Judicial Code in order to allow anonymous childbirth. Tabled by Valérie Van Peel (N-VA), no. 183/1, 16 July 2019. (Chambre des représentants. 2019. Proposition de loi modifiant le Code civil et le Code judiciaire en vue de permettre l'accouchement discret. Déposée par Valérie Van Peel (N-VA), no. 183/1, 16 juillet.)

House of Representatives. 2019. Bill decriminalising abortion and updating the law on the voluntary termination of pregnancy. Tabled by Marco Van Hees, Raoul Hedebouw, Maria Vindevoghel, Nadia Moscufo, Sofie Merckx, Greta Daems and Nabil Boukili (PVDA-PTB), no. 458/1, 30 September. (Chambre des représentants. 2019. Proposition de loi dépénalisant l'avortement et actualisant la loi relative à l'interruption volontaire de grossesse. Déposée par Marco Van Hees, Raoul Hedebouw, Maria Vindevoghel, Nadia Moscufo, Sofie Merckx, Greta Daems et Nabil Boukili (PVDA-PTB), no. 458/1, 30 septembre.)

House of Representatives. 2019. Bill decriminalising the voluntary termination of pregnancy. Tabled by Sarah Schlitz, Jessika Soors, Séverine de Laveleye, Evita Willaert, Cécile Thibaut, Barbara Creemers, Marie-Colline Leroy, Kim Buyst, Julie Chanson and Laurence Hennuy (Ecolo-Groen), no. 614/1, 16 October 2019. (Chambre des représentants. 2019. Proposition de loi visant à dépénaliser l'interruption volontaire de grossesse. Déposée par Sarah Schlitz, Jessika Soors, Séverine de Laveleye, Evita Willaert, Cécile Thibaut, Barbara Creemers, Marie-Colline Leroy, Kim Buyst, Julie Chanson et Laurence Hennuy (Écolo-Groen), no. 614/1, 16 octobre.)

House of Representatives. 2019. Bill decriminalising the voluntary termination of pregnancy and to relax the conditions for its use. Tabled by Sophie Rohonyi and François De Smet (Défi), no. 385/1, 17 September. (Chambre des représentants. 2019. Proposition de loi visant à dépénaliser l'interruption volontaire de grossesse et à assouplir les conditions pour y recourir. Déposée par Sophie Rohonyi et François De Smet (Défi), no. 385/1, 17 septembre.)

House of Representatives. 2019. Bill on abortion. Tabled by Katja Gabriëls, Egbert Lachaert and Goedele Liekens (Open VLD), no. 652/1, 22 October. (Chambre des représentants. 2019. Proposition de loi relative à l'avortement. Déposée par Katja Gabriëls, Egbert Lachaert et Goedele Liekens (Open Vld), no. 652/1, 22 octobre.)

House of Representatives. 2019. Bill on easing the conditions for the termination of a pregnancy. Tabled by Karin Jiroflée (SP.A), no. 676/1, 23 October. (Chambre des représentants. 2019. Proposition de loi assouplissant les conditions pour recourir à une interruption de grossesse. Déposée par Karin Jiroflée (sp.a.), no. 676/1, 23 octobre.)

House of Representatives. 2019. Bill on the voluntary termination of pregnancy. Tabled by Kattrin Jadin, David Clarinval, Philippe Goffin, Caroline Taquin, Florence Reuter, Daniel Bacquelaine, Emmanuel Burton and Michel De Maegd (MR), no. 740/1, 12 November. (Chambre des représentants. 2019. Proposition de loi relative à l'interruption volontaire de grossesse. Déposée par Kattrin Jadin, David Clarinval, Philippe Goffin, Caroline Taquin, Florence Reuter, Daniel Bacquelaine, Emmanuel Burton et Michel De Maegd (MR), no. 740/1, 12 novembre.)

House of Representatives. 2019. Bill to insert Article 1383bis in the Civil Code specifying that there is no prejudice due to the mere fact of one's birth. Tabled by Daniel Bacquelaine, Philippe Goffin, Emmanuel Burton, Caroline Taquin, Michel De Maegd and David Clarinval (MR), no. 531/1, 3 October

2019. (Chambre des représentants. 2019. Proposition de loi insérant un article 1383bis dans le Code civil précisant qu'il n'y a pas de préjudice du seul fait de sa naissance. Déposée par Daniel Bacquelaine, Philippe Goffin, Emmanuel Burton, Caroline Taquin, Michel De Maegd et David Clarinval (MR), no. 531/1, 3 octobre.)

House of Representatives. 2019. Bill to relax the conditions for the voluntary termination of pregnancy. Tabled by Éliane Tillieux, Caroline Désir, Patrick Prévot, Özlem Özen, Laurence Zanchetta, Mélissa Hanus, Jean-Marc Delizée and Sophie Thémont (PS), no. 158/1, 16 July. (Chambre des représentants. 2019. Proposition de loi visant à assouplir les conditions pour recourir à l'interruption volontaire de grossesse. Déposée par Éliane Tillieux, Caroline Désir, Patrick Prévot, Özlem Özen, Laurence Zanchetta, Mélissa Hanus, Jean-Marc Delizée et Sophie Thémont (PS), no. 158/1, 16 juillet.)

House of Representatives. 2019. Bill to relax the conditions for the voluntary termination of pregnancy: amendments. Tabled by Éliane Tillieux (PS), Karin Jiroflée (SP.A), Sophie Rohonyi (Défi), Sofie Merckx (PVDA-PTB), Kattrin Jadin (MR), Jessika Soors (Ecolo-Groen), Sarah Schlitz (Ecolo-Groen) and Katja Gabriëls (Open VLD), no. 158/3, 13 November. (Chambre des représentants. 2019. Proposition de loi visant à assouplir les conditions pour recourir à l'interruption volontaire de grossesse. Amendements. Déposés par Éliane Tillieux (PS), Karin Jiroflée (SP.A), Sophie Rohonyi (Défi), Sofie Merckx (PVDA-PTB), Kattrin Jadin (MR), Jessika Soors (Écolo-Groen), Sarah Schlitz (Écolo-Groen) et Katja Gabriëls (Open Vld), no. 158/3, 13 novembre.)

House of Representatives. 2019. Bill to relax the conditions for the voluntary termination of pregnancy: amendment submitted at the second reading. Tabled by Katja Gabriëls (Open VLD), Sarah Schlitz (Ecolo-Groen), Jessika Soors (Ecolo-Groen), Sophie Rohonyi (Défi), Sofie Merckx (PVDA-PTB), Kattrin Jadin (MR) and Éliane Tillieux (PS), no. 158/6, 16 December. (Chambre des représentants. 2019. Proposition de loi visant à assouplir les conditions pour recourir à l'interruption volontaire de grossesse. Amendement déposé en deuxième lecture. Déposé par Katja Gabriëls (Open Vld), Sarah Schlitz (Écolo-Groen), Jessika Soors (Écolo-Groen), Sophie Rohonyi (Défi), Sofie Merckx (PVDA-PTB), Kattrin Jadin (MR) et Éliane Tillieux (PS), no. 158/6, 16 décembre.)

House of Representatives. 2019. Bill to relax the conditions for the voluntary termination of pregnancy: amendments submitted at the second reading. Tabled by Éliane Tillieux (PS), Sophie Rohonyi (Défi), Sofie Merckx (PVDAPTB), Jessika Soors (Ecolo-Groen), Karin Jiroflée (SP.A), Sarah Schlitz (Ecolo-Groen), Kattrin Jadin (MR) and Katja Gabriëls (Open VLD), no. 158/7, 20 December. (Chambre des représentants. 2019. Proposition de loi visant à assouplir les conditions pour recourir à l'interruption volontaire de grossesse. Amendements déposés en deuxième lecture. Déposés par Éliane Tillieux (PS), Sophie Rohonyi (Défi), Sofie Merckx (PVDA-PTB), Jessika Soors (Écolo-Groen), Karin Jiroflée (sp.a.), Sarah Schlitz (Écolo-Groen), Kattrin Jadin (MR) et Katja Gabriëls (Open Vld), no. 158/7, 20 décembre.)

House of Representatives. 2020. Biennial reports of the National Evaluation Commission of the Law of 3 April 1990 on the voluntary termination of pregnancy: hearings. No. 1201/1, 28 April. (Chambre des représentants. 1990. Rapports bisannuels de la Commission nationale d'évaluation de la loi du 3 avril 1990 relative à l'interruption volontaire de grossesse. Auditions. No. 1201/1, 28 avril.)

House of Representatives. 2020. Bill amending various legislative provisions in order to relax the conditions for the voluntary termination of pregnancy: amendments submitted in the plenary session. No. 158/13, 30 June. (Chambre des représentants. 2020. Proposition de loi modifiant diverses dispositions législatives en vue d'assouplir les conditions pour recourir à l'interruption volontaire de grossesse. Amendements déposés en séance plénière.No. 158/13, 30 juin.)

House of Representatives. 2020. Bill amending various legislative provisions in order to relax the conditions for the voluntary termination of pregnancy: amendments submitted in the plenary session. No. 158/15, 15 July. (Chambre des représentants. 2020. Proposition de loi modifiant diverses dispositions législatives en vue d'assouplir les conditions pour recourir à l'interruption volontaire de grossesse. Amendements déposés en séance plénière. No. 158/15, 15 juillet.)

House of Representatives. 2020. Bill amending various legislative provisions in order to relax the conditions for the voluntary termination of pregnancy: Council of State opinion no. 67.122/AG of 19 June 2020. No. 158/12, 22 June. (Chambre des représentants. 2020. Proposition de loi modifiant diverses dispositions législatives en vue d'assouplir les conditions pour recourir à l'interruption volontaire de grossesse. Avis du Conseil d'État no. 67.122/AG du 19 juin 2020. No. 158/12, 22 juin.)

House of Representatives. 2020. Bill amending various legislative provisions in order to relax the conditions for the voluntary termination of pregnancy: Council of State opinion no. 67.732/AV of 10 July 2020. No. 158/14, 10 July. (Chambre des représentants. 2020. Proposition de loi modifiant diverses dispositions législatives en vue d'assouplir les conditions pour recourir à l'interruption volontaire de grossesse. Avis du Conseil d'État no. 67.732/AV du 10 juillet 2020. No. 158/14, 10 juillet.)

House of Representatives. 2020. Bill to relax the conditions for the voluntary termination of pregnancy: amendments submitted in the plenary session. No. 158/11, 12 March. (Chambre des représentants. 2020. Proposition de loi visant à assouplir les conditions pour recourir à l'interruption volontaire de grossesse. Amendements déposés en séance plénière. No. 158/11, 12 mars.)

House of Representatives. 2020. Bill to relax the conditions for the voluntary termination of pregnancy: Council of State opinion no. 66.881/AG of 24 February 2020. No. 158/10, 2 March. (Chambre des représentants. 2020. Proposition de loi visant à assouplir les conditions pour recourir à l'interruption volontaire de grossesse. Avis du Conseil d'État no. 66.881/AG du 24 février 2020. No. 158/10, 2 mars.)

House of Representatives. 2020. *Full Report* (31), 19 March. (Chambre des représentants. 2020. *Compte rendu intégral* (31), 19 mars.)

House of Representatives. 2020. *Summary Record* (49), 2 July. (Chambre des représentants. 2020. *Compte rendu analytique* (49), 2 juillet.)

House of Representatives. 2020. *Summary Record* (52), 15 July. (Chambre des représentants. 2020. *Compte rendu analytique* (52), 15 juillet.)

House of Representatives, Committee on Public Health, Environment and Social Renewal. 2017. Bill amending Royal Decree no. 78 of 10 November 1967 on the practice of the health care professions in order to allow the free distribution of contraceptives and the morning-after pill via family planning centres by means of a "Contraception Pass"; bill amending the coordinated acts of 10 May 2015 on the practice of the health care professions in order to allow the distribution of emergency contraception and contraceptives that are not likely to present a danger to health by approved bodies: report. No. 1456/5, 2 June 2017. (Chambre des représentants, Commission de la Santé publique, de l'Environnement et du Renouveau de la société. 2017. Proposition de loi modifiant l'arrêté royal no. 78 du 10 novembre 1967 relatif à l'exercice des professions des soins de santé, afin de permettre la distribution gratuite de moyens contraceptifs et de la pilule du lendemain via les Centres de planning familial au moyen d'un "Pass contraception" ; proposition de loi modifiant les lois coordonnées du 10 mai 2015 relatives à l'exercice des professions des soins de santé, afin de permettre la distribution de moyens de contraception d'urgence et non susceptibles de présenter un danger pour la santé par des organismes agréés. Rapport. No. 1456/5, 2 juin.)

House of Representatives, Committee on Justice. 2018. Bill on the voluntary termination of pregnancy; bill amending the Criminal Code and the law of 22 August 2002 on the rights of the patient aimed at decriminalising the voluntary termination of pregnancy; bill to remove the voluntary termination or pregnancy from the Criminal Code and to introduce it into the law of 22 August 2002 on the rights of the patient; bill on the voluntary termination of pregnancy; bill decriminalising abortion and updating the law on the voluntary termination of pregnancy; bill on the voluntary termination of pregnancy; bill decriminalising the voluntary termination of pregnancy; bill on the termination of pregnancy: first reading of the report. No. 3216/3, 1 August. (Chambre des représentants, Commission de la Justice. 2018. Proposition de loi relative à l'interruption volontaire de grossesse ; proposition de loi modifiant le Code pénal et la loi du 22 août 2002 relative aux droits du patient, visant à dépénaliser l'interruption volontaire de grossesse ; proposition de loi visant à sortir l'interruption volontaire de grossesse du Code pénal et à l'introduire au sein de la loi du 22 août 2002 relative aux droits du patient ; proposition de loi relative à l'interruption volontaire de grossesse ; proposition de loi dépénalisant l'avortement et actualisant la loi relative à l'interruption volontaire de grossesse ; proposition de loi relative à l'interruption volontaire de grossesse ; proposition de loi dépénalisant l'interruption volontaire de grossesse ; proposition relative à l'interruption de grossesse. Rapport de la première lecture. No. 3216/3, 1 août.)

House of Representatives, Committee on Justice. 2019. Bill to relax the conditions for the voluntary termination of pregnancy: report of the first reading. No. 158/4, 6 December. (Chambre des représentants, Commission de la Justice. 2019. Proposition de loi visant à assouplir les conditions pour recourir à l'interruption volontaire de grossesse. Rapport de la première lecture. No. 158/4, 6 décembre.)

House of Representatives, Committee on Justice. 2019. Bill to relax the conditions for the voluntary termination of pregnancy: report of the second reading. No. 158/8, 30 December. (Chambre des représentants, Commission de la Justice. 2019. Proposition de loi visant à assouplir les conditions pour recourir à l'interruption volontaire de grossesse. Rapport de la deuxième lecture. No. 158/8, 30 décembre.)

House of Representatives, Committee on Justice. 2019. Bill to relax the conditions for the voluntary termination of pregnancy: articles adopted at the first reading. No. 158/5, 6 December. (Chambre des représentants, Commission de la Justice. 2019. Proposition de loi visant à assouplir les conditions pour recourir à l'interruption volontaire de grossesse. Articles adoptés en première lecture. No. 158/5, 6 décembre.)

House of Representatives, Committee on Justice. 2019. Bill to relax the conditions for the voluntary termination of pregnancy: text adopted at the second reading. No. 158/9, 30 December. (Chambre des représentants, Commission de la Justice. 2019. Proposition de loi visant à assouplir les conditions pour recourir à l'interruption volontaire de grossesse. Texte adopté en deuxième lecture. No. 158/9, 30 décembre.)

Senate. 1986. Bill on the voluntary termination of pregnancy to amend Articles 348, 350 and 351 of the Criminal Code and to repeal Articles 352 and 353 of the same Code. Tabled by Roger Lallemand (PS), Lucienne Herman-Michielsens (PVV), Jozef Wyninckx (SP), Robert Henrion (PRL), Jean-François Vaes (Ecolo), Magda Aelvoet (Agalev), Jacques Lepaffe (FDF), Paul Pataer (SP) and Monique Rifflet-Knauer (PS), no. 189/1, 6 March. (Sénat. 1986. Proposition de loi relative à l'interruption de grossesse, tendant à modifier les articles 348, 350 et 351 du Code pénal et à abroger les articles 352 et 353 du même Code. Déposée par Roger Lallemand (PS), Lucienne Herman-Michielsens (PVV), Jozef Wyninckx (SP), Robert Henrion (PRL), Jean-François Vaes (Écolo), Magda Aelvoet (Agalev), Jacques Lepaffe (FDF), Paul Pataer (SP), Monique Rifflet-Knauer (PS), no. 189/1, 6 mars.)

Senate. 1988. Bill on the voluntary termination of pregnancy to amend Articles 348, 350 and 351 of the Criminal Code and to repeal Articles 352 and 353 of the same Code. Tabled by Lucienne Herman-Michielsens (PVV), France Truffaut-Denef (PS), Jozef Wyninckx (SP), Robert Henrion (PRL), Jean-François Vaes (Ecolo), Magda Aelvoet (Agalev) and Paul Pataer (SP), no. 247/1, 19 April. (Sénat. 1988. Proposition de loi relative à l'interruption de grossesse, tendant à modifier les articles 348, 350 et 351 du Code pénal et à abroger les articles 352 et 353 du même Code. Déposée par Lucienne Herman-Michielsens (PVV), France Truffaut-Denef (PS), Jozef Wyninckx (SP),

Robert Henrion (PRL), Jean-François Vaes (Écolo), Magda Aelvoet (Agalev), Paul Pataer (SP), no. 247/1, 19 avril.)

Senate and House of Representatives. 2012. Report of the National Commission for the Evaluation of the Law of 3 April 1990 on the termination of pregnancy: report to Parliament; 1 January 2010–31 December 2011. No. 1784/1 (Senate) and no. 2399/1 (House), 27 August. (Sénat et Chambre des représentants. 2012. Rapport de la Commission nationale d'évaluation de la loi du 3 avril 1990 relative à l'interruption de grossesse. Rapport à l'attention du Parlement : 1er janvier 2010-31 décembre 2011. No. 1784/1 (Sénat) et no. 2399/1 (Chambre), 27 août.)

Documents of Belgian courts and tribunals

Constitutional Court. 2019. Action for annulment of the law of 15 October 2018 lodged by the de facto association *Citoyens pour la vie* on 26 April 2019, received by the Court on 29 April 2019, roll number 7168. Announced in the *Moniteur belge*, 4 June.

Court of Cassation. 2013. Judgement no. S.12.0076.F, 18 November.

Council of Europe documents

Council of Europe. 2018. Report of the Independent Investigation Body on the allegations of corruption within the Parliamentary Assembly. 15 April 2018.

Council of Europe, Commissioner for Human Rights. 2017. Women's sexual and reproductive health and rights in Europe. Strasbourg.

Council of Europe, Commissioner for Human Rights. 2020. Submission by the Council of Europe Commissioner for Human Rights. Strasbourg, 27 January.

Council of Europe, Commissioner for Human Rights. 2021. Third party intervention by the Council of Europe Commissioner for Human Rights under Article 36, paragraph 3, of the European Convention on Human Rights. Strasbourg, 10 November.

Council of Europe, Committee of Ministers. 2021. Decisions, supervision of the execution of the European Court's judgments, concerning Tysiąc and R. R. (Applications nos. 5410/03, 27617/04), P. and S. (application no. 57375/08) v. Poland. CM/Del/Dec (2021) 1419/H46-25, 2 December.

Parliamentary Assembly of the Council of Europe. 2008. Access to safe and legal abortion in Europe. Resolution no. 1607, 16 April.

Parliamentary Assembly of the Council of Europe. 2010. The right to conscientious objection in lawful medical care. Resolution no. 1763, 20 July.

Parliamentary Assembly of the Council of Europe, Social, Health and Family Affairs Committee. 2010. Women's access to lawful medical care: the problem of unregulated use of conscientious objection. Christine McCafferty (rapporteur), Doc. 12347, 20 July.

European Union documents

Draft legal act tabled under the European Citizens' Initiative "One of us", registered by the European Commission as ECI(2012)000005, 11 May 2012. URL: https://register.eci.ec.europa.eu/core/api/register/document/1499.

European Commission. 2010. Strategy for the effective implementation of the Charter of Fundamental Rights by the European Union. COM (2010) 573 final, 19 October.

European Commission. 2014. Appendices to the Communication from the Commission on the European Citizens' Initiative "One of us". Appendix 1, COM(2014) 355 final, Brussels, 28 May.

European Commission. 2014. Communication from the Commission on the European Citizens' Initiative "One of us". COM(2014) 355 final, Brussels, 28 May.

European Commission. 2015. *Guide to the European Citizens' Initiative*. Luxembourg: Publications Office of the European Union.

European Parliament. 2002. European Parliament Resolution on sexual and reproductive health. 2001/2128 (INI), 6 June.

European Parliament. 2010. European Parliament Resolution on equality between women and men in the European Union. 2009/2101 (INI), 10 February.

European Parliament. 2013. European Parliament Resolution on sexual and reproductive health and rights. 2013/2040 (INI), 10 December.

European Parliament. 2015. European Parliament Resolution on progress made on gender equality in the EU in 2013. 2014/2217(INI), 10 March.

European Parliament. 2015. European Parliament Resolution on the EU Strategy for equality between women and men post 2015. 2014/2152 (INI), 9 June.

European Parliament. 2016. European Parliament Resolution on the situation of women refugees and asylum seekers in the EU. 2015/2325 (INI), 8 March.

European Parliament. 2019. European Parliament Resolution on the criminalisation of sex education in Poland. 2019/2891 (RSP), 14 November.

European Parliament. 2019. European Parliament Resolution on the decline in women's rights and gender equality in the EU. 2018/2684 (RSP), 13 February.

European Parliament. 2019. European Parliament Resolution on the situation of fundamental rights in the European Union in 2017. 2018/2103 (INI), 16 January.

European Parliament. 2020. European Parliament Resolution on the de facto ban on the right to abortion in Poland. 20/2876 (RSP), 26 November.

European Parliament. 2021. European Parliament Resolution on the first anniversary of the de facto abortion ban in Poland. 2021/2925 (RSP), 11 November.

European Parliament. 2021. European Parliament Resolution on sexual and reproductive health and rights in the EU, in the frame of women's health. 2020/2215 (INI), 24 June.

European Parliament. 2021. European Parliament Resolution on the state law relating to abortion in Texas, USA. 2021/2910 (RSP), 7 October.

European Parliament, Committee on Women's Rights and Gender Equality. 2013. Report on sexual and reproductive health and rights. (2013/ 2040(INI)). Edite Estrela (rapporteur), Meeting Document A7-0426/2013, 2 December.

European Parliament, the Council of the European Union and the European Commission. N.D. EU Transparency Register. URL: https://ec.europa.eu/transparencyregister.

European Union. 1957. Treaty on the Functioning of the European Union.

European Union Agency for Fundamental Rights. 2017. Challenges to Women's Human Rights in the EU.

Documents of international organisations

European Committee of Social Rights: Complaints

Confederazione Generale Italiana del Lavoro (CGIL) v. Italy. Complaint no. 91/2013, decision on admissibility and merits of 12 October 2015.

Federation of Catholic Family Associations in Europe (FAFCE) v. Sweden. Complaint no. 99/2013, decision on the merits of 17 March 2015.

International Planned Parenthood Federation – European Network (IPPF EN) v. Italy. Complaint no. 87/2012, decision on the merits of 10 September 2013.

European Court of Human Rights

Applications

A, B and C v. Ireland. Application no. 25579/05, judgement of 16 December 2010.

A. L.-B. v. Poland and 3 other applications. Application no. 3801/21, judgement of 1 July 2021.

Case of Tysiąc v. Poland. Application no. 5410/03, judgement of 20 March 2007.

Case of Vo v. France. Application no. 53924/00, judgement of 8 July 2004.

I. G. and Others v. Slovakia. Application no. 15966/04, judgement of 13 November 2012.

K. B. v. Poland and 3 other applications. Application no. 1819/21, judgement of 1 July 2021.

K. C. v. Poland and 3 other applications. Application no. 3639/21, judgement of 1 July 2021.

P. and S. v. Poland. Application no. 57375/08, judgement of 30 October 2012.

R. R. v. Poland. Application no. 27617/04, judgement of 26 May 2011.

V. C. v. Slovakia. Application no. 18968/07, judgement of 8 November 2011.

Concluding Observations

Ireland, CCPR/C/IRL/CO/4, 19 August 2014.

Malta, CCPR/C/MLT/CO/2, 20 November 2014.
Poland, CCPR/POL/CO/6, 15 November 2010.

UN Committee on the Elimination of Discrimination against Women: Concluding Observations

Croatia, CEDAW/C/HRV/CO/4-5, 28 July 2015.
Germany, CEDAW/C/DEU/CO/7-8, 9 March 2017.
Greece, CEDAW/C/GRC/CO/7, 26 March 2013.
Hungary, CEDAW/C/HUN/CO/7-8, 26 March 2013, 17 June 2013 and 10 August 2013.
Poland, CEDAW/C/POL/CO/7-8, 14 November 2014.
Slovakia, CEDAW/C/SVK/CO/5-6, 25 November 2015.

UN Committee on the Rights of the Child

UN Committee on the Rights of the Child. 2012. Consideration of reports submitted by States parties under article 44 of the Convention. CRC/C/VAT/2, 22 October.

Concluding Observations

Slovakia, CRC/C/SVK/CO/3-5, 25 November 2015 and 20 July 2016.

UN Human Rights Committee

UN Human Rights Committee. 2016. Communication submitted by Amanda Jane Mellet (represented by the Center for Reproductive Rights) v. Ireland. CCPR/116/D/2324/2013, 17 November.
UN Human Rights Committee. 2017. Communication submitted by Siobhán Whelan (represented by the Center for Reproductive Rights) v. Ireland. CCPR/C/119/D/2425/2014, 11 July.

Concluding Observations

Ireland, CCPR/C/IRL/CO/4, 19 August 2014.
Malta, CCPR/C/MLT/CO/2, 20 November 2014.
Poland, CCPR/POL/CO/6, 15 November 2010.

UN Committee on Economic, Social and Cultural Rights: Concluding Observations

Poland, E/C.12/POL/CO/5, 2 December 2009.

United Nations

United Nations. 1995. Report of the International Conference on Population and Development: Cairo, 5–13 September 1994. A/CONF.171/13/Rev.1. New York: UN.

United Nations. 1996. Report of the Fourth World Conference on Women: Beijing, 4–15 September 1995. A/CONF.177/20/Rev.1. New York: UN.

United Nations. 2017. Global abortion policies database. URL: https://abortion-policies.srhr.org.

World Health Organization

Cook, Rebecca J. 1994. *Women's Health and Human Rights*. Geneva: WHO.

World Health Organization. 1977. *International Classification of Diseases: Manual of the International Statistical Classification of Diseases, Injuries and Causes of Death; Revision 1975*, volume 1. Geneva: WHO.

World Health Organization. 2006. Defining sexual health: report of a technical consultation on sexual health, 28–31 January 2002.

World Health Organization. 2006. Definition of sexual health and sexual rights in the framework of reproductive health.

World Health Organization. 2012. *Safe Abortion: Technical and Policy Guidance for Health Systems*. Geneva: WHO.

World Health Organization. 2013. *Safe Abortion: Technical and Policy Guidance for Health Systems*, 2nd edition. Geneva: WHO.

World Health Organization. 2015. *Sexual Health and its Linkages to Reproductive Health: An Operational Approach*. Geneva: WHO.

World Health Organization. 2015. *Sexual Health, Human Rights and the Law*. Geneva: WHO.

World Health Organization. 2021. Model list of essential medicines: 22nd list. World Health Organization. 2017. *Selected Practical Recommendations on the Use of Contraceptive Methods*, 3rd edition. Geneva: WHO.

World Health Organization. 2022. Abortion care guidelines.

World Health Organization, Regional Office for Europe. 1987. *Concepts of Sexual Health: Report on a Working Group*. Copenhagen: WHO.

Documents of the Holy See and the Belgian Catholic Church

1994: Year of the Family; Letter [of Pope John Paul II] to Families. 1994. Rome: Libreria Editrice Vaticana.

Apostolic Exhortation, Evangelii Gaudium of Pope Francis to Bishops, Priests and Deacons, Consecrated Persons and All the Lay Faithful on the Proclamation of the Gospel in Today's World. 2013. Rome: Libreria Editrice Vaticana.

Apostolic Exhortation, Familiaris Consortio of His Holiness Pope John Paul II to the Episcopate, the Clergy and the Faithful of the Whole Catholic Church on the Role of the Christian Family in the Modern World. 1981. Rome: Libreria Editrice Vaticana.

Apostolic Letter, Mulieris Dignitatem of the Supreme Pontiff John Paul II on the Dignity and Vocation of Women on the Occasion of the Marian Year. 1988. Rome: Libreria Editrice Vaticana.

Belgian Bishops' Conference. 2018. Supprimer l'avortement du Code pénal : une décision symboliquement lourde. Press Release, 15 June. URL: http//info. catho.be.

Benedict XVI (Pope). 2008. Address to the Roman Curia on the occasion of the traditional meeting for Christmas greetings. 22 December. URL: www.v2.vatican.va.

Charter of the Rights of the Family presented by the Holy See to all persons, institutions and authorities concerned with the mission of the family in today's world. 22 October 1983. URL: www.vatican.va.

Declaration on Religious Freedom, Dignitatis Humanae. 1965. Rome, Libreria Editrice Vaticana.

de Kesel, Joseph (Cardinal), et al. 2019. Nouvel élargissement des conditions de l'avortement : déclaration des évêques de Belgique. 12 November. URL: www.cathobel.be.

Encyclical Letter, Evangelium Vitae of the Supreme Pontiff John Paul II to Bishops, Priests and Deacons, Religious Men and Women, Lay Faithful and All People of Good Will on the Value and Inviolability of Human Life. 1995. Rome: Libreria Editrice Vaticana.

Encyclical Letter, Veritatis Splendor of the Supreme Pontiff John Paul II to all the Bishops of the Catholic Church on Some Fundamental Questions of the Church's Moral Teaching. 1993. Rome: Libreria Editrice Vaticana.

Francis (Pope). 2014. Not just good, but beautiful. Address to participants at the international colloquium on the complementarity between man and woman sponsored by the Congregation for the Doctrine of the Faith, 17 November. URL: http://humanum.it.

Francis (Pope). 2015. *General Audience: St. Peter's Square, Wednesday 15 April and Wednesday 22 April 2015*. Rome: Libreria Editrice Vaticana.

Francis (Pope). 2015. General audience: the family; 10 – male and female (I). *Vatican Online Archive*, April 15. URL: https://w2.vatican.va.

Humanae Vitae: Encyclical Letter of the Supreme Pontiff, Pope Paul VI, on the Regulation of Birth. 1968. Rome, Libreria Editrice Vaticana.

Letter to the Bishops of the Catholic Church on the collaboration of men and women in the Church and in the world. 31 May 2004. URL: www.vatican.va.

Letter to Women from Pope John Paul II. 1995. Rome: Libreria Editrice Vaticana. Pastoral Constitution on the Church in the Modern World, Gaudium et Spes. 1965. Rome: Libreria Editrice Vaticana.

Permanent Observer Mission of the Holy See to the United Nations. 2011. 55th Commission on the Status of Women, explanation of position of the Holy See on the agreed conclusions. E.CN.6/2011/L.6, New York, 14 March.

Permanent Observer Mission of the Holy See to the United Nation. 2013. 57th Commission on the Status of Women, intervention of the Holy See. New York, 12 March.

Permanent Observer Mission of the Holy See to the United Nations. 2014. 8th session of the Open Working Group on the Sustainable Development Goals: "Promoting equality, including social equity, gender equality, and women's empowerment". New York, 6 February.

Permanent Observer Mission of the Holy See to the United Nations. 2014. 69th session of the United Nations General Assembly Third Committee, agenda item 68(b,c): "Human rights". New York, 29 October 2014.

Permanent Observer Mission of the Holy See to the United Nations. 2015. 70th session of the General Assembly Third Commission, agenda item 72(b,c): "Promotion and protection of human rights". New York, 30 October.

Permanent Observer Mission of the Holy See to the United Nations. 2015. Remarks of H.E. Archbishop Bernardito Auza, Permanent Observer of the Holy See to the United Nations, at the conference on "Defending human dignity in reproductive health". New York, 19 March.

Permanent Observer Mission of the Holy See to the United Nations. 2015. Remarks of H.E. Archbishop Bernardito Auza, Permanent Observer of the Holy See to the United Nations, at the conference on "Women promoting human dignity". New York, 18 March.

Permanent Observer Mission of the Holy See to the United Nations. 2016. 60th Commission on the Status of Women, explanation of position of the Holy See on the resolution "Women, the girl child and HIV and AIDS". E.CN.6/2016/L.5, New York.

Permanent Observer Mission of the Holy See to the United Nations. 2018. 73rd session of the General Assembly Third Commission, agenda item 74(a,b,c): "Promotion and protection of human rights". New York, 17 October.

Pontifical Council for the Family. 2005. *Lexique des termes ambigus et controversés sur la famille, la vie et les questions éthiques [Lexicon: Ambiguous and Debatable Terms Regarding Family Life and Ethical Questions]*. Paris: Pierre Téqui.

Suenens, Léon-Joseph, et al. 1973. *Déclaration sur l'avortement*. Brussels: Licap.

Books, articles, theses and papers

Alzamora, Revoredo Oscar. 2005. Genre : dangers et portée de cette idéologie. In *Lexique des termes ambigus et controversés sur la famille, la vie et les questions éthiques [Lexicon: Ambiguous and Debatable Terms Regarding Family Life and Ethical Questions]*, by the Pontifical Council for Family. Paris: Pierre Téqui.

Amy, Jean-Jacques. 2009. Homage to Willy Peers. *European Journal of Contraception and Reproductive Health Care* 14(6), 383–384.

Amy, Jean-Jacques. 2009. The shortest lecture on fertility control. *European Journal of Contraception and Reproductive Health Care* 14(5), 321–323.

Amy, Jean-Jacques. 2019. *"Anoniem" is een vrouw. De strijd voor gelijke rechten.* Brussels: VUB Press.

Arruzza, Cinzia, Tithi Bhattacharya and Nancy Fraser. 2019. *Féminisme pour les 99 %. Un manifeste.* Paris: La Découverte.

Arthur, Joyce, Christian Fiala, Kristina Gemzell Danielsson, Oskari Heikinheimo and Jens A. Guðmundsson. 2017. The dishonourable disobedience of not providing abortion. *European Journal of Contraception and Reproductive Health Care* 22(1), 81.

Ayoub, Philip M., and David Paternotte. 2016. L'International Lesbian and Gay Association (ILGA) et l'expansion du militantisme LGBT dans une Europe unifiée. *Critique internationale* (70), 55–70.

Bajos, Nathalie, and Michèle Ferrand. 2006. La condition foetale n'est pas la condition humaine. *Travail, genre et société* 1(15), 176–182.

Bajos, Nathalie, and Michèle Ferrand. 2011. De l'interdiction au contrôle : les enjeux contemporains de la légalisation de l'avortement. *Revue française des affaires sociales* (1), 42–60.

Baubérot, Jean. 2007. *Les laïcités dans le monde.* Paris: Presses universitaires de France.

Benford, Robert D., and David A. Snow. 2012. Processus de cadrage et mouvements sociaux : présentation et bilan. *Politix* (99), 219–255.

Benhabib, Seyla. 2007. Twilight of sovereignty or the emergence of cosmopolitan norms? Rethinking citizenship in volatile times. *Citizenship Studies* 11(1), 19–36.

Benhabib, Seyla. 2008. The legitimacy of human rights. *Daedalus* 137(3), 94–104.

Berer, Marge. 2017. Abortion law and policy around the world: in search of decriminalization. *Health and Human Rights Journal* 19(1), 1–26.

Bernard, Diane, Sahra Datoussaid, Eugénie d'Ursel and Valérie Eloy. 2019. L'autonomie reproductive et les droits des femmes à l'aune de trois nouvelles lois "symboliques" : du glissement au recul ? *Journal des tribunaux* (6771), 4 May, 344–347.

Bitzer, Johannes. 2016. Conscientious objection: to be or not to be. *European Journal of Contraception and Reproductive Health Care* 21(3), 195–197.

Blaise, Pierre, Jean Faniel, and Caroline Sägesser. 2022. *Introduction à la Belgique fédérale*. Brussels: CRISP.

Boltanski, Luc. 2004. *La condition foetale. Une sociologie de l'engendrement et de l'avortement*. Paris: Gallimard.

Bracke, Sarah, Wannes Dupont and David Paternotte. 2018. Personne n'est prophète en son pays : le militantisme catholique anti-genre en Belgique. In *Campagnes anti-genre en Europe. Des mobilisations contre l'égalité*, edited by Roman Kuhar and David Paternotte, pp. 79–98. Lyon: Presses universitaires de Lyon.

Brébant, Émilie, and Cécile Vanderpelen. 2015. Pourquoi le ventre des femmes est-il sacré ? Quand les catholiques belges s'engagent contre l'IVG (de 1990 à aujourd'hui). *Sextant* (31), 223–238.

Bruyère, Lynn, Anne-Sophie Crosetti, Jean Faniel and Caroline Sägesser. 2019. Introduction. Sécularisation, déconfessionnalisation et pluralisme : les piliers résistent. In *Piliers, dépilarisation et clivage philosophique en Belgique*, edited by Lynn Bruyère, Anne-Sophie Crosetti, Jean Faniel and Caroline Sägesser, pp. 5–22. Brussels: CRISP.

Buss, Doris E. 1998. Robes, relics and rights: the Vatican and the Beijing conference on women. *Social and Legal Studies* 7(3), 339–363.

Case, Mary Anne. 2016. The role of the Popes in the invention of complementarity and the Vatican's anathematization of gender. *Religion and Gender* 6(2), 155–172.

Casini, Carlo. 2005. Interruption volontaire de grossesse. In *Lexique des termes ambigus et controversés sur la famille, la vie et les questions éthiques [Lexicon: Ambiguous and Debatable Terms Regarding Family Life and Ethical Questions]*, by the Pontifical Council for the Family. Paris: Pierre Téqui.

Celis, Karen. 2001. The abortion debates in Belgium (1974–1990). In *Abortion Politics, Women's Movements, and the Democratic State: A Comparative Study of State Feminism*, edited by Dorothy McBride Stetson, pp. 39–61. Oxford: Oxford University Press.

Celis Karen, and Gily Coene. 2017. Still a woman's right? Feminist and other discourses in Belgium's abortion struggles. In *A Fragmented Landscape*, edited by Silvia De Zordo, Joanna Mishtal and Lorena Anton, pp. 123–143. Abortion Governance and Protest Logics in Europe. New York/Oxford: Berghahn.

Chassagnard-Pinet, Sandrine. 2008, La désobéissance civile face à la normativité du droit. In *La désobéissance civile. Approches politique et juridique*, edited by David Hiez and Bruno Villalba, pp. 51–66. Villeneuve d'Ascq: Presses universitaires du Septentrion.

Chatzistavrou, Filippa. 2005. L'usage du *soft law* dans le système juridique international et ses implications sémantiques et pratiques sur la notion de règle de droit. *Le Portique* (15), 1–12.

Chavkin, Wendy, Laurel Swerdlow and Jocelyn Fifield. 2017. Regulation of conscientious objection to abortion: an international comparative multiple-case study. *Health and Human Rights Journal* 19(1), 55–68.

Chetouani, Lamria. 1995. Procréation ou contraception ? De la bioéthique à la biopolitique. Mots. *Les langages du politique* (44), 73–98.

Ciccone, Lino. 2005. Santé reproductive. In *Lexique des termes ambigus et controversés sur la famille, la vie et les questions éthiques [Lexicon: Ambiguous and Debatable Terms Regarding Family Life and Ethical Questions]*, by the Pontifical Council for the Family. Paris: Pierre Téqui.

Coates, Amy L., Peter S. Hill, Simon Rushton and Julie Balen. 2014. The Holy See on sexual and reproductive health rights: conservative in position, dynamic in response. *Reproductive Health Matters* 22(44), 114–124.

Cook, Rebecca J., Joanna Erdman and Bernard Dickens (eds). 2014. *Abortion Law in Transnational Perspective: Cases and Controversies*. Philadelphia, PA: University of Pennsylvania Press.

Corrêa, Sonia. 1994. *Population and Reproductive Rights. Feminist Perspectives from the South*. London: Zed Books.

Corrêa, Sonia. 1997. From reproductive health to sexual rights: achievements and future challenges. *Reproductive Health Matters* 5(10), 107–116.

Couture, Denise. 2012. L'antiféminisme du "nouveau féminisme" préconisé par le Saint-Siège. *Recherches féministes* 25(1), 15–35.

de Bonald, Louis-Ambroise. 1965. *Théorie du pouvoir politique et religieux*. Paris: Union générale d'éditions (original edition: 1796).

de Coorebyter, Vincent. 2008. Clivages et partis en Belgique. *Courrier hebdomadaire* (2000), CRISP.

de La Hougue, Claire. 2016. L'avortement en raison du sexe de l'enfant. In *Droit et prévention de l'avortement en Europe*, edited by Grégor Puppinck, pp. 163–184. Bordeaux: LEH.

de La Hougue, Claire, and Grégor Puppinck. 2015. Enfants survivant à l'avortement et infanticides en Europe. *Revue générale de droit médical* (57), 111–134.

Delfosse, Marie-Luce. 2019. Vers la loi du 28 mai 2002 relative à l'euthanasie. *Courrier hebdomadaire* (2427–2428 and 2429–2430), CRISP.

Delgrange, Xavier, and David Koussens. 2019. Les nouveaux arcs-boutants de la laïcité belge pilarisée. In *Piliers, dépilarisation et clivage philosophique en Belgique*, edited by Lynn Bruyère, Anne-Sophie Crosetti, Jean Faniel and Caroline Sägesser, pp. 83–99. Brussels: CRISP.

de Maistre, Joseph. 1998. *Considérations sur la France*. Brussels: Complexe (original edition: 1796).

de Saint-Moulin, Élise. 2019. Les actions en grossesse et vie préjudiciables. État des lieux critique au regard de la jurisprudence récente de la Cour de cassation. *Journal des tribunaux* (6759), 2 February, 81–93.

Descarries, Francine. 1998. Le projet féministe à l'aube du XXIe siècle : un projet de libération et de solidarité qui fait toujours sens. *Cahiers de recherche sociologique* (30), 179–210.

Deschouwer, Kris. 2012. *The Politics of Belgium: Governing a Divided Society*, 2nd edition. Basingstoke: Palgrave Macmillan.

De Zordo, Silvia, Joanna Mishtal and Lorena Anton (eds). 2017. *A Fragmented Landscape: Abortion Governance and Protest Logics in Europe*. New York/ Oxford: Berghahn.

Diamantopoulou, Elisa. 2005. Les enjeux politico-religieux de la corporéité féminine en Grèce, à travers les questions de la contraception et de l'avortement. *Revista de Estudos da Religião* (3), 63–77.

Dieckhoff, Alain. 2019. Les populistes au pouvoir : perspective comparée. In *Populismes au pouvoir*, edited by Alain Dieckhoff, Christophe Jaffrelo and Élise Massicard, pp. 13–29. Paris: Presses de Sciences Po.

Dieckhoff, Alain, Christophe Jaffrelo and Élise Massicard (eds). 2019. *Populismes au pouvoir*. Paris: Presses de Sciences Po.

Dieckhoff, Alain, and Philippe Portier (eds). 2017. *Religion et politique*. Paris: Presses de Sciences Po.

Dworkin, Andrea. 2012. *Les femmes de droite*. Montreal: Éditions du remue-ménage (original edition: 1983).

Dworkin, Ronald. 1993. *Life's Dominion: An Argument about Abortion, Euthanasia, and Individual Freedom*. New York: Knopf.

El Berhoumi, Mathias, and John Pitseys. 2016. L'obstruction parlementaire en Belgique. *Courrier hebdomadaire* (2289–2290), CRISP.

Engeli, Isabelle. 2009. The challenges of abortion and assisted reproductive technologies policies in Europe. *Comparative European Policies* 7(1), 56–74.

Engeli, Isabelle. 2012. Political struggles on reproduction: doctors, women and Christians. *Political Research Quarterly* 2(65), 330–345.

Engeli, Isabelle, and Fréderic Varone. 2012. Governing morality issues through procedural policies. *Swiss Political Science Review* 17(3), 239–258.

Englert, Marion, Sarah Luyten, David Hercot and Déogratias Mazina. 2014. *Rapport sur l'état de la pauvreté 2013. Baromètre social 2013*. Brussels: Commission communautaire commune, Observatoire de la Santé et du Social de Bruxelles-Capitale. URL: www.ccc-ggc.brussels.

Erdman, Joanna. 2014. The procedural turn: abortion at the European court of human rights. In *Abortion Law in Transnational Perspective: Cases and Controversies*, edited by Rebecca J. Cook, Joanna Erdman and Bernard Dickens, pp. 121–142. Philadelphia, PA: University of Pennsylvania Press.

Errazuriz, Ossa Francisco J. 2005. Femme : discrimination et CEDAW. In *Lexique des termes ambigus et controversés sur la famille, la vie et les questions éthiques [Lexicon: Ambiguous and Debatable Terms Regarding Family Life and Ethical Questions]*, by the Pontifical Council for the Family. Paris: Pierre Téqui.

Evans, David. 1993. *Sexual Citizenship: The Material Construction of Sexualities*. London: Routledge.

Faniel, Jean, Corinne Gobin and David Paternotte. 2020. Introduction. La Belgique des mouvements sociaux. In Se mobiliser en Belgique. Raisons, cadres et formes de la contestation sociale contemporaine, edited by Jean Faniel, Corinne Gobin and David Paternotte, pp. 5–42. Louvain-la-Neuve: Academia-L'Harmattan.

Fiala, Christian, and Joyce H. Arthur. 2017. There is no defence for "conscientious objection" in reproductive health. European Journal of Obstetrics and Gynecology and Reproductive Biology (216), 254–258.

Fiala, Christian, Kristina Gemzell Danielsson, Oskari Heikinheimo, Jens A. Guðmundsson and Joyce H. Arthur. 2016. Yes we can! Successful examples of disallowing "conscientious objection" in reproductive health care. European Journal of Contraception and Reproductive Health Care 21(3), 201–206.

Foltzenlogel, Christophe, Claire de La Hougue and Grégor Puppinck. 2016. La prévention de l'avortement : garantir le "droit de ne pas avorter". In *Droit et prévention de l'avortement en Europe*, edited by Grégor Puppinck, pp. 73–106. Bordeaux: LEH.

Foret, François. 2014. Introduction: religion at the European Parliament; purposes, scope and limits of a survey on the religious beliefs of MEPs. *Religion, State and Society* 42(2–3), 108–129.

Foret, François (ed.). 2015. *The Secular Canopy*. New York: Cambridge University Press.

Fraisse, Geneviève. 2007. *Du consentement*. Paris: Seuil.

Freedman, Lynn P., Stephen L. Isaacs. 1993. Human rights and reproductive choice. *Studies in Family Planning* 24(1), 18–30.

Garbagnoli, Sara. 2015. L'hérésie des "féministes du genre" : genèse et enjeux de l'antiféminisme "antigenre" du Vatican. In *Les antiféminismes. Analyse d'un discours réactionnaire*, edited by Diane Lamoureux and Francis Dupuis-Déri, pp. 107–127. Montreal: Éditions du remue-ménage.

Garbagnoli, Sara. 2019. De quoi le "gender" des campagnes "anti-genre" est-il le nom ? Sur une contre-révolution straight et ses succès. In *Antiféminismes et masculinismes d'hier et d'aujourd'hui*, edited by Christine Bard, Mélissa Blais and Francis Dupuis-Déri, pp. 241–270. Paris: Presses universitaires de France.

Gautier, Arlette. 2012. *Genre et biopolitiques. L'enjeu de la liberté*. Paris: L'Harmattan.

Giami, Alain. 2015. Sexualité, santé et droits de l'homme : l'invention des droits sexuels. *Sexologies* 24(3), 105–113.

Govaert, Serge. 2016. La montée des nationalistes flamands au pouvoir dans les gouvernements fédéraux, 1977–2014. *Courrier hebdomadaire* (2313), CRISP.

Haarscher, Guy. 2004. *La laïcité*. Paris: Presses universitaires de France.

Habermas, Jürgen. 1996. *Droit et démocratie. Entre faits et normes*. Paris: Gallimard.

Habermas, Jürgen. 2008. *Entre naturalisme et religion. Les défis de la démocratie*. Paris: Gallimard.

Halsaa, Beatrice, Sasha Roseneil and Sümer Sevil (eds). 2012. *Remaking Citizenship in Multicultural Europe: Women's Movements, Gender and Diversity*. Basingstoke: Palgrave Macmillan.

Heinen, Jacqueline. 2015. Assauts tous azimuts contre le droit à l'avortement. La Pologne fait-elle école ? In *Genre et religion : des rapports épineux. Illustration à partir des débats sur l'avortement*, edited by Ana Amuchástegui, Edith

Flores, Evelyn Aldaz, Jacqueline Heinen and Christine Verschuur, pp. 55–90. Paris: L'Harmattan.

Heino, Anna, Mika Gissler, Dan Pater and Christian Fiala. 2013. Conscientious objection and induced abortion in Europe. *European Journal of Contraception and Reproductive Health Care* 18(4), 231–233.

Held, David. 1995. *Democracy and the Global Order: From the Modern State to Cosmopolitan Governance.* Cambridge: Polity Press.

Hessini, Leila. 2008. Islam and abortion: the diversity of discourses and practices. *IDS Bulletin* 39(3), 18–27.

Hirschman, Albert O. 1995. Deux siècles de rhétorique réactionnaire. Paris: Fayard.

Jacquot, Sophie. 2011. Le lobby européen des femmes : de l'exception à la marginalisation ? Conference paper, Fourth International Congress of Francophone Political Science Associations, Brussels, April.

Jacquot, Sophie. 2017. "Nous étions des militantes, maintenant ce sont des fonctionnaires ma chère" : la professionnalisation de la politique européenne d'égalité entre les femmes et les hommes. In *La professionnalisation des luttes pour l'égalité : genre et féminisme*, edited by Petra Meier and David Paternotte, pp. 47–66. Louvain-la-Neuve: Academia-L'Harmattan.

Jenson, Jane. 2007. Des frontières aux lisières de la citoyenneté. In *L'état des citoyennetés en Europe et dans les Amériques*, edited by Jane Jenson, Bérengère Marques-Pereira and Éric Remacle, pp. 23–30. Montreal: Presses de l'Université de Montréal.

Jenson, Jane. 2017. The new maternalism: children first; women second. In *Reassembling Motherhood: Procreation and Care in a Globalized World*, edited by Yasmine Ergas, Jane Jenson and Sonya Michel, pp. 269–286. New York: Columbia University Press.

Keck, Margaret, and Kathrijn Sikking. 1998. *Activists Beyond Borders: Advocacy Networks in International Politics.* Ithaca, NY: Cornell University Press.

Kuhar, Roman, and David Paternotte (eds). 2018. *Campagnes anti-genre en Europe. Des mobilisations contre l'égalité.* Lyon: Presses universitaires de Lyon.

Lacroix, Justine, and Jean-Yves Pranchère. 2016. *Le procès des droits de l'homme. Généalogie du scepticisme démocratique.* Paris: Seuil.

Lamoureux, Diane. 2019. L'antiféminisme comme conservatisme. In *Antiféminismes et masculinismes d'hier et d'aujourd'hui*, edited by Christine Bard, Mélissa Blais and Francis Dupuis-Déri, pp. 51–77. Paris: Presses universitaires de France.

Legros, Robert. 1983. 1830–1980. Droit pénal et société. *Revue belge d'histoire contemporaine* 14(1–2), 177–199.

Le Méné, Jean-Marie. 2005. Interruption médicale de grossesse (IMG). In *Lexique des termes ambigus et controversés sur la famille, la vie et les questions éthiques [Lexicon: Ambiguous and Debatable Terms Regarding Family Life and Ethical Questions]*, by the Pontifical Council for the Family. Paris: Pierre Téqui.

Lister, Ruth. 1997. *Citizenship: Feminist Perspectives*. Basingstoke: Palgrave Macmillan.

Lister, Ruth. 2002. Sexual citizenship. In *Handbook of Citizenship Studies*, edited by Engin Isin and Bryan Turner, pp. 191–208. London: Sage.

Lister, Ruth. 2007. Inclusive citizenship: realizing the potential. *Citizenship Studies* 11(11), 49–61.

Lister, Ruth, et al. 2007. *Gendering Citizenship in Western Europe: New Challenges for Citizenship Research in a Cross-National Context*. Bristol: Policy Press.

Lochak, Danièle. 1998. Désobéir à la loi. In *Pouvoir et liberté. Études offertes à Jacques Mourgeon*, pp. 191–208. Brussels: Bruylant.

Lochak, Danièle. 1998. Les bornes de la liberté. *Pouvoirs* (84), 15–30.

Locoge, Thérèse. 2018. Le passage de la réflexion éthique vers le biodroit. Paper presented at World Bioethics Day, UNESCO Chair, Ghent, 19 October.

Louissaint, Cherline. 2016. Les conséquences médicales et sociales de l'avortement. In *Droit et prévention de l'avortement en Europe*, edited by Grégor Puppinck, pp. 52–56. Bordeaux: LEH.

Mabille, François. 2017. Le Saint-Siège, weak state et soft power. In *Religion et politique*, edited by Alain Dieckhoff and Philippe Portier, pp. 177–184. Paris: Presses de Sciences Po.

Mabille, Xavier. 1986. *Histoire politique de la Belgique. Facteurs et acteurs de changement*. Brussels: CRISP.

Mabille, Xavier. 1990. Le débat politique d'avril 1990 sur la sanction et la promulgation de la loi. *Courrier hebdomadaire* (1275), CRISP.

Mabille, Xavier. 2011. *Nouvelle histoire politique de la Belgique*. Brussels: CRISP.

MacKinnon, Catherine. 1987. *Feminism Unmodified: Discourses on Life and Law*. Cambridge, MA: Harvard University Press.

Magnette, Paul, and Jean-Benoit Pilet. 2008. La Belgique. In *Les démocraties européennes*, edited by Jean-Michel De Waele and Paul Magnette, pp. 51–68. Paris: Armand Colin.

Marques-Pereira, Bérengère. 1986. L'interruption volontaire de grossesse. *Courrier hebdomadaire* (1127), CRISP.

Marques-Pereira, Bérengère. 1989. *L'avortement en Belgique. De la clandestinité au débat politique*. Brussels: Éditions de l'Université de Bruxelles.

Marques-Pereira, Bérengère. 2018. Abortion rights: rights and practices in a multilevel setting. In *Citizenship as a Regime: Canadian and International Perspectives*, edited by Mireille Paquet, Nora Nagels and Aude-Claire Fourot, pp. 238–254. Montreal: McGill–Queen's University Press.

Marques-Pereira, Bérengère, and Sophie Pereira. 2014. Abortion in Belgium: a precarious right? *About Gender: International Journal of Gender Studies* 3(5), 225–244.

Marshall, Thomas H. 1950. *Citizenship and Social Class*. Cambridge: Cambridge University Press.

Marshall, Thomas H. 1963. *Class, Citizenship and Social Development*. Chicago, IL: Chicago University Press.

Meaney, Joseph, and Michael Meaney. 2005. Le libre choix de la vie : l'option "Pro Choice". In *Lexique des termes ambigus et controversés sur la famille, la vie et les questions éthiques [Lexicon: Ambiguous and Debatable Terms Regarding Family Life and Ethical Questions]*, by the Pontifical Council for the Family. Paris: Pierre Téqui.

Mercier, Stéphane. 2017. *La philosophie pour la vie. Contre un prétendu "droit de choisir" l'avortement.* Roosdaal: Quentin Moreau.

Mill, John Stuart. 1859. *On Liberty.* London: John W. Parker and Sons.

Miller, Alice, and Mindy Roseman. 2011. Sexual and reproductive rights at the United Nations: frustration or fulfilment? *Reproductive Health Matters* 19(38), 102–118.

Mishtal, Joanna. 2017. "Quietly beating the system": the logics of protest and resistance under the Polish abortion ban. In *A Fragmented Landscape: Abortion Governance and Protest Logics in Europe*, edited by Silvia De Zordo, Joanna Mishtal and Lorena Anton, pp. 226–244. New York/Oxford: Berghahn.

Mondo, Émilie. 2018–19. European culture wars? Abortion and human embryonic stem cells research (1998–2015). PhD Thesis, Université libre de Bruxelles.

Mondo, Émilie, and Caroline Close. 2018. Morality politics in the European Parliament: a qualitative insight into MEPs' voting behaviour on abortion and human embryonic stem cell research. *Journal of European Integration* 40(7), 1001–1018.

Morgan, Lynn N. 2017, The Dublin Declaration on Maternal Health Care and anti-abortion activism: examples from Latin America. *Health and Human Rights Journal* 19(1), 41–53.

Moreau, Caroline, et al. 2021. Abortion regulation in Europe in the era of COVID-19: a spectrum of policy responses. *BMJ Sexual and Reproductive Health* 47(14), 1–8.

Mouffe, Chantal. 2016. *Le paradoxe démocratique.* Paris: Beaux-Arts de Paris.

Mounier, Emmanuel. 2016. *Le personnalisme.* Paris: Presses universitaires de France (original edition: 1950).

Nouailhat, Yves-Henri. 2006. Le Saint-Siège, l'ONU et la défense des droits de l'homme sous le pontificat de Jean-Paul II. *Relations internationales* (127), 95–110.

Oja Liiri, Yamin, and Ely Alicia. 2016. "Woman" in the European human rights system: how is the reproductive rights jurisprudence of the European Court of Human Rights constructing narratives of women's citizenship? *Columbia Journal of Gender and Law* 32(1), 62–95.

Okin, Susan Moller. 1991. Gender, the public and the private. In *Political Theory Today*, edited by David Held, pp. 67–90. Cambridge: Polity Press.

Orr, Judith. 2017. *Abortion Wars: The Fight for Reproductive Rights.* Bristol: Policy Press.

Outshoorn, Joyce (ed.). 2015. *European Women's Movements and Body Politics: The Struggle for Autonomy.* Basingstoke: Palgrave Macmillan.

Pateman, Carole. 1988. *The Sexual Contract.* Cambridge: Polity Press.

Paternotte, David. 2015. Introduction: Habemus Gender! Autopsie d'une obsession vaticane. *Sextant* (31), 7–22.

Pavard, Bibia, Florence Rochefort and Michelle Zancarini-Fournal. 2012. *Les lois Veil*. Paris: Armand Colin.

Peña-Ruiz, Henri. 2003. *Qu'est-ce que la laïcité ?* Paris: Gallimard.

Peris, Cancio Alfredo. 2005. Droits sexuels et reproductifs. In *Lexique des termes ambigus et controversés sur la famille, la vie et les questions éthiques [Lexicon: Ambiguous and Debatable Terms Regarding Family Life and Ethical Questions]*, by the Pontifical Council for the Family. Paris: Pierre Téqui, 2005.

Petchesky, Rosalind Pollack. 1990. *Abortion and Woman's Choice: The State, Sexuality and Reproductive Freedom*. Boston, MA: Northeastern University Press (original edition: 1984).

Phillips, Anne. 1991. *Engendering Democracy*. Cambridge: Polity Press.

Plummer, Ken. 2001. The square of intimate citizenship: some preliminary proposals. *Citizenship Studies* 5(3), 237–253.

Plummer, Ken. 2003. *Intimate Citizenship: Private Decisions and Public Dialogues*. Seattle, WA: University of Washington Press.

Pontifical Council for the Family. 2005. *Lexique des termes ambigus et controversés sur la famille, la vie et les questions éthiques [Lexicon: Ambiguous and Debatable Terms Regarding Family Life and Ethical Questions]*. Paris: Pierre Téqui.

Portier, Philippe. 2017. Les régimes de laïcité en Europe. In *Religion et politique*, edited by Alain Dieckhoff and Philippe Portier, pp. 211–221. Paris: Presses de Sciences Po.

Proeschel, Claude. 2017. La conscience en politique. In *Religion et politique*, edited by Alain Dieckhoff and Philippe Portier, pp. 287–296. Paris: Presses de Sciences Po.

Profeta, Paola, Ximena Calo and Roberto Occhiuzzi. 2021. Covid-19 and its economic impact on women and women's poverty:insights from 5 European Countries, European Parliament, May.

Puppinck, Grégor. 2016. Objection de conscience et droits de l'homme. Essai d'analyse systématique. *Société, Droit et Religion* 1(6), 209–275.

Puppinck, Grégor (ed.). 2016. *Droit et prévention de l'avortement en Europe*. Bordeaux: LEH.

Puppinck, Grégor, and Claire de La Hougue. 2016. Les enfants survivant à l'avortement et les infanticides néonatals. In *Droit et prévention de l'avortement en Europe*, edited by Grégor Puppinck, pp. 137–161. Bordeaux: LEH.

Rancière, Jacques. 1995. *La mésentente*. Politique et philosophie. Paris: Galilée.

Rawls, John. 1971. *A Theory of Justice*. Cambridge, MA: Harvard University Press.

Revault, d'Allones Myriam. 2018. *La faiblesse du vrai*. Paris: Seuil.

Richardson, Diane. 2017. Rethinking sexual citizenship. *Sociology* 51(2), 208–224.

Richardson, Diane. 2018. *Sexuality and Citizenship*. Cambridge: Polity Press.

Richardson, Eileen, and Bryan Turner. 2001. Sexual, intimate or reproductive citizenship? *Citizenship Studies* 5(3), 329–338.

Roseneil, Sasha (ed.). 2013. *Beyond Citizenship? Feminism and the Transformation of Belonging*. Basingstoke: Palgrave Macmillan.

Roseneil, Sasha, et al. 2011. Intimate citizenship and gendered well-being: the claims and interventions of women's movements in Europe. In *Transforming Gendered Well-Being in Europe: The Impact of Social Movements*, edited by Alison Woodward, Jean-Michel Bonvin and Mercè Renom, pp. 187–206. Farnham: Ashgate.

Roseneil, Sasha, et al. 2012. Remaking intimate citizenship in multicultural Europe: experiences outside the conventional family. In *Remaking Citizenship in Multicultural Europe: Women's Movements, Gender and Diversity*, edited by Beatrice Halsaa, Sasha Roseneil and Sevil Sümer, pp. 41–69. Basingstoke: Palgrave Macmillan.

Roseneil, Sasha, Isabel Crowhurst, Ana Cristina Santos and Mariya Stoilova. 2013. Reproduction and citizenship/reproducing citizens: editorial introduction. *Citizenship Studies* 17(8), 901–911.

Rowlands, Sam. 2014. A global view of conscientious objection in abortion care provision. Paper presented at the European Society of Contraception, Lisbon, May.

Sägesser, Caroline. 2020. La formation du gouvernement De Croo (mai 2019 - octobre 2020). *Courrier hebdomadaire* (2471–2472), CRISP.

Schmidt Vivien. 2008. Discursive institutionalism: the explanatory power of ideas and discourse. *Annual Review of Political Science* (12), 303–326.

Schouppe, Jean-Pierre. 2016. La dimension institutionnelle de l'objection de conscience. In *Droit et prévention de l'avortement en Europe*, edited by Grégor Puppinck, pp. 249–267. Bordeaux: LEH.

Schreiber, Jean-Philippe. 2017. En conclusion : Église et sexualité. In *La Sainte Famille. Sexualité, filiation et parentalité dans l'Église catholique*, edited by Cécile Vanderpelen-Diagre and Caroline Sägesser, pp. 223–232. Brussels: Éditions de l'Université de Bruxelles.

Scott, Joan W. 2012. *De l'utilité du genre*. Paris: Fayard.

Séhier, Véronique. 2019. *Droits sexuels et reproductifs en Europe : entre menaces et progrès*. Paris: Conseil économique, social et environnemental.

Siegel, Reva. 2014. The constitutionalization of abortion. In *Abortion Law in Transnational Perspective: Cases and Controversies*, edited by Rebecca J. Cook, Joanna Erdman and Bernard Dickens, pp. 13–35. Philadelphia, PA: University of Pennsylvania Press.

Siim, Birte. 2000. *Gender and Citizenship: Politics and Agency in France, Britain and Denmark*. Cambridge: Cambridge University Press.

Sintomer, Yves. 2001. Droit à l'avortement, propriété de soi et droit à la vie privée. *Les Temps modernes* (615–616), 206–239.

Snow, David A. 2004. Framing processes, ideology, and discursive fields. In *The Blackwell Companion to Social Movements*, edited by David A. Snow, Sarah A. Soule and Hanspeter Kriesi, pp. 380–412. Oxford: Blackwell Publishing.

Sorbonne University. N.D. Encyclopédie d'histoire numérique de l'Europe. URL: https://ehne.fr.

Stoeckl, Kristina. 2016. The Russian Orthodox Church as moral norm entrepreneur. *Religion, State and Society* 44(2), 132–151.

Swennen, Béatrice. 2001. Évaluation de la politique d'interruption volontaire de grossesse. In *Évaluer les politiques publiques. Regards croisés sur la Belgique*, edited by Christian de Visscher and Frédéric Varone, pp. 103–114. Louvain-la-Neuve: Academia-Bruylant.

Tarrow, Sidney, and Charles Tilly. 2008. *Politique(s) du conflit. De la grève à la révolution.* Paris: Presses de Sciences Po.

Tartakowsky, Eva, and Paul Zawadski. 2017. Politique et religion en Pologne. In *Religion et politique*, edited by Alain Dieckhoff, Philippe Portier, pp. 297–305. Paris: Presses de Sciences Po.

Tilly, Charles. 1984. Les origines du répertoire de l'action collective contemporaine en France et en Grande-Bretagne. *Vingtième Siècle* (4), 89–108.

Tilly, Charles. 2006. *Regimes and Repertoires.* Chicago, IL: University of Chicago Press.

Turner, Bryan. 2008. Citizenship, reproduction and the state: international marriage and human rights. *Citizenship Studies* 12(1), 45–54.

Verleden, Frederik. 2019. *Aux sources de la particratie. Les relations entre les partis politiques belges et leurs parlementaires (1918–1970).* Brussels: CRISP.

Wenham, Clare. 2020. The gendered impact of the Covid-19 crisis and post-crisis period. European Parliament, September.

Whitaker, Robin, and Goretti Horgan. 2017. Abortion governance in the new Northern Ireland. In *A Fragmented Landscape: Abortion Governance and Protest Logics in Europe*, edited by Silvia De Zordo, Joanna Mishtal and Lorena Anton, pp. 245–265. New York/Oxford: Berghahn.

Witte, Els. 1990. Twintig jaar politieke strijd rond de abortuswetgeving in Belgë (1970–1990). *Res Publica* 32(4), 427–487.

Yamin, Alicia Ely, Neil Datta and Ximena Andión. 2018. Behind the drama: the roles of transnational actors in legal mobilization over sexual and reproductive rights. *Georgetown Journal of Gender and the Law* 19(3), 533–569.

Yuval-Davis, Nira. 1996. Women and the biological reproduction of "the nation". *Women's Studies International Forum* 19(1), 17–24.

Yuval-Davis, Nira. 1997. *Gender and Nation.* London: Sage.

Zacharenko, Elena. 2016. Perspectives on anti-choice lobbying in Europe: study for policy makers on opposition to sexual and reproductive health and rights in Europe. The Greens/EFA in the European Parliament, Brussels.

Zampas, Christina. 2017. Legal and political discourses on women's right to abortion. In *A Fragmented Landscape: Abortion Governance and Protest Logics in Europe*, edited by Silvia De Zordo, Joanna Mishtal and Lorena Anton, pp. 23–45. New York/Oxford: Berghahn.

Zampas, Christina, and Jaime M. Gher. 2008. Abortion as a human right: international and regional standards. *Human Rights Law Review* 8(2), 249–294.

Open letters and petitions

Bartholomeeusen, Henri. 2016. Le droit à l'avortement pourrait être mis à mal. Open Letter, *Le Soir*, 19 April.

Bartholomeeusen, Henri. 2018. Humaniser le deuil ou les foetus. Open Letter, *Le Soir*, 25 September.

European Centre for Law and Justice, Fédération des associations familiales catholiques en Europe and International Catholic Child Bureau. 2015. Pétition pour les droits des nouveau-nés survivant à leur avortement. Submitted to the Parliamentary Assembly of the Council of Europe, January. URL: https://eclj.org.

La Libre Belgique. 2019. Nous, personnel soignant opposé à la proposition de loi sur l'avortement. Open Letter, 26 November.

Le Soir. 2018. Appel à un débat parlementaire pour réellement légaliser l'IVG. Open Letter, 9 July (see also www.manifestedes350.be).

Les Soir. 2019. IVG : respectons le choix des femmes et leur droit à la santé ! Petition, 16 December.

Websites

https://abortion-policies.srhr.org
https://adfinternational.org/campaign/defund-ippf
https://adfmedia.org
https://lobbyfacts.eu
https://treaties.un.org
www.adfinternational.org
www.afterbaiz.com
www.agendaeurope.org
www.astra.org.pl
www.cathobel.be
www.catholicsforchoice.org
www.citizengo.org
www.comece.eu
www.cpdh.org
www.demens.nu
www.dignitatishumanae.com
www.droitavortement.com
www.ec.europa.eu/citizens-initiative
www.eclj.org
www.ecouteivg.org
www.epfweb.org
www.euro.who.int
www.europeandignitywatch.org
www.fafce.org

www.famillechretienne.fr
www.federation-pro-europa-christiana.org
www.femmesprevoyantessocialistes.be
www.groupe-croissance.be
www.hazteoir.org
www.health.belgium.be
www.highgroundalliance.eu
www.humanistfederation.eu
www.humanum.it
www.ieb-eib.org
www.ilga-europa.org
www.ippf.org
www.ivg.net
www.jeunespourlavie.org
www.jongereninfolife.be
www.laicite.be
www.manifestedes350.be
www.mariestopes.org
www.novaterrae.eu
www.oneofus.eu
www.ordoiuris.org
www.reproductiverights.org
www.souffledevie.be
www.treaties.un.org
www.ultramontain.be
www.vatican.va and www.v2.vatican.va
www.viefeminine.be
www.womenlobby.org

About the author

Bérengére Marques-Pereira was a full professor at the Université libre de Bruxelles in political and social sciences until September 2011 and is currently a guest professor at the same university. She is a member of the METICES research centre (Migrations, Spaces, Work, Institutions, Citizenship, Epistemology and Health) of the Institute of Sociology. Between 2000 and 2003 she was president of the ABSP (the Belgian Francophone Political Science Association), where she founded the Gender and Politics working group. Her publications focus on women's social and political citizenship in Europe and Latin America, Latin American politics, and abortion rights.